A Practical Rhetoric for Writers

Revised Edition

Steve Sansom
Cher Brock

North Harris College
Houston, TX

Harcourt Brace *Custom Publishers*
Harcourt Brace College Publishers
Fort Worth   Philadelphia   San Diego   New York   Orlando   Austin
San Antonio   Toronto   Montreal   London   Sydney   Tokyo

Custom Publisher	Felix Frazier
Senior Production Manager	Sue Dunaway

A Practical Rhetoric for Writers

Copyright © 1998 by Cheryl A. Brock and Steve Sansom

Permissions Department
Harcourt Brace & Company
6277 Sea Harbor Drive
Orlando, FL 32887-6777

Portions of this Work were published in previous editions.

Printed in the United States of America

0-03-044487-x

CONTENTS

PART THREE: EXERCISES

Acknowledgments

The first time we published this book, it was with the blessing of the English department. We were motivated by what we saw as the need of our students for more direction in adopting a logical rhetorical stance and for essays directed at the kinds of essay writing the students are required to do in and out of the formal academic environment. Our colleagues at North Harris College, especially Katie and Danel Olson, Mim Freiter, and Robert Miller, have, again, generously assessed the usefulness of the essays in the first edition and have helped in the selection of those for this edition. We are particularly indebted to Robert Miller for writing Chapter Five and for making several editorial contributions elsewhere. We are also grateful to Olin Joynton for providing several exercises on logic. The staff at Harcourt Brace have changed but have been flexible and helpful; Felix Frazier and Athena Noal may be the "new kids," but they follow worthily in the footprints of Brian Hickman. For preparing the text from "scratch" (The wonders of modern technology are always mysterious!), Judy McCann and Kathleen Carpenter deserve–and have–our heartfelt thanks. Whatever success this text enjoys we share with our families, all these our friends, the omnipresent Meta, and our students. Whatever its shortcomings, they are ours alone--and always in the process of change.

S. S.
C. B.

May, 1995

PART ONE

A GUIDE TO WRITING

CHAPTER ONE
The Elements of Rhetoric

From the time of the ancient Greeks and Romans to our present day, someone has always attempted to alter the lives of others through words; witness the eloquent phrases in the Declaration of Independence, Lincoln's "Gettysburg Address, "Martin Luther King's "I Have a Dream" speech, John F. Kennedy's inaugural address, even the demagoguery of Adolph Hitler and Saddam Hussein. The major power of their words is the power of rhetoric, the art or discipline of writing effectively and persuasively, used to inform or motivate an audience. While Aristotle defined rhetoric as discovering the best means of persuasion in any given situation, this definition might include not only the argumentative but the expository or informative mode of discourse as well. In fact, rhetoric operates in almost every form of writing we find. For this reason, rhetoric is still an important concern of each of us today, primarily because none of us can escape it—not the lawyer, the teacher, the politician, the computer analyst, or the student. We all indulge in and are exposed to rhetoric daily. Therefore, the goal of the class in which you are enrolled and the goal of this text are to raise your awareness of the rhetorical components all around you so you might be more effective in expressing your own ideas as well as more alert to others' use and misuse of rhetoric. This text, through its instructions and exercises, can serve as a guide for you in your move toward communicating your thoughts and feelings through words.

Your tasks as a writer can range from giving the directions for planting a garden to persuading an audience that capital punishment should or should not be abolished. Whether you choose to use the expository or persuasive method, you should understand and be able to use certain rhetorical elements in order to make your ideas more convincing or persuasive. These elements include the writer's purpose, audience, voice, and the situation. While all four elements play a role in every composition, they do not always have equal roles. For example, audience would obviously assume a greater place in process analysis and persuasive essays than in a comparison and contrast essay, and voice might play a minimal role in definition and a major role in narration and description. Nevertheless, each principle must be present for you to achieve your goal of communicating your ideas. However varying their presence in an essay, all four elements must be included.

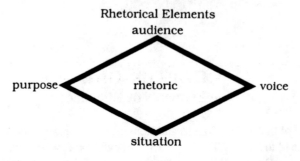

Rhetorical Elements

audience

purpose   rhetoric   voice

situation

Figure 1-A

PURPOSE

Writing always has a purpose. Every writer must have a reason for writing, and that reason, or purpose, determines which of the other three elements of rhetoric will be emphasized. The general purpose of various writing methods is to know what we think and how best to communicate those thoughts. Therefore, we must always determine what particular message we want to convey and what method would likely be most effective. Do we wish simply to report or inform, to explain, or to persuade? During your college career and afterwards, you might be required to report on a given project or to inform your audience as to the progress of a particular project. In addition, you might be expected to explain to a co-worker the step-by-step procedure for seeking advancement in the company, or you may wish to persuade your supervisor that your particular ideas warrant attention over the proposals of a co-worker. Whichever rhetorical mode you select to write your essay, it must have a purpose, and the purpose must be clearly evident to the reader. The rhetorical purpose is sometimes determined by the specific assignment. If a topic is assigned, your task of deciding on a purpose may already have been done for you. However, often you will have to determine the purpose yourself. If it cannot be discovered immediately, the purpose can emerge from your preliminary brainstorming of the assigned general topic and from the early stages of organizing your random thoughts. Until a purpose is clearly in your mind, though, it is best not to begin writing the essay, else you will likely waste time and effort. Time spent in determining your purpose is far better used than time spent in wandering from point to point without direction. Knowing your purpose helps you sharpen your focus. Make certain, too, that your goals are reasonable and that you can manage what you tell your audience you will accomplish in your statement of purpose, or your thesis. Then you can decide which method of presentation is the most efficient and can best accomplish your purpose. These rhetorical methods are discussed in specific detail in Chapter Three.

AUDIENCE

Your audience is your intended listener or reader. Every word we utter is directed toward something or someone, even if we are only talking to ourselves. When we speak to someone, we have the advantage of immediate feedback, of noting the reaction, either verbal or nonverbal, and so we are able to determine whether or not he understands us. When speaking, therefore, we can adjust our voice, gestures, or language to accommodate our listener, thus increasing our chances of being understood. In writing, however, the advantages of instant feedback and subsequent adjustments are not available to us. Therefore we must be more aware of who our audience is and what he or she knows. If we want to achieve an intended effect (purpose), we must be able to make certain assumptions about our audience. In adapting your ideas to meet your particular audience, you must bear in mind the interests and values of those you want to reach. Estimate what their backgrounds are, their education, age, sex, political and religious inclinations, and experiences. What can they expect to gain by reading your ideas? These concerns help you establish which approach to use in presenting your ideas and what to stress or to omit in your essay. Identifying the audience will assist you in anticipating questions and in being prepared to address those questions in your essays. This procedure is not unlike a job applicant's research into a company with whom he intends to interview.

Students are correct in assuming their audience is their instructor. But most writing instructors will want you to specify a variety of audiences, real or imagined, in order to sharpen your rhetorical skills to meet the demands of different situations. This task is not always easy. Addressing a variety of audiences in a variety of essays places restraints on students, but these situations more than likely reflect the situations you may encounter in life. You will always be confronted with different audiences, different situations, and different subjects. It is best, then, to keep in mind that you will likely have more than one audience for your essay–your instructor and some other designated audience. This dual audience requires you to adapt to each one's needs and expectations, just as a newspaper reporter must write a news item with his editor as well as the general reading public in mind. Knowing your audience and writing to them does not mean you have to sacrifice your own beliefs in order to accommodate those of your audience. You must not feel you have to choose between your integrity and reader appeal. If you are skillful in the use of rhetoric, you can maintain an honest and authentic voice and at the same time still be a successful strategist.

VOICE

Having defined your audience, you must now determine the role that you want to assume with your audience. This stance, or voice, that you must assume is much like the different masks you prepare daily "to meet the faces that you meet" or the face that you "keep in a jar by the door." You present yourself one way when attending class, and you present yourself quite differently when you are on a date or visiting your in-laws. While these masks are different, your identity is still the same. Each role is sincere, but each allows you the flexibility to select the appropriate demeanor and words for a specific occasion and audience. This role-playing is similar to the role you assume in presenting your ideas in your essay to a given audience. Consider how you would express yourself in a personal letter to a friend as compared to how you would express yourself in a letter of application for scholarship funds. Authenticity and sincerity are imperative. They guide the voice in its attempt to demonstrate you are serious about your subject and respectful of your audience. Be genuine in whatever voice you assume. You can be sympathetic, neutral, angry, or humorous, but most of all be yourself. What you say and how you say it, therefore, are determined by your purpose, audience, and subject matter.

SITUATION

The fourth element of the rhetorical process is the situation. It is the most important of all four elements because without it you would have no basis for an essay. The remainder of this text is concerned with the steps in putting together your ideas and deciding on the appropriate method of presenting those ideas to a designated audience in a given situation. Which arrangement to use in presenting your essay depends upon the situation, your audience, your voice or the stance you take in offering your ideas, and your purpose. The rules for the art and craft of rhetoric are not written in stone, nor are they "writ in water." A great deal of rhetorical flexibility in regard to these rules is available to writers of compositions, but sometimes the refusal to concern yourself with these rules can have disastrous consequences. In the classroom the results can be an inferior grade, while in the marketplace they can mean unemployment. The rules that are discussed in the following pages represent the methods of writing that are time-proven, that have served people in almost every endeavor–mostly, but not always, for good purposes. We can only hope that you use your rhetorical skills for the general good, never to be abused or misused.

So now we arrive at our starting place; through language and the expression of ideas we begin to understand our world and ourselves.

CHAPTER TWO
The Writing Process

The first rule of writing a composition is "Don't panic." The task of writing does not have to be a dreadful undertaking, but neither should it be taken too casually. Instead, view it as an opportunity to express your ideas. Even if you presently lack the confidence to take on such a task comfortably, you will discover that it is within your abilities if you understand the general principles of what constitutes good, effective writing. Most of your assignments will require observations, feelings, or opinions. This explanation is the general substance of expository writing. In addition, you may be asked to defend your opinions or observations or to attempt to convince your readers of your opinions, that is, to use persuasive writing. Knowing the fundamental components of each of these types of composition will reduce much of your tendency toward panic and will, at the same time, provide you with the proper tools to begin your writing assignment. Finally, you may be asked to write a critical analysis, i.e., your interpretation of observations about a short story, a poem, or a nonfiction essay. This project, too, requires the basic components of expository and persuasive writing.

Writing is a recursive process: each step overlaps another step. You may begin and proceed through the process in several ways. However, a logical approach is to follow certain prewriting steps to get started.

THE BEGINNING

Finding a Topic

Beginning an essay can be extremely frustrating when you have the freedom to choose your own topic. Coming up with a fresh, original subject and having something unique to say about it can be overwhelming. Finding a topic does not have to be stressful, however; it can be turned to your advantage. It will allow you to focus on what you know, what you have experienced, and what you would prefer to discuss. Your own experiences are your best sources, whether you decide to write a narrative of your harrowing experiences during registration or you have to argue your views on the irrelevancy of the grading system.

No matter what the assignment is, first consider what you know the most about—yourself. Your own experiences and perceptions will always play a major part in your writing. Maybe your career or studies toward a career can provide some interesting topics. Perhaps you have just read a book or seen a play or movie that deals with a subject that intrigues you. Perhaps you want to make known your views about a particular controversial issue that is important to you. Sources for potential topics are all around you, but you must be observant. Many instructors prefer that you keep your journal entries to record experiences as they occur. This practice not only provides you with personal explorations and possible source material for your essays, but it also affords you the chance to practice your writing skills. Finally, your general reading research will provide supplementary information for your opinions and observations. Your preparation for writing depends on how involved you are with the world around you.

Brainstorming/Gathering Details

Whether your topic is assigned or you have a choice of subjects, you should first brainstorm to help you determine what you want to say about your subject. First, select a topic you find interesting or one with which you are most familiar. If you are undecided about what to write, brainstorm two or three possible topics and then see which subject generates the most ideas. One advantage of brainstorming is that it is graphic: it reveals to you the topic about which you know the most.

Once you have settled upon a topic and a general approach, determine for whom you will be writing your essay–your audience. This decision is crucial before you brainstorm further because it will determine what to include in and exclude from your discussion.

An essay about the benefits of attending a community college that is to be read by a college professor will include quite different information than would the same essay aimed at an audience of graduating high school seniors. Be aware of your audience: it determines your approach. In a writing course, however, you must realize that you are writing for two audiences: your designated reader and your instructor. Therefore, even though your designated reader may vary with each assignment, you always have to keep in mind the requirements of your other reader–your instructor.

Finally, clarify your purpose. Ask yourself, "What do I want to accomplish?" "What do I want my audience to do or to understand?" Purpose is largely dependent upon audience. If you are discussing the advantages of a community college for an instructor, chances are your purpose is to inform. But if the essay will be read by a high school senior, your purpose is probably to persuade. Without knowing your purposes before you organize your ideas, you risk misdirection and increased frustration, not to mention the loss of precious time and energy.

Once you have gone through this initial exercise, begin brainstorming. Brainstorm alone or with others and write down as quickly as you can anything–any random fragments, words, or sentences–that relate even remotely to your subject. Do not pause to consider the relevance of any item that surfaces, its spelling, grammar, or level of importance; that step will come later. Anything jotted down at this stage is relevant and valid and, even though you might ultimately reject some ideas, they might possibly generate other useable thoughts. The example below is a brainstorming exercise on the assigned topic "The Qualities of a Good Teacher." The student determined that his audience would be a group of his peers on the occasion of a teacher awards ceremony, and his purpose would be to inform them of what he believes constitutes excellence in teaching.

QUALITIES OF A GOOD TEACHER

has high expectations of students
competent
shows relevance of field of study
patience w/ students
stimulates interest
prepared and organized
accessible after class
rarely absent
fair, unbiased
flexible
creative
enthusiastic
open-minded
brings ideas to discussion not in textbook
clear instructions
asks questions
interested in students' ideas
keeps up to date in field
never uses yellow lecture notes
no favorites
never embarrasses students
variety of teaching styles
can answer any question
can "tell stories"
drives a Corvette

wide knowledge, not just of
    subject
no spoonfeeding
praises good work
not monotone
encourages critical
    thinking
organized notes
command of
    language
doesn't patronize
doesn't speak down
loves subject & enjoys it
considerate, tactful
attractive
listens to opposing views
clear expectations
grades consistently
interesting lectures
doesn't repeat readings
values student contributions
motivates, inspires
prompt
fair tests
Mrs. Jones–history
young
single

Obviously not everything from this list will make its way to the final draft of the essay. Much will be cut and much will be incorporated into more general topics. You can see from this list that "good teachers" is a topic that produces a wealth of material.

Once your brainstorming session seems to have exhausted itself, group together those items that share some common characteristics. After forming these tentative groups, eliminate everything that does not fit into any of these groups. Now these groups and the details that remain should help shape an approach that will eventually become the focus of your thesis. Notice how the details from our original brainstorming of "good teachers" are grouped in the following example:

Relationships with students
    –has high expectations of students
    –no spoonfeeding
    –praises good work
    –patience with students
    –doesn't patronize
    –doesn't speak down
    –considerate
    –tactful
    –listens to opposing views
    –interested in students' ideas
    –provides additional help if needed
    –accessible after class
    –fair, unbiased
    –flexible
    –open-minded
    –values student contributions
    –motivates, inspires
    –no favorites
    –doesn't ridicule or embarrass students

Style of teaching
    –sense of humor
    –loves subject and enjoys it
    –stimulates student interest
    –asks questions
    –not a monotone
    –encourages critical thinking
    –creative
    –clear expectations & instructions
    –grades consistently
    –interesting lectures
    –doesn't repeat readings
    –fair tests
    –enthusiastic
    –variety of teaching styles
    –can adapt methods spontaneously

Knowledge of subject
    –competent
    –prepared and organized
    –command of language
    –brings ideas to discussion not in text
    –keeps up to date in field
    –doesn't lecture from yellow notes
    –wide knowledge, not just of subject
    –shows relevance of field of study
    –can "tell stories"
    –knows incidental information
    –can answer almost any question

Grouping shows that the details we save can be sorted into three general groups: relationship with students, teaching style, and knowledge of the subject matter. However, if we had to deal with all three subtopics, we would have quite a long essay, much longer than what is required for a typical writing assignment. We can pick any of these three groups and use it alone as the topic for our essay. Since most of our brainstorming ideas fall into the category of relationship with students, we choose that grouping as the narrowed topic of our essay.

At this point in the writing process you have a specific subject, an audience and purpose, and a general idea of what you want to discuss. The next step is to construct a statement that will incorporate your primary ideas into a workable thesis.

Formulating a Thesis Statement

Many beginning writers make the mistake of underestimating the importance of a thesis statement or of confusing it with the topic or a statement of purpose of the essay. The thesis is an explicit statement, a single sentence that expresses the central point the writer wishes to make. It is the summary of all the individual elements in your paper that relate to your topic. The thesis is what holds the essay together and gives it direction. Without a good thesis you will likely have a poorly organized essay. The steps suggested below should help you formulate a thesis statement that will work to your advantage by giving coherence and organization to your essay.

Step One
After you have discovered your topic and have brainstormed it thoroughly, as in the earlier exercise regarding good teachers, you now must state what is a key component of the thesis statement–the subject. The subject of your thesis sentence states the narrowed, restricted topic of your essay. It tells what your essay will be about. The subject part of the thesis sentence says, simply, that you will discuss, not just "teachers," but "good teachers." Putting a subject in a thesis statement is easy now since by brainstorming you have already arrived at a fairly restricted

subject. However, that is not to say that you cannot further revise the subject at this stage. Remember that we limited our topic further to "the relationship good teachers have with their students." Be sure that the subject you choose is restricted enough to give the reader a clear and thorough treatment of it in the length of the essay required. Too broad a subject will result in a discussion that is too general and superficial, while too narrow a subject will leave you with nothing to say after one or two sentences.

Step Two
The other key component of a thesis statement, the focus, is usually the predicate portion of your sentence, that portion which asserts exactly what you intend to say about your subject. The focus is not as easy to formulate as the subject, and many beginning writers tend to neglect it. This oversight is a fatal mistake. Imagine an essay that begins, "There are many good teachers at my school." The reader, right before falling asleep or throwing the paper into the trash, will reply, "So what?" It is not enough to say that there are good teachers out there; you must be able to say something about them: "The best teachers have three qualities in common," or "Mrs. Jones, the best teacher I ever had, cared about her students both in and out of the classroom."

To arrive at a focus, let's take another look at our subtopic "Relationship with students" and see how we can group the details there.

Motivation/Inspiration
    has high expectations of students
    no spoonfeeding
    praises good work
    motivates, inspires
    makes class interesting

Respect for students
    patience with students
    doesn't patronize
    doesn't speak down
    considerate
    tactful
    listens to opposing views
    fair, unbiased
    flexible
    open-minded
    values student contributions
    no favorites
    doesn't ridicule or embarrass students

Personal interest in students
    provides additional help if needed
    accessible after class
    interested in extra-curricular activities

As well as helping to restrict your subject, the groupings furnish you the specific terms with which to compose a tentative thesis statement. From the groupings above we can formulate the following thesis sentence: *A good teacher respects students, has a personal interest in them, and motivates them to do their best.* Now that you have a specific subject and a clearer focus in front of you, you are better prepared to organize and present your material. You have taken your random thoughts and formed them into a cohesive whole.

Step Three

Because you have identified a specific audience that may not be easy to convince, make certain your thesis is precise, concise, and unified. By being precise, you make certain that no word is ambiguous or unclear. Say clearly what you mean and what you intend to discuss. Don't tell your reader that "Mrs. Jones, my favorite teacher, was interesting and nice," although she probably was both. Even if your audience is the least bit interested in this insightful observation, the point will be almost impossible to prove. How does one define "nice"? Was she friendly? polite? cheerful? caring? "Nice" means all of these things and none of them. And the word "interesting" runs the gamut from being able to tell the best jokes of anyone on the faculty to having an extensive collection of World War II artillery shells. Use specific, concrete words rather than vague general terms. Being concise comes from taking the time to choose the most precise words and phrases, those that say exactly what you want to say and that will be easy to develop in the body of the essay. In addition, you must state succinctly what your intention is and no more. Consider this thesis sentence: "Mrs. Jones was the best teacher I ever had because she cared for her students; that is, she always had a kind word for everyone and she helped us study for the tests." After a thesis like that, there will be little left to discuss in the rest of the paper. Remember, although your purpose in the essay is to present, explain, or argue an idea, the thesis statement is not the place to begin your argument or explanation. It is only to sum up or to defend your position, sometimes referred to as the "method of approach." "Mrs. Jones was the best teacher I ever had because she cared for her students" indicates what you are going to discuss, but does not reveal the whole essay in the opening paragraph.

Finally, unless your essay is a lengthy one, make certain your thesis statement contains a single issue or idea; otherwise, the scope of your essay will be too broad and your supporting examples too general to be convincing. A unified thesis statement reduces the possibilities of unity violations in the body of the essay. "Mrs. Jones, the best teacher I ever had, cared about her students: that is, she always had a kind word for everyone, even though she never had much to say to my friend Hortense." Aside from being wordy and too precise, this sentence violates unity in that it wanders off to the subject of Hortense. A unified thesis statement reduces the ever-present potential for violations of unity in the body of the essay.

A final word about the thesis statement.

Here are a few things to remember in order to make your thesis sentence work for you and not against you:

1. Avoid the obvious. While you want to make it clear to your audience what you intend to do, never say, "In this paper I will . . . ." Statements like this are dull, plodding, and unsubtle. Make your wording original and fresh.

2. Be direct and forceful in stating your opinion without alienating the reader. Make it clear that you are taking a stand and are allied with a certain position.

3. Do not, however, say, "It is my opinion that . . . ." The reader will know that the opinions in the essay are yours. Phrasing a sentence thus only makes for another dull and plodding sentence. If the ideas are not yours, they must be correctly documented.

4. Make sure that your thesis sentence indicates the organization of your paper. If you have three characteristics of excellence in teachers to discuss, mention each briefly in the thesis sentence and mention them in the order you wish to discuss them in the body of the paper. This method of organization creates confidence in the readers regarding the writer's ability to be clear, logical, and organized from the outset.

5. Make certain the length of your sentence is appropriate for the length of your paper. A 45-word thesis statement is too long for a 600-word essay. Your introductory paragraph should not consist only of a thesis. This paragraph introduces your thesis as well as the entire essay.

6. The thesis statement should be ONE sentence only. A compound sentence is okay, but do not make it merely a string of independent clauses. Selective wording will eliminate a "rambling" sentence.

7. Finally, never hesitate to revise your thesis statement at any stage in drafting your essay if you feel you can improve it. Even though it may mean additional adjustments in the body of the essay, your extra effort will usually pay off. You should make at least two revisions.

THE MIDDLE

Now that you have a thesis statement to control the essay, you must organize the body of your discussion. To begin this process, look back at your notes from your brainstorming once again and notice the way you grouped the details. Why did you group certain things together? What did they have in common? What "heading" could you give each group? Each of the groupings that you made in your brainstorming now will become a main element in the body of your essay and will be mentioned in your thesis statement. Next, formulate the ideas generated in each of the brainstorming categories into a working statement that summarizes all the ideas in the category. This sentence will serve as your topic sentence for each category; it will be formed eventually into a paragraph composed of subtopics and examples. This topic sentence functions as the controlling idea of the paragraph. Just as your thesis statement states your purpose for the entire essay, your topic sentence directs your audience's attention to the single idea you will discuss in each particular paragraph. Each topic sentence, just like the thesis statement, has a subject and a focus. This focus will signal to the reading audience precisely what you intend to illustrate in the course of that paragraph and how it relates to the thesis. The same rules of clarity, conciseness, and unity required of your thesis statement apply to the topic sentence as well, for, regardless of its length and complexity, the paragraph should contain only one central idea.

Outlining/Developing A Plan

While the word "outline" itself provokes scurrilous mutterings and utter contempt from most composition students, it need not be treated as an adversarial force to be conquered or endured. It must, however, be done *before* you write the essay, not *after*. Once you become familiar enough with the benefits of outlining, you will discover it is the most critical step in all the pre-writing stage. The outline functions much like the blueprints of an architectural project. It is the framework on which to build your essay. You must overcome the tendency to resist this key step in the stage of writing, for, regardless of which rhetorical mode you select for your essay, good planning is essential. Likewise, poor planning is quickly evident. The value is endless for the writer as well as the reader. Consider the following advantages:

1. For the writer, the outline encourages brevity.

2. It can keep you from violating unity by indicating that an idea does not belong. At the same time, the outline will often suggest that some additional idea might be included.

3. The outline can ensure that important ideas are placed in the appropriate places according to relative value.

4. Its format allows you to check for stylistic consistency, continuity, and clarity.

5. It keeps you focused on the separate ideas and lets you actually visualize the level of generality among your ideas. Your ideas in the outline format are simply easier to see.

6. Finally, the outline will provide you with a psychological boost. Having succeeded in organizing your ideas logically, you enjoy a sense of

accomplishment that should allow you to move on to the next writing stage with increased confidence.

There are two basic outline forms–the topic outline and the sentence outline. Regardless of the assignment, you will want to consider using both forms at strategic stages in the prewriting phase. Now that your purpose is clear, your audience is designated, and you have a workable thesis clearly in mind, it is time to impose the standard outline system of organization on your thoughts. The following system is the *universal format for outlining ideas*:

Thesis
I.   [First topic related to discussion of thesis]
    A.
        1.
           a.
           b.
           c.
        2.
           a.
           b.   (Note: the old adage "If
           c.   you have a 1, you must have
                        a 2" is a valid point. The
    B.   same holds true of any
        1.   subheading or level of
           a.   development. A good rule
           b.   to remember is that a *pair*
           c.   *is the required minimum.*)
        2.
           a.
           b.
           c.
II.   [Second topic related to thesis statement]
    A. [etc.]

Each Roman numeral is a major division of the thesis of the essay, and each of the subheadings, capital letters, Arabic numerals, and lower case letters are more specific information that develop each division (paragraph).

Topic Outline
The topic outline is helpful in the preliminary organization of the essay when you want to determine the main points of your discussion and the order in which you will discuss them. Each entry in a topic outline is just what the term implies: a topic heading, much like a title, not a complete sentence, but a "bare bones" phrase.

The topic outline delineates the areas to be discussed but does not yet deal with what specifically will be said about them. Even at the topic outline level, however, you should be grammatically consistent. If you want to use nouns, nouns plus a verb form, or prepositional phrases, make certain you use them at each letter or number level in order to create a parallel structure. This consistency will assist you later when transforming your topic outline to the body paragraphs of the essay.

Topic Outline Example

Good Teachers

Thesis: A good teacher respects students, has a personal interest in them, and motivates them to do their best.

I. Respect for students
   A. Considerate
      1. Tactful
      2. Non-ridiculing
      3. Patient
      4. Non-patronizing
   B. Fair
      1. Flexible
      2. Fair in testing
      3. Objective in grading
      4. No favoritism
   C. Values students' contributions
      1. Compliments students' work
      2. Praises student involvement
II. (etc.)

Sentence Outline

Whether it is used initially or instead of the topic outline, the sentence outline requires more effort. You will still be required to list, categorize, and order your ideas by relative importance. This time, however, you must write your thoughts in complete sentences. The first stage of a sentence outline might look like this:

Good Teachers

Thesis: A good teacher respects students, has a personal interest in them, and motivates them to do their best.

I. A good teacher respects her students.
   A. She is considerate of her students.

1. She criticizes them tactfully.
2. She does not ridicule them or embarrass them.
3. She is patient with them.
4. She never patronizes her students.
B. She treats her students fairly.
   1. She is flexible and open-minded.
   2. Her tests are fair.
   3. She grades objectively and consistently.
   4. She does not have favorites.
C. She shows that she values the contributions of everyone in the class.
   1. She compliments her students on their work.
   2. She praises them for their involvement even when she disagrees with them.
  II. (etc.)

A note about outlining. Regardless of which outline form you use, it is a good idea to write down all the headings/sentences for the Roman numerals before going on to the capital letters and all the capital letter headings before going on to the next level. Doing so helps keep the levels of development, the subtopics and details, clear. With this systematic organizational plan behind you, you can now concentrate on the next phase: development.

The Paragraph

The standard paragraph is made up of a topic sentence, subtopic headings and various levels of specific examples. The topic sentence functions in the paragraph just as the thesis statement functions in the essay. The topic sentence also supports the thesis statement by offering a main point in the discussion and announces what specifically will be discussed in the paragraph. Likewise, each subtopic heading (the A, B, etc. of the outline) will support the specific focus of the paragraph. Finally, the examples under each subtopic heading offer illustrations that support the assertions of the subheading. Thus, in a well-organized paragraph, the relationship of every detail to the topic sentence is obvious, and, in turn, the connection with the thesis is obvious. Remember that the paragraph is a miniature essay. Mastering the principles of paragraph form offers greater assurance toward mastering the essay. This mastery involves being familiar with unity, development, coherence, and continuity within the paragraph.

Paragraph Unity
For a paragraph to have unity, each sentence in a body paragraph must directly relate to the purpose indicated in the topic sentence. The paragraph must hang together as a whole, creating an unmistakable sense of oneness. Any departure from the single purpose of the paragraph violates paragraph unity. For example, if you were to bring into your discussion of good teachers the idea that teachers' salaries need to be

raised, you would be shifting the focus away from the main idea, thus breaking the unity in the paragraph. *Stick to your topic sentence!* Keep in mind that a paragraph is, by definition, a unified statement of a particular idea. A way to test paragraph unity is to try to link each sentence to a word or phrase in the topic sentence. Draw lines and arrows if you must. Any sentence that you cannot obviously link to the topic sentence is probably irrelevant and, therefore, will undermine the effectiveness of your paper.

Paragraph Development

Just because you have said in your thesis statement that a good teacher respects her students, shows interest in them, and motivates them, that does not mean that your readers have to accept your viewpoint automatically. You must convince your audience that what you have to say is sound, sensible, and well-supported. In other words, even if you are informing, you are still persuading your readers. You must explore your main idea explicitly, concretely, and thoroughly, and you must strive to include enough supporting evidence in each paragraph to present your point convincingly. *Inadequate paragraph development* is one of the most serious weaknesses of beginning writers. No matter how organized and unified your ideas are, if they are not developed fully, you will have failed to communicate to your audience. Supporting evidence or examples come from your own experiences, from hypothetical examples, research material, authoritative evidence, facts, or from just about any sound, reliable source.

Many students ask, "What is enough support?" The answer is arbitrary, but some general guidelines apply. You want enough support to convince your audience of the soundness of your argument. Whose opinion, for example, is more likely to be accepted in a court of law: a defense attorney's claim that her client is innocent because the defendant's family and friends know he is innocent or the prosecuting attorney's claim that the defendant is guilty because of fourteen eyewitnesses and his fingerprints on the murder weapon? Valid evidence is convincing and supports opinions and observation. The same is true of paragraph development. You must provide enough information to convince them of the soundness of your argument. As a rule, the average length of a paragraph in a college-level essay might run approximately three-fourths of a typed page. While striving arduously for quantity, however, NEVER forget that quality is more important. The fact that Aunt Zona Gail believes men make better teachers than women is not the strong evidence you want to support your contentions about good teachers. But surveying students or speaking with teachers who have won awards or recognition for excellence in teaching would serve as appropriate proof.

In moving from topic sentence to supporting evidence in a paragraph, you are moving from general to specific. The order and progression of this movement is essential to effective paragraphs, and the outline is the most efficient method of making certain this progression occurs logically. This order ranks and demonstrates the levels of generality in a paragraph. For example:

I. [topic sentence–general statement]
   Igor was a poor student. **LEVEL ONE**
   A. [subtopic–less general] He was not conscientious. **LEVEL TWO**
      1. [example–specific] He never handed in assignments on time.
         LEVEL THREE
         a. [more specific] He handed in his first English
            composition two weeks late. **LEVEL FOUR**

These levels constitute the arrangement of ideas in the paragraph, from general statement to specific examples. <u>Always develop your ideas in the outline of your paragraph at least to level three</u>. The logic behind this recommendation is that you most likely will have to reach level three before you can provide examples that are specific and concrete enough to persuade your readers of your general assertion (level one). In addition, the *ideal* number of level two or level three statements is *three*; that is, A, B, C and 1, 2, and 3. If you offer only two examples, you could risk sounding dogmatic and inflexible. Four or more examples under the same subtopic, however, suggest you wish to appeal emotionally to your readers. Some readers might cry out "Enough already!" There is such a thing as overkill, especially if your examples tend to be repetitious. You will not always be able to provide three examples, but the goal is a worthy one. Make sure you understand and can recognize the different levels so you can create good, effective outlines and, consequently, good paragraphs. Note in the following outline how we have added level four to our sentence outline.

I. A good teacher respects her students. **LEVEL ONE**
   A. She is considerate of her students. **LEVEL TWO**
      1. She criticizes them tactfully. **LEVEL THREE**
         a. She always tells them something positive about their work
            along with suggestions on how to improve it. **LEVEL FOUR**

Finally, if your paragraph is a long one, you might consider including a summary sentence, a "clincher," to close your paragraph. The inclusion of such a sentence serves at least two purposes. First, it brings closure to the main idea of the paragraph, especially if you have provided extensive examples. Closure helps your audience by returning them to your central idea and reminding them of your specific intention in the paragraph. Second, the summary sentence is on the same level of generality as your topic sentence; therefore, it will make your task of bridging the connection between this paragraph and the next easier than it would be if you had to move from a very specific level of generality, a minor support statement, to a new topic sentence in a new paragraph. This final summary sentence "clinches" the discussion and emphasizes the main idea. Some writers prefer to provide in this final sentence some notion of what is to come in the next paragraph through some kind of transition device.

Continuity in the Paragraph

Continuity means literally "holding together." It is achieved through good organization and unity, as we have seen, and also by the language you use to illustrate to your readers how your ideas fit together. The language you use will serve as *transitions*, devices that link sentences to each other. Transitions are also used to connect paragraphs, thus linking your ideas together in a smooth, logical order.

Transitional devices include pronouns and demonstrative adjectives, repetition of key words, the use of synonyms, transitional expressions, and parallel construction.

1. Pronouns and demonstrative adjectives–When their antecedents are clearly understood, pronouns (*they, it, she, he*) help the reader recognize that the phrase or sentence in which they appear is linked to the preceding idea. Example: "Steinbeck is fascinated by the animal motivation behind human behavior. Frequently in *his* fiction, *he* equates human and animal conduct to show *their* similarities.

Demonstrative adjectives also clearly link the sentence containing them with the preceding sentences. These adjectives are words like *that, this, these*, and *those*. Notice how the demonstrative adjective links the following two sentences: "Recognition of the unity of all life is the basis for John Steinbeck's artistic use of nature. One of the major expressions of *this* unity is the kinship that man feels with the land."

2. Repetition of key words and use of synonyms–the important rule here is to repeat key words, those words that keep your focus in the minds of your audience. Notice how the word *unity* is repeated in the example above. Be careful, however, that you do not rely too heavily on the transitional technique; too much repetition becomes monotonous. If you feel you are repeating the same word too often, substitute a synonym. Instead of *unity* try *oneness* or *harmony* occasionally if it fits the context of your meaning.

3. Transitional words–The most recognizable and most effective transitional words include "furthermore," "moreover," "likewise," "similarly," "nevertheless," "on the other hand," "conversely," "first," "second," "third," and so on. Each of these words has a definite function, whether it is to show logical order or to indicate logical relationships between ideas and sentences. Without these expressions, your sentences would make little sense and certainly would not fit together to develop your idea. A word of caution, however: be sure the transitional expression you choose does precisely what you want it to do. Do not simply close your eyes and select a transitional word from the list. Use an appropriate term for the meaning or connection you wish to convey. Never use "furthermore" when "however" is what you need to alter the direction or to qualify a statement. Consult your handbook or thesaurus for additional help.

4. Parallel construction–This transitional device links your sentences and ideas by repeating a grammatical structure, thereby forcing your audience not only to keep the focus in mind but to realize fully the connection between your ideas. Note, for example, President Lincoln's use of parallel construction in his famous "Gettysburg Address" and the power of its connected ideas to hold his audience:

It is rather for us to be here dedicated to the great task remaining before us; **that** from these honored dead we take increased devotion to that cause for which they gave the last full measure of devotion; **that** we here highly resolve that these dead shall not have died in vain; **that** this nation, under God, shall have a new birth of freedom, and **that** government of the people, by the people, for the people, shall not perish from the earth.

All transitional devices assist you, the writer, in avoiding dull repetition by making the expression of your ideas more interesting and more varied. These devices keep you and your reader from having to leap from one idea to another because they offer convenient and persuasive bridges which add to the coherence and logic of your ideas. Most writers find that they naturally include the transitional devices within paragraphs, but additional editing might be required during revising to make certain that there is adequate bridging between paragraphs.

The following excerpt is written with the transitional devices italicized. Notice how the transitional devices make the argument easy to follow and make the writing style more fluid.

Kinship between man and the land is only one aspect of Steinbeck's celebration of the unity of all life. As *man* is one with the *land*, so is *he one* with the *animal life* that inhabits the *land*. *Man* is part of nature, and *his* social and biological behavior is not unlike the lower forms of *animal life*. *Furthermore*, the *biologist* who observes the living habits of animals can correctly apply *his observations* to human nature. Steinbeck the *biologist* is fascinated by the *animal* motivation behind *human behavior*. Frequently in *his* fiction, *he* equates *human and animal conduct* to show *their* similarities.

Steinbeck uses *animal life* symbolically in three ways. *First*, he frequently describes the *human community* with the image of a many-celled organism, a "group-man" whose individual cells contribute to *his* total function. *This image* is a basic one and it's the foundation of much of Steinbeck's social theorizing. *Second*, many of his individual characters display obvious *animal* characteristics and are closely associated with, and often symbolized by, particular *animals*. *Third*, he uses animals to *symbolize* many of the human problems, emotions, and activities appearing in the novels and the short stories. Both the *human community* and the *individual*, *then*, are related to *animal life*.

From Paragraph To Essay

When you understand the principles that constitute a good paragraph, you will understand the general organization of the essay. Remember that a paragraph is a miniature essay. Only the scope of a paragraph changes to meet the requirements of the essay. The system remains the same, but the form expands. Consider the diagram below and note the simple changes that occur when the components of the paragraph are converted to the essay.

Paragraph		Essay
I. Topic sentence	——— becomes———	Thesis statement
A. Subtopic	——— becomes———	I. Topic sentence
1. Example	——— becomes———	A. Subtopic
2. Example	——— becomes———	B. Subtopic
B. Subtopic	——— becomes———	II. Topic sentence
1. Example	——— becomes———	A. Subtopic
2. Example	——— becomes———	B. Subtopic
C. Subtopic	——— becomes———	III. Topic sentence

What is needed now in the essay is an additional level of development. Under the subtopics in the above essay format, you would add specific, supporting examples to complete the essential skeleton of the essay (i.e., add 1., 2., 3. under A. and B., etc.). In general, most of your writing will have an introductory paragraph, usually three or more body paragraphs, and a concluding paragraph. Regardless of the length of the essay, the principles of organization remain the same.

THE END

Now you are ready to conclude the writing process by putting the finishing touches on your essay. This stage of your writing actually includes several steps. Not only does it involve the concluding paragraph, but it also includes constructing the introductory paragraph and a title for the essay. Having completed the heart of your thoughts in your body paragraphs (the middle), you now need to introduce those thoughts in an opening paragraph that includes your thesis and to conclude your discussion by offering closure. Although the techniques vary considerably regarding these two paragraphs, the primary function is to provide the framework for the ideas you convincingly present to your audience. This stage completes the writing phase.

Introductory Paragraph

Because the opening paragraph is the audience's first contact with you and with what you have to say, it is of utmost importance. Traditionally, however, writers have discovered that this paragraph is the most difficult to write, perhaps because of its importance and uniqueness or perhaps because of the "mental block" associated with the dreaded "blank page syndrome." There are at least two options in putting your introductory paragraph together. Some writers prefer to write their opening paragraph first, knowing what they intend to discuss in the body paragraphs and what their thesis statement is. If they feel that the introductory paragraph needs to be altered after having written the essay, they simply revise it accordingly. However, some writers prefer to wait until the essay is complete before they tackle this paragraph. Perhaps it is easier to explain to someone where you are going if you have already been there. Since you have had your thesis in mind throughout the organizing and writing stages, and since you now know what ground you have traveled in your body discussion, you can more confidently address the issue of putting an introduction of your ideas together, capped, of course, by your thesis statement. You now must show your audience precisely which path you will travel together.

To begin, you must keep in mind the four primary functions of the introductory paragraph:

1. to get the reader's attention;
2. to set the tone for the rest of the essay;
3. to show the audience why they should continue to read your essay;
4. to make a commitment, to take a stand that tells the audience what to expect from your discussion in the essay.

To help you determine what kind of opening paragraph you need, you must remind yourself of your audience and purpose. When you write an essay, you make a commitment to your audience. You are obligated to live up to your commitment; therefore, you want to fulfill that obligation by explaining and supporting your ideas with as much information as you can. By learning what your commitment and purpose are in your opening paragraph, your readers know what to expect. If you fail to interest them in the introductory paragraph or renege on your obligation, your audience might decide to read no further. In short, you want your audience to read all the way through your discussion; therefore, you want to do what you said you would do.

The opening paragraph also sets the tone for the rest of the essay. If your topic is a serious one, the opening paragraph should be sufficiently serious. Conversely, if your essay is humorous, the opening should establish a light tone. Nothing is more disconcerting to a reader and self-defeating to a writer than inconsistency in tone.

The introductory paragraph for an average college-level essay usually will require no more than five or six sentences, depending upon how specific you are in your opening comments. The paragraph moves from a general statement introducing the subject to a specific thesis statement. The organization might be diagrammed as an inverted pyramid, thus:

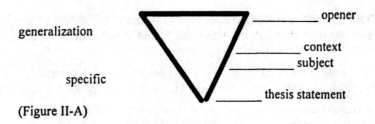

generalization

specific

opener

context
subject

thesis statement

(Figure II-A)

The thesis is the most specific statement in the paragraph and generally will appear as the last sentence of the paragraph. In the following introductory paragraph, notice how the writer moves from a general statement about the treatment of minor medical emergencies, to the independent emergency clinic, to her own experiences with such a clinic, to her thesis that the independent clinic will soon replace the hospital emergency ward:

In the past several years, a new concept in the treatment of minor medical emergencies has emerged. The independent emergency clinic is devoted to the patient with minor problems. In the past, I have had the misfortune of seeking minor emergency care in the hospital emergency ward. Even though I always received excellent medical care, I did encounter some disadvantages. Upon visiting this new type of facility as both observer and patient, I found the medical care equal to the hospital without many of the disadvantages. **The independent clinic may very well replace the hospital emergency ward in the treatment of minor medical emergencies in the future.**

Even though you will move in the paragraph from general to specific, you should avoid beginning with too broad a generalization. The more general you are at first, the longer it will take you to get around to your thesis and the more you risk losing your audience's attention. A first sentence about the quality of health care in the United States today would have been much too general for the introductory paragraph on independent clinics.

Begin with a sentence that is not so general that it fails to get the readers' attention but that gets them involved in your discussion. There are several effective methods of achieving this goal:

1. Use a relevant anecdote or personal narrative. The writer of the paragraph on independent clinics could have had a much more compelling introduction if she had recounted one of the times when she had to go to an emergency ward. The anecdote might include the "attention-getter" sentence, or it can follow a separate "attention-getter" sentence.

2. Ask a question. "In this day of rising medical costs, what can the consumer do to get the best emergency health care at the best price?"

3. Offer a startling opening statement: "Medical technology has advanced as never before, yet more than 20% of Americans cannot afford even the most basic of health care."

4. Use an analogy or comparison. "Many health care professionals scornfully refer to the independent clinic as 'Doc-in-the-Box' or 'Quack Shack.'"

5. Offer an informal definition. Without referring to the dictionary (denotative) definition, state your own meaning of a term that will allow you to introduce your subject and its discussion.

No matter which of these methods you select, make certain your beginning is interesting and says something important and relevant to your subject. Make sure that your opening anecdote, analogy, or startling statistic fits smoothly into the rest of your introductory paragraph and leads logically to your thesis statement. Too many beginning writers come up with an attention-getting first sentence but then fail to tie it in smoothly to the rest of the opening paragraph; such a failure stops the reader cold.

The suggestions listed above certainly do not exhaust the possibilities. As you develop as a writer, you will discover other methods of introduction that might be even more suitable to your own taste, style, or technique. But never lose sight of the general purpose and function of the introductory paragraph.

Concluding Paragraph

While your final paragraph is not as important as your introductory paragraph, it is vital to your purpose because it is your last chance to make an impression on your audience. This paragraph should achieve at least the following goals:

1. Restate the thesis but reword it this time;
2. Summarize the key topics presented in the discussion (This goal is optional. Inquire about your instructor's preference);
3. Suggest larger implications than you could have offered before you presented all your evidence, especially in persuasive writing;
4. Give the audience a sense of closure.

You want to realize that much of what your readers will remember about your discussion is what you present in your concluding paragraph. You have kept their attention long enough to bring them to your closing remarks; don't lose them now! Offer something that is memorable. What you have said in the body paragraphs has surely taken your readers beyond the boundaries of your thesis statement. Now you must relate to your audience what your purpose and thesis imply. Do not, however, claim more than your presentation justifies or you can deliver. Make your point and close. Never give the impression that you have simply stopped writing.

The readers desire and expect a sense of closure–an end or conclusion. Never mention a new idea in your conclusion that could or should have been discussed earlier in the essay. Not much can be added at this point that might convince readers if it has not already been said in the body paragraphs. Close while you still have their attention, avoiding platitudes, overused generalities, or noble-sentiment endings. Sometimes the methods suggested earlier for opening your introductory paragraph can work for the closure of your final paragraph as well. Do not, however, merely repeat your opening sentence or your thesis. Make your closure interesting, provocative, informative, or inspiring. Whatever works for you, use it.

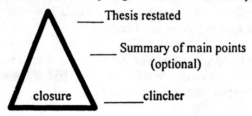

(Figure II-B)

Titles

Most writers prefer to consider a title after they have completed their entire draft. Now that your subject and focus, your tone, and your audience and purpose are all clearly determined and you have the full picture of what you have said in the essay, you might try to capture the essence of this writing in a few words. After all, the title is the first thing your audience sees of your essay; therefore, why not establish an initial greeting that captures your whole discussion? *Be accurate and specific* in your title, providing more than the mere subject of your essay. The title should let the reader see the link between what it promises and what the essay delivers. You might include a key word from the focus of your discussion, but never let a sentence be your title. Be consistent with the tone; a serious essay is undermined by a flippant title. In short, use your imagination and be creative; strive to get the attention of your audience. Instead of titling your essay "Good Teachers," why not "How Good Teachers Treat their Students," or better yet, "Good Teachers: Respect Begetting Respect."

Revising the Draft

Revision is the third and final phase of constructing a good essay. Its importance lies in the fact that it is your final involvement with the essay; therefore, you need to make sure you have corrected all the problems and put the finishing touches to your draft. Many students neglect this "polishing" step for one reason or another, but the difference between an excellent essay and a mediocre one can depend on how thoroughly you proofread and revise your ideas.

Once you have completed your first draft, you should allow some time to pass before you begin to revise it. If you wait until you are fresh and a bit removed from your essay, you will be able to detect the problems in it more easily. Some writers have found that if they transfer their hand-written draft to a typed or printed form (or from screen to hard copy), they can more readily recognize and correct their errors. Typing allows you to view the essay more objectively. Because there are so many areas to be reviewed, you should plan to read your draft several times, determining in advance what specific potential problems you are searching for and correcting. You should also consider reading the draft aloud. You will be surprised to discover that your ears will detect an awkward sentence or phrase that your eyes overlooked. Never blink when you are proofreading!

Next, proofread your essay with the following checklist in mind. Examine your draft for effectiveness in these four areas: (1) subject matter, (2) organization, (3) style, and (4) mechanics and grammar.

Checklist

1. Subject matter
   a. Are your examples valid? Do they contribute to the validity of your opinions?
   b. Have you provided an adequate number of examples to develop each topic sentence?
   c. Does each topic sentence directly relate to the thesis statement?
   d. Do your paragraphs maintain unity? Have you taken out any material that is irrelevant, unnecessary, or vague?

2. Organization
   a. Is your purpose clearly implied, and is your thesis statement specifically stated?
   b. Are your paragraphs in logical order?
   c. Do your transitions function effectively? Do your ideas flow smoothly and logically from one sentence to the next? from one paragraph to the next? Do your transitional devices eliminate vagueness?
   d. Does your introductory paragraph get the readers' attention, does it establish the context for your subject, and does your thesis statement have a limited subject and a restricted focus?
   e. Have you summarized your main points (if you are required to do so) and provided effective closure in your final paragraph?

3. Style
   a. Have you offered a variety of sentence constructions (i.e., simple, compound, complex sentences)? Could some sentences be combined through modification or subordination for more effective expression? Can you improve sentence structure for better emphasis or focus?
   b. Are your language and examples appropriate for your specified purpose and audience? Have you selected the best word for the meaning you wish to convey?
   c. Have you removed all "deadwood," those phrases or words that are unnecessary or fail to contribute directly to your purpose? Remember that more is not always better. For example, rather than saying "due to the fact that," simply say "because."
   d. Is your diction consistent with the tone you want to convey? Have you avoided jargon and slang expressions?
   e. Are your ideas clear, appropriate, and interesting?

4. Mechanics and Grammar
   a. Always check for the following:
      1. spelling errors
      2. subject-verb agreement errors
      3. sentence fragments

4. fused sentences
5. comma splices
6. punctuation errors
7. reference agreement errors
8. dangling or misplaced modifiers
9. verb tense inconsistencies
10. clichés

Make minor corrections in the text of your draft if they can be done neatly; otherwise, retype or rewrite the essay.

b. Is your handwritten draft legible? Is it neat? If not, make it so.

c. If your essay is a research assignment, have you complied with the MLA style form? Consult your handbook for specific guidelines and procedures.

d. Are you convinced that this essay represents you and your best ideas? Can you submit it to your instructor with pride and certainty? Remember that the final draft suggests to your reader that it is the best you can do. Is it? If not, revise further. Rumor has it that when asked why he revised the last page of his novel *A Farewell to Arms* thirty-nine times, Ernest Hemingway replied "Getting the words right." This many revisions might be a little extreme for a freshman essay. Nevertheless, when you are satisfied with the essay and you feel you cannot improve upon it any more (and by now you are probably sick of the whole thing anyway), turn it in for evaluation, and feel confident that you have accomplished what you set out to do in the beginning.

CHAPTER THREE
EXPOSITION

In any writing you do, you must determine who your audience is, what your purpose is, what the situation is, and what voice you will use to meet the challenges established. In order to write well, you will need to consider the best possible organizational plan to communicate clearly. In exposition, there are several useful rhetorical strategies including description and narration, process analysis, definition, illustration/exemplification, comparison/contrast, classification/division, and causal analysis.

In this chapter these rhetorical strategies will be discussed as separate units. Each will be presented as a means to an end, but in actual writing situations, you will find that you must use multiple strategies. In almost any essay you write, your purpose will be served by paying attention to specific details in order to describe, by exemplifying and illustrating any generalizations you make, by keeping in mind that all writing is an on-going process, and by keeping cause-effect relationships clear. You may need to develop each paragraph using one or the other of the rhetorical strategies while your overall purpose calls for a broader organizational plan.

You will find that your understanding of these rhetorical strategies, sometimes called *modes,* will assist you in developing your ideas clearly, whether for an essay, an essay exam, or some other purpose. Your thesis, in any case, will be determined by the situation, your audience, and your particular purpose.

DESCRIPTION AND NARRATION

Description

In nearly every essay-writing situation, we use description, especially in providing vivid examples. When we describe, we try to recreate for the audience the sensations we may have felt in a similar situation. The basis of any good description is, of course, close observation and a careful consideration of the audience and purpose. Remember the last time you were asked where you had parked your car and you had to rely on description to explain exactly what your car looked like and generally how to get there? Unless you observe the details, explaining anything clearly for your audience is difficult.

Implementation

Description is used in almost any rhetorical mode. It is often not an end in itself. It clarifies your point in narration, explains in comparison and classification, makes definition interesting, and creates strong emotional appeals in persuasive writing.

Technique

In addition to observing closely, choosing the right word is an essential feature of any writing experience. When we use any word in context, we must take several different things into consideration, including the degree of specificity and the nuances of the words. Beginning any discussion with a generalization or an abstraction is entirely possible. However, leaving the subject at that level does not create a very clear image or impression for the audience. In order to write evocatively, the writer must aim toward the specific rather than the general and the concrete rather than the abstract. Introducing an abstraction like *loyalty* is a beginning; however, describing the black and white terrier named Scotty sleeping on his master's grave in the cemetery night after night becomes more specific. Certain techniques help create vivid writing.

Attention to diction

Every writer understands the differences between denotation and connotation. Denotation is the dictionary definition of a particular word. If you look up *mother* in the dictionary, you find it means "female parent"–no real surprise.

The connotational value of a word, however, includes the associations our experience brings to that word. For some, the connotations of *mother* bring images of hot dogs, station wagons, and apple pies while for others it connotes a busy, organized woman with a briefcase. Connotations can be positive, neutral, or negative as well. If we refer to a person as obstinate or principled, we mean that person has a tendency to stick tenaciously to convictions. A person with conviction might also be called stubborn or, in some contexts, pig headed: in each case the connotations become progressively more negative. Our choices of words indicate how we want the reader to understand what we mean. Using the wrong word in certain contexts communicates something to the reader that we never meant! Suppose you were writing about water pollution, for instance, and you found yourself repeating *pure* over and over again in the conclusion. You might open your thesaurus to find another word to vary the way you present your summation of evidence. Among the synonyms, you will find "chaste." Now, chaste does mean purity in some contexts, but it would give your reader an unusual perception of water! Diction–your choice of the right word in the right place–makes a major difference in how your audience understands your point.

Comparisons

Communicating means putting yourself in the place of the audience well enough for you to figure out what the audience knows and to fill the gaps so you can get your point across. One way to do so is to use *literal comparisons*. That is, by comparing an unfamiliar thing to a familiar one, one the audience understands, you can clarify the unfamiliar. The literal comparison usually requires finding likenesses in two things that are basically similar in nature. Have you ever eaten fried alligator? What does it taste like? Chicken? Your answer is an example of a literal comparison: two things of *like* nature (sources of protein) compared in order to make the unfamiliar more familiar.

Another kind of comparison used in description is the *figurative comparison*. Figures of speech usually compare two things of essentially *unlike* nature. Common figures of speech include some of the following:

simile: a comparison of two essentially unlike things using words that make the comparison clear ("like," "as," "resembles," "than," and similar words). When you say that a certain child eats like a horse, you are using a simile to indicate a single aspect of the two subjects where the qualities of one make the qualities of the other vivid or interesting by comparison.

metaphor: a comparison of two essentially unlike things not using words that emphasize the comparison. The metaphor is a more implicit comparison. When we say a person *turns beet red* or is *a mad dog* when he is angry, we are using metaphor.

personification: a comparison of two essentially unlike things in which inanimate objects are given human or animal characteristics, abstractions are given qualities of humans or animals, animals are given human characteristics, and so forth. People who give their cars a name are personifying. If your car coughs and dies, you have given it (a machine with internal problems) human characteristics.

synecdoche: a comparison of two unlike things, in this case a part with the whole. If a farmer hires extra help during harvest, he may say he hires four hands. He actually hires four people with eight hands, but the essential aspect of his help is their ability to work with their hands, of course. In class it does not take you long to figure out which students are quick to catch on or which students have come to class well prepared. You may call those students "brains" to indicate their essential characteristics. You do not mean that they sit in the back of the class in a beaker.

Rhetorical Devices
Closely allied to figurative language, these devices are often included in descriptions. They are often examples of verbal irony, a discrepancy between what we say and what we mean.

hyperbole: a deliberate exaggeration for a particular effect. Anyone who lives in Texas understands the basic focus of hyperbole (pronounced hi per bo le, not "hyper bowl"–which sounds like a game played between two champion teams who have had too much sugar). When we say a mountain of dirty dishes is in the sink, we are using hyperbole. No matter where you park on campus, your car is 7000 miles from any class you have–truth or hyperbole?

understatement: a deliberate undercutting or downplaying of importance to create a particular effect. If the rain begins unexpectedly during class, catching you unprepared, and if it rains forty days and forty nights in an hour and a half (hyperbole), and if your car is 7000 miles from any shelter near a parking lot, and some character wanders past you in a yellow slicker, an umbrella, and hip boots and says, "Damp out, isn't it?" he is understating the situation.

paradox: an apparent contradiction that proves to be true upon reflection. Wordsworth's statement that the "child is father of the man" seems backwards but says something about the relative understanding of the two generations. *Everything I Needed to Know I Learned in Kindergarten* would seem to operate upon the same paradox. An **oxymoron** is a paradox in which the seeming contradiction is contained within a single phrase. The usual examples are "jumbo shrimp" and "sophomore" ("wise fool"). Some more literary references to "darkness visible" and "wintry fever" also fit the definition.

Imagery

Appeals to the senses. Obviously you must describe sensory impressions if you are to involve the reader in the point you are trying to make. The five kinds of sensory appeals include visual imagery (appeals to the way things look), tactile imagery (the way things feel), auditory/aural imagery (the way things sound), gustatory imagery (the way things taste), and olfactory imagery (the way things smell). In English there are more words to describe the way things look than to describe any other single image. Usually, the first three kinds of images are used more often in expository writing, but every once in a while, you may be called upon to use all the senses to vivify your writing. While you may start a discussion by saying that something looks good or that it sounds great, you really have not told the audience anything to expand understanding. You must use specific adjectives to create particular images to evoke corresponding sensations in the audience, to recreate for them the same sensations that you as the writer experienced.

Other descriptive words you may use also include certain devices involving sound, often associated with poetic language. Two that may lend unity and lyricism to your writing are alliteration and onomatopoeia.

Alliteration is the repetition of initial consonant sounds. All tongue twisters exemplify this device: "Peter Piper picked a peck of pickled peppers."

Onomatopoeia is language which imitates natural sounds. "Buzz," "clatter," and "bang," for instance, create images for the reader.

Organization

No descriptive passage exists in a vacuum: it is designed to fit your audience and your purpose. Therefore, most descriptions are used within examples to support whatever point you are making. Descriptions usually support a dominant impression you are trying to convey in your discussion and are organized to present the information in the most clearly logical way for your audience: *spatially* or *emphatically*. You may choose to arrange according to where things are in space or how they relate to each other (spatial). You may choose, on the other hand, to arrange your description according to the relative importance of your details (emphatic). No matter what the arrangement, the details you select will communicate your point to the reader. In certain circumstances you may want to present on objective description, trying to be as complete and unbiased in your presentation as possible. In other cases, your dominant impression may be subjective. You will want to involve your audience emotionally in your subject.

Consider the following description from Michael McFarland's short story "The False Country":

The center stripe was the bright line to which the dark world vibrated. It was the flashing middle marker stretching all the way from the horizon of the flat farm land. Far off at its origin was a point that Stephen aimed his car toward. Although it was night, he could see many other dimmer lines–made by the freeway's painted edge, the ditches, the endless fences, even the horizon, and–above the horizon–the tree line. They all seemed to begin at this central point and they came toward him at different speeds–sadly, slowly. Finally, reaching him, they slipped by until they were no longer in sight but probably converged at some equidistant point behind. The painted lines were the most dramatic, especially the center one. It constantly started up slowly and crept towards him, gathering speed until it flashed under. Finally it gave itself to the roar of the engine. The car seemed almost to be running on this energy like the toy cars he had played with as a boy. He had pushed them along the floor hard, until the momentum gave them life and they whirred off under their own power.

You will quickly notice the vivid visual and auditory images he creates. Comparison–literal and figurative–and rhetorical devices also contribute to the effect McFarland seeks to convey. At least one comparison appears as he likens the car to "the toy cars he had played with as a boy," and he personifies the lines as "[creeping] towards him," moving toward Stephen "sadly, slowly," examples of alliteration. The fences are called "endless"–a hyperbole, of course. The engine roars and the lines whir onomatopoeically: the evocative language involves the reader in the description. The dominant impression is subjective. From Stephen's point of view there is much movement and the lines are the central focus. Read E. B. White's essay "Once More to the Lake." As you read, note the descriptive techniques he uses, paying particular attention to the figures of speech and vivid images.

ONCE MORE TO THE LAKE
E. B. WHITE

August 1941

One summer, along about 1904, my father rented a camp on a lake in Maine and took us all there for the month of August. We all got ringworm from some kittens and had to rub Pond's Extract on our arms and legs night and morning, and my father rolled over in a canoe with all his clothes on; but outside of that the vacation was a success and from then on none of us ever thought there was any place in the world like that lake in Maine. We returned summer after summer–always on August 1 for one month. I have since become a salt-water man, but sometimes in summer there are days when the restlessness of the tides and the fearful cold of the sea water and the incessant wind that blows across the afternoon and into the evening make me wish for the placidity of a lake in the woods. A few weeks ago this feeling got so strong I bought myself a couple of bass hooks and a spinner and returned to the lake where we used to go, for a week's fishing and to revisit old haunts.

I took along my son, who had never had any fresh water up his nose and who had seen lily pads only from train windows. On the journey over to the lake I began to wonder what it would be like. I wondered how time would have marred this unique, this holy spot–the coves and streams, the hills that the sun set behind, the camps and the paths behind the camps. I was sure that the tarred road would have found it out, and I wondered in what other ways it would be desolated. It is strange how much you can remember about places like that once you allow your mind to return into the grooves that lead back. You remember one thing, and that suddenly reminds you of another thing. I guess I remembered clearest of all the early mornings, when the lake was cool and motionless, remembered how the bedroom smelled of the lumber it was made of and of the wet woods whose scent entered through the screen. The partitions in the camp were thin and did not extend clear to the top of the rooms, and as I was always the first up I would dress softly so as not to wake the others, and sneak out into the sweet outdoors and start out in the canoe, keeping close along the shore in the long shadows of the pines. I remembered being very careful never to rub my paddle against the gunwale for fear of disturbing the stillness of the cathedral.

The lake had never been what you would call a wild lake. There were cottages sprinkled around the shores, and it was in farming country although the shores of the lake were quite heavily wooded. Some of the cottages were owned by nearby farmers, and you would live at the shore and eat your meals at the farmhouse.

That's what our family did. But although it wasn't wild, it was a fairly large and undisturbed lake and there were places in it that, to a child at least, seemed infinitely remote and primeval.

I was right about the tar: it led to within half a mile of the shore. But when I got back there, with my boy, and we settled into a camp near a farmhouse and into the kind of summertime I had known, I could tell that it was going to be pretty much the same as it had been before–I knew it, lying in bed the first morning smelling the bedroom and hearing the boy sneak quietly out and go off along the shore in a boat. I began to sustain the illusion that he was I, and therefore, by simple transposition, that I was my father. This sensation persisted, kept cropping up all the time we were there. It was not an entirely new feeling, but in this setting it grew much stronger. I seemed to be living a dual existence. I would be in the middle of some simple act, I would be picking up a bait box or laying down a table fork, or I would be saying something and suddenly it would be not I but my father who was saying the words or making the gesture. It gave me a creepy sensation.

We went fishing the first morning. I felt the same damp moss covering the worms in the bait can, and saw the dragonfly alight on the tip of my rod as it hovered a few inches from the surface of the water. It was the arrival of this fly that convinced me beyond any doubt that everything was as it always had been, that the years were a mirage and that there had been no years. The small waves were the same, chucking the rowboat under the chin as we fished at anchor, and the boat was the same boat, the same color green and the ribs broken in the same places, and under the floorboards the same fresh water leavings and debris–the dead hellgrammite, the wisps of moss, the rusty discarded fishhook, the dried blood from yesterday's catch. We stared silently at the tips of our rods, at the dragonflies that came and went. I lowered the tip of mine into the water, tentatively, pensively dislodging the fly, which darted two feet away, poised, darted two feet back, and came to rest again a little farther up the rod. There had been no years between the ducking of this dragonfly and the other one–the one that was part of memory. I looked at the boy, who was silently watching his fly, and it was my hands that held his rod, my eyes watching. I felt dizzy and didn't know which rod I was at the end of.

We caught two bass, hauling them in briskly as though they were mackerel, pulling them over the side of the boat in a businesslike manner without any landing net, and stunning them with a blow on the back of the head. When we got back for a swim before lunch, the lake was exactly where we had left it, the same number of inches from the dock, and there was only the merest suggestion of a breeze. This seemed an utterly enchanted sea, this lake you could leave to its own devices for a few hours and come back to, and find that it had not stirred, this constant and trustworthy body of water. In the shallows, the dark, water-soaked sticks and twigs, smooth and old, were undulating in clusters on the bottom against the clean ribbed sand, and the track of the mussel was plain. A school of minnows swam by, each minnow with its small individual shadow, doubling the attendance, so clear and sharp in the sunlight. Some of the other campers were in swimming, along the shore, one of them with a cake of soap, and the water felt thin and clear and unsubstantial. Over the years there had been this person with the cake of soap, this cultist, and here he was. There had been no years.

Up to the farmhouse to dinner through the teeming dusty field, the road under our sneakers was only a two-track road. The middle track was missing, the one with the marks of the hooves and the splotches of dried, flaky manure. There had always been three tracks to choose from in choosing which track to walk in; now the choice was narrowed down to two. For a moment I missed terribly the middle alternative. But the way led past the tennis court, and something about the way it lay there in the sun reassured me the tape had loosened along the backline, the alleys were green with plantains and other weeds, and the net (installed in June and removed in September) sagged in the dry noon, and the whole place steamed with midday heat and hunger and emptiness. There was a choice of pie for dessert, and one was blueberry and one was apple, and the waitresses were the same country girls, there having been no passage of time, only the illusion of it as in a dropped curtain–the waitresses were still fifteen; their hair had been washed, that was the only difference–they had been to the movies and seen the pretty girls with the clean hair.

Summertime, oh, summertime, pattern of life indelible with fade-proof lake, the wood unshatterable, the pasture with the sweetfern and the juniper forever and ever, summer without end; this was the background, and the life along the shore was the design, the cottages with their innocent and tranquil design, their tiny docks with the flagpole and the American flag floating against the white clouds in the blue sky, the little paths over the roots of the trees leading from camp to camp and the paths leading back to the outhouse and the can of lime for sprinkling, and at the souvenir counters at the store the miniature birch-bark canoes and the postcards that showed things looking a little better than they looked. This was the American family at play, escaping the city heat, wondering whether the newcomers in the camp at the head of the cove were "common" or "nice," wondering whether it was true that the people who drove up for Sunday dinner at the farmhouse were turned away because there wasn't enough chicken.

It seemed to me, as I kept remembering all this, that those times and those summers had been infinitely precious and worth saving. There had been jollity and peace and goodness. The arriving (at the beginning of August) had been so big a business in itself, at the railway station the farm wagon drawn up, the first smell of the pineladen air, the first glimpse of the smiling farmer, and the great importance of the trunks and your father's enormous authority in such matters, and the feel of the wagon under you for the long ten-mile haul, and at the top of the last long hill catching the first view of the lake after eleven months of not seeing this cherished body of water. The shouts and cries of the other campers when they saw you, and the trunks to be unpacked, to give up their rich burden. (Arriving was less exciting nowadays, when you sneaked up in your car and parked it under a tree near the camp and took out the bags and in five minutes it was all over, no fuss, no loud wonderful fuss about trunks.)

Peace and goodness and jollity. The only thing that was wrong now, really, was the sound of the place, an unfamiliar nervous sound of the outboard motors. This was the note that jarred, the one thing that would sometimes break the illusion and set the years moving. In those other summertimes all motors were inboard; and when they were at a little distance, the noise they made was a sedative, an ingredient of summer sleep. They were one-cylinder and two-cylinder engines, and some were make-and-break and some were jump-spark, but they all made a sleepy sound across the lake. The one-lungers throbbed and fluttered, and the twin cylinder ones purred and purred, and that was a quiet sound, too. But now the campers all had outboards. In the daytime, in the hot mornings, these motors made a petulant, irritable sound; at night in the still evening when the afterglow lit the water, they whined about one's ears like mosquitoes. My boy loved our rented outboard, and his great desire was to achieve single-handed mastery over it, and authority, and he soon learned the trick of choking it a little (but not too much), and the adjustment of the needle valve. Watching him I would remember the things you could do with the old one-cylinder engine with the heavy flywheel, how you could have it eating out of your hand if you got really close to it spiritually. Motorboats in those days didn't have clutches, and you would make a landing by shutting off the motor at the proper time and coasting in with a dead rudder. But there was a way of reversing them, if you learned the trick, by cutting the switch and putting it on again exactly on the final dying revolution of the flywheel, so that it would kick back against compression and begin reversing. Approaching a dock in a strong following breeze, it was difficult to slow up sufficiently by the ordinary coasting method, and if a boy felt he had complete mastery over his motor, he was tempted to keep it running beyond its time and then reverse it a few feet from the dock. It took a cool nerve, because if you threw the switch a twentieth of a second too soon you would catch the flywheel when it still had speed enough to go up past center, and the boat would leap ahead, charging bull-fashion at the dock.

We had a good week at the camp. The bass were biting well and the sun shone endlessly, day after day. We would be tired at night and lie down in the accumulated heat of the little bedrooms after the long hot day and the breeze would stir almost imperceptibly outside and the smell of the swamp drift in through the rusty screens. Sleep would come easily and in the morning the red squirrel would be on the roof, tapping out his gay routine. I kept remembering everything, lying in bed in the mornings–the small steamboat that had a long rounded stern like the lip of a Ubangi, and quietly she ran on the moonlight sails, when the older boys played their mandolins and the girls sang and we ate doughnuts dipped in sugar, and how sweet the music was on the water in the shining night, and what it had felt like to think about girls then. After breakfast we would go up to the store and the things were in the same place–the minnows in a bottle, the plugs and spinners disarranged and pawed over by the youngsters from the boy's camp, the Fig Newtons and the

Beeman's gum. Outside, the road was tarred and cars stood in front of the store. Inside, all was just as it had always been, except there was more Coca-Cola and not so much Moxie and root beer and birch beer and sarsaparilla. We would walk out with the bottle of pop apiece and sometimes the pop would backfire up our noses and hurt. We explored the streams, quietly, where the turtles slid off the sunny logs and dug their way into the soft bottom; and we lay on the town wharf and fed worms to the tame bass. Everywhere we went I had trouble making out which was I, the one walking at my side, the one walking in my pants.

One afternoon while we were at that lake a thunderstorm came up. It was like the revival of an old melodrama that I had seen long ago with childish awe. The second-act climax of the drama of the electrical disturbance over a lake in America had not changed in any important respect. This was the big scene, still the big scene. The whole thing was so familiar, the first feeling of oppression and heat and a general air around camp of not wanting to go very far away. In midafternoon (it was all the same) a curious darkening of the sky, and a lull in everything that had made life tick; and then the way the boats suddenly swung the other way at their moorings with the coming of a breeze out of the new quarter, and the premonitory rumble. Then the kettle drum, then the snare, then the bass drum and cymbals, then crackling light against the dark, and the gods grinning and licking their chops in the hills. Afterward the calm, the rain steadily rustling in the calm lake, the return of light and hope and spirits, and the campers running out in joy and relief to go swimming in the rain, their bright cries perpetuating the deathless joke about how they were getting simply drenched, and the children screaming with delight at the new sensation of bathing in the rain, and the joke about getting drenched linking the generations in a strong indestructible chain. And the comedian who waded in carrying an umbrella.

When the others went swimming my son said he was going in, too. He pulled his dripping trunks from the line where they had hung all through the shower and wrung them out. Languidly, and with no thought of going in, I watched him, his hard little body, skinny and bare, saw him wince slightly as he pulled up around his vitals the small, soggy, icy garment. As he buckled the swollen belt, suddenly my groin felt the chill of death.

Narration

Description is often used in conjunction with narrative. Every time you tell your friends and family about a particular event in your day, you use narration. Any time you tell a story to answer "What happened?" you use narration. Usually, there is a point to the details you choose to include in your recitation. Your details support a central idea. If the day was horrendous, your details turn into a long whine; if the day was wonderful, your details bolster the effect. A joke, a journal entry, a story, an historical perspective–all require narrative.

Implementation

Narration may be used any number of ways:

1. as an introductory or concluding technique to gain the reader's interest and create a vivid beginning or ending for the essay.

2. as an essay in itself to explain an event, a process, or to make a point.

3. throughout an essay to provide personal examples.

Technique

The sequence of events, called **plot** in fiction, indicates the order in which events happen. You may want to use chronological order to show how events unfold. Begin with the setting and situation and proceed to tell the story from first to last. In the process you will pay attention, again, to logical details necessary to fulfill your purpose. Narrative should usually develop causally: an event should follow any preceding one logically. You may want to present events out of their normal order to emphasize an important effect you are trying to create. Be careful with this kind of development, however. No matter what order you choose, you must describe the beginning, middle, and end to make causal relationships clear. As you present your narrative, you will find that some kind of conflict is intrinsic to your discussion.

Conflict is, of course, a clash of wills, characters, or forces. It can be internal (within you or the central character you are presenting) or external (between two people or forces). Presenting conflict in an extended narrative creates an essential tension necessary to good narrative writing. Unless there is conflict, there really is not much suspense–or interest–generated in the reader.

Setting, for the most part, establishes where and when the events take place. It may be used straightforwardly to emphasize your point or it may be used ironically.

Selection of details: In realistic fiction the author chooses details that create the illusion of reality for the reader, verisimilitude. Your selection of details helps you make your point and create vivid impressions for the audience. The point of your story will be emphasized by your handling of setting, sequence, and people or characters.

Characters are the people involved: how you introduce and describe them gives the reader an understanding of your point. They may be described physically or psychologically or both, but the effect is much more vivid if you do not tell the reader how to feel. Instead you need to describe the character in such a way that the reader knows what kind of person he or she is. Mark Twain once said that it is not enough to tell about an old lady who shows up and is unhappy; "bring her on and let her scream" her head off.

Time: When you describe, you are probably more interested in spatial relationships, but in narrative the important relationships are most concerned with time. You will use chronological order most of the time to indicate the beginning, middle, and end of the incident, but as a writer you must decide whether to compress time or to emphasize or de-emphasize certain aspects. Sometimes, you will want to start *in medias res*, in the midst of the action, to vivify the events and put the reader into the action. No matter which kind of sequence you choose, be particularly careful with verb tenses. In most cases present tense makes sense unless you are referring to incidents which occur in the past of the characters.

Dialogue: Another way to make your narrative vivid and immediate is to use direct dialogue rather than referring to conversation indirectly. In other words, you must check your handbook for the proper use of quotation marks and punctuation to allow your characters to speak for themselves.

Point of view: While you often use third person ("she," "he") in academic writing, in personal narrative, especially, you may be told to use first person ("I") in order to create immediacy and interest. All your choices in any kind of writing are determined by your audience and your particular purpose. Your audience and purpose are essential to the way you present your point. Keep your readers firmly in mind and present significant details in descriptive language tailored to them. All the stories in *"The Eighth of January" and Other Stories* by Michael McFarland are examples of narration. In "The Girl in the Orange" the narrator is an English teacher in a community college who questions his effectiveness. A part of the story (not dealing with the girl in orange at all) tells of his past:

This morning I am driving in to start my second semester of teaching college English since I stopped being an administrator. When I graduated with my teaching degree, my wife had wanted me to go into business with her brother selling pressure pumps for oil rigs. But that was not my idea of a fulfilling job, so I compromised. The community college needed a business manager in a hurry and my other degree was in business. After a few years, however, the job took its toll. I gradually developed a rigid code which I felt highly protective of, as if one chink in it would open me up to criticism and certain death. Anyone working under me during that time could really have told you some stories.

But finally I got enough of it. I was tired of the insidious habit of putting institutional prestige above basic human needs. It happened that some kid had to withdraw from school and couldn't get his refund for two weeks. That would have been all right, but the kid was really destitute and nobody at the college could do anything to expedite his money. I couldn't even wrangle a simple hand-written check so he could put food on the table that night. The assistant B.M. (Business Manager) had been no help at all. He could talk only in negatives. "I don't want to know what you can't do," I said when I got him on the horn. "I want to know what you can do to solve this problem." His most creative idea was to look for some church group that might give out meals.

That was it for me. I went into the classroom in order to live with myself again, though everyone says the dean is concerned about what kind of teacher I'll be.

In this narrative about the instructor's experience with a girl in an orange dress whom he sees from time to time in a car behind him, in the cafeteria, and finally in class, he does not talk about the significance of the girl; he focuses the quoted part instead on revealing his character by discussing his past. The details he chooses show his priorities. His attitudes are shown by his tone and the language he uses, and the basic conflict of a person interested in people as people with a stereotypical administrative outlook is emphasized–all in a relatively short space. Maya Angelou's "Graduation" is a good example of a narrative. What point does she make? What narrative techniques does she employ?

GRADUATION
MAYA ANGELOU

The children in Stamps trembled visibly with anticipation. Some adults were excited too, but to be certain the whole young population had come down with graduation epidemic. Large classes were graduating from both the grammar school and the high school. Even those who were years removed from their own day of glorious release were anxious to help with preparations as a kind of dry run. The junior students who were moving into the vacating classes' chairs were tradition-bound to show their talents for leadership and management. They strutted through the school and around the campus exerting pressure on the lower grades. Their authority was so new that occasionally if they pressed a little too hard it had to be overlooked. After all, next term was coming, and it never hurt a sixth grader to have a play sister in the eighth grade, or a tenth-year student to be able to call a twelfth grader Bubba. So all was endured in a spirit of shared understanding. But the graduating classes themselves were the nobility. Like travelers with exotic destinations on their minds, the graduates were remarkably forgetful. They came to school to secure replacements for the missing equipment. When accepted, the willing workers might or might not be thanked, and it was of no importance to the pregraduation rites. Even teachers were respectful of the now quiet and aging seniors, and tended to speak to them, if not as equals, as beings only slightly lower than themselves. After tests were returned and grades given, the student body, which acted like an extended family, knew who did well, who excelled, and what piteous ones had failed.

Unlike the white high school, Lafayette County Training School distinguished itself by having neither lawn, nor hedges, nor tennis court, nor climbing ivy. Its two buildings (main classrooms, the grade school and home economics) were set on a dirt hill with no fence to limit either its boundaries or those of bordering farms. There was a large expanse to the left of the school which was used alternately as a baseball diamond or basketball court. Rusty hoops on swaying poles represented the permanent recreational equipment, although bats and balls could be borrowed from the P.E. teacher if the borrower was qualified and if the diamond wasn't occupied.

Over this rocky area relieved by a few shady tall persimmon trees the graduating class walked. The girls often held hands and no longer bothered to speak to the lower students. There was a sadness about them, as if this old world was not their home and they were bound for higher ground. The boys, on the other hand, had become more friendly, more outgoing. A decided change from the closed attitude they projected while studying for finals. Now they seemed not ready to give up the old school, the familiar paths and classrooms. Only a small percentage would be continuing on to college—one of the South's A&M (agricultural and mechanical) schools, which trained Negro youths to be carpenters, farmers, handymen, masons, maids, cooks and baby nurses. Their future rode heavily on their shoulders, and blinded them to the collective joy that had pervaded the lives of the boys and girls in the grammar school graduating class.

Parents who could afford it had ordered new shoes and ready-made clothes for themselves from Sears and Roebuck or Montgomery Ward. They also engaged the best seamstresses to make the floating graduating dresses and to cut down secondhand pants which would be pressed to a military slickness for the important event.

Oh, it was important, all right. Whitefolks would attend the ceremony, and two or three would speak of God and home, and the Southern way of life, and Mrs. Parsons, the principal's wife, would play the graduation march while the lower-grade graduates paraded down the aisles and took their seats below the platform.

The high school seniors would wait in empty classrooms to make their dramatic entrance.

In the Store I was the person of the moment. The birthday girl. The center. Bailey had graduated the year before, although to do so he had had to forfeit all pleasures to make up for his time lost in Baton Rouge.

My class was wearing butter-yellow pique dresses, and Momma launched out on mine. She smocked the yoke into tiny crisscrossing puckers, then shirred the rest of the bodice. Her dark fingers ducked in and out of the lemony cloth as she embroidered raised daisies around the hem. Before she considered herself finished she had added a crocheted cuff on the puff sleeves, and a pointy crocheted collar.

I was going to be lovely. A walking model of all the various styles of fine hand sewing and it didn't worry me that I was only twelve years old and merely graduating from the eighth grade. Besides, many teachers in Arkansas Negro schools had only that diploma and were licensed to impart wisdom.

The days had become longer and more noticeable. The faded beige of former times had been replaced with strong and sure colors. I began to see my classmates' clothes, their skin tones, and the dust that waved off pussy willows. Clouds that lazed across the sky were objects of great concern to me. Their shiftier shapes might have held a message that in my new happiness and with a little bit of time I'd soon decipher. During that period I looked at the arch of heaven so religiously my neck kept a steady ache. I had taken to smiling more often, and my jaws hurt from the unaccustomed activity. Between the two physical sore spots, I suppose I could have been uncomfortable, but that was not the case. As a member of the winning team (the graduating class of 1940) I had outdistanced unpleasant sensations by miles. I was headed for the freedom of open fields.

Youth and social approval allied themselves with me and we trammeled memories of slights and insults. The wind of our swift passage remodeled my features. Lost tears were pounded to mud and then to dust. Years of withdrawal were brushed aside and left behind, as hanging ropes of parasitic moss.

My work alone had awarded me a top place and I was going to be one of the first called in the graduating ceremonies. On the classroom blackboard, as well as on the bulletin board in the auditorium, there were blue stars and white stars and red stars. No absences, no tardiness, and my academic work was among the best of the year. I could say the preamble to the Constitution even faster than Bailey. We timed ourselves often: "We the people of the United States in order to form a more perfect union. . . ." I had memorized the Presidents of the United States from Washington to Roosevelt in chronological as well as alphabetical order.

My hair pleased me too. Gradually the black mass had lengthened and thickened, so that it kept at last to its braided pattern, and I didn't have to yank my scalp off when I tried to comb it.

Louise and I had rehearsed the exercises until we tired out ourselves. Henry Reed was class valedictorian. He was a small, very black boy with hooded eyes, a long, broad nose and an oddly shaped head. I had admired him for years because each term he and I vied for the best grades in our class. Most often he bested me, but instead of being disappointed I was pleased that we shared top places between us. Like many Southern Black children, he lived with his grandmother, who was as strict as Momma and as kind as she knew how to be. He was courteous, respectful and softspoken to elders, but on the playground he chose to play the roughest games. I admired him. Anyone, I reckoned, sufficiently afraid or sufficiently dull could be polite. But to be able to operate at a top level with both adults and children was admirable.

His valedictory speech was entitled "To Be or Not to Be." The rigid tenth grade teacher had helped him write it. He'd been working on the dramatic stresses for months.

The weeks until graduation were filled with heady activities. A group of small children were to be presented in a play about buttercups and daisies and bunny rabbits. They could be heard throughout the building practicing their hops and their little songs that sounded like silver bells. The older girls (non-graduates, of course) were assigned the task of making refreshments for the night's festivities. A tangy scent of ginger, cinnamon, nutmeg and chocolate wafted around the home economics building as the budding cooks made samples for themselves and their teachers.

In every corner of the workshop, axes and saws split fresh timber as the woodshop boys made sets and stage scenery. Only the graduates were left out of the general bustle. We were free to sit in the library at the back of the building or look in quite detachedly, naturally, on the measures being taken for our event.

Even the minister preached on graduation the Sunday before. His subject was, "Let your light so shine that men will see your good works and praise your Father, Who is in Heaven." Although the sermon was purported to be addressed to us, he used the occasion to speak to backsliders, gamblers and general ne'er do-wells. But since he had called our names at the beginning of the service we were mollified.

Among Negroes the tradition was to give presents to children going only from one grade to another. How much more important this was when the person was graduating at the top of the class. Uncle Willie and Momma had sent away for a Mickey Mouse watch like Bailey's. Louise gave me four embroidered handkerchiefs. (I gave her crocheted doilies.) Mrs. Sneed, the minister's wife, made me an undershirt to wear for graduation, and nearly every customer gave me a nickel or maybe even a dime with the instruction "Keep on moving to higher ground," or some such encouragement.

Amazingly the great day finally dawned and I was out of bed before I knew it. I threw open the back door to see it more clearly, but Momma said, "Sister, come away from that door and put your robe on."

I hoped the memory of that morning would never leave me. Sunlight was itself young, and the day had none of the insistence maturity would bring it in a few hours. In my robe and barefoot in the backyard, under cover of going to see about my new beans, I gave myself up to the gentle warmth and thanked God that no matter what evil I had done in my life He had allowed me to live to see this day.

Somewhere in my fatalism I had expected to die, accidentally, and never have the chance to walk up the stairs in the auditorium and gracefully receive my hard-earned diploma. Out of God's merciful bosom I had won reprieve.

Bailey came out in his robe and gave me a box wrapped in Christmas paper. He said he had saved his money for months to pay for it. It felt like a box of chocolates, but I knew Bailey wouldn't save money to buy candy when we had all we could want under our noses.

He was as proud of the gift as I. It was a soft-leather-bound copy of a collection of poems by Edgar Allan Poe, or, as Bailey and I called him, "Eap." I turned to "Annabel Lee" and we walked up and down the garden rows, the cool dirt between our toes, reciting the beautifully sad lines.

Momma made a Sunday breakfast although it was only Friday. After we finished the blessing, I opened my eyes to find the watch on my plate. It was a dream of a day. Everything went smoothly and to my credit. I didn't have to be reminded or scolded for anything. Near evening I was too jittery to attend to chores, so Bailey volunteered to do all before his bath.

Days before, we had made a sign for the Store, and as we turned out the lights Momma hung the cardboard over the doorknob. It read clearly: CLOSED. GRADUATION.

My dress fitted perfectly and everyone said that I looked like a sunbeam in it. On the hill, going toward the school, Bailey walked behind with Uncle Willie, who muttered, "Go on, Ju." He wanted him to walk ahead with us because it embarrassed him to have to walk so slowly. Bailey said he'd let the ladies walk together, and the men would bring up the rear. We all laughed, nicely.

Little children dashed by out of the dark like fireflies. Their crepe-paper dresses and butterfly wings were not made for running and we heard more than one rip, dryly, and the regretful "uh uh" that followed.

The school blazed without gaiety. The windows seemed cold and unfriendly from the lower hill. A sense of ill-fated timing crept over me, and if Momma hadn't reached for my hand I would have drifted back to Bailey and Uncle Willie, and possibly beyond. She made a few slow jokes about my feet getting cold, and tugged me along to the now-strange building.

Around the front steps, assurance came back. There were my fellow "greats," the graduating class. Hair brushed back, legs oiled, new dresses and pressed pleats, fresh pocket handkerchiefs and little handbags, all homesewn. Oh, we were up to snuff, all right. I joined my comrades and didn't even see my family go in to find seats in the crowded auditorium.

The school band struck up a march and all classes filed in as had been rehearsed. We stood in front of our seats, as assigned, and on a signal from the choir director, we sat. No sooner had this been accomplished than the band started to play the national anthem. We rose again and sang the song, after which we recited the pledge of allegiance. We remained standing for a brief minute before the choir director and the principal signaled to us, rather desperately I thought, to take our seats. The command was so unusual that our carefully rehearsed and smooth-running machine was thrown off. For a full minute we fumbled for our chairs and bumped into each other awkwardly. Habits change or solidify under pressure, so in our state of nervous tension we had been ready to follow our usual assembly pattern: the American national anthem, then the pledge of allegiance, then the song every Black person I knew called the Negro National Anthem. All done in the same key, with the same passion and most often standing on the same foot.

Finding my seat at last, I was overcome with a presentiment of worse things to come. Something unrehearsed, unplanned, was going to happen, and we were going to be made to look bad. I distinctly remember being explicit in the choice of pronoun. It was "we," the graduating class, the unit, that concerned me then.

The principal welcomed "parents and friends" and asked the Baptist minister to lead us in prayer. His invocation was brief and punchy, and for a second I thought we were getting on the high road to right action. When the principal came back to the dais, however, his voice had changed. Sounds always affected me profoundly and the principal's voice was one of my favorites. During assembly it melted and lowed weakly into the audience. It had not been in my plan to listen to him, but my curiosity was piqued and I straightened up to give him my attention.

He was talking about Booker T. Washington, our "late great leader," who said we can be as close as the fingers on the hand, etc. . . . Then he said a few vague things about friendship and the friendship of kindly people to those less fortunate than themselves. With that his voice nearly faded, thin, away. Like a river diminishing to a stream and then to a trickle. But he cleared his throat and said, "Our speaker tonight, who is also our friend, came from Texarkana to deliver the commencement address, but due to the irregularity of the train schedule, he's going to, as they say, 'speak and run.'" He said that we understood and wanted the man to know that we were most grateful for the time he was able to give us and then something about how we were willing always to adjust to another's program, and without more ado— "I give you Mr. Edward Donleavy."

Not one but two white men came through the door off-stage. The shorter one walked to the speaker's platform, and the tall one moved to the center seat and sat down. But that was our principal's seat, and already occupied. The dislodged gentleman bounced around for a long breath or two before the Baptist minister gave him his chair, then with more dignity that the situation deserved, the minister walked off the stage.

Donleavy looked at the audience once (on reflection, I'm sure that he wanted only to reassure himself that we were really there), adjusted his glasses and began to read from a sheaf of papers.

He was glad "to be here and to see the work going on just as it was in the other schools.

At the first "Amen" from the audience I willed the offender to immediate death by choking on the word. But Amens and Yes, sir's began to fall around the room like rain through a ragged umbrella.

He told us of the wonderful changes we children in Stamps had in store. The Central School (naturally, the white was Central) had already been granted improvements that would be in use in the fall. They were going to have the newest microscopes and chemistry equipment for their laboratory. Mr. Donleavy didn't leave us long in the dark over who made these improvements available to Central High. Nor were we to be ignored in the general betterment scheme he had in mind.

He said that he had pointed out to people at a very high level that one of the first-line football tacklers at Arkansas Agricultural and Mechanical College had graduated from good old Lafayette County Training School. Here fewer Amen's were heard. Those few that did break through lay dully in the air with the heaviness of habit.

He went on to praise us. He went on to say how he had bragged that "one of the best basketball players at Fisk sank his first ball right here at "Lafayette County Training School."

The white kids were going to have a chance to become Galileos and Madame Curies and Edisons and Gauguins, and our boys (the girls weren't even in on it) would try to be Jesse Owenses and Joe Louises.

Owens and the Brown Bomber were great heroes in our world, but what school official in the white-goddom of Little Rock had the right to decide that those two men must be our only heroes? Who decided that for Henry Reed to become a scientist he had to work like George Washington Carver, as a bootblack, to buy a lousy microscope? Bailey was obviously always going to be too small to be an athlete, so which concrete angel glued to what country seat had decided that if my brother wanted to become a lawyer he had to first pay penance for his skin by picking cotton and hoeing corn and studying correspondence books at night for twenty years?

The man's dead words fell like bricks around the auditorium and too many settled in my belly. Constrained by hard-learned manners I couldn't look behind me, but to my left and right the proud graduating class of 1940 had dropped their heads. Every girl in my row had found something new to do with her handkerchief. Some folded the tiny squares into love knots, some into triangles, but most were wadding them, then pressing them flat on their yellow laps.

On the dais, the ancient tragedy was being replayed. Professor Parsons sat, a sculptor's reject, rigid. His large, heavy body seemed devoid of will or willingness, and his eyes said he was no longer with us. The other teachers examined the flag (which was draped stage right) or their notes or the windows which opened on our now-famous playing diamond.

Graduation, the hush-hush magic time of frills and gifts and congratulations and diplomas, was finished for me before my name was called. The accomplishment was nothing. The meticulous maps, drawn in three colors of ink, learning and spelling decasyllabic words, memorizing the whole of *The Rape of Lucrece*–it was for nothing. Donleavy had exposed us.

We were maids and farmers, handymen and washerwomen, and anything higher that we aspired to was farcical and presumptuous.

Then I wished that Gabriel Prosser and Nat Turner had killed all whitefolks in their beds and that Abraham Lincoln had been assassinated before the signing of the Emancipation Proclamation, and that Harriet Tubman had been killed by that blow on her head and Christopher Columbus had drowned in the *Santa Maria*.

It was awful to be a Negro and have no control over my life. It was brutal to be young and already trained to sit quietly and listen to charges brought against my color with no chance of defense. We should all be dead. I thought I should like to see us all dead, one on top of the other. A pyramid of flesh with the whitefolks on the bottom, as the broad base, then the Indians with their silly tomahawks and teepees and wigwams and treaties, the Negroes with their mops and recipes and cotton sacks and spirituals sticking out of their mouths. The Dutch children should all stumble in their wooden shoes and break their necks. The French should choke to death on the Louisiana Purchase (1803) while silkworms ate all the Chinese with their stupid pigtails. As a species, we were an abomination. All of us.

Donleavy was running for election, and assured our parents that if he won we could count on having the only colored paved playing field in that part of Arkansas. Also–he never looked up to acknowledge the grunts of acceptance–also, we were bound to get some new equipment for the home economics building and the workshop.

He finished, and since there was no need to give any more than the most perfunctory thank-you's, he nodded to the men on the stage, and the tall white man who was never introduced joined him at the door. They left with the attitude that now they were off to something really important. (The graduation ceremonies at Lafayette County Training School had been a mere preliminary.)

The ugliness they left was palpable. An uninvited guest who wouldn't leave. The choir was summoned and sang a modern arrangement of "Onward, Christian Soldiers," with new words pertaining to graduates seeking their place in the world. But it didn't work. Elouise, the daughter of the Baptist minister, recited "Invictus" and I could have cried at the impertinence of "I am the master of my fate, I am the captain of my soul."

My name had lost its ring of familiarity and I had to be nudged to go and receive my diploma. All my preparations had fled. I neither marched up to the stage like a conquering Amazon, nor did I look in the audience for Bailey's nod of approval. Marguerite Johnson, I heard the name again, my honors were read, there were noises in the audience of appreciation, and I took my place on the stage as rehearsed.

I thought about colors I hated: ecru, puce, lavender, beige and black.

There was shuffling and rustling around me, then Henry Reed was giving his valedictory address, "To Be or Not to Be." Hadn't he heard the whitefolks? We couldn't be, so the question was a waste of time. Henry's voice came out clear and strong. I feared to look at him. Hadn't he got the message? There was no "nobler in the mind" for Negroes because the world didn't think we had minds, and they let us know it. "Outrageous fortune"? Now, that was a joke. When the ceremony was over I had to tell Henry Reed some things. That is, if I still cared. Not "rub," Henry, "erase." "Ah, there's the erase." Us.

Henry had been a good student in elocution. His voice rose on tides of promise and fell on waves of warnings. The English teacher had helped him to create a sermon winging through Hamlet's soliloquy. To be a man, a doer, a builder, a leader, or to be a tool, an unfunny joke, a crusher of funky toadstools. I marveled that Henry could go through with the speech as if we had a choice.

I had been listening and silently rebutting each sentence with my eyes closed; then there was a hush, which in an audience warns that something unplanned is happening. I looked up and saw Henry Reed, the conservative, the proper, the A student, turn his back to the audience and turn to us (the proud graduating class of 1940) and sing, nearly speaking,

> "Lift ev'ry voice and sing
> Till earth and heaven ring
> Ring with the harmonies of Liberty . . ."

It was the poem written by James Weldon Johnson. It was the music composed by J. Rosamond Johnson. It was the Negro National Anthem Out of habit we were singing it.

Our mothers and fathers stood in the dark hall and joined the hymn of encouragement. A kindergarten teacher led the small children onto the stage and the buttercups and daisies and bunny rabbits marked time and tried to follow:

> "Stony the road we trod
> Bitter the chastening rod
> Felt in the days when hope, unborn, had died.
> Yet with a steady beat
> Have not our weary feet
> Come to the place for which our fathers sighed?"

Each child I knew had learned that song with his ABC's and along with "Jesus Loves Me This I Know." But I personally had never heard it before. Never heard the words, despite the thousands of time I had sung them. Never thought they had anything to do with me.

On the other hand, the words of Patrick Henry had made such an impression on me that I had been able to stretch myself tall and trembling and say, "I know not what course others may take, but as for me, give me liberty or give me death."

And now I heard, really for the first time:

> "We have come over a way that with tears
> has been watered,
> We have come, treading our path through
> the blood of the slaughtered."

While echoes of the song shivered in the air, Henry Reed bowed his head, said "Thank you," and returned to his place in the line. The tears that slipped down many faces were not wiped away in shame.

We were on top again. As always, again. We survived. The depths had been icy and dark, but now a bright sun spoke to our souls. I was no longer simply a member of the proud graduating class of 1940; I was a proud member of the wonderful, beautiful Negro race.

Oh, Black known and unknown poets, how often have your auctioned pains sustained us? Who will compute the lonely nights made less lonely by your songs, or the empty pots made less tragic by your tales?

If we were a people much given to revealing secrets, we might raise monuments and sacrifice to the memories of our poets, but slavery cured us of that weakness. It may be enough, however, to have it said that we survive in exact relationship to the dedication of our poets (include preachers, musicians and blues singers).

(1969)

PROCESS ANALYSIS

We use process analysis all the time. When we read and follow the directions on a pay telephone or a self-service gas pump, we are using process. Process is a habit of mind involving ideas in logical sequences. There is an orderly and efficient way to do almost everything, although nearly everyone thinks his or her way is best. Basically there are two kinds of processes: directional and informational. The **directional** process explains **how** to do something so that the reader can duplicate the action suggested while the **informational** process explains how a more complicated process is done but not with the intent of duplication. You do not have to be a miner to understand how strip mining works, nor are you expected to run right out and create a strip mine in your back yard if you read about how the process is done.

Implementation

Process analyses are used in almost anything that requires a step-by-step explanation. When you explain the steps of a chemistry experiment, you are presenting a directional process. You use informational processes every time you explain how the Indians were disenfranchised, how a bill becomes law, or how the writing process works. Chapter Two in this book specifically discusses the writing process, for instance.

Technique

When you explain a process, particularly a directional one, you should take several things into consideration.

1. Provide an overview of general principles. Give your reader an understanding of the way you intend to develop your plan.

2. Provide complete details. All the techniques you use in describing anything will, of course, be applicable to describing how to do a process or how a particular process is done.

3. Define any technical terms. Keep your audience in mind and try to

53

make your explanation clear enough to communicate effectively.

4. Provide reasons for the steps you include. You should tell why it is important to include certain elements of the process as well as how to do them.

5. Include negative directions as well as the reasons for doing things a certain way in a certain order. You must warn the reader in key places about what not to do. Since cyanide is difficult to remove from all kinds of surfaces, including glass, it is probably better not to mix Kool-Aid for the neighborhood kids in a beaker you usually use for cyanide experiments.

6. Illustrate your process using descriptive techniques. Normally, you will not have diagrams or other visual aids in your writing; therefore, you need to create images to make your process clear.

7. You will have noticed in the course of this discussion that its point of view violates the rules you may have been told about using second person and shifting points of view. Since this book is designed as a set of directions or instructions for the reader, it often uses second person. The purpose and audience determine the point of view you will use in your writing. Sometimes your instructor will insist that you use third person ("one,""he,""she") in order to practice appealing to certain audiences of the type you will write for in many academic settings. One way to implement the consistent use of third person in a process is to introduce an actor–someone who is logically involved in the process–early in your discussion. If you are describing how to bake bread, the person involved in the process is the baker. When you refer to the baker as the actor in the process, you refer to him or her in the third person. Sometimes you may be asked to use the imperative: a command or request whose implied subject is "you." An old Paul Simon song advises the audience about "fifty ways to leave a lover" and uses the imperative: "Get on the bus, Gus"; "Make a new plan, Stan"; "No need to be coy, Roy." The directions on the pay phone are consistently imperative:

1. Lift the receiver; 2. Listen for the dial tone; 3. Deposit a quarter; 4. Dial the number.

No matter what the assignment requires, you must maintain a consistent point of view. Do not slip from "I" to "you" to "he" and back again. Keep your audience firmly in mind.

Organization

In writing process papers, the same general steps that apply to all writing situations are also important. As you outline, you should group steps logically. You will not put each step in a single short paragraph. The reader should be aware that you have a plan, an outline, but it should not be intrusive. Your outline is the skeleton of your essay; the essay should flesh out that skeleton. Be sure you choose a process which is a suitable length for the paper required, and organize logically, usually chronologically. The thesis statement should indicate the specific groups of steps you will discuss, corresponding to the paragraphs you develop. Throughout the paper, keep your reader firmly in mind: the audience and the purpose will determine your tone, your techniques, and your direction. Do not condescend to or patronize your audience; explain clearly. In a directional process you may want to use personal narrative, especially in the introduction, to indicate how you became familiar with the process or why you think knowing about this process is important or worthwhile. Transitions are particularly important in process, usually indicating that the steps are chronological for a reason. Generally you will use transitions like "first", "next", "then," "additionally," and "finally" in addition to any devices you need to make your ideas clearly logical for your reader. You may want to include phrases like "Be sure to ___ before you try to ___" or "Under no circumstance should you do ___ before doing ___." In your conclusion, you should indicate the results of the procedure–a fluffy soufflé, a law, a well-written essay, an embalmed corpse–and their significance.

As you read the following student essay, pay particular attention to its structure and organization.

Planting a Vegetable Garden

There are three major steps in planting a summer vegetable garden. Besides being good exercise, gardening can bring pleasant family activity to the back yard for a nominal investment. Many a back yard gardener has become addicted after his first harvest. With a little planning and preparation, as is described below, one may enjoy the fruit of his labor for several weeks during the picking season.

The first major step is preparation. As the gardener begins to prepare for his garden, he needs to be aware of the last predicted date for frost in his area. Also, he should consider the types of crops which would likely flourish in his region. Other considerations are the proper spot, in terms of size, for projected yield, location for a minimum of six hours of sunlight daily, and elevation of the plot for purposes of drainage. Once these factors have been decided, he must gather the proper tools and supplies. These may include gloves, a garden hoe, rotary tiller, water hose, prepared commercial fertilizer of a five-ten-five ration, previously composted material, seeds and plants such as tomatoes to be set, and, perhaps, some bottomless paper cups for use as support collars.

The second major step to vegetable gardening is that of action. First, the soil must be prepared. This is done by tilling the desired area to remove grass and weeds and to loosen the dirt. Once the grass and weeds are loose, they may be manually picked up and discarded. At this time the gardener should add four pounds, per one hundred square feet, of commercially prepared fertilizer of a five-ten-five ration. Also helpful is adding three to four inches in depth of composted matter for richness and moisture retention. Re-tilling this mixture into the soil will insure proper blending. At this stage, the furrows may be formed by using a hoe and burrowing along in the fluffy ground. The excess dirt may be lightly tossed to each side to form the mounds for planting. When shallow trenches are made in the furrows, the seeds may be planted. Three seeds at a time may be sown at specified intervals noted on the envelope in which they were packaged. When the seeds are planted, the trench may be closed up by pinching the soil back in place over the mound. At this point young seedlings may be set in the remaining garden area, at one foot intervals.

Now that the actual planting is done, the finishing stage remains. One final touch might be to cover weak or spindly seedlings with inverted paper cups which are bottomless. Also, the gardener should quench this thirsty new crop with the water hose before spraying clean the tiller blades and hoe. The implements may be put away along with the gloves, unused fertilizer, leftover paper cups, remaining seeds, and the recoiled water hose. Of course, any trash generated by the project needs to be discarded at this time.

The original planning and maintaining of a vegetable garden are a lot of work and not very cost effective for the average family's consumption. Most backyard gardens are small and puny in comparison to amber waves of grain. However, the sore back, the callused hands, and the hours of pulling weeds are usually forgotten with the first juicy bite of a "Big Boy" variety tomato picked from the vine only minutes ago.

In his essay "How to Give a Speech," Walter Kiechel III takes the novice speech-giver through the process of preparing a speech for an unfamiliar audience. Note how he offers a step-by-step process of giving a speech from the choice of a topic to the actual delivery itself.

HOW TO GIVE A SPEECH
Walter Keichel

Looking for an easy way to reduce even a strong, self-confident manager to a nail-biting mass of insecurities? Just ask him to give a speech to an unfamiliar audience. If he can't get out of accepting, he'll probably devote several sweaty hours to writing out his remarks or, if he is senior enough, delegate the awful task of composition to some underling. When the hour of execution arrives, he will stride manfully to the podium, assume a quasi-fetal stance, and proceed to read his text word by droning word. Not for nothing does pop research indicate the average American fears speaking before a group more than he fears death. As Paul Nelson, Dean of Ohio University's college of communication, observes, "Death is faster."

Choose life, even if it means working to become a better speaker. Why don't more managers take up the challenge? "Most businessmen are worried that they're going to come across like someone else," argues Charles Windhorst, co-founder of

Communispond. It's a firm that teaches executives that the trick in fact is to have all the mechanical stuff down so pat that the authentic, worth-listening-to you comes through undistorted. Learn the basics and get out of your own way.

The basics begin when you're invited to speak. While the folks asking may have a foggy idea of what they want you to talk on, their none-too-clear guidelines probably leave you ample room to set your own topic. Don't be in a hurry here. First, the experts universally agree, you should find out as much as you can about your audience.

Who are these people–what age, sex, and line of work–and why will they be assembled? If they're mostly women, you will want to use more examples that feature you know whom. Are they coming to hear you more or less voluntarily, or is their attendance required? Captive audiences are harder to grab. When are you supposed to talk to them? If it's right after a meal or at the end of the day, expect Coma City; leading off in the morning often means that you'll lose 15 minutes to your hosts' unavailing attempts to start on time. Maybe most important, why do they want to hear from you, of all people? Much of this dope
you can get by grilling the person who had the temerity to invite you. For the ultimate in analysis, though, nothing beats spending a little time with your prospective audience. Robert Waterman, Jr., whose co-authorship of *In Search of Excellence* propelled him into big-time speakerdom, finds that if he's to exhort some company's troops, for example, it helps a lot to poke around the corporation for a day or so beforehand talking to everybody he can. He can then address their specific concerns.

Once you have a feel for your audience, consult your mental inventory of what interests you these days. Not just what you know or can amass facts on, but what you care about. Dale Carnegie said it 70 years ago, and the experts are still saying it: If you're not excited about your subject, you won't be able to excite your audience about it either. To find your topic, look for where your concerns intersect with their wants and needs. Decide on your purpose–whether to inform, persuade, or entertain. Then give your impending address what Max Wortman, a management professor at the University of Tennessee and a popular speaker, calls a "schmaltzy" title. Not "Current Realities and Future Trends in the Brake Shoe Industry"; rather "What the Future Holds, and Why We Probably Can't Get There From Here."

Now all you have to do is compose and deliver the sucker. In putting it together, bear in mind that this is an oral, not a written communication. This means you should use short, simple words, go long on personal pronouns I, me, you, we–and repeat your main points, since the listener won't be able to go back and reread whatever puzzled him. To achieve the right effect, try composing initially with a Dictaphone or cassette recorder, says Fern Johnson, a professor of communication at the University of Massachusetts at Amherst. If others write the talk for you, make sure that they too observe the basic principle. Dorothy Sarnoff, a

Manhattanite who has taught public speaking to many a celebrity, tells of asking 20 or so U.S. State Department speechwriters whether they ever spoke aloud the remarks they prepared for senior diplomats. None ever did. And you wondered why we're in trouble around the globe.

In thinking about how to structure what you say, go back to the purpose you decided on. As Communispond's Windhorst observes, the standard tell-'em-what-you're-gonna-tell-'em, tell-'em, and tell-'em-what-you-told-'em works fine if your goal is to inform. If you're out to persuade, though, you're probably better off laying out the problem, marshaling the evidence for your view, then ending with a call to action.

At the beginning of your remarks, you want to get the audience on your side–and fast. Research suggests that they make up their minds on whether to like you, and to listen to you, within a minute or two after you start out. Audacious you can, of course, attempt to win them over with a joke. Be careful, though: Make sure that you can actually tell a funny story–not everyone can–and that the joke leads naturally into the body of your speech. The best openers, the experts advise, are probably tales from your own experience: sometimes self-deprecating, not necessarily thigh-slappers, but calculated to show the audience that you're pretty much like them. Or worse.

The standard wisdom says you probably can't hope to put across more than three main points. Listeners should get a sense of movement, of progression, from one part of the speech to the next. Consider using rhetorical questions to alert them to transitions. You needn't be highfalutin, though. Some of the hottest speakers on the corporate circuit–Tom Peters, Waterman's co-author, for example–seem to do nothing but string together story after story.

In framing your conclusion, figure out precisely what you want your listeners to take away. An impulse to act? Lay out with gory specificity what they should do, whether it's writing their Congressman, selling more brake shoes, or razing Carthage. A better understanding of your subject? Summarize your main points. A warm, happy feeling? Leave 'em laughing. Time your remarks to run a bit shorter than the period allotted; besides surprising your listeners no end, this may cause them to want more, and to invite you back another time.

Once you know what you're going to say, put it into a form you can talk from. To keep you from reading, the Communispond firm recommends using your own miserably hand-drawn pictures, or ideographs, one for each major idea. If you simply must have the words in front of you, at least break down your text into natural five- or six-word phrases, one to a line, triple-spaced with brackets to indicate the phrases that make up a single thought.

You can now attend to the truly mechanical. If you're going to use so-called visual aids–and you probably should if your audience is large–keep them simple, one phrase or idea per slide or overhead transparency. Determine in as much detail as possible how the room will be set up. Will there be a podium, for instance? How tall? If the answer is two inches below your height in stiletto heels, ask that other arrangements be made. Ensure that someone checks out the microphone before you go on.

Rehearse, but try to avoid getting it down so well that you're bored with it. A final pre-speaking tip from Ohio Univeristy's Nelson: Write your own introduction. The audience is going to form an impression about you so quickly that if Mr. It-Gives-Me-Great-Pleasure stumbles through your entire potted bio–the four degrees, the military service, the time you spent heading the Thule office–you may lose them before you stand up. Furnish him instead with a brief, down-to-earth account of yourself that stresses what you have in common with your listeners.

With appropriate fanfare, you take the podium. Stand up straight, look out at your audience, smile if it's appropriate, and then launch right in, with no boring "Thank you" or "Madam President, Mr. First Vice President. . ." Put more energy into talking than you usually do; this isn't the time or place for the stuffy nonsense that says that a good manager never raises his voice or gestures with his hands. Indeed, if you can just forget about the appendages, you may free them to do their own helpful thing, whether it's the grand sweep of a big idea, a short jab for emphasis, or the clenched fist of intensity.

Maintain eye contact with your audience. If you're a novice, and nervous, try to find two or three friendly faces, people who seem to be laughing at your stories and nodding along with your witty aperçus. When you look up from your text, look at them. As Dean Nelson notes, the nodders are more likely to be women, who aren't socialized like males to keep a poker face. As you grow more experienced, you'll be able to sweep the room with your gaze, exchanging glances with the neutrals and eventually even with the hostiles. What you're looking for is not just encouragement, but also any sense that you may be losing the crowd. When you see them beginning to stare at the floor, react: Rephrase your last point to make it clearer, tell them again how vital your subject is to them, trot out one of your punchier anecdotes. You may also want to hasten to the close, dropping the lesser points that stand in your way.

Finish strong, not trailing off or adding another feeble "thank you." Give 'em a great quote, a passionate, punctuated request, or a sure-fire gag line. Leave the vivid air signed with your honor, to borrow Stephen Spender's phrase. Then sit down and just wait for the applause.

(1987)

Jessica Mitford's "Behind the Formaldehyde Curtain" is an excerpt from *The American Way of Death* (1963), a detailed examination of the funeral industry. In the essay she presents the process of preparing a corpse for viewing, focusing particularly on the procedure of embalming. Consider the satirical tone of the author and determine what effect Ms. Mitford achieves through such a lavish process analysis.

BEHIND THE
FORMALDEHYDE CURTAIN
JESSICA MITFORD

The drama begins to unfold with the arrival of the corpse at the mortuary.

Alas, poor Yorick! How surprised he would be to see how his counterpart of today is whisked off to a funeral parlor and is in short order sprayed, sliced, pierced, pickled, trussed, trimmed, creamed, waxed, painted, rouged and neatly dressed–transformed from a common corpse into a Beautiful Memory Picture. This process is known in the trade as embalming and restorative art, and is so universally employed in the United States and Canada that the funeral director does it routinely, without consulting corpse or kin. He regards as eccentric those few who are hardy enough to suggest that it might be dispensed with. Yet no law requires embalming, no religious doctrine commends it, nor is it dictated by considerations of health, sanitation, or even of personal daintiness. In no part of the world but in Northern America is it widely used. The purpose of embalming is to make the corpse presentable for viewing in a suitably costly container; and here too the funeral director routinely, without first consulting the family, prepares the body for public display.

Is all this legal? The processes to which a dead body may be subjected are after all to some extent circumscribed by law. In most states, for instance, the signature of next of kin must be obtained before an autopsy may be performed, before the deceased may be cremated, before the body may be turned over to a medical school for research purposes, or such provision must be made in the decedent's will. In the case of embalming, no such permission is required nor is it ever sought. A textbook, *The Principles and Practices of Embalming*, comments on this: "There is some question regarding the legality of much that is done within the preparation room." The author points out that it would be most unusual for a responsible member of a bereaved family to instruct the mortician, in so many words, to "embalm" the body of a deceased relative. The very term "embalming" is so seldom used that the mortician must rely upon custom in the matter. The author concludes that unless the family specifies otherwise, the act of entrusting the body to the care of a funeral establishment carries with it an implied permission to go ahead and embalm.

Embalming is indeed a most extraordinary procedure, and one must wonder at the docility of Americans who each year pay hundreds of millions of dollars for its perpetuation, blissfully ignorant of what it is all about, what is done, how it is done. Not one in ten thousand has any idea of what actually takes place. Books on the subject are extremely hard to come by. They are not to be found in most libraries or bookshops.

In an era when huge television audiences watch surgical operations in the comfort of their living rooms, when, thanks to the animated cartoon, the geography of the digestive system has become familiar territory even to the nursery school set, in a land where the satisfaction of curiosity about almost all matters is a national pastime, the secrecy surrounding embalming can, surely, hardly be attributed to the inherent gruesomeness of the subject. Custom in this regard has within this century suffered a complete reversal. In the early days of American embalming, when it was performed in the home of the deceased, it was almost mandatory for some relative to stay by the embalmer's side and witness the procedure. Today, family members who might wish to be in attendance would certainly be dissuaded by the funeral director. All others, except apprentices, are excluded by law from the preparation room.

A close look at what does actually take place may explain in large measure the undertaker's intractable reticence concerning a procedure that has become his major *raison d'être*. Is it possible he fears that public information about embalming might lead patrons to wonder if they really want this service? If the funeral men are loath to discuss the subject outside the trade, the reader may, understandably, be equally loath to go on reading at this point. For those who have the stomach for it, let us part the formaldehyde curtain. . . .

The body is first laid out in the undertaker's morgue–or rather, Mr. Jones is reposing in the preparation room–to be readied to bid the world farewell.

The preparation room in any of the better funeral establishments has the tiled and sterile look of a surgery, and indeed the embalmer-restorative artist who does his chores there is beginning to adopt the term "dermasurgeon" (appropriately corrupted by some mortician-writers as "demi-surgeon") to describe his calling. His equipment, consisting of scalpels, scissors, augers, forceps, clamps, needles, pumps, tubes, bowls and basins, is crudely imitative of the surgeon's, as is his technique, acquired in a nine- or twelve-month post high-school course in an embalming school. He is supplied by an advanced chemical industry with a bewildering array of fluids, sprays, pastes, oils, powders, creams, to fix or soften tissue, shrink or distend it as needed, dry it here, restore the moisture there. There are cosmetics, waxes and paints to fill and cover features, even plaster of Paris to replace entire limbs. There are ingenious aids to prop and stabilize the cadaver: a Vari-Pose Head Rest, the Edwards Arm and Hand Positioner, the Repose Block (to support the shoulders during the embalming), and the Throop Foot Positioner, which resembles an old-fashioned stocks.

Mr. John H. Eckels, president of the Eckels College of Mortuary Science, thus describes the first part of the embalming procedure: "In the hands of a skilled practitioner, this work may be done in a comparatively short time and without mutilating the body other than by slight incision–so slight that it scarcely would cause serious inconvenience if made upon a living person. It is necessary to remove the blood, and doing this not only helps in the disinfecting, but removes the principal cause of disfigurements due to discoloration."

Another textbook discusses the all-important time element: "The earlier this is done, the better, for every hour that elapses between death and embalming will add to the problems and complications encountered. . . ." Just how soon should one get going on the embalming? The author tells us, "On the basis of such scanty information made available to this profession through its rudimentary and haphazard system of technical research, we must conclude that the best results are to be obtained if the subject is embalmed before life is completely extinct–that is, before cellular death has occurred. In the average case, this would mean within an hour after somatic death." For those who feel that there is something a little rudimentary, not to say haphazard, about this advice, a comforting thought is offered by another writer. Speaking of fears entertained in early days of premature burial, he points out, "One of the effects of embalming by chemical injection, however, has been to dispel fears of live burial." How true; once the blood is removed, chances of live burial are indeed remote.

To return to Mr. Jones, the blood is drained out through the veins and replaced by embalming fluid pumped in through the veins and the arteries. As noted in *The Principles and Practices of Embalming,* "every operator has a favorite injection and drainage point–a fact which becomes a handicap only if he fails or refuses to forsake his favorites when conditions demand it." Typical favorites are the carotid artery, femoral artery, jugular vein, subclavian vein. There are various choices of embalming fluid. If Flextone is used, it will produce a "mild, flexible rigidity. The skin retains a velvety softness, the tissues are rubbery and pliable. Ideal for women and children." It may be blended with B and G Products Company's Lyf-Lyk tint, which is guaranteed to reproduce "nature's own skin texture . . . the velvety appearance of living tissue." Suntone comes in three separate tints: Suntan; Special Cosmetic tint, a pink shade "especially indicated for young female subjects"; and Regular Cosmetic Tint, moderately pink.

About three to six gallons of a dyed and perfumed solution of formaldehyde, glycerin, borax, phenol, alcohol and water is soon circulating through Mr. Jones, whose mouth has been sewn together with a "needle directed upward between the upper lip and gum and brought out through the left nostril," with the corners raised slightly "for a more pleasant expression." If he should be bucktoothed, his teeth are cleaned with Bon Ami and coated with colorless nail polish. His eyes, meanwhile, are closed with flesh-tinted eye caps and eye cement.

The next step is to have at Mr. Jones with a thing called a trocar. This is a long, hollow needle attached to a tube. It is jabbed into the abdomen, poked around the entrails and chest cavity, the contents of which are pumped out and replaced with "cavity fluid." This done, and the hole in the abdomen sewn up, Mr. Jones's face is heavily creamed (to protect the skin from burn which may be caused by leakage of the chemicals), and he is covered with a sheet and left unmolested for a while. But not for long–there is more, much more, in store for him. He has been embalmed, but not yet restored, and the best time to start the restorative work is eight to ten hours after embalming, when the tissues have become firm and dry.

The object of all this attention to the corpse, it must be remembered, is to make it presentable for viewing in an attitude of healthy repose. "Our customs require the presentation of our dead in the semblance of normality . . . unmarred by the ravages of illness, disease or mutilation," says Mr. J. Sheridan Mayer in his *Restorative Art*. This is rather a large order since few people die in the full bloom of health, unravaged by illness and unmarked by some disfigurement. The funeral industry is equal to the challenge: "In some cases the gruesome appearance of a mutilated or disease-ridden subject may be quite discouraging. The task of restoration may seem impossible and shake the confidence of the embalmer. This is the time for intestinal fortitude and determination. Once the formative work is begun and affected tissues are cleaned or removed, all doubts of success vanish. It is surprising and gratifying to discover the results which may be obtained."

The embalmer, having allowed an appropriate interval to elapse, returns to the attack, but now he brings into play the skill and equipment of sculptor and cosmetician. Is a hand missing? Casting one in plaster of Paris is a simple matter. "For replacement purposes, only a cast of the back of the hand is necessary; this is within the ability of the average operator and is quite adequate." If a lip or two, a nose or an ear should be missing, the embalmer has at hand a variety of restorative waxes with which to model replacements. Pores and skin texture are simulated by stippling with a little brush, and over this cosmetics are laid on. Head off? Decapitation cases are rather routinely handled. Ragged edges are trimmed, and head joined to torso with a series of splints, wires and sutures. It is a good idea to have a little something at the neck–a scarf or a high collar–when time for viewing comes. Swollen mouth? Cut out tissue as needed from inside the lips. If to much is removed, the surface contour can easily be restored by padding with cotton. Swollen necks and cheeks are reduced by removing tissue through vertical incisions made down each side of the neck. "When the deceased is casketed, the pillow will hide the suture incisions . . . as an extra precaution against leakage, the suture may be painted with suture sealer."

The opposite condition is more likely to present itself–that of emaciation. His hypodermic syringe now loaded with massage cream, the embalmer seeks out and fills the hollowed and sunken areas by injection. In this procedure the backs of the hands and fingers and the under-chin area should not be neglected. Positioning the lips is a problem that recurrently challenges the ingenuity of the embalmer. Closed too tightly, they tend to give a stern, even disapproving expression. Ideally, embalmers feel, the lips should give the impression of being ever so lightly parted, the upper lip protruding slightly for a more youthful appearance. This takes some engineering, however, as the lips tend to drift apart. Lip drift can sometimes be remedied by pushing one or two straight pins through the inner margin of the lower lip and then inserting them between the two front upper teeth. If Mr. Jones happens to have no teeth, the pins can just as easily be anchored in his Armstrong Face Former and Denture Replacer. Another method to maintain lip closure is to dislocate the lower jaw, which is then held in its new position by a wire run through holes which have been drilled through the upper and lower jaws at the midline. As the French are fond of saying, *il faut souffrir pour être belle.*

If Mr. Jones has died of jaundice, the embalming fluid will very likely turn him green. Does this deter the embalmer? Not if he has intestinal fortitude. Masking pastes and cosmetics are heavily laid on, burial arrangements and casket interiors are color-correlated with particular care, and Jones is displayed beneath rose-colored lights. Friends will say "How *well* he looks." Death by carbon monoxide, on the other hand, can be rather a good thing from the embalmer's viewpoint: "One advantage is the fact that this type of discoloration is an exaggerated form of a natural pink coloration." This is nice because the healthy glow is already present and needs but little attention.

The patching and filling completed, Mr. Jones is now shaved, washed and dressed. Cream-based cosmetic, available in pink, flesh, suntan, brunette and blond, is applied to his hands and face, his hair is shampooed and combed (and, in the case of Mrs. Jones, set), his hands manicured. For the horny-handed son of toil special care must be taken; cream should be applied to remove ingrained grime, and the nails cleaned. "If he were not in the habit of having them manicured in life, trimming and shaping is advised for better appearance–never questioned by kin."

Jones is now ready for casketing (this is the present participle of the verb "to casket"). In this operation his right should be depressed slightly "to turn the body a bit to the right and soften the appearance of lying flat on the back." Positioning the hands is a matter of importance, and special rubber positioning blocks may be used. The hands should be cupped slightly for a more lifelike, relaxed appearance. Proper placement of the body requires a delicate sense of balance. It should lie as high as possible in the casket, yet not so high that the lid, when lowered, will hit the nose.

On the other had, we are cautioned, placing the body too low "creates the impression that the body is in a box."

Jones is next wheeled into the appointed slumber room where a few last touches may be added–his favorite pipe placed in his hand or, if he was a great reader, a book propped into position. (In the case of little Master Jones a Teddy bear may be clutched.) Here he will hold open house for a few days, visiting hours 10 A.M. to 9 P.M.

All now being in readiness, the funeral director calls a staff conference to make sure that each assistant knows his precise duties. Mr. Wilber Kriege writes: "This makes your staff feel that they are a part of the team, with a definite assignment that must be properly carried out if the whole plan is to succeed. You never heard of a football coach who failed to talk to his entire team before they go on the field. They have drilled on the plays they are to execute for hours and days, and yet the successful coach knows the importance of making even the bench-warming third-string substitute feel that he is important if the game is to be won." The winning of *this* game is predicated upon glass-smooth handling of the logistics. The funeral director has notified the pallbearers whose names were furnished by the family, has arranged for the presence of clergyman, organist, and soloist, has provided transportation for everybody, has organized and listed the flowers sent by friends. In *Psychology of Funeral Service* Mr. Edward A. Martin points out: "He may not always do as much as the family thinks he is doing, but it is his helpful guidance that they appreciate in knowing they are proceeding as they should. . . . The important thing is how well his services can be used to make the family believe they are giving unlimited expression to their own sentiment."

The religious service may be held in a church or in the chapel of the funeral home; the funeral director vastly prefers the latter arrangement, for not only is it more convenient for him but it affords him the opportunity to show off his beautiful facilities to the gathered mourners. After the clergyman has had his say, the mourners queue up to file past the casket for a last look at the deceased. The family is *never* asked whether they want an open-casket ceremony; in the absence of their instruction to the contrary, this is taken for granted. Consequently well over 90 percent of all American funerals feature the open casket–a custom unknown in other parts of the world. Foreigners are astonished by it. An English woman living in San Francisco described her reaction in a letter to the writer:

I myself have attended only one funeral–that of an elderly fellow worker of mine. After the service I could not understand why everyone was walking towards the coffin (sorry, I mean casket), but thought I had better follow the crowd. It shook me rigid to get there and find the casket open and poor old Oscar lying there in his brown tweed suit, wearing a suntan makeup and just the wrong shade of lipstick. If I had not been extremely fond of the old boy, I have a horrible feeling that I might have giggled. Then and there I decided that I could never face another American funeral–even dead.

The casket (which has been resting throughout the service on a Classic Beauty Ultra Metal Casket Bier) is now transferred by a hydraulically operated device called Porto-Lift to a balloon-tired, Glide Easy casket carriage which will wheel it to yet another conveyance, the Cadillac Funeral Coach. This may be lavender, cream, light green–anything but black. Interiors, of course, are color-correlated, "for the man who cannot stop short of perfection."

At graveside, the casket is lowered into the earth. This office, once the prerogative of friends of the deceased, is now performed by a patented mechanical lowering device. A "Lifetime Green" artificial grass mat is at the ready to conceal the sere earth, and overhead, to conceal the sky, is a portable Steril Chapel Tent ("resists the intense heat and humidity of summer and the terrific storms of winter . . .available in Silver Grey, Rose or Evergreen"). Now is the time for the ritual scattering of earth over the coffin, as the solemn words "earth to earth, ashes to ashes, dust to dust" are pronounced by the officiating cleric. This can today be accomplished "with a mere flick of the wrist with the Gordon Leak-Proof Earth Dispenser. No grasping of a handful of dirt, no soiled fingers. Simple, dignified, beautiful, reverent! The modern way!" The Gordon Earth Dispenser (at $5) is of nickel-plated brass construction. It is not only "attractive to the eye and long wearing"; it is also "one of the 'tools' for building better public relations" if presented as "an appropriate non-commercial gift" to the clergyman. It is shaped something like a saltshaker.

Untouched by human hand, the coffin and the earth are now united.

It is in the function of directing the participants through this maze of gadgetry that the funeral director has assigned to himself his relatively new role of "grief therapist." He has relieved the family of every detail, he has revamped the corpse to look like a living doll, he has arranged for it to nap for a few days in the slumber room, he has put on a well-oiled performance in which the concept of *death* has played no part whatsoever–unless it was inconsiderately mentioned by the clergyman who conducted the religious service. He has done everything in his power to make the funeral a real pleasure for everybody concerned. He and his team have given their all to score an upset victory over death.

(1963)

ILLUSTRATION/EXAMPLE

One of the most commonly used patterns of expository writing is the development of a thesis, idea, or statement by means of illustration/example or exemplification. If, for example, you wish to tell your audience that, in your opinion, Marvin is not the best choice for the position of Chief Cashier at Citibank, you might proceed to illustrate your opinion with examples of Marvin's behavior. You might provide three examples to illustrate your assertion: (1) Marvin is a chain smoker and lights his cigarettes with $10 bills. (2) Although his salary is now only $100 a week and his parents live in a one-room apartment, Marvin drives a new Lexus and goes on vacations in Bora Bora. (3) Two months ago Marvin returned after another kind of vacation in Huntsville, Texas, where he was serving 10 to 20 years for embezzling two hundred thousand dollars from the Second Interstate Bank. Each of these examples serves to show your reader why you do not think highly of Marvin as a bank employee. You have made a statement (Don't make Marv Chief Cashier) and illustrated your statement with three effective examples of his behavior that should disqualify him from the job. In the *exemplification essay*, you make a statement and then provide examples to clarify your statement for the audience. The examples should be clear, concrete, appropriate, interesting, and supportive of the thesis statement.

Implementation

The purpose of developing an essay or a paragraph through illustration and example is to make clear the thesis, idea, or subject that you are trying to get across to your readers. You give your audience an illustration in order to explain a more general statement. The examples are samples of the general thesis, giving your readers more specific and concrete illustrations of the idea. The example thus acts as a kind of bridge from you to the readers, making the idea or subject clearer.

Suppose you want to convey to your history professor your idea that the war in Vietnam did a great deal of damage to the American spirit. This is a general, broad idea, and your audience would like (1) to have it made clearer and more specific for them and easier to understand, and they might like you (2) to give some evidence for your assertion or at least offer them some reasons to believe that what you say about the war and America is true. You can give them both of these things by providing them with good examples.

You could, for instance, include in your essay either a single extended example or several examples that will show that what you say is true. In order to demonstrate that the war has damaged the American spirit, you might choose the following examples:

1. Historical documents of public polls indicate that in 1972 over 70% of the Americans surveyed felt that the war in Vietnam was bad for America and the U.S. should get out of Indo-China.

2. In 1972 a large number of Vietnam veterans, organized as "Veterans Against the War," gathered in Washington, made speeches against U.S. involvement in Vietnam, and threw to the ground the medals they had won in Vietnam.

3. In order to avoid fighting in Vietnam, many young men left this country to live in Canada or Sweden. The government regarded them as draft-dodgers and criminals, while many of them said that they left the U.S. because the war was immoral and unjust. The American people seemed divided over whether to let these young men return from exile.

Your method is thus to illustrate your general statement (that the war has damaged the American spirit) with three examples that make clear to the audience precisely what you mean. You could also have chosen only one of the examples and presented an extended discussion of even greater detail to illustrate your point. Whether an essay is formally called exemplification or not, every composition needs concrete, detailed examples. In either case the examples clarify your basic point.

Technique

Effective examples have a number of common characteristics: they are clear, concrete, appropriate, vivid, interesting, and supportive of your thesis statement.

Good examples are clear.
Since the purpose of using examples is to make your general idea clearer to your audience, it should be obvious that the examples must be carefully chosen for their clarity. How clear the example is will depend to some extent on who the readers of the essay are likely to be. If you want to illustrate the economic principle of Supply and Demand, for instance, you would choose different examples for a professor of business administration than you would for a 9th-grade history textbook. The professor will understand references to Gross National Product, and a good example for her might be a fairly complicated graph showing annual consumption of fuel oil per capita. The 9th-grader, however, would probably not find these examples helpful because they would not be clear to him. He would probably benefit more from an illustration based on a sporting goods store and the different prices of baseball caps at various time of the year. When you show him that ball caps cost more in January than in July because there were fewer caps available in January, he will begin to see what you mean by "Supply and Demand." Whenever you choose an example, therefore, you should be sure that it will be clear to your intended audience and that it will make your general statement or thesis clearer to them.

Good examples are concrete.
This characteristic is closely allied to clarity since most examples are clearer when they are most concrete. Because of the way most of us think, readers are attracted to and benefit most from particular, specific, detailed examples. In the example already suggested–the illustration of Supply and Demand by a reference to the price of baseball caps in January–the example will be more effective if you specify

"baseball cap" than if you use a more abstract term like "wearing apparel." Referring to specific months, like January and July, to explain why production is lowest, too, will probably be more effective than talking about felicitous and infelicitous manufacturing periods. To illustrate your point, you might even decide to write a short narrative in which Coach Neander complains in a rage to Mr. Strapp, the manager of the sporting goods store (frightening him and causing him to knock down an 8-foot replica of a Dallas Cowboy linebacker display he was putting up), that the caps the coach wants for this team cost $20. The idea is to make the example specific, particular, and concrete because then the thesis will be easier for your audience to understand.

Good examples are appropriate.
In order to be effective, to do a good job of illustrating your point, an example should be appropriate; it should be suitable to the idea it illustrates (valid, reasonable) and also to the intended audience (appropriate for their experience, background, and knowledge of the subject). If you wanted to choose an appropriate example of how advertising can sway the consumer and force him to buy something he does not really want or need, you probably would not use the Ford Motor Company's greatest flop, the Edsel, as your example. Such an example would be neither valid nor reasonable since it suggests the opposite of what you want to demonstrate. The Edsel was heavily advertised, but it looked so awful that people refused to buy it. By the same token, you do not want to choose an example that is so outlandish or exaggerated that it fails to convince your readers because it is not representative. Such an example to demonstrate how advertising can influence the consumer might be "subliminal" advertising. Some years ago there were allegations that advertising messages like "Buy a Coke" were inserted on single frames of motion pictures. The message would flash on the screen for only a fraction of a second, and the movie patrons would not even be aware they had seen it. They supposedly got thirsty, and Coke sales in the lobby went up. Now this example might illustrate the power of advertising, and it can made clear and concrete enough, but it probably is not a good example because it is not appropriate. It is too exceptional and, therefore, unlikely to convince your audience. The charges were never proven, few theaters would have been involved anyway, and it is unlikely that your audience would feel such tactics applicable to them. The example, therefore, is not appropriate for your thesis. A more appropriate example could be the number of poor people who can barely afford to feed their families, but who buy the so-called "miracle drugs" advertised on television and in the newspapers. The drugs are often worthless, but clever advertising succeeds in selling them anyway.

Good examples are vivid and interesting.
No example is very useful if the reader does not read it because it is boring. Some of the characteristics already discussed are relevant to interesting examples since an interesting example will probably be clear, appropriate, and (especially) concrete. While some examples are vivid and interesting because of the material presented, almost all examples will gain by presentation in very specific and descriptive terms.

If for some reason you had to write an essay about "The Best Teacher I have Known," you would write a more effective and interesting essay if, instead of talking about the "vast knowledge" and "truly wonderful personality" of the teacher, you illustrated your essay with a vividly described example of the time the teacher taught you about propulsion and Newton's laws of motion by having the class build and launch a 29" rocket. If you want to write a propaganda leaflet about the awful food in your school cafeteria, don't talk vaguely about inedible food and slime in the ice machine. Instead, describe in sickening detail the barbecued cockroach nestled in your friend's cheeseburger or the ability of the coffee to etch glass and dissolve your spoon in 18 seconds. Make your reader participate in the essay to get your point across more quickly and thoroughly than you could with any amount of general verbiage about the teacher's "immense contribution to learning" or the cafeteria's wretched cuisine. Vivid examples can make an essay interesting, exciting, and effective. Dull, generalized examples will put your reader to sleep faster than ether, a rubber hammer, or an interview with Michael Jackson.

Organization

These characteristics obviously apply to essays that use illustration and examples as the structural principle, but it is important to note that we use examples in all of our rhetorical patterns, in every kind of expository and persuasive writing. Examine almost any good piece of writing, and you will find examples that are vivid, concrete, clear, interesting, and appropriate. Essays developed by definition, classification, comparison and contrast, process analysis, causal analysis, argumentation, and critical analysis depend on examples to help get their ideas across to their audience. The difference is that an essay developed by illustration uses examples as the structural principle on which it is organized. Review the general principles of composition and the checklist discussed in Chapter Two of this text. The general method of development in that chapter is based on the structure of illustration/example.

In the following essay written by Allison K. Hinson, an NHC student, notice the organization of the paragraphs and their relationship to the thesis statement. Also important are the specific examples used to discuss each of the divisions.

Horror Novels as Therapy

We humans have a coping mechanism for dealing with the world's problems. Instead of going to a therapist we go to a movie or open a book. In the fifties, to help America accept the fear caused by the Atom bomb, Hollywood gave us *Them!* and a series of "big bug" movies. To escape the social ills of today, we open a horror novel. Horror is defined as a feeling of extreme fear or dislike, a disgust that makes one shudder. However, people pay for the pleasure of being horrified. In fiction, the horror genre can be recognized by Gothic settings, psychological conflicts, and supernatural events.

Gothic horror draws us into a gloomy setting with the beauty of its prose. One of the best examples is Shirley Jackson's *The Haunting of Hill House*: "[W]alls continued upright, bricks met neatly, floors were firm, and doors were sensibly shut; silence lay steady against the wood and stone of Hill House, and whatever walked there, walked alone." With this beautifully paced opening, Ms. Jackson sets the tone for her frightening tale. In Edgar Allan Poe's "The Cask of Amontillado" we see the cobwebs and feel the nitre seep into our bones as we follow our narrator on his dark journey: "'The nitre!' I said; 'see, it increases. It hangs like moss upon the vaults. . . . The drops of moisture trickle among the bones.'" Similarly, we know that no good will come from Dracula's castle as Bram Stoker weaves his tale around us.

While Gothic settings can set the mood, psychological horror creates terror in the actual plot. Psychological horror disturbs reality, changing the way we think and act. Horror novels that are based on psychological conflicts create a feeling of terror in the reader because they are plausible. It is conceivable to experience the terror that the young mother and child feel in Stephen King's *Cujo* when they are trapped by the rabid dog. In Anthony Burgess's *A Clockwork Orange* the real horror is not that Alex and his "droogs" are on a rampage in England, but rather that the state forces mind control on him. The psychological conflict in V.C. Andrews' *Flowers in the Attic* is a struggle for power as a mother is slowly brainwashed into giving up her children. Likewise, Robert Louis Stevenson's *Dr. Jekyll and Mr. Hyde* creates horror by bringing attention to the destructive evil inside us all, symbolized by the werewolf. We all possess to some degree the split personalities between what we are and what we know. Thus, it is our identification with these psychological conflicts that makes these novels horrifying.

Supernatural horror, on the other hand, does the opposite of psychological horror; it brings us outside the known laws of nature. Mary Shelley's *Frankenstein* shows us men reaching beyond set boundaries and finding only pain. Certainly the monster was furious at being brought to life and then denied companionship, and the doctor's irresponsibility brought disaster. In Ira Levin's *Rosemary's Baby* the terror is in the powerlessness Rosemary feels against the supernatural Satanic forces at work within her body. In Stephen King's *Tommyknockers* we find alien ghosts hoping to take over the world by gaining a foothold in a small town in Maine. This story gives us Pandora's box and allows us to open it, spilling forth the horrors that we knew were inside. Supernatural horror scares us because we feel so helpless before such powerful and mysterious forces.

These three components of horror fiction provide the basis of what makes horror fiction so entertaining and cathartic. The human mind can handle only so much horror in daily life. It is better to release this horror by opening a good book than to succumb to it by opening a vein.

In his essay "Courtship Through the Ages," James Thurber discusses in careful detail the courtship rituals of animals, often comparing them to the courtship rituals of human beings. Through humor, the author reveals the stereotypical views of his generation over half a century ago (1930s). Compare his views with your views of courtship today.

COURTSHIP
THROUGH THE AGES

JAMES THURBER

Surely nothing in the astonishing scheme of life can have nonplussed nature so much as the fact that none of the females of any of the species she created really cared very much for the male, as such. For the past ten million years Nature has been busily inventing ways to make the male attractive to the female, but the whole business of courtship, from the marine annelids up to man, still lumbers heavily along, like a complicated musical comedy. I have been reading the sad and absorbing story in Volume 6 (Cole to Dama) of the *Encyclopedia Britannica*. In this volume you can learn about cricket, cotton, costume designing, crocodiles, crown jewels, and Coleridge, but none of these subjects is so interesting as the Courtship of Animals, which recounts the sorrowful lengths to which all males must go to arouse the interest of a lady.

We all know, I think, that Nature gave man whiskers and a mustache with the quaint idea in mind that these would prove attractive to the female. We all know that, far from attracting her, whiskers and mustaches only made her nervous and gloomy, so that man had to go in for somersaults, tilting with lances, and performing feats of parlor magic to win her attention; he also had to bring her candy, flowers, and the furs of animals. It is common knowledge that in spite of all these "love displays" the male is constantly being turned down, insulted, or thrown out of the house. It is rather comforting, then, to discover that the peacock, for all his gorgeous plumage, does not have a particularly easy time in courtship; none of the males in the world do. The first peahen, it turned out, was only faintly stirred by her suitor's beautiful train. She would often go quietly to sleep while he was whisking it around. The *Britannica* tells us that the peacock actually had to learn to vibrate his quills so as to make a rustling sound. In ancient times man himself, observing the ways of the peacock, probably tried vibrating his whiskers to make a rustling sound; if so, it didn't get him anywhere. He had to go in for something else; so, among other things, he went in for gifts. It is not unlikely that he got this idea from certain flies and birds who were making no headway at all with rustling sounds.

One of the flies of the family Empidae, who had tried everything, finally hit on something pretty special. He contrived to make a glistening transparent balloon which was even larger than himself. Into this he would put sweetmeats and tidbits and he would carry the whole elaborate envelope through the air to the lady of his choice. This amused her for a time, but she finally got bored with it. She demanded silly little colorful presents, something that you couldn't eat but that would look nice around the house. So the male Empis had to go around gathering flower petals and pieces of bright paper to put into his balloon. On a courtship flight a male Empis cuts quite a figure now, but he can hardly be said to be happy. He never knows how soon the female will demand heavier presents, such as Roman coins and gold collar buttons. It seems probable that one day the courtship of the Empidae will fall down, as man's occasionally does, of its own weight.

The bowerbird is another creature that spends so much time courting the female that he never gets any work done. If all the male bowerbirds became nervous wrecks within the next ten or fifteen years, it would not surprise me. The female bowerbird insists that a playground be built for her with a specially constructed bower at the entrance. This bower is much more elaborate than an ordinary nest and is harder to build; it costs a lot more, too. The female will not come to the playground until the male has filled it up with a great many gifts: silvery leaves, red leaves, rose petals, shells, beads, berries, bones, dice, buttons, cigar bands, Christmas seals, and the Lord knows what else. When the female finally condescends to visit the playground, she is in a coy and silly mood and has to be chased in and out of the bower and up and down the playground before she will quit giggling and stand still long enough even to shake hands. The male bird is, of course, pretty well done in before the chase starts, because he has worn himself out hunting for eyeglass lenses and begonia blossoms. I imagine that many a bowerbird, after chasing a female for two or three hours, says the hell with it and goes home to bed. Next day, of course, he telephones someone else and the same trying ritual is gone through with again. A male bowerbird is as exhausted as a night-club habitue before he is out of his twenties.

The male fiddler crab has a somewhat easier time, but it can hardly be said that he is sitting pretty. He has one enormously large and powerful claw, usually brilliantly colored, and you might suppose that all he had to do was reach out and grab some passing cutie. The very earliest fiddler crabs may have tried this, but, if so, they got slapped for their pains. A female fiddler crab will not tolerate any caveman stuff; she never has and doesn't intend to start now. To attract a female, a fiddler crab has to stand on tiptoe and brandish his claw in the air. If any female in the neighborhood is interested–and you'd be surprised how many are not–she comes over and engages him in light badinage, for which he is not in the mood. As many as a hundred females may pass the time of day with him and go on about their business. By nightfall of an average courting day, a fiddler crab who has been standing on tiptoe for eight or ten hours waving a heavy claw in the air is in pretty sad shape. As in the case of the male of all species, however, he gets out of bed next morning, dashes some water on his face, and tries again.

The next time you encounter a male web-spinning spider, stop and reflect that he is too busy worrying about his love life to have any desire to bite you. Male web-spinning spiders have a tougher life than any other males in the animal kingdom. This is because the female web-spinning spiders have very poor eyesight. If a male lands on a female's web, she kills him before he has time to lay down his cane and gloves, mistaking him for a fly or a bumblebee who has tumbled into her trap. Before the species figured out what to do about this, millions of males were murdered by ladies they called on. It is the nature of spiders to perform a little dance in front of the female, but before a male spinner could get near enough for the female to see who he was and what he was up to, she would lash out at him with a flat-iron or a pair of garden shears. One night, nobody knows when, a very bright male spinner lay awake worrying about calling on a lady who had been killing suitors right and left. It came to him that this business of dancing as a love display wasn't getting anybody anywhere except the grave. He decided to go in for web-twitching, or strand-vibrating. The next day he tried it on one of the nearsighted girls. Instead of dropping in on her suddenly, he stayed outside the web and began monkeying with one of its strands. He twitched it up and down and in and out with such a lilting rhythm that the female was charmed. The serenade worked beautifully; the female let him live. The *Britannica's* spider-watchers, however, report that this system is not always successful. Once in a while, even now, a female will fire three bullets into a suitor or run him through with a kitchen knife. She keeps threatening him from the moment he strikes the first low notes on the outside strings, but usually by the time he has got up to the high notes played around the center of the web, he is going to town and she spares his life.

Even the butterfly, as handsome a fellow as he is, can't always win a mate merely by fluttering around and showing off. Many butterflies have to have scent scales on their wings. Hepialus carries a powder puff in a perfumed pouch. He throws perfume at the ladies when they pass. The male tree cricket, Oecanthus, goes Hepialus one better by carrying a tiny bottle of wine with him and giving drinks to such doxies as he has designs on. One of the male snails throws darts to entertain the girls. So it goes, through the long list of animals, from the bristle worm and his rudimentary dance steps to man and his gift of diamonds and sapphires. The golden-eye drake raises a jet of water with his feet as he flies over a lake; hepialus has his powder puff, Oecanthus his wine bottle, man his etchings. It is a bright and melancholy story, the age-old desire of the male for the female, the age-old desire of the female to be amused and entertained. Of all the creatures on earth, the only males who could be figured as putting any irony into their courtship are the grebes and certain other diving birds. Every now and then a courting grebe slips quietly down to the bottom of a lake and then, with a mighty "Whoosh!" pops out suddenly a few feet from his girl friend, splashing water all over her. She seems to be persuaded that this is a purely loving display, but I like to think that the grebe always has a faint hope of drowning her or scaring her to death.

I will close this investigation into the mournful burdens of the male with *Britannica's* story about a certain Argus pheasant. It appears that the Argus displays himself in front of a female who stands perfectly still without moving a feather. . . . The male Argue the *Britannica* tells about was confined in a cage with a female of another species, a female who kept moving around, emptying ashtrays and fussing with lampshades all the time the male was showing off his talents. Finally, in disgust, he stalked away and began displaying in front of his water trough. He reminds me of a certain male (*Homo sapiens*) of my acquaintance who one night after dinner asked his wife to put down her detective magazine so that he could read a poem of which he was very fond. She sat quietly enough until he was well into the middle of the thing, intoning with great ardor and intensity. Then suddenly there came a sharp, disconcerting *slap!* It turned out that all during the male's display, the female had been intent on a circling mosquito and had finally trapped it between the palms of her hands. The male in this case did not stalk away and display in front of a water trough; he went over to Tim's and had a flock of drinks and recited the poem to the fellows. I am sure they all told bitter stories of their own about how their displays had been interrupted by females. I am also sure that they all ended up singing "Honey, Honey, Bless Your Heart."

(1942)

DEFINITION

We are all curious beings. We begin asking questions in early childhood, and we develop this inquisitive nature throughout our lives. Our curiosity leads us to seek meanings constantly in order to learn or to clarify our understanding. In addition, we are often asked to explain our own ideas or to clarify, through more specific language, something we have said, whether we are having a friendly discussion among friends or responding orally or in writing to an instructor's question. One of the methods of making ourselves more precise is through *definition*. When someone asks, "What do you mean by that?" your answer may be a constructed definition, relating precisely what the specific idea or term means. In putting together that definition, we often have to "translate" what we mean so our audience will understand our meaning better; we literally put our thoughts into other words in order to convey our message in an understandable language. When a definition is precise enough, it enables the audience to distinguish the particular term being defined from other similar terms with which it could be confused. The rhetorical pattern called *definition* is a convenient method of clarifying or analyzing a word or concept while you examine the term for a broader understanding.

Implementation

There are at least three types of definitions: the informal definition, the formal definition, and the extended definition. Although the first two require little more than a word or perhaps a sentence, the third method of definition may run into a paragraph or even several pages. Definition can be used as a method to introduce your essay, to clarify your terms within other methods of expository writing, or as a means to an end in itself.

Techniques

1. Informal definition (synonyms) – This definition is usually associated
    with the speaker's or writer's own explanation of the word with his
    particular purpose in mind. This is the connotative meaning of the word
    being defined. It defines the term by offering a synonym, a word
    that has a meaning similar to that of another word in the same   language.
    The use of a synonym lets the writer clarify his expression by   providing
    a word or term that is more familiar to the audience.   For example, if you
    were asked what you meant by the word "mooncalf," you could simply
    respond with a synonym like "idiot."

Remember that a definition requires a common ground between the writer and his
audience. This common ground implies that the definition is for a specific person
or persons involved in the exchange of ideas. Consider the following conversation
between a father and his 16-year-old son:

Son: "I want a new Supercharged Model X1100 convertible, Dad. It's so *bad*!"
Dad: "You mean you don't like it then?"
Son: "No, man. I mean it's *rad*!
Dad: "Then I'm really confused, son."

It is no wonder that dad is confused. There is no common ground of understanding
here between him and his son. For the son's meaning to be understood, his
audience, Dad in this case, must know that "rad" means "awesome." Some terms,
however, require more than just a synonym. The term "sexual harassment" could
be defined as "office abuse." Because this synonymous term does not quite reflect
a true parallel meaning, you can see why "sexual harassment" might require further
explanation through a formal definition or an extended definition.

2. Formal definition – This type of definition is that which is most likely to
    to be found in dictionaries and other reference sources. It provides the
    denotative meaning of the word being defined and is composed of two
    distinct parts. You must first classify the term to be defined and then
    distinguish it from other similar terms in the same classification. Note
    the three steps in the following examples:

Term	Classification	Distinguishing Characteristics
A *mooncalf*	*is a person*	*who is congenitall foolish or mentally defective.*
A *wife*	*is a woman*	*who is married to a man.*

Note that the above two terms–mooncalf and wife–are placed into a broader category or class, limiting the terms to a kind of person or woman, respectively. Then we add the characteristics that distinguish that person or woman from all the other people or women. Not all definitions, however, are this simple. Some are more complex and require even more specific descriptions of the distinguishing traits. Consider the following:

Existentialism	*is a philosophy*	*that focuses on the uniqueness and isolation of individual experiences in an indifferent universe, regards human existence as explainable, and emphasizes man's freedom of choice and responsibility for the consequences of his actions.*
Sexual harassment	*is a human social interaction*	*whereby a person violates federal law by compelling another person to submit or to feel obligated to submit to sexual pressure.*

3.   Extended definition – You will most likely want to use the extended definition method when your definition is as complex as those for existentialism or sexual harassment. This method of definition is what your instructor will most likely expect from you in analyzing some term, phrase, or concept in an essay of several hundred words. Such an examination involves writing an essay on this concept, delving more deeply into its meaning and citing examples that illustrate the term and the difficulties in defining it. Definition, however, is not just an academic exercise. In the matter of sexual harassment, for instance, much work has gone into arriving at an explicit legal definition, for company policy and civil rights cases before the courts all hinge on how the term is defined. The two essays containing the opening speeches by Clarence Thomas and Anita Hill that appear at the end of this text illustrate the difficulties in defining sexual harassment.

Organization

Extended definitions may include one or several methods of development: synonyms, antonyms, formal definitions, narration and description, illustration, comparison or contrast, classification, or causal analysis. Regardless of which method of development you use to define your term or phrase, you will probably want to use the formal definition for your thesis statement and then develop your essay according to the requirements of that particular rhetorical method. Notice how, in his essay later in this section, Gordon Bigelow uses illustration to define existentialism so the reader will have a clearer understanding of the term and how it works. He could just as well have written a comparison/contrast essay showing how existentialism is similar to or different from another 20th-century philosophy. Likewise, he could have classified existentialism by dividing its class into the religious or non-religious groups of existentialists. But he chose to use a combination of techniques to be certain that the audience would understand fully the meaning of the term. In addition, you may wish to define what your term means by negation, that is, by telling your audience what your term does not mean. Dr. Samuel Johnson once defined darkness as the "want of light." If you wanted to define the term wife, you may choose to tell your audience that a wife is not a nanny, a maid, or a mistress. While negation is effective in explaining what a term does not mean, it must be accompanied by additional methods of definition. Negation can only help to clarify other statements about what your term does mean.

Regardless of which method you use to write your definition, you should realize in the process that definition is a flexible method of expository writing. It can accommodate you and persuade your audience through almost any format you choose. It helps us to understand the things we see and sometimes the things we do not see.

Checklist for definition essay

1. Is your audience clearly determined and is your purpose clearly stated?
2. Is the method of development you used the best means for reaching your audience and achieving your purpose?
3. Is your organization logical and suitable for your purpose?
4. Did you avoid repeating in your predicate or in your discussion the term you are defining, thus avoiding circularity? For instance, you should not define sexual harassment as "harassment of a sexual nature."
5. Does your definition avoid vagueness and generalities? Are you precise and clear?

Although you have already looked at the term *existentialism* in the above discussion, the term can certainly bear further explanation. George E. Bigelow's "A Primer of Existentialism" extends the definition of existentialism by discussing six specific divisions that characterize this modern philosophy.

A PRIMER OF
EXISTENTIALISM
GEORGE BIGELOW

For some years I fought the word by irritably looking the other way whenever I stumbled across it, hoping that like dadaism and some of the other "isms" of the French *avant garde* it would go away if I ignored it. But existentialism was apparently more than the picture it evoked of uncombed beards, smoky basement cafes, and French beatniks regaling one another between sips of absinthe with brilliant variations on the theme of despair. It turned out to be of major importance to literature and the arts, to philosophy and theology, and of increasing importance to the social sciences. To learn more about it, I read several of the self-styled introductions to the subject, with the baffled sensation of a man who reads a critical introduction to a novel only to find that he must read the novel before he can understand the introduction. Therefore, I should like to provide here something most discussions of existentialism take for granted, a simple statement of its basic characteristics. This is a reckless thing to do because there are several kinds of existentialism and what one says of one kind may not be true of another, but there is an area of agreement, and it is this common ground that I should like to set forth here. We should not run into trouble so long as we understand from the outset that the six major themes outlined below will apply in varying degrees to particular existentialists. A reader should be able to go from here to the existentialists themselves, to the more specialized critiques of them, or be able to recognize an existentialist theme or coloration in literature when he sees it.

A word first about the kinds of existentialism. Like transcendentalism of the last century, there are almost as many varieties of this *ism* as there are individual writers to whom the word is applied (not all of them claim it). But without being facetious we might group them into two main kinds, the *ungodly* and the *godly*. To take the ungodly or atheistic first, we would list as the chief spokesmen among many others Jean-Paul Sartre, Albert Camus, and Simone de Beauvoir. Several of this important group of French writers had rigorous and significant experience in the Resistance during the Nazi occupation of France in World War II. Out of the despair which came with the collapse of their nation during those terrible years they found unexpected strength in the single indomitable human spirit, which even under severe torture could maintain the spirit of resistance, the unextinguishable ability to say "No." From this irreducible core in the human spirit, they erected after the war a philosophy which was a twentieth-century variation of the philosophy of Descartes.

But instead of saying "I think, therefore I am," they said "I can say No, therefore I exist." As we shall presently see, the use of the word "exist" is of prime significance. This group is chiefly responsible for giving existentialism its status in the popular mind as a literary-philosophical cult.

Of the godly or theistic existentialists we should mention first a mid nineteenth-century Danish writer, Søren Kierkegaard; two contemporary French Roman Catholics, Gabriel Marcel and Jacques Maritain; two Protestant theologians, Paul Tillich and Nicholas Berdyaev; and Martin Buber, an important contemporary Jewish theologian. Taken together, their writings constitute one of the most significant developments in modern theology. Behind both groups of existentialists stand other important figures, chiefly philosophers, who exert powerful influence upon the movement–Blaise Pascal, Friedrich Nietzsche, Henri Bergson, Martin Heidegger, Karl Jaspers, among others. Several literary figures, notably Tolstoy and Dostoievsky, are frequently cited because existentialist attitudes and themes are prominent in their writings. The eclectic nature of this movement should already be sufficiently clear and the danger of applying too rigidly to any particular figure the general characteristics of the movement which I now make bold to describe:

1. Existence before essence. Existentialism gets its name from an insistence that human life is understandable only in terms of an individual man's existence, his particular experience of life. It says that a man *lives* (has existence) rather than *is* (has being or essence), and that every man's experience of life is unique, radically different from everyone else's and can be understood truly only in terms of his involvement in life or commitment to it. It strenuously shuns that view which assumes an ideal of Man or Mankind, a universal of human nature of which each man is only one example. It eschews the question of Greek Philosophy, *"What is mankind?"* which suggests that man can be defined if he is ranged in his proper place in the order of nature; it asks instead the question of Job and St. Augustine, *"Who am I"* with its suggestion of the uniqueness and mystery of each human life and its emphasis upon the subjective or personal rather than the objective or impersonal. From the outside a man appears to be just another natural creature; from the inside he is an entire universe, the center of infinity. The existentialist insists upon this latter radically subjective view, and from this grows much of the rest of existentialism.

2. Reason is impotent to deal with the depths of human life. There are two parts to this proposition–first, that human reason is relatively weak and imperfect, and second, that there are dark places in human life which are "nonreason" and to which reason scarcely penetrates. Since Plato, Western civilization has usually assumed a separation of reason from the rest of the human psyche, and has glorified reason as suited to command the nonrational part. The classic statement of this separation appears in the Phaedrus where Plato describes the psyche in the myth of the chariot which is drawn by white steeds of the emotions and the black unruly steeds of the appetites. The driver of the chariot is Reason who holds the reins which control the horses and the whip to subdue the surging black steeds of passion. Only the driver, the rational nature, is given human form; the rest of the psyche, the nonrational part, is given a lower, animal form. This separation and exaltation of reason is carried further in the allegory of the cave in the *Republic*. You recall the sombre picture of human life with which the story begins: men are chained in the dark in a cave, with their backs to a flickering firelight, able to see only uncertain shadows moving on the wall before them, able to hear only confused echoes of sounds. One of the men, breaking free from his chains, is able to turn and look upon the objects themselves and the light which casts the shadows; even, at last, he is able to work his way entirely out of the cave into the sunlight beyond. All this he is able to do through his reason; he escapes from the bondage of error, from time and change, from death itself, into the realm of changeless eternal ideas or Truth, and the lower nature which had chained him in darkness is left behind.

Existentialism in our time, and this is one of its most important characteristics, insists upon reuniting the "lower" or irrational parts of the psyche with the "higher." It insists that man must be taken in his wholeness and not in some divided state, that whole man contains not only intellect but also anxiety, guilt, and the will to power—which modify and sometimes overwhelm the reason. A man seen in this light is fundamentally ambiguous, if not mysterious, full of contradictions and tensions which cannot be dissolved simply by taking thought. "Human life," said Berdyaev, "is permeated by underground streams." One is reminded of D.H. Lawrence's outburst against Franklin and his rational attempt to achieve moral perfection: "The Perfectability of man! . . . The perfectability of which man? I am many men. Which of them are you going to perfect? I am not a mechanical contrivance. . . . It's a queer thing is a man's soul.. It is the whole of him. Which means it is the unknown as well as the known. . . . The soul of man is a dark vast forest, with wild life in it." The emphasis in existentialism is not on idea but upon the thinker who has the idea. It accepts not only his power of thought, but his contingency and fallibility, his frailty, his body, blood, and bones, and above all his death. Kierkegaard emphasized the distinction between *subjective* truth (what a person *is*) and *objective* truth (what the person *knows*), and said that we encounter the true self not in the detachment of thought but in the involvement and agony of choice and in the pathos of commitment to our choice. This distrust of rational systems helps to explain why many existential writers in their own expression are paradoxical or prophetic or gnomic, why their works often belong more to literature than to philosophy.

    3. Alienation or estrangement. One major result of the dissociation of reason from the rest of the psyche has been the growth of science, which has become one of the hallmarks of Western civilization, and an ever-increasing rational ordering of men in society. As the existentialists view them, the main forces of history since the Renaissance have progressively separated man from concrete earthly existence, have forced him to live at ever higher levels of abstraction, have collectivized individual man out of existence, have driven God from the heavens, or what is the same thing, from the hearts of men. They are convinced that modern man lives in a fourfold condition of alienation: from God, from nature, from other men, from his own true self.

The estrangement from God is most shockingly expressed by Nietzsche's anguished cry, "God is dead," a cry which has continuously echoed through the writings of the existentialists, particularly the French. This theme of spiritual barrenness is a commonplace in literature of this century, from Eliot's "Hollow Men" to the novels of Dos Passos, Hemingway, and Faulkner. It often appears in writers not commonly associated with the existentialists as in this remarkable passage from *A Story-Teller's Story*, where Sherwood Anderson describes his own awakening to his spiritual emptiness. He tells of walking alone late at night along a moonlit road when,

I had suddenly an odd, and to my own seeming, a ridiculous desire to abase myself before something not human and so stepping into the moonlit road, I knelt in the dust. Having no God, the gods having been taken from me by the life about me, as a personal God has been taken from all modern men by a force within that man himself does not understand but that is called the intellect, I kept smiling at the figure I cut in my own eyes as I knelt in the road. . . .

There was no God in the sky, no God in myself, no conviction in myself that I had the power to believe in a God, and so I merely knelt in the dust in silence and no words came to my lips.

In another passage Anderson wondered if the giving of itself by an entire generation to mechanical things was not really making all men impotent, if the desire for a greater navy, a greater army, taller public buildings, was not a sign of growing impotence. He felt that Puritanism and the industrialism which was its offspring had sterilized modern life, and proposed that men return to a healthful animal vigor by renewed contact with simple things of the earth, among them untrammeled sexual expression. One is reminded of the unkempt and delectable raffishness of Steinbeck's *Cannery Row* or of D.H. Lawrence's quasi-religious doctrine of sex, "blood-consciousness" and the "divine otherness" of animal existence.

Man's estrangement from nature has been a major theme in literature at least since Rousseau and the Romantic movement, and can hardly be said to be the property of existentialists. But this group nevertheless adds its own insistence that one of modern man's most urgent dangers is that he builds ever higher the brick and steel walls of technology which shut him away from a healthy-giving life according to "nature." Their treatment of this theme is most commonly expressed as part of a broader insistence that modern man needs to shun abstraction and return to "concreteness" or "wholeness."

A third estrangement has occurred at the social level and its sign is growing dismay at man's helplessness before the great machine-like colossus of industrialized society. This is another major theme of Western literature, and here again, though they hardly discovered the danger or began the protest, the existentialists in our time renew the protest against any pattern or force which would stifle the unique and spontaneous in individual life. The crowding of men into cities, the subdivision of centralized government, the growth of advertising, propaganda, and mass media of entertainment and communication–all the things which force men into Riesman's "Lonely Crowd"–these same things drive men asunder by destroying their individuality and making them live on the surface of life, content to deal with things rather than people. "Exteriorization," says Berdyaev, "is the source of slavery, whereas freedom is interiorization. Slavery always indicated alienation, the ejection of human nature into the external." This kind of alienation is exemplified by Zero, in Elmer Rice's play "The Adding Machine." Zero's twenty-five years as a bookkeeper in a department store have dried up his humanity, making him incapable of love, of friendship, of any deeply felt, freely expressed emotion. Such estrangement is often given as the reason for man's inhumanity to man, the explanation of injustice in modern society. In Camus' short novel, aptly called *The Stranger*, a young man is convicted by a court of murder. This is a homicide which he has actually committed under extenuating circumstances. But the court never listens to any of the relevant evidence, seems never to hear anything that pertains to the crime itself; it convicts the young man on wholly irrelevant grounds– because he had behaved in an unconventional way at his mother's funeral the day before the homicide. In this book one feels the same dream-like distortion of reality as in the trial scene in *Alice in Wonderland*, a suffocating sense of being enclosed by events which are irrational or absurd but also inexorable. Most disturbing of all is the young man's aloneness, the impermeable membrane of estrangement which surrounds him and prevents anyone else from penetrating to his experience of life or sympathizing with it.

The fourth kind of alienation, man's estrangement from his own true self, especially as his nature is distorted by an exaltation of reason, is another theme having an extensive history as a major part of the Romantic revolt. Of the many writers who treat the theme, Hawthorne comes particularly close to the emphasis of contemporary existentialists. His Ethan Brand, Dr. Rappaccini, and Roger Chillingworth are a recurrent figure who represents the dislocation in human nature which results when an overdeveloped or misapplied intellect severs "the magnetic chain of human sympathy." Hawthorne is thoroughly existential in his concern for the sanctity of the individual human soul, as well as in his preoccupation with sin and the dark side of human nature, which must be seen in part as his attempt to build back some fullness to the flattened image of man bequeathed to him by the Enlightenment. Whitman was trying to do this when he added flesh and bone and a sexual nature to the spiritualized image of man he inherited from Emerson, though his image remains diffused and attenuated by the same cosmic optimism. Many of the nineteenth-century depictions of man represent him as a figure of power or of potential power, sometimes as daimonic, like Melville's Ahab, but after World War I the power is gone; man is not merely distorted or truncated, he is hollow, powerless, faceless. At the time when his command over natural forces seems to be unlimited, man is pictured as weak, ridden with nameless dread. And this brings us to another of the major themes of existentialism.

    4. *"Fear and trembling," anxiety.* At Stockholm when he accepted the Nobel Prize, William Faulkner said that "Our tragedy today is a general and universal

physical fear so long sustained by now that we can even bear it. There are no longer problems of the spirit. There is only one question: When will I be blown up?" The optimistic vision of the Enlightenment which saw man, through reason and its extensions in science, conquering all nature and solving all social and political problems in a continuous upward spiral of Progress, cracked open like a melon on the rock of World War I. The theories which held such high hopes died in that sickening and unimaginable butchery. Here was a concrete fact of human nature and society which the theories could not contain. The Great Depression and World War II deepened the sense of dismay which the loss of these ideals brought, but only with the atomic bomb did this become an unbearable terror, a threat of instant annihilation which confronted all men, even those most insulated by the thick crust of material goods and services. Now the most unthinking person could sense that each advance in mechanical technique carried not only a chromium and plush promise of comfort but a threat as well.

Sartre, following Kierkegaard, speaks of another kind of anxiety which oppresses modern man—"the anguish of Abraham"—the necessity which is laid upon him to make moral choices on his own responsibility. A military officer in wartime knows the agony of choice which forces him to sacrifice part of his army to preserve the rest, as does a man in high political office, who must make decisions affecting the lives of millions. The existentialists claim that each of us might make moral decisions in our own lives which involve the same anguish. Kierkegaard finds that this necessity is one thing which makes each life unique, which makes it impossible to speculate or generalize about human life, because each man's case is irretrievably his own, something in which he is personally and passionately involved. His book *Fear and Trembling* is an elaborate and fascinating commentary on the Old Testament story of Abraham, who was commanded by God to sacrifice his beloved son Isaac. Abraham thus becomes the emblem of man who must make a harrowing choice, in this case between love for his son and love for God, between the universal moral law which says categorically, "thou shalt not kill," and the unique inner demand of his religious faith. Abraham's decision, which is to violate the abstract and collective moral law, has to be made not in arrogance but in fear and trembling, one of the inferences being that sometimes one must make an exception to the general law because he is (existentially) an exception, a concrete being whose existence can never be completely subsumed under any universal.

   5. *The encounter with nothingness.* For the man alienated from God, from nature, from his fellow man and from himself, what is left at last but Nothingness? The testimony of the existentialists is that this is where modern man now finds himself, not on the highway of upward Progress toward a radiant Utopia but on the brink of a catastrophic precipice, below which yawns the absolute void, an uncompromised black Nothingness. In one sense this is Eliot's Wasteland inhabited by his Hollow Man who is

> Shape without form, shade without color
>
> Paralyzed force, gesture without motion.

That is what moves E.A. Robinson's Richard Cory, the man who is everything that might make us wish that we were in his place, to go home one calm summer night and put a bullet through is head.

One of the most convincing statements of the encounter with Nothingness is made by Leo Tolstoy in "My Confession." He tells how in good health, in the prime of life, when he had everything that a man could desire—wealth, fame, aristocratic social position, a beautiful wife and children, a brilliant mind and great artistic talent in the height of their powers, he nevertheless was seized with a growing uneasiness, a nameless discontent which he could not shake or alleviate. His experience was like that of a man who falls sick, with symptoms which he disregards as insignificant; but the symptoms return again and again until they merge into a continuous suffering. And the patient suddenly is confronted with the overwhelming fact that what he took for mere indisposition is more important to him than anything else on earth, that it is death! "I felt the ground on which I stood was crumbling, that there was nothing for me to stand on, that what I had been living for was nothing, that I had no reason for living. . . . To stop was impossible, to go back was impossible; and it was impossible to shut my eyes so as to see that there was nothing before me but suffering and actual death, absolute annihilation." This is the Sickness Unto Death" of Kierkegaard, the despair in which one wishes to die but cannot. Hemingway's short story, "A Clean, Well-Lighted Place" gives an unforgettable expression of this theme. At the end of the story, the old waiter climbs into bed late at night saying to himself, "What did he fear? It was not fear or dread. It was a nothing which he knew too well. It was all a nothing and a man was nothing too. . . . Nada y pues nada, y nada y pues nada." and then because he has experienced the death of God he goes on to recite the Lord's Prayer in blasphemous despair: "Our Nothing who are in Nothing, nothing be thy nothing. . . ." And then the Ave Maria, "Hail nothing, full of nothing. . . ." This is stark, even for Hemingway, but the old waiter does no more than name the void felt by most people in the early Hemingway novels, a hunger they seek to assuage with alcohol, sex, and violence in an aimless progress from bar to bed to bullring. It goes without saying that much of the despair and pessimism in other contemporary authors springs from a similar sense of the void in modern life.

6. *Freedom.* Sooner or later, as a theme that includes all the others, the existentialist writings bear upon freedom. The themes we have outlined above describe either some loss of man's freedom or some threat to it, and all existentialists of whatever sort are concerned to enlarge the range of human freedom.

For the avowed atheists like Sartre freedom means human autonomy. In a purposeless universe man is *condemned* to freedom because he is the only creature who is "self-surpassing," who can become something other than he is. Precisely because there is no God to give purpose to the universe, each man must accept individual responsibility for his own becoming, a burden made heavier by the fact that in choosing for himself he chooses for all men "the image of man as he ought to be. A man *is* the sum total of the acts that make up his life—no more, no less—and though the coward has made himself cowardly, it is always possible for him to change and make himself heroic. In Sartre's novel, *The Age of Reason*, one of the least likable of the characters, almost overwhelmed by despair and self-disgust at his homosexual tendencies, is on the point of solving his problem by mutilating himself with a razor, when in an effort of will he throws the instrument down, and we are given to understand that from this moment he will have mastery over his aberrant drive. Thus in the daily course of ordinary life must men shape their becoming in Sartre's world.

The religious existentialists interpret man's freedom differently. They use much the same language as Sartre, develop the same themes concerning the predicament of man, but always include God as a radical factor. They stress the man of faith rather than the man of will. They interpret man's existential condition as a state of alienation from his essential nature which is God-like, the problem of his life being to heal the chasm between the two, that is, to find salvation. The mystery and ambiguity of man's existence they attribute to his being the intersection of two realms. "Man bears within himself," writes Berdyaev, "the image which is both the image of man and the image of God, and is the image of man as far as the image of God is actualized." Tillich describes salvation as "the act in which the cleavage between the essential being and the existential situation is overcome." Freedom here, as for Sartre, involves an acceptance of responsibility for choice and a *commitment* to one's choice. This is the meaning of faith, a faith like Abraham's, the commitment which is an agonizing sacrifice of one's own desire and will and dearest treasure to God's will.

A final word. Just as one should not expect to find in a particular writer all of the characteristics of existentialism as we have described them, he should also be aware that some of the most striking expressions of existentialism in literature and the arts come to us by indirection, often through symbols or through innovations in conventional form. Take the preoccupation of contemporary writers with time. In *The Sound and the Fury*, Faulkner both collapses and expands normal clock time, or by juxtapositions of past and present blurs time into a single amorphous pool. He does this by using various forms of "stream of consciousness" or other techniques which see life in terms of unique, subjective experience—that is, existentially. The conventional view of externalized life, a rational orderly progression cut into uniform segments by the hands of a clock, he rejects in favor of a view which sees life as opaque, ambiguous, and irrational—that is, as the existentialist sees it. Graham Greene does something like this in *The Power and the Glory*. He creates a scene isolated in time and cut off from the rest of the world, steamy and suffocating as if a bell jar had been placed over it. Through this atmosphere fetid with impending death and human suffering, stumbles the whiskey priest, lonely and confused, pursued by a police lieutenant who has experienced the void and the death of God.

Such expressions in literature do not mean necessarily that the authors are conscious existentialist theorizers, or even that they know the writings of such theorizers. Faulkner may never have read Heidegger–or St. Augustine–both of whom attempt to demonstrate that time is more within a man and subject to his unique experience of it than it is outside him. But it is legitimate to call Faulkner's views of time and life "existential" in this novel because in recent years existentialist theorizers have given such views a local habitation and a name. One of the attractions, and one of the dangers, of existential themes is that they become like Sir Thomas Browne's quincunx: once one begins to look for them, he sees them everywhere. But if one applies restraint and discrimination, he will find that they illuminate much of contemporary literature and sometimes the literature of the past as well. (1961)

COMPARISON AND CONTRAST

Although comparison and contrast are seldom used entirely by themselves (often being combined with other rhetorical patterns in the same essay), you have used them yourself and others have used them to make things clear to you. When you were a child, you might have asked your father what a "giraffe" was. His response might have been something like this: "It is an animal that looks something like a horse, except that it has long legs and a very long neck–much longer than a horse's neck. Its color is much like a leopard's, yellow with black spots, but the giraffe's spots are larger and he has fewer of them than a leopard has. A giraffe has a black tongue, too–very different from cats and dogs and most other animals." Your father answered your question by comparing and contrasting the giraffe's size, legs, neck, color, and tongue with those of other animals. Because the giraffe is an animal, the best things to compare it with are other animals, members of the same classification. It would be possible to compare the giraffe to a Chevrolet (the giraffe is taller, not a machine, and a different color; it lacks bucket seats and a vinyl roof) or to a telephone pole (the giraffe is not as tall, can move around better, and does/does not smell better), but the comparisons and contrasts possible would not be as useful as the animal comparisons are in giving a child an idea of what a giraffe is. In general, then, we usually compare and contrast things in a group or class defined by our interest, things that have important similarities as well as differences.

Implementation

There are three reasons for developing an essay by comparison and contrast. The first is that we might want to describe or define one item, and we do so by relating it to another item with which our reader is familiar. If you wanted to tell your reader how the Texas Senate operates, you might do it by comparing and contrasting the Texas Senate with the United States Senate. You assume that your reader knows something about the U.S. Senate and that he will be able to make the correct associations with the Texas Senate. Obviously, it is important to choose one item with which your reader is already familiar. Comparing the Texas Senate to England's Parliament will not do much good if your reader has no idea how that Parliament operates.

The second reason for developing an essay by comparison and contrast is to tell your reader something about both of the subjects by discussing them in relation to some general principle. The general principle should be applicable in both and familiar to the reader. So you might compare and contrast the Texas Senate and England's Parliament, about neither of which your reader knows anything, by relating them to principles of democratic government that your reader understands. You might begin by showing that both the Texas Senate and England's Parliament use forms of representative government. The people elect representatives to these legislative bodies, and the elected legislators make laws on behalf of the electorate. Here you have compared the Texas Senate and England's Parliament in relation to representative government. Because our reader understands how representative government works (the people elect representatives to the legislative body), he now knows something about the Texas Senate and England's Parliament.

Finally, you may compare and contrast several things with which the reader is already familiar in order to help him understand some general principles or ideas with which he is not familiar. If you want your reader to understand what government is, you might compare and contrast American democracy, British parliamentary rule, and the emerging Russian system to show what they have in common. If you want your reader to get an idea of what "Social Science" is, you can compare and contrast the academic disciplines of psychology, history, and economics to show what they have in common. In these cases you would be using comparison and contrast to move from your examples with which the reader is already familiar (American democracy, psychology) to a general description of the classes under which your examples belong (government, social science) and about which your reader knows very little or nothing.

Organization

Once you decide to use comparison and contrast, there are two basic ways of organizing your essay. You can present one item fully and then discuss the other, called the *block method*, or you can present a part of one item, then a part of the other, and so on until both are fully demonstrated, which is called the *alternating method*.

Block Pattern
The first method, sometimes called the block pattern, is usually most appropriate when the elements of comparison and contrast are rather simple, broad, and obvious. The assumption the writer makes when presenting the whole of one subject and then the whole of the other is that his reader will be able to remember

the first subject while reading the comparisons and contrasts of the second. Since a complex or extended comparison/contrast would probably be difficult for the reader to remember, we normally use the first method for simple subjects. Here is a short example of the first method of organization; watch the organization of the essay as you read.

The Scientist and the Humanitarian

One of the best places for a people watcher to practice his observations is on any college campus. Close examination of the large flocks of students will soon lead the dedicated observer to the conclusion that there are at least two easily identifiable subgroups among the student population. These kinds have been classified as *studens scientiae* (scientists) and *studens humani* (humanitarians); they are identifiable by their appearance, natural habitats, and conversations.

The scientist can be recognized by his appearance, his general residence away from home, and his customary language. The male of the species is characterized by a bow tie (usually polka-dotted), numerous pens and mechanical pencils in a plastic folder in his shirt pocket and a pocket calculator in a leather case protruding from his pants pocket. It is extremely unusual, but not impossible, to observe facial hair on the male. Both male and female are generally drab and colorless in appearance, the male tending to white shirts and brown polyester slacks, while the female wears severely tailored beige tweed suits and little or no makeup. She wears her hair tied neatly in a bun and often exhibits yellow nitric acid stains on the fingers of her right hand. In addition, the normal habitat of the scientist is the laboratory or computer center, where he drinks coffee from a beaker and turns dials. When forced to move from these sites by hunger, examination, or fire, scientists travel in small groups at a very rapid pace, as if hurrying to a meeting or an explosion. If the observer can get close enough to hear their conversation, he will hear repeated utterances of "integer, integer." When excited or animated, the species emits a shrill repeated cry of "valence," interspersed with numerical and alphabetical designations on such recitations as "approximating the irrational zeros of polynomial functions." When away from their laboratory or computer sites, scientists become nervous and irritable, refusing to approach other species.

A very different picture is evident when the humanitarian is scrutinized. He is much more brightly colored, though usually less neatly groomed. Males tend to blue jeans, black Metallica T-shirts, and tennis shoes. The females are difficult to distinguish from the males of the species, except that long facial hair is more often characteristic of the male while the female may have two or three more pierced earrings in each ear. Hair length for both male and female is uniformly long, and in either case it may hide the face completely or be shaved on one side of the head. The habitat and habits of the humanitarian, too, present a striking contrast with those of the scientist. The humanitarian avoids the laboratory and computer sites of the scientist, congregating instead on grassy knolls in the front of the campus or beneath campus trees. Humanitarians move as little as possible and never in accelerated fashion. Their favorite position is to lie fully extended and apparently asleep in the sun. The observer should recognize approaching humanitarians fairly easily since they are often dozing beneath earphones, or engaged in desultory conversations on the lawn or in the courtyard. Their normal call when at rest is a plaintive "Kierkegaard, Kierkegaard," with an occasional variation of "Existential Phenomenology." When aroused or excited, though, humanitarians can be quite dangerous. They collect quickly into large groups; their call changes to a shrill "Save the whales," and their behavior is marked by chanting and the waving of protest signs.

We can see, then, a clear profile of each dominant type and how each differs in several ways. Although there are other species of student life on campus, the scientists and humanitarians form two of the most colorful, distinctive, and intriguing subjects for the interested observer. These two types of appearances, natural habitats, and conversations mark these groups as two very distinctive classes of student life.

The author of this essay wanted to acquaint his reader with two types of college students. He illustrated one of these types, which he calls "scientists," with examples of their appearance, habits, and conversations. Then, assuming that the reader will be able to remember the description of the scientists, he compares and contrasts them with another group, which he calls humanitarians. He describes this group, giving examples of their appearance, habits, and conversations that point up the differences between the scientists and humanitarians.

Alternating Pattern

In the second basic organizational method, the alternating pattern, the writer structures his essay differently. He discusses one characteristic of the first subject and then a corresponding characteristic of the second subject. He continues alternating the two subjects until the comparison/contrast is complete and both subjects are fully revealed. This pattern is better than the block pattern for long, complex comparison/contrast essays where the subjects are related at a number of points or where the comparisons and contrasts require extensive explanation. The writer decides on the alternating pattern when use of the block pattern would make it too difficult for his reader to remember the details of the first description while reading the second. In the example of the alternating pattern that follows, we will use the same humanitarian-scientist subject matter as was used in the previous example. You have seen the essay structure according to the block pattern; now read the following portion of an essay using the alternating pattern and notice the structural differences.

The Scientist and the Humanitarian

One of the best places for a people watcher to practice his observations is on any college campus. Close examination of the large flocks of students will soon lead the dedicated observer to the conclusion that there are at least two easily identifiable subgroups among the student population These kinds have been classified as *studens scientiae* (scientists) and *studens humani* (humanitarians), distinctive for their appearance, natural habitats, and conversations.

The two types are easily discernible from their appearance alone. The scientist can be recognized by his appearance and grooming habits. The male of the species is characterized by a bow tie (usually polka dotted), numerous pens and mechanical pencils in a plastic folder in his shirt pocket, and a pocket calculator in a leather case protruding from his pants pocket. It is extremely unusual, but not impossible, to observe facial hair on the male. Both male and female are generally drab and colorless in appearance, the male tending to white shirts and brown polyester slacks, while she wears her hair tied neatly in a bun and often exhibits yellow nitric acid stains on the fingers of the right hand. The humanitarian, by contrast, is much more interestingly attired, though usually less neatly groomed. The males tend to blue jeans, black Metallica T-shirts, and tennis shoes, combat boots, or Birkenstock sandals. The females are difficult to distinguish from the males of the species, except that long facial hair is more often characteristic of the male, while the female exhibits three or more pierced earrings on each ear. Hair length for both male and female is uniformly long, and, in either case, it may hide the face completely or be shaved on one side of the head. The two types are differentiated with little difficulty at forty paces.

The contrast in appearance extends to the normal habits and habitats of the two species as well. etc., etc.

Technique

These two essays have a number of things in common. The first (introductory) paragraphs are the same; it is only when they get midway into the second paragraph (first body paragraph) that the essays begin to vary. Both contrast the humanitarian and the scientist, and both use a mock-scientific tone, implying that the students are species of animals or birds. The differences between the two are organizational and can be represented in outline form. An outline of the first essay, using the block pattern, looks like this:

Introduction (with thesis statement)
Body
I.   The Scientist
        A. Appearance
        B. Habits and Habitats
        C. Conversations

II.   The Humanitarian
        A. Appearance
        B. Habits and Habitats
        C. Conversations
Conclusion

The second essay (or portion of it) uses the alternating pattern and looks like this in outline form:

Introduction (with thesis statement)
Body
I. Appearance (Only this paragraph appears in the example above)
    A. The Scientist
    B. The Humanitarian

II. Habits and Habitats
    A. The Scientist
    B. The Humanitarian

III. Conversations
    A. The Scientist
    B. The Humanitarian
Conclusion

As is obvious from these two outlines, the first essay treats the scientist first (I, A & B), and then the humanitarian.(II, A & B). The second essay treats both the scientist and the humanitarian in turn, first according to appearance (I), then according to habits and habitats (II), and then according to conversations of both (III).

While the two organizational patterns so far identified are the basic and usual ones for an essay of comparison and contrast, it is possible to combine the two if the writer feels that would make his essay clearer or better. In this combined pattern the first subject is presented fully, just as in the sample essay illustrating the block pattern. Then in the second part of the essay the reader is referred, point by point, to the first subject. The writer provides a brief summary of the relevant part of the full presentation and then compares and contrasts the relevant part of the second subject to it. Either of the two basic patterns or the combined pattern should be chosen based on the determination of which is most suitable for the subject, the purpose, and the audience.

The block method, remember, is generally most suitable for a fairly simple and straightforward comparison/contrast, while the alternating pattern works better for complex and lengthy subject matter. The combined method, too, is generally used for a more difficult or extended comparison and contrast than the block pattern–one in which it will be useful to be able to refer the reader, point by point, back to the full description in the first section. While the patterns are presented here as expository, they may be used to structure your argument in a persuasive essay, where rather than merely presenting the alternatives informatively, you must make choices. You will take a stand and use comparison and contrast as your major method of development.

Checklist

Does your essay

1. use the appropriate pattern of comparison/contrast for your subject matter, audience, and purpose?
2. include topic sentences that contain references to *both* items if you have chosen the alternating pattern?
3. contain a thesis statement that indicates your purpose (i.e., comparing or contrasting or both), that mentions both items to be discussed, that makes clear the point you intend to show in the essay?
4. offer the best logical order for the purpose you want to achieve?
5. avoid commonplace comparisons and contrasts?

Read the following student essay by Kathleen Saunders and determine which pattern she uses.

Too Perfect for Me

Watching a comedy sitcom like *The Cosby Show* is a great way to unwind from a stressful day at work. The show's characters are likeable and the story line is humorous, but halfway through the program I usually turn the television off and return to the kitchen to wash the dinner dishes. Watching *The Cosby Show* makes me feel guilty. The Huxtables are too perfect. Their house is too perfect. In comparison to the Huxtables I feel like an unfit mother in a slovenly, dysfunctional family. The characters on *The Cosby Show* should be portrayed in a more realistic manner; in fact, the program could be far more entertaining, not to mention relaxing, if certain aspects of the program such as weekday mornings, sibling quarrels and housework were made more believable.

To begin with, mornings are just too perfect at the Huxtables' house, unlike the chaos in my house. In the Huxtable kitchen the table is set; fresh flowers are in a vase, and milk is in a glass pitcher. The entire family is simultaneously dressed and ready in clean, ironed, coordinated clothes. Everyone's hair is perfect and Mrs. Huxtable's makeup is flawless. The Huxtables even eat breakfast together. The family is relaxed, in a cheerful mood, and politely take turns discussing their schedules for the day. The children have their lunches made, their shoes on, and their bookbags ready. And if that is not enough, Mr. and Mrs. Huxtable never have to hunt for their car keys. On the other hand, my family's day begins in complete chaos. To begin with, my kids never agree as to whose turn it is to set the table. My kids would rather go hungry than perform a chore that could possibly be someone else's. I cannot afford fresh flowers, and I have never owned a glass pitcher. Next, my family is never ready together or on time for that matter because of the time spent looking for shoes, ironing clothes and fighting over hot rollers. If I do happen to be in the kitchen with my kids, I am in a ratty bathrobe, hair half-set, and mascara on only one eye. I am making last minute lunches, slurping coffee and ignoring my husband's bellowing for someone to bring another roll of toilet paper to him in the upstairs bathroom. My kids and my husband never discuss their daily plans with me, but they do enjoy adding a little suspense to my day.

Another difference between our two families is the matter of quarrels. A farfetched scene from *The Cosby Show* is Mr. and Mrs. Huxtable's mediation of sibling quarrels. When a quarrel begins, Mr. and Mrs. Huxtable are usually sitting on the couch with nothing better to do than anticipate a problem. The children come down and rationally explain the problem and their side of the story. If there is any name calling, the children use harmless words like "stupid" and "meanie." Meanwhile Mr. and Mrs. Huxtable serenely listen to each child's point of view. With infinite patience they wisely mediate a truce with a brilliant compromise acceptable to both sides. Everyone is happy; the problem is solved. On the contrary, in my family we do not have quarrels; we have combat situations which erupt at the most inopportune times, such as when I'm plunging a toilet and my husband is under his car. The cause of the problem and the kids' points of view are irrelevant to us because my husband and I are dodging airborne objects. Preventing physical injuries is our primary mission. With battle cries like "dork-vomit" and "sewer-breath" raging in the background, compromise during the mediation of the fight seems unimportant to either my husband or me. Consequently, as Commander-in-Chief I issue an irrational order which always leaves one kid gloating and prancing while the other kid is scowling, stomping, and plotting revenge.

Housekeeping is another major distinction between the two families. The Huxtable's house is far too perfect to be inhabited by children. The tables gleam; the floors shine. The rugs are not littered with shoes, books, and toys. I have never seen anyone in *The Cosby Show* do housework or laundry, nor have I ever seen a pile of dirty clothes, and the Huxtables do not seem to have a maid. In contrast I go to Herculean efforts to keep the Health Department from knocking on my door. I do not have the time to dust. When I'm not picking up shoes, washing clothes, and screaming for anyone to vacuum, I'm on my hands and knees scraping goo off the floor with a butter knife.

I always wonder who does the housework on *The Cosby Show*. Perhaps the Huxtables are naturally perfect, and we are natural slobs by comparison. Nevertheless, when I watch television I do not want to feel guilty. I want to relax and laugh at others in realistic situations. Just once I would love to see Mrs. Huxtable wake up late, be unable to decide what to wear, scream at the kids, and have to call a taxi because she can't find her car keys.

Gilbert Highet uses the block pattern to contrast two contemporary figures of ancient Greece and their values in "Diogenes and Alexander." You might try to determine what these two very different men had in common.

DIOGENES AND ALEXANDER
GILBERT HIGHET

Lying on the bare earth, shoeless, bearded, half-naked, he looked like a beggar or a lunatic. He was one, but not the other. He had opened his eyes with the sun at dawn, scratched, done his business like a dog at the roadside, washed at the public fountain, begged a piece of breakfast bread and a few olives, eaten them squatting on the ground, and washed them down with a few handfuls of water scooped from the spring. (Long ago he had owned a rough wooden cup, but he threw it away when he saw a boy drinking out of his hollowed hands.) Having no work to go to and no family to provide for, he was free. As the market place filled up with shoppers and merchants and gossipers and sharpers and slaves and foreigners, he had strolled through it for an hour or two. Everybody knew him, or knew of him. They would throw sharp questions at him and get sharper answers. Sometimes they threw jeers, and got jibes; sometimes bits of food, and got scant thanks; sometimes a mischievous pebble, and got a shower of stones and abuse. They were not quite sure whether he was mad or not. He knew they were mad, each in a different way; they amused him. Now he was back at his home.

It was not a house, not even a squatter's hut. He thought everybody lived far too elaborately, expensively, anxiously. What good is a house? No one needs privacy; natural acts are not shameful; we all do the same things, and need not hide them. No one needs beds and chairs and such furniture: the animals live healthy lives and sleep on the ground. All we require, since nature did not dress us properly, is one garment to keep us warm, and some shelter from rain and wind. So he had one blanket–to dress him in the daytime and cover him at night–and he slept in a cask. His name was Diogenes. He was the founder of the creed called Cynicism (the word means "doggishness"); he spent much of his life in the rich, lazy, corrupt Greek city of Corinth, mocking and satirizing its people, and occasionally converting one of them.

His home was not a barrel made of wood: too expensive. It was a storage jar made of earthenware, something like a modern fuel tank–no doubt discarded because a break had made it useless. He was not the first to inhabit such a thing: the refugees driven into Athens by the Spartan invasion had been forced to sleep in casks. But he was the first who ever did so by choice, out of principle.

Diogenes was not a degenerate or a maniac. He was a philosopher who wrote plays and poems and essays expounding his doctrine; he talked to those who cared to listen; he had pupils who admired him. But he taught chiefly by example. All should live naturally, he said, for what is natural is normal and cannot possibly be evil or shameful. Live without conventions, which are artificial and false; escape complexities and superfluities and extravagances: only so can you live a free life. The rich man believes he possesses his big house with its many rooms and its elaborate furniture, his pictures and his expensive clothes, his horses and his servants and his bank accounts. He does not. He depends on them, he worries about them, he spends most of his life's energy looking after them; the thought of losing them makes him sick with anxiety. They possess him. He is their slave. In order to produce a quantity of false, perishable goods he has sold the only true, lasting good, his own independence.

95

There have been many men who grew tired of human society with its complications, and went away to live simply—on a small farm, in a quiet village, in a hermit's cave, or in the darkness of anonymity. Not so Diogenes. He was a not a recluse, or a stylite, or a beatnik. He was a missionary. His life's aim was clear to him: it was "to restamp the currency." (He and his father had once been convicted for counterfeiting, long before he turned to philosophy, and this phrase was Diogenes's bold, unembarrassed joke on the subject.) To restamp the currency: to take the clean metal of human life, to erase the old false conventional markings, and to imprint it with its true values.

The other great philosophers of the fourth century before Christ taught mainly their own private pupils. In the shady groves and cool sanctuaries of the Academy, Plato discoursed to a chosen few on the unreality of this contingent existence. Aristotle, among the books and instruments and specimens and archives and research-workers of his Lyceum, pursued investigations and gave lectures that were rightly named *esoteric* "for those within the walls." But for Diogenes, laboratory and specimens and lecture halls and pupils were all to be found in a crowd of ordinary people. Therefore he chose to live in Athens or in the rich city of Corinth, where travelers from all over the Mediterranean world constantly came and went. And, by design, he publicly behaved in such ways as to show people what real life was. He would constantly take up their spiritual coin, ring it on a stone, and laugh at its false superscription.

He thought most people were only half-alive, most men only half-men. At bright noonday he walked through the market place carrying a lighted lamp and inspecting the face of everyone he met. They asked him why. Diogenes answered, "I am trying to find a *man*."

To a gentleman whose servant was putting on his shoes for him, Diogenes said, "you won't be really happy until he wipes your nose for you: that will come after you lose the use of your hands."

Once there was a war scare so serious that it stirred even the lazy, profit-happy Corinthians. They began to drill, clean their weapons, and rebuild their neglected fortifications. Diogenes took his old cask and began to roll it up and down, back and forward. "When you are all so busy," he said, "I feel I ought to do *something!*"

And so he lived—like a dog, some said, because he cared nothing for privacy and other human conventions, and because he showed his teeth and barked at those whom he disliked. Now he was lying in the sunlight, as contented as a dog on the warm ground, happier (he himself used to boast) than the Shah of Persia. Although he knew he was going to have an important visitor, he would not move.

The little square began to fill with people. Page boys elegantly dressed, spearmen speaking a rough foreign dialect, discreet secretaries, hard-browed officers, suave diplomats, they all gradually formed a circle centered on Diogenes. He looked them over, as a sober man looks at a crowd of tottering drunks, and shook his head. He knew who they were. They were the attendants of the conqueror of Greece, the servants of Alexander, the Macedonian king, who was visiting his newly subdued realm.

Only twenty, Alexander was far older and wiser than his years. Like all Macedonians he loved drinking, but he could usually handle it; and toward women he was nobly restrained and chivalrous. Like Macedonians he loved fighting; he was a magnificent commander, but he was not merely a military automaton. He could think. At thirteen he had become a pupil of the greatest mind in Greece, Aristotle. No exact record of his schooling survives. It is clear, though, that Aristotle took the passionate, half-barbarous boy and gave him the best of Greek culture. He taught Alexander poetry: the young prince slept with the *Illiad* under his pillow and longed to emulate Achilles, who brought the mighty power of Asia to ruin. He taught him philosophy, in particular the shapes and uses of political power: a few years later Alexander was to create a supranational empire that was not merely a power system but a vehicle for the exchange of Greek and Middle Eastern cultures.

Aristotle taught him the principles of scientific research: during his invasion of the Persian domains Alexander took with him a large corps of scientists, and shipped hundreds of zoological specimens back to Greece for study. Indeed, it was from Aristotle that Alexander learned to seek out everything strange which might be instructive. Jugglers and stunt artists and virtuosos of the absurd he dismissed with a shrug; but on reaching India he was to spend hours discussing the problems of life and death with naked Hindu mystics, and later to see one demonstrate Yoga self-command by burning himself impassively to death.

Now, Alexander was in Corinth to take command of the League of Greek States which, after conquering them, his father Philip had created as a disguise for the New Macedonian Order. He was welcomed and honored and flattered. He was the man of the hour, of the century: he was unanimously appointed commander-in-chief of a new expedition against old, rich, corrupt Asia. Nearly everyone crowded to Corinth in order to congratulate him, to seek employment with him, even simply to see him: soldiers and statesmen, artists and merchants, poets and philosophers. He received their compliments graciously. Only Diogenes, although he lived in Corinth, did not visit the new monarch. With that generosity which Aristotle had taught him was a quality of the truly magnanimous man, Alexander determined to call upon Diogenes. Surely Diogenes, the God-born, would acknowledge the conqueror's power by some gift of hoarded wisdom.

With his handsome face, his fiery glance, his strong supple body, his purple and gold cloak, and his air of destiny, he moved through the parting crowd, toward the Dog's kennel. When a king approaches, all rise in respect. Diogenes did not rise, he merely sat up on one elbow. When a monarch enters a precinct, all greet him with a bow or an acclamation. Diogenes said nothing.

There was a silence. Some years later Alexander speared his best friend to the wall, for objecting to the exaggerated honors paid to His Majesty; but now he was still young and civil. He spoke first, with a kindly greeting. Looking at the poor broken cask, the single ragged garment, and the rough figure lying on the ground, he said: "Is there anything I can do for you, Diogenes?"

"Yes," said the Dog. "Stand to one side. You're blocking the sunlight."

There was silence, not the ominous silence preceding a burst of fury, but a hush of amazement. Slowly, Alexander turned away. A titter broke out from the elegant Greeks, who were already beginning to make jokes about the cur that looked at the King. The Macedonian officers, after deciding that Diogenes was not worth the trouble of kicking, were starting to guffaw and nudge one another. Alexander was still silent. To those nearest him he said quietly, "If I were not Alexander, I should be Diogenes." They took it as a paradox, designed to close the awkward little scene with a polite curtain line. But Alexander meant it. He understood cynicism as the others could not. Later he took one of Diogenes's pupils with him to India as a philosophical interpreter (it was he who spoke to the naked *saddhus*). He was what Diogenes called himself, a *cosmopolites*, "citizen of the world." Like Diogenes, he admired the heroic figure of Hercules, the mighty conqueror who labors to help mankind while all others toil and sweat only for themselves. He knew that of all men then alive in the world only Alexander the conqueror and Diogenes the beggar were truly free.

1993

In his essay "The English and the Americans," Edward T. Hall contrasts the people of two countries, employing a mix of block and alternating patterns. Notice, too, how he incorporates other strategies of causal analysis, illustration, and classification.

THE ENGLISH AND THE AMERICANS
EDWARD T. HALL

It has been said that the English and the Americans are two great people separated by one language. The differences for which language gets blamed may not be due so much to words as to communications on other levels beginning with English intonation (which sounds affected to many Americans) and continuing to ego-linked ways of handling time, space, and materials. If there ever were two cultures in which differences of the proxemic details are marked it is in the educated (public school) English and the middle-class Americans. One of the basic reasons for this wide disparity is that in the United States we use space as a way of classifying people and activities, whereas in England it is the social system that determines who you are. In the United States, your address is an important cue to status (this applies not only to one's home but to the business address as well). The Joneses from Brooklyn and Miami are not as "in" as the Joneses from Newport and Palm Beach. Greenwich and Cape Cod are worlds apart from Newark and Miami. Businesses located on Madison and Park avenues have more tone than those on Seventh and Eighth avenues. A corner office is more prestigious than one next to the elevator or at the end of a long hall. The Englishman, however, is born and brought up in a social system. He is still Lord–no matter where you find him, even if it is behind the counter in a fishmonger's stall. In addition to class distinctions, there are differences between the English and ourselves in how space is allotted.

The middle-class American growing up in the United States feels he has a right to have his own room, or at least part of a room. My American subjects, when asked to draw an ideal room or office, invariably drew it for themselves and no one else. When asked to draw their present room or office, they drew only their own part of a shared room and then drew a line down the middle. Both male and female subjects identified the kitchen and master bedroom as belonging to the mother or the wife, whereas Father's territory was a study or a den, if one was available; otherwise, it was "the shop," "the basement," or sometimes only a workbench or the garage. American women who want to be alone can go to the bedroom and close the door. The closed door is the sign meaning "Do not disturb" or "I'm angry." An American is available if his door is open at home or at his office. He is expected not to shut himself off but to maintain himself in a state of readiness to answer the demands of others. Closed doors are for conferences, private conversations, and business, work that requires concentration, study, resting, sleeping, dressing, and sex.

The middle-and upper-class Englishman, on the other hand, is brought up in a nursery shared with brothers and sisters. The oldest occupies a room by himself which he vacates when he leaves for boarding school, possibly even at the age of nine or ten. The difference between a room of one's own and early conditioning to shared space, while seeming inconsequential, has an important effect on the Englishman's attitude toward his own space. He may never have a permanent "room of his own" and seldom expects one or feels he is entitled to one. Even Members of Parliament have no offices and often conduct their business on the terrace overlooking the Thames. As a consequence, the English are puzzled by the American need for a secure place in which to work, an office. Americans working in England may become annoyed if they are not provided with what they consider appropriate enclosed work space. In regard to the need for walls as a screen for the ego, this places the Americans somewhere between the Germans and the English.

The contrasting English and American patterns have some remarkable implications, particularly if we assume that man, like other animals, has a built-in need to shut himself off from others from time to time. An English student in one of my seminars typified what happens when hidden patterns clash. He was quite obviously experiencing strain in his relationships with Americans. Nothing seemed to go right and it was quite clear from his remarks that we did not know how to behave. An analysis of his complaints showed that a major source of irritation was that no American seemed to be able to pick up the subtle clues that there were times when he didn't want his thoughts intruded on. As he stated it, "I'm walking around the apartment and it seems that whenever I want to be alone my roommate starts talking to me.

Pretty soon he's asking 'What's the matter?' and wants to know if I'm angry. By then I am angry and say something."

It took some time but finally we were able to identify most of the contrasting features of the American and British problems that were in conflict in this case. When the American wants to be alone he goes into a room and shuts the door–he depends on architectural features for screening. For an American to refuse to talk to someone else present in the same room, to give them the "silent treatment," is the ultimate form of rejection and a sure sign of great displeasure. The English, on the other hand, lacking rooms of their own since childhood, never developed the practice of using space as a refuge from others. They have in effect internalized a set of barriers, which they erect and which others are supposed to recognize. Therefore, the more the Englishman shuts himself off when he is with an American the more likely the American is to break in to assure himself that all is well. Tension lasts until the two get to know each other. The important point is that the spatial and architectural needs of each are not the same at all.

CLASSIFICATION AND DIVISION

Classification and division are forms of analysis used often by most of us even if we do not know the name of the techniques. Although they are methods of expository writing, classification and division are also ways of looking at the world around us and of thinking about things. Like illustration and comparison and contrast, *classification* is a process that involves bringing order out of experience. Like these other methods of expository writing, classification and division are concerned with the general (class) and the relationship to its parts.

Almost all parts fall into a class of some kind, sharing certain characteristics that allow these parts to be classified with a certain group. Thus, a class is determined by a network of significant characteristics shared by all members of the category. If you see a heavy-set man about 25 years old walking down the street, you will probably pass by him without thinking about him much. Put him into a blue uniform and give him a badge and a gun, and you will both notice him and make judgments about him (he is a police officer, or he is a fascist pig cop). If the man is not dressed in a uniform but is carrying a baby, you think of him as a father and assume that the woman with him is his wife and the mother of the child. In each of these cases you are classifying the man; you are putting him into a category and seeing him as a part of a whole (class). He is a policeman, father or husband. We are always classifying that which we experience in the world around us even when we have not the slightest intention of writing an essay of classification.

In the same way, *division* is a way of thinking about and reacting to the world around us. We know that things have parts, and we talk about things in terms of those parts. In fact, we often define terms by identifying the parts that make up those terms. A sailboat can be divided into hull, mast, and sails. Social Science is made up of history, economics, sociology, geography, and psychology. The government of the United States has three main branches: the executive, legislative, and judicial.

Classification

Implementation

The need for care in setting up classifications can be demonstrated by examples of the two kinds of classification used in analysis. The kinds are called *simple* and *complex* classifications.

Simple classification–This form of classification involves grouping your subject into two categories only. For example, if your purpose is to investigate your experiences with good male teachers, a simple classification merely involves separating the subject "teachers" into good teachers and those who were not considered good (level one of classification). Step two would be to take the good teachers classification and organize it again (level two) into two classes–male and female. If your purpose is to determine how many good male teachers you have had in your academic experience, you pursue only the male classification and abandon the female portion. We call this a simple classification because at each stage or level the analysis makes only two groups–those that fit a certain category and those that do not.

Complex classification–You most likely will decide to select the complex classification for your composition assignments because this method demands that you delve more deeply into the multiple categories required by your instructor. For instance, if you are expected to consider the full range of your experiences with teachers, you would choose the complex classification method, beginning with level one. You could, therefore, classify your teachers as good, bad, and mediocre. Next, if you have chosen bad teachers as your focus, you would further classify that group, organizing it into several types of bad teachers (level two)–the boring ones, the incomprehensible ones, and the impossibly demanding ones. Although this level does not exhaust the types of bad teachers you have known, it does include those specific types you wish to discuss in your present analysis. You should note that this classification requires more than two categories for each level; therefore, it is called a complex classification.

ORGANIZATION

The following diagram illustrates the process of *complex classification.*

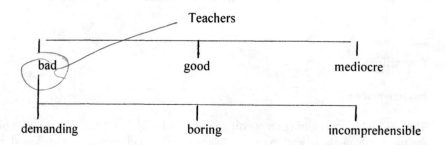

Figure III-A

You should develop your classification as completely as is necessary for your purpose in the analysis. Your thesis and your discussion, then, will include only those types with whom you are personally familiar although there exist other categories of bad teachers. Just make certain that your reader understands that your classification is limited by your focus. As you read the following essay, note how the writer sets up and sticks to a clear basis for his classification–the bad teachers that all students talk about.

One of the normal topics of conversation in a college cafeteria or Student Union is teachers. Students enjoy talking about their instructors as much as elderly people enjoy talking about their ailments. After all, everybody likes to complain. If one learns to recognize and avoid three basic kinds of bad teachers—the boring, the incomprehensible, and the demanding—that form the subject of most of this student conversation, his college days will be much more pleasant.

> *use for emphasis*

The first kind of bad teacher is exemplified by Dr. Lackluster. His kind tends to concentrate in subject areas that require lists and facts. One may find him in a scientific lecture course, pointing out the details of the Periodic Table of the Elements or discussing the major dates and rulers of the Byzantine Empire in a history class. Whenever one finds him, Dr. Lackluster is recognizable by the quality of his instruction and by his effect on his students. His voice is high, monotonous, and droning, and he speaks at a regular pace, his gaze fixed on a corner of the ceiling at the back of the room. He uses yellowed, crumbling lecture notes he compiled his first year of teaching forty years earlier, but they serve as props, since he has given the same lecture so many times he could do it in his sleep—and often does. The effect of his delivery on his students is unmistakable. They slump in their seats, resigned, glassy-eyed, or they simply turn their ball caps around backwards and instantly go to sleep. The gentle hum of suppressed snoring provides harmony for the professor's dreary lists. The single student ever known to gain anything from Dr. Lackluster's class was a compulsive doodler who filled 141 notebook pages with pen drawings in one semester. The Museum of Modern Art has given an exhibition of the drawings (entitled "Ode to Tedium"), and the young artist was launched on a promising career by his unknowing instructor. It is Dr. Lackluster's single triumph in a long teaching career.

The second kind of bad teacher, exemplified by Professor Fervor, is almost the opposite of Dr. Lackluster. Professor Fervor is usually found in the humanities—philosophy, English, or languages. She is frantic in her love of her subject and her enthusiasm for it. Her lectures resound down the halls, crashing and clanging with the apostolic vigor of an intellectual barroom brawl. Her eyes light with ecstasy as she describes the more arcane subtleties of Spinoza's *Tractatus Theologico-Politicus* or plurisignation in *Beowulf*. The problem is that she is completely incomprehensible to anyone lacking a Ph.D. in her field (and maybe to the Ph.D.'s, too, although they refuse to admit it). A look at her students confirms the diagnosis: there is a vast scratching of heads and tugging at ears; muttered conferences ("What does 'infrangible nominalism' mean?"); gestures of pain and dismay. The lady is intelligent, cultured, enthusiastic, and genuinely devoted to her subject. Unfortunately, she is also disorganized, unintelligible, and ultimately of no use to any of her students.

The third kind of bad teacher is Dr. Adamantine. He combines the virtues (such as they are) of the two preceding and has none of their vices. He is organized, systematic, and understandable; he is also enthusiastic, interesting, witty, and intelligent. He has the profile of a Greek god, flashing white teeth, a deep tan, and a Porsche 928S. He was captain of the football team at Princeton, was a Rhodes Scholar, and beats the Academic Dean regularly at tennis. In his classes students are ignited by his delivery and by his grasp of the subject, and they remain alert and questing for knowledge throughout the class period. And yet Dr. Adamantine, too, is the subject of scathing remarks and moans of despair in the cafeteria and snackbar. The problem is that he is a hard grader and demands a great deal from his students. This is the final disaster, the cruelest blow of all. One can get an A from Dr. Lackluster by coming to class (he takes roll) and secreting a chart of the Periodic Table or the Byzantine Empire in one's sleeve at exams. One can get an A from Professor Fervor by staying after class once a week and saying, "I was really interested in your discussion of Schopenhauer today, Professor. Are there any books in the library I could read to assuage my burning thirst for knowledge about him?" But to get an A from Dr. Adamantine it is necessary to work for it. And what student in his right mind would go to such an extreme?

These three kinds of college teachers give college a bad name. In fact, if we could get rid of teachers altogether, then there would be no problem. Etc. . . .

Observe how each category listed in level two of the diagram becomes the focus of each paragraph in the body of the essay. In this case, the writer has used illustration as a method of development by describing specific teachers who represent that particular classification. Also, he has used comparison and contrast in his paragraph development to distinguish each type from the others. Classification necessarily involves comparison and contrast. Note, too, that the purpose of the classification in the essay is clearly stated in the thesis and the designated classes are listed in the order of discussion and, therefore, in the essay itself.

Technique

When writing a classification essay, make sure you adhere to the following:

1. You must set up a clear basis for the classification, and you must follow the classification through logically and thoroughly. This means you must be careful to classify your subject distinctly at each level of the analysis. To say that there are three types of bad teachers–the boring, the incomprehensible, and those who drive pickup trucks–is using an indistinct method of classification. Then make certain you discuss each category in relation to those elements that link the category to the other categories of the same class, in this case, approach to instruction. This basis of comparison is used similarly in your comparison and contrast; it is essential in classification as well to make your purpose clear to your audience in examining your categories by classifying them.

2. You should develop your analysis by classification as completely as is necessary for your purpose. Your purpose determines how complete and extensive the classification will be. Your analysis will always be based on some specific interest in the subject being analyzed, and that specific interest must be clearly stated for your reader in the thesis. For example,

teachers can be classified in a large variety of ways (professional workers, parents, union members, political affiliates), but in this case we chose good, bad, and mediocre–focusing on the bad teachers and the general characteristics (bases of comparison) that explain to the reader why students' conversations center on these types of teachers.

Checklist for classification essay

Be sure that

1.   your purpose for classification is clear to your audience and is included in your thesis statement.
2.   the classification is applied to a plural subject (like different types of pumpers at a gas station, for instance, or teachers), and that the focus is on types, categories, or kinds.
3.   the basis of the classification is consistent with your purpose and audience.
4.   the classification is complete; all pertinent categories to your specific interest are included.
5.   the categories are arranged in logical or emphatic order.
6.   the categories do not overlap. If an individual member of one category can also be put into another category (i.e., an incomprehensible teacher who drives a pickup truck) then your categories need rethinking. They must be mutually exclusive.

Division

Having studied one part of the process of analysis, classification, let us now look at its partner, division. *Division* is a way of analyzing a subject, too. But instead of sorting the subject-matter into categories as we do in classification, we *divide* a single subject into its **component parts**. When we say that *Hamlet* has five acts or that a certain book has fifteen chapters, we are dividing *Hamlet* and the book into parts. When a sports-car lover talks of the engine, transmission, and body of a new Ferrari, he is talking about parts of the whole.

Organization
The same rules that apply to a successful analysis by classification apply to division as well. First, a clear basis for the division must be established. If we divide water into its chemical elements, we divide it into hydrogen and oxygen. We do not say that water is composed of hydrogen, oxygen, and the ability to freeze at 0 degrees centigrade; since we are only interested in the chemical makeup of water, this third attribute is irrelevant to our division. Every division, just like every classification, is made on the basis of some particular interest in the subject, and the division must confine itself to the parts of the subject that relate to that interest. Also, as in

classification, you must continue your analysis by division logically and completely until it is finished. (You cannot discuss only four acts of *Hamlet*, for example.) If you plan to divide a subject only into its main parts or focus on particular parts, you must make this limitation clear to your audience. This focus should appear in your introductory paragraph, preferably in your thesis statement. Otherwise, your readers have the right to expect a complete division. If you tell them that you are going to discuss the organization of the police force and talk only about the Narcotics Squad and the Police Laboratory, they will wonder what happened to the Vice Squad, the Traffic Bureau, and the Homicide Division. If you want to discuss only two of the parts of the police force, then you must say something like "The control and suppression of narcotics traffic are the responsibility of two allied parts of the police force, the Narcotics Squad and the Police Laboratory, whose operation and organization are important parts of one aspect of the police force." Here you have made clear to your audience your intention to discuss only two of the parts that make up the police force, and your audience will not expect to read about the Homicide Division or the Vice Squad.

The following skeletal outline is an example of *division*. As you read it, notice what the subject is that is being divided, into what parts it is being divided, and how the division is structured.

Hamiltonian America

Thesis: Unlike Jefferson's democratic governmental theories, Hamilton's picture of the future of America was based on three main ideas–centralized government, aristocratic rule, and progress through industrialization.

1. Hamilton believed in a strong, centralized government, not in the decentralized regionally-oriented government of Jefferson.

II. While Jefferson believed in the common man's right to democratic process, Hamilton felt that the aristocratic, well-educated minority was better equipped to govern.

III. Finally, Hamilton based the two preceding principles on his vision of America as a strong industrial country with an emphasis on progress and technology.

The subject of analysis is Alexander Hamilton's political theory. This rather scant outline divides his philosophy into three main ideas or parts. Hamilton had other ideas (he believed, for example, in a pro-British foreign policy), but the writer is specifically interested only in "three main ideas," which he tells his readers in his thesis statement. Not only does the writer's thesis state the specific ideas to be discussed in the division process, it also provides a clear notion of what specific point the writer wishes to make about those three parts, that they differed from Jefferson's ideas.

It is worth noting, too, that the intended essay will not be developed by division alone. Although the writer's chief subject is Alexander Hamilton's political philosophy, he finds it impossible to discuss Hamilton's ideas without reference to Hamilton's great opponent, Thomas Jefferson. The essay, then, also employs comparison and contrast; the writer should observe the guidelines for comparison and contrast by following the rule of consistency in comparison throughout the essay. However, division remains the writer's main method of organization and development. It is not unusual to find several different strategies of expository prose being used in a single essay.

Technique

Checklist for Division Essay

Be sure that the division

1. is applied to a *singular* subject. Only one thing at a time can be divided.
2. is consistent with your purpose.
3. is complete in fulfilling your purpose.
4. is clearly stated in your thesis statement and that your point is appropriate for your audience.
5. uses logical subdivisions to make the point and arranges them in a logical or emphatic order.

Read the following essay by Jade Whelihan and note the kinds of details she uses for each category:

Pumpers

There are many types of people who purchase gasoline, but three types are easy to spot. All three have an obvious physical appearance which sets them apart from other gas purchasers. Each also has a distinctive pumping technique and freely vocalizes his opinion. Finally, each type has a particular way of annoying every other patron at the same location.

The first type of gas purchaser is Leisure Lou. He can be identified immediately by his appearance. He drives a station wagon with wooden side panels and a bumper sticker that tells the world that he is retired. His Hawaiian print shirt captures everyone's attention. He wears Bermuda shorts and black socks with sandals. On his head sits a fly fisherman's hat which is his obvious display of a continuous state of leisure. His pumping technique also sets him apart from the normal crowd. When he parks his car. he stops at the first pump. preventing the use of the pump in front of him. He always pays for his gas in advance so that the attendant can preset the pump, and he will not have to worry about stopping the pump himself. He activates the pump before opening the access door and unscrewing the tank lid. He tucks the hose under his elbow and spills gas on his hip while opening the tank. As

Leisure Lou leans against the side of his car, he pumps his gas absent-mindedly, confident that the pump will stop before gas pours onto the ground. Once the pump stops, he replaces the hose and screws on the tank lid but forgets to close the access door. Leisure Lou even vocalizes his not-a-care-in-the-world attitude. He whistles some melodic tune from *The Sound of Music* while pumping his gas. When inside the convenience store, he tells everyone how wonderful retirement is. But Leisure Lou can be a tremendous annoyance. He blocks the use of two pumps while he performs a number of time-consuming tasks. First he browses through the store with no intention of making a purchase. Then he washes his car's windshield. Next he visits the restroom to wash his hands and looks at the stain on his hip. Last, he walks his dog around the small patches of grass that serve as landscaping. Leisure Lou is a man who cannot be ignored.

The second type of gasoline purchaser is Strictly-Business Betty. Her physical appearance is also very distinctive. She drives an economical, imported car that has a lock on the access door so that she can safely hide a spare key inside. She wears closed-toe pumps instead of flirty sandals. Her skirt and blazer are of a classical line with no frills. Strictly-Business Betty's pumping technique is equally distinctive. She unscrews the lid to her tank before removing the hose from the pump. She pumps her gas until the tank is nearly full and then slows the volume to prevent the gas from spewing from the tank. Next she turns off the pump and gives the handle a final squeeze to empty the hose. Finally, she replaces the hose, seals the tank, and closes the access door as if following instructions. Now Strictly-Business Betty's most tell-tale characteristic is voiced. She announces to the cashier that she must have a legible receipt for her expense-account report. Then she preaches about the economic virtues of owning an import. Finally she distinguishes herself in a way that annoys everyone. She spends more than her fair share of time at the cashier's counter but pays no attention to the amount of purchase because she plans to pay with a credit card. But when the cashier announces the price, Strictly-Business Betty has to double check the accuracy of the computer. Then she borrows a calculator to check the gas mileage that she has received from her last tank. In the end no one has missed Strictly-Business Betty's presence, but the other customers hope they miss her the next time she purchases gas.

The last type of gas purchaser is Lawnmower Larry. He can generally be recognized by his physical appearance. He drives a pickup truck that has a dented fender with a red and yellow gas can in the bed. He wears a sweat-stained shirt and jeans that sag to his hips. Glaring over the waistband of his jeans is his underwear. He has on a baseball cap to protect his face from the sun and stuffed in his pocket is a red shop rag. He has a streak of grease across his brow where he has obviously wiped his sweat off with a dirty hand. Also unique is Lawnmower Larry's pumping technique. He pays his two dollars in advance but always overpumps the gas by one cent or two. He has no change and borrows the needed pennies from the courtesy jar on the cashier's counter. Lawnmower Larry can be distinguished from the other patrons by his conversation. He complains about the difficulty he has trying to get that blankety-blank lawnmower started. Also, now that the mower is running, it is too hot to mow. Lawnmower Larry's annoyances are only two, but they distinctly identify him. First, he leaves sweat on the counter where he has leaned. Second, he always returns later in the day for more gas and repeats his earlier routine. While sympathetic to his plight, the normal patrons do not miss Lawnmower Larry when he has gone.

In conclusion, these three types of patrons can add more frustration to the life of the average patron than the price of gas. While somewhat humorous, these three could test the patience of a saint. Most people can identify with one or two characteristics of each type, but these are extreme characters. If any patron misses Leisure Lou, Strictly-Business Betty, or Lawnmower Larry, he should consider himself lucky.

In his essay "Some American Types." Max Lerner classifies six different categories by which Americans can be identified. Consider which classifications he has neglected and consider whether or not his ideas seem applicable to us today after three and a half decades.

Some American Types
Max Lerner

Seventeenth-century England produced a number of books on *Characters* depicting English society through the typical personality patterns of the era. Trying something of the same sort for contemporary America, the first fact one encounters is the slighter emphasis on a number of character types that stand out elsewhere in Western society: to be sure, they are to be found in the scholar, the aesthete, the priest or "parson," the "aristocratic" army officer, the revolutionary student, the civil servant, the male schoolteacher, the marriage broker, the courtesan, the mystic, the saint. Anyone familiar with European literature will recognize these characters as stock literary types and therefore as social types. Each of them represents a point of convergence for character and society. Anyone familiar with American literature will know that it contains stock portraits of its own which express social types. I want to use these traditional types as backdrops and stress some of the social roles that are new and still in process of formation.

Thus there is the *fixer*, who seems an organic product of a society in which the middleman function eats away the productive one. He may be a public relations man or influence peddler; he may get your traffic fine settled, or he may be able–whatever the commodity–to "get it for you wholesale." He is contemptuous of those who take the formal rules seriously; he knows how to cut corners–financial, political, administrative, or moral. At best there is something of the iconoclast in him, an unfooled quality far removed from the European personality types that always obey authority. At worst he becomes what the English call a "spiv" or cultural procurer.

Related to the fixer is the *inside dopester*, as Riesman has termed him. He is oriented not so much toward getting things fixed as toward being "in the know" and" wised up" about things that innocents take at face value. He is not disillusioned because he has never allowed himself the luxury of illusions. In the 1920s and 1930s he consumed the literature of "debunking"; in the current era he knows everything that takes place in the financial centers of Wall Street, the political centers of Capitol Hill, and the communications centers of Madison Avenue–yet among all the things he knows there is little he believes in. His skepticism is not the wisdom which deflates pretentiousness but that of the rejecting man who knows ahead of time that there is "nothing in it," whatever the "it" may be. In short, he is "hep."

Another link leads to the *neutral* man. He expresses the devaluing tendency in a culture that tries to avoid commitments. Fearful of being caught in the crosscurrents of conflict that may endanger his safety or status, he has a horror of what he calls "controversial figures"–and anyone becomes "controversial" if he is attacked. As the fixer and the inside dopester are the products of a middleman's society, so the neutral man is the product of a technological one. The technician's detachment from everything except effective results becomes–in the realm of character–an ethical vacuum that strips the results of much of their meaning.

From the neutral man to the *conformist* is a short step. Although he is not neutral–in fact, he may be militantly partisan–his partisanship is on the side of the big battalions. He lives in terror of being caught in a minority where his insecurity will be conspicuous. He gains a sense of stature by joining the dominant group, as he gains security by making himself indistinguishable from that group. Anxious to efface any unique traits of his own, he exacts conformity from others. He fears ideas whose newness means they are not yet accepted, but once they are firmly established he fights for them with a courage born of the knowledge that there is no danger in championing them. He hates foreigners and immigrants. When he talks of the "American way," he sees a world in which other cultures have become replicas of his own.

It is often hard to distinguish the conformist from the *routineer*. Essentially he is a man in uniform, sometimes literally, always symbolically. The big public service corporations–railroads, airlines, public utilities–require their employees to wear uniforms that will imprint a common image of the enterprise as a whole. City employees, such as policemen and firemen, wear uniforms. Gas-station attendants, hotel clerks, bellhops, must similarly keep their appearance within prescribed limits. Even the sales force in big department stores or the typists and stenographers in big corporations tend toward the same uniformity. There are very few young Americans who are likely to escape the uniform of the Armed Services. With the uniform goes an urge toward pride of status and a routineering habit of mind. There is the confidence that comes of belonging to a large organization and sharing symbolically in its bigness and power. There is a sense of security in having grooves within which to move. This is true on every level of corporate enterprise, from the white-collar employee to "the man in the gray flannel suit," although it stops short of the top executives who create the uniforms instead of wearing them. Even outside the government and corporate bureaus there are signs of American life becoming bureaucratized, in a stress on forms and routines, on "going through the channels."

Unlike the conformist or routineer, the *status seeker* may possess a resourceful energy and even originality, but he directs these qualities toward gaining status. What he wants is a secure niche in a society whose men are constantly being pulled upward or trodden down. Scott Fitzgerald has portrayed a heartbreaking case history of this character type in *The Great Gatsby*, whose charm and energy are invested fruitlessly in an effort to achieve social position. The novels of J.P. Marquand are embroideries of a similar theme, narrated through the mind of one who already has status and is confronted by the risk of losing it. At various social levels the status seeker becomes a "joiner" of associations which give him symbolic standing. (1957)

CAUSE AND EFFECT

Any time we respond to the question "Why?" we are concerned with the causes of an event.

Q.   Why did you wreck your new car?
A.   I was busy selecting a cassette tape to play and was not paying attention to the changing signal light.

Q.   Why did you perform so poorly on the biology final exam?
A.   I spent all the previous night bailing water out of my bedroom after our subdivision flooded from the heavy rains.

We look for causes when we want to know why something happened. Similarly, when we want to know what happened as a result of the cause or causes, we attempt to determine the effects. When we respond to the questions "What happened then?" or "What would happen if...?" we engage in discovering the effect.

Q.   What happened because you performed so poorly on the biology final exam?
A.   I was placed on scholastic probation for a semester.

Q.   What will happen if you cannot raise your GPA sufficiently next semester?
A.   I will be forced to drop out of school and to get a job.

We are constantly being required to use causal analysis in our attempt to understand and explain the world around us.

Implementation

Causal analysis may be simple or complex. Sometimes a causal analysis simply involves determining the cause or the effect of, say, why your car would not start. However, a more complex analysis might be required when the cause and effect arrangement involves a causal chain. The process requires that the writer begin with either a cause or an effect and then work backward or forward to determine related causes and effects. For example, consider the following scenario. Mr. Strump failed to pay his income tax this year, and the investigating Internal Revenue Service agent discovers that Mr. Strump died on January 1 and thus had no income for the year. Here is an example of a simple causal analysis. The effect (Mr. Strump's not paying taxes) can be traced to a specific cause (he died on January 1). A more thorough analysis may be required, however, and thorough analyses can be quite complicated. The IRS agent will probably be satisfied with the reason Mr. Strump paid no income taxes. He dies, he has no income, he pays no tax: case closed. But suppose the agent mentions Mr. Strump's death to Detective Sergeant Wexley of the police department. The sergeant might want to undertake a more thorough analysis. Here, Mr. Strump's death becomes the "effect" in question, and the sergeant goes looking for the causes of that death.

He discovers that Mr. Strump's corpse contains enough potassium cyanide to kill an elephant, much less a 92 year-old millionaire. He also finds that Miss Goldie May Goodbody, Mr. Strump's faithful 22-year old secretary and ex-Miss International Seafood, has inherited Mr. Strump's six million dollar fortune and now lives in a penthouse in Miami Beach. Mr. Strump had his fatal "heart attack" after drinking the special tea Miss Goodbody always brought him at his bedtime. The teacup was washed, but Sergeant Wexley discovers a bottle of potassium cyanide crystals with Miss Goodbody's fingerprints on it and a note from the old gentleman telling her that he is changing his will. Instead of leaving everything to her, Mr. Strump was planning to endow a foundation for the study of the mating habits of the bubble-eyed goldfish, and he had an appointment with his lawyer for the morning after he died. Sergeant Wexley reconstructs the cause-effect sequence like this: (1) Miss Goodbody is such a good secretary that old Mr. Strump makes a will leaving her $6,000,000. (2) Mr. Strump develops a mania for bubble-eyed goldfish and tells Miss Goodbody that the fish, not she, will get the fortune once he talks to his lawyer. (3) Miss Goodbody feeds the old boy a cup of cyanide tea to help him sleep. (4) Mr. Strump has his "heart attack," and Miss Goodbody has six million dollars. As a matter of fact, we could follow the sequence further since Sergeant Wexley retired abruptly from the police department and married the lovely Miss Goodbody. They moved to their Kentucky estate where the ex-sergeant raises quarter horses. The fingerprints, cyanide, and note strangely disappeared.

Anyway, before retiring from the force, the sergeant unearthed a cause-effect relationship leading up to Mr. Strump's death. He went further than the IRS agent, who was only concerned with nonpayment of taxes. It would be possible to carry the analysis further than the sergeant did to discover not only the immediate causes of the death but also the ultimate or remote causes–the basic, underlying factors that explain the more obvious ones. Why, for example, did Mr. Strump turn from the attractions of Miss Goodbody (blond, 5'9" tall, 39-24-37) to those of the bubble-eyed goldfish (also blond, 3" long, 1-2-1)? What reasons did Miss Goodbody have for changing from a beauty queen to a secretary, and why did she want to work for Mr. Strump? (The six million dollars may have had something to do with it.) The point to be made here is that the writer must decide how far to take any causal analysis, and the writer will make the decision to suit the purpose of the analysis to the audience for whom it is intended. The IRS agent was interested only in the nonpayment of taxes, and the purpose of his analysis was accomplished when he found out that Mr. Strump was dead. He did not need to continue the analysis. If Sergeant Wexley had been doing his analysis for publication in a psychological journal, he would have had to discover the underlying psychological reasons for Mr. Strump's sudden love of goldfish and Miss Goodbody's deep love of six million dollars. Because he was analyzing the events for a police report, however, he needed only to go as far as a determination of guilt for Mr. Strump's death. As you can see from the example above, causality involves two questions.

1. What caused the effect to occur?
2. Under certain conditions, what will be the resulting effect or effects?

The first question involves tracing backward the relationship between cause and effect; the second question involves tracing the relationship forward from cause to effect.

Causes

The rules of causation are twofold. (1) Without event A, effect B will not occur, and (2) whenever event A occurs, B will later occur. Several types of causes exist, and the writer must be able to distinguish them in order to sort out the essential events that result in causation. Three types of causes include the following:

1. **necessary cause**—this cause must be present for an effect to occur; without it the effect cannot happen. For example, in order to have light in your kitchen at home, you must turn on the light switch. The switch mechanism is a necessary cause, but it will not provide light by itself. Electricity must also be present. Event A (switch), in other words, must be present for B (light) to occur.

2. **contributing cause**—this cause may determine a particular effect but cannot singly determine it. For instance, you may make a good grade

on an exam if you study your class notes thoroughly; however, other factors come into play as well, such as the quality of your notes, regular attendance in class, and your ability to remember what you reviewed in your notes. Event A (study) may be present for event B (good grade) to occur, but event A does not automatically result in event B. Other factors may also have contributed to your good grade.

3.   **sufficient cause**--this cause can determine a particular effect by itself, but the effect does not always follow as a result of the cause. For example, a student may fail a course because of poor attendance, but this cause alone does not always lead to failure. A grade average below 60 must be present as well. Event A (poor attendance) can be present for event B (failure), but A does not automatically result in event B.

Causal analysis, then, is concerned with the reasons that things happen. Because of this concern, it is one of the basic techniques of reasoning. When a writer decides to write an essay based on causal analysis, it is very important that he be convincing, for he is discussing something more complex than a light switch. The writer's aim is to demonstrate for the reader why event B (effect) occurred. Why, for example, does high cholesterol cause heart disease? Why did my daughter fail her college courses? In order to do the job convincingly, the writer must make the reader appreciate the logic and thoroughness of the essay. The writer is actually engaged in an intellectual process, and because he is usually appealing to the reader's mind, he must be sure that his analysis is rationally satisfying.

Organization

Causal chain. The causal chain works like a series of dominoes aligned in a row. If you knock the first over, the second and the third dominoes will fall in succession, and so on until they have all tumbled. In a causal chain, the remote cause is like the fall of the first domino in the chain, which causes an effect (fall of second domino). This effect becomes the cause of the next effect (fall of second domino). This sequence continues until the immediate cause (the third domino) results in the final event (effect) of the chain process. The causal chain process looks like the following figure:

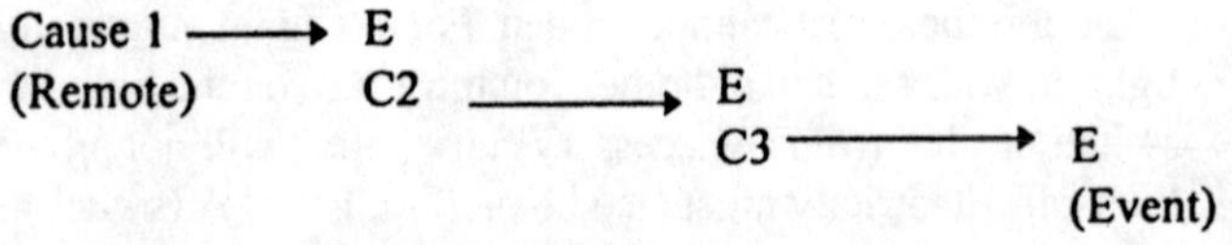

Cause 1 ⟶ E
(Remote)   C2 ⟶ E
                    C3 ⟶ E
                                (Event)

Figure III-B

There are several ways to structure a causal analysis. Ordinarily, either the writer will work logically from the most immediate cause back toward the most basic or

114

remote cause, or he will start with the basic/remote cause and work forward to the immediate cause. An example of the immediate to remote sequence would be an analysis of the reasons for today's high cost of living. The writer might begin with high and rising prices for meat and clothing, suggest inflation as the reason for the price trend, point out high demand and limited supplies as the reason for inflation, discuss the basic economic law of supply and demand as responsible for the situation, and finally blame the whole thing on our capitalistic, money oriented society. This analysis would have moved from the immediate level (the high price of food and clothing items), through an intermediate level (inflation and the supply and demand principles), to a very basic cause (the economic structure of the country). An example of the second pattern (basic/remote to immediate) would be an analysis of the reasons for American involvement in Vietnam, which begins with a discussion of the American spirit as dominated by a Protestant ethic of aggressive morality (remote cause). The author might assert that this morality makes Americans want to assert their own ideas of justice and ethical behavior on the world (intermediate cause) and finally suggest that our desire to impose "righteousness" on others (immediate cause) was the reason we became involved in Southeast Asia. Here the analysis has moved from the author's basic premise (the American spirit of aggressive morality) to the effect of that premise (U.S. involvement in Vietnam).

When putting together a *causal chain analysis*, you must remember to observe some very important guidelines. First, because your analysis depends on demonstrating a causal chain, you must make clear to your reader how each cause is directly linked to the other causes included in your essay. For example, after you have discussed one of the causes in the first body paragraph, make certain that you show the connection of your second cause with the one already discussed, whether the second cause is the effect of the first or the cause of the first cause discussed, depending upon whether you began your analysis with the remote or the immediate cause. The same rule applies to the next paragraph. *This causal link must be clearly shown in the topic sentence of each paragraph.* Otherwise, the chain process will not be apparent to your audience. Study the two following outlines and note how the structure of each differs slightly. The first outline contains several causes that are not linked together but are combined to create a single effect.

I.   Introduction/thesis–Thesis identifies single effect (subject) and multiple causes (focus).

Body
II.   Cause #1
III.   Cause #2
IV.   Cause #3

V.   Conclusion (restates effect and three causes)

An outline indicating a causal chain analysis looks similar to the one above, but some distinctions should be noted. Consider the following example.

I.   Introduction/thesis–Thesis identifies single effect (subject) and multiple causes connected by a causal chain (focus)

Body
II.   Cause #1 remote/basic cause
III.   Cause #2 intermediate cause (effect of cause #1)
IV.   Cause #3 immediate cause (effect of cause #2)
V.   Conclusion

Effects

Sometimes a single cause may have multiple effects. For example, what would be the effects on a student who failed a college course? His failure may lead to low self esteem (effect #1), he may have to forfeit his financial aid (effect #2), and his parents may refuse to pay for any further education (effect #3). Note that these three effects are independent of one another; in other words, one effect does not lead to another. Determining the effects of an event means we are predicting into the future what we assume will happen based on the evidence we have at the present time. We use this method of analysis every day. Before we commit ourselves to a particular act or opt for a specific choice, we often consider the consequences of such an act or choice. In this case, we are speculating about the future results of our decision today. Economic trends and weather predictions are determined by people who are informed enough about certain historical conditions to make educated prognostications regarding the future. You know what the potential effects would be if you failed to succeed in college. Causal analysis is the process that sets this same process into a coherent, logical structure. Just like the essay outline shown above that lists the causes for a single effect, the outline traces the multiple effects of a single cause and arranges them in a similar fashion.

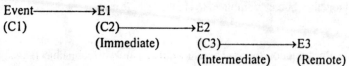

Figure III-C

The thesis statement will contain the cause (subject of thesis) and the effects (focus of thesis), listing the effects in the order that you will discuss them in the subsequent paragraphs, moving downward either to the most important effect (if there is no causal chain of effects) or to the remote/basic effect or the immediate effect (in a causal chain process), depending on your purpose in the essay. If you wish to write

an essay that discusses the effects in some preferential/emphatic order, the outline
will have the following format:

I.   Introduction/thesis–Identifies single event (subject) and multiple effects
            (focus)
Body
II.   Effect #1   least important
III   Effect #2   more important
IV.   Effect #3   most important
[A fourth body paragraph can be added to discuss the initial event (single cause) if
you wish.]
V.   Conclusion

The same general outline will serve as the format for an essay that discusses the
causal chain resulting in the multiple effects of a single event/cause. The major
difference here will be the arrangement of effects usually from immediate effect to
remote or remote to immediate effect. Consider the following example.

I.   Introduction/thesis – single cause (subject of thesis) multiple effects
                        (focus of thesis) listed by a time sequence (chain)
Body
II.   Effect #1 immediate effect (cause of effect #2)
III.   Effect #2 intermediate effect (cause of effect #3)
IV.   Effect #3   remote effect (result of effect #2)
V.   Conclusion

Should you be required to write a causal analysis that examines both causes and
effects, the process is a bit more complex but is consistent with the outlines
described above. Whether you choose to write a causal chain or simply an essay
showing multiple causes and effects, you must be consistent in considering your
method. For instance, if you use the causal chain in tracing the causes, make certain
that you use the causal chain also in examining the multiple effects. For a sample
outline of the causal chain of both causes and effects of failing a course, consider the
following outline.

I. Introduction/thesis –Effect #1 (subject of thesis–the failure of the course) and
            the causes and effects of failure (focus of thesis statement) in a logical
            order.
Body
II.   Cause #1
III.   Cause #2
IV.   Cause #3
V.   Effect #1
VI.   Effect #2   (One option might be to include all three

VII.   Effect #3   effects into a single paragraph. Consult your instructor for
                           preferred format.)

VIII.   Conclusion

Technique

There are several potential hazards the writer of a causal analysis must be aware of if
he wishes his essay to be convincing. (1) One is the *post hoc ergo propter hoc*
fallacy. The Latin words mean "after this; therefore, because of this" and suggest
that because one event follows another event, the first necessarily is the cause of the
second. An extreme example might be to say that, as you were driving to class one
day, a black cat crossed in front of your car and soon afterwards you were involved
in a collision. You then conclude that black cats are omens of bad luck. This is an
example of the post hoc fallacy and is obviously silly, but the writer must beware of
asserting that just because something happened first (failure of the final exam) it
caused something else (failure of the course) to happen. (2) Another hazard can be
avoided if the writer makes sure that his analysis considers all the relevant causes
and factors leading up to a certain effect. It may be true that the student's failing the
final exam was a cause of his failure of the course, but other causes (poor
attendance, poor daily quiz average, sleeping through lectures, assignments usually
submitted late if at all, never purchasing the textbook, having a serious attitude
problem, to name a few) may also have to be considered. (3) In order to be
convincing, the writer should also offer evidence for his assertions. Simply saying
that something was caused by something else is not enough. Because the writer
wants his reader's intellectual assent, he must accompany his assertions with proof.
If, for example, the writer says that the student's social life was responsible for his
failure, then he must give evidence of how it was responsible: that it kept him from
studying and that it was more important to him than his academic responsibilities.
This third hazard can be avoided if the writer is objective, reasonable, and honest. If
it becomes evident to the audience that the writer is condemning the failing student
because of his hedonistic, immoral social behavior, and his love of heavy metal
music and companions with fried brains, then the reader will not be convinced of
the validity of the essay's analysis.

Checklist

As you prepare to write your causal analysis, keep the following in mind:

1. Focus on your purpose. A causal analysis can be primary or supplementary. Its
    purpose can be to inform, to speculate on possibilities, and/or to persuade.
    Regardless of the essay's primary purpose, your purpose is, of course, to
    persuade your audience of the legitimacy of your analysis.

2. Think logically. Indicate the complexity of the situation and look beyond the
    obvious and superficial. Recognize reasonable probability and do not overstate.
    Neither should you settle for simplistic explanations. Determine and

differentiate between immediate and remote causes or effects and provide facts, statistics, details, and/or a personal narrative to explain and exemplify your reasoning.

3. Write a thesis statement that focuses on your purpose and your approach. Indicate whether you intend to talk about causes, effects, or both to show your order and development. Make your point clear and remember who your audience is.

4. Choose an organizational plan. Some causal analyses are organized *chronologically*: causes and effects are presented in the order in which they happen, but a strict time sequence can be a problem if the primary causes are buried in the middle of the essay. Your causal analysis should be arranged *emphatically* with the most significant cause or effect reserved for last.

5. Use effective language that hints at the complexity of cause and effect relationships. While you should qualify what you say, you should be careful not to undercut your own thinking.

In the following student essay, identify the method Kathy Crosby uses to examine her decision to go into nursing.

A New Career

I am presently attending college to obtain an Associate Degree in Nursing. There are a number of factors which led me to make this choice such as the great demand for this particular profession as well as the opportunities available in the area medical center. However, there are three important elements that allowed me to make this very important decision. They are the direct observation and personal contact I experienced, the strong desire and ambition I obtained as a result of this contact, and the encouragement and support of others as they became aware of my strong desire to pursue a career outside the home.

The basic and perhaps most subtle factor which brought me to realize a career in nursing was the influence I experienced from the nurses assigned to care for my terminally ill mother. For a period of six months I had a considerable amount of contact with these very caring people, and I was able to observe many things. All their routine duties were performed with dedication. They encouraged my mother to ask for pain medication whenever necessary, which is very important for the cancer patient. They would spend hours trying to get her temperature down, for she was subject to night fevers. There were no heroics involved. It was done strictly for her comfort. Every night they would come to give her a back rub. She looked forward to these. These same nurses were compassionate and understanding. If time allowed, they would just sit and visit with my mother. I also found them to be sensitive to the needs of the family, allowing us to hope when despair was often present or sometimes just offering their prayers. They provided a sense of humor, which I found to be so necessary for both my mother and our family. Due to the nurses' dedication, many of my mother's fears, along with those of the family, were lessened. As her last months of life were spent with this new family, it was reassuring for all involved to know that her basic needs and comforts were being taken care of. I was grateful to her new friends. They made her last few months bearable. From this steady diet of their daily routines and personal care of this special patient, each day I became more and more interested in doing the same.

As a result of all this exposure, I acquired a strong desire and ambition to pursue a career in nursing. I find this ambition to be an ever-present, necessary ingredient and a principal element for success. It is a quiet resolve that does not quit even when it would be convenient to do so. Sometimes I will ask myself, "Why am I doing this? I don't really need a career. Isn't it enough just being a wife and mother?" But I do go on because of my ambition. My conscience tells me I must continue even though I'd rather be doing something else. It is this same conscience telling me, "I must succeed; I will succeed." I am filled with much hope of attaining this success in school, thus allowing me to provide the necessary care needed by so many individuals. I want to make the difference in the quality of patient care. I want to help alleviate fears and anxieties, ease pain and suffering, maybe help someone to smile or laugh, as I so often witnessed with those who surrounded my mother. I find this ambition to be a very necessary factor in pursuing my new career. Moreover, I find that as I am more and more successful in school, my ambition grows. Also, I do believe strongly that my personal experience afforded me the opportunity to attain this ambition.

Subsequently, as my ambition became known, I was deluged with encouragement and support from family and friends. In this particular situation, I believe this to be the most important factor in my decision regarding careers. I experienced some feelings of apprehension, which were alleviated by the presence of this encouragement. It was reassuring to know that others had confidence in me. Their confidence reinforced the little confidence I had in myself. There were some misconceptions I held which were later discounted through this encouragement. I am thankful for this encouragement. It has allowed me to feel comfortable about attending school. I truly believe that without the support and encouragement of my immediate family, I would not be seeking this new career. There are some sacrifices we have all had to make. My husband is very considerate, supportive, and proud of his wife. My two sons think it is great their mom goes to college. The older one can't wait for school to begin so we can study together. The younger one thinks it is great we get to eat out more often. This encouragement and support I receive helps me balance out the juggling act I sometimes feel I'm performing as I balance the duties of wife and mother versus student. Most of all, I'm not made to feel I am neglecting them in any way. I would not be pursuing this career without their support and encouragement.

In summary, I believe the decision I made to become a nurse began with the experience my mother had with her nurses. She was fortunate to have wonderful and caring nurses. I was fortunate to be able to receive something positive from an unfortunate experience. This experience brought forth a strong desire to enter the field of nursing. And as a result, I have been the object of much encouragement and support, which helped me to make my final decision. I will reach my goal eventually. I will become a nurse. My past experience will provide me with the ambition to finish school with the encouragement and support of my family and friends. One day I'll be working in a hospital caring for people who need compassion and dedication, and I will be able to give them just that and more.

In "Who Killed Benny Paret?" (1961), Norman Cousins traces the causes for the death of a young Cuban boxer. Using a causal chain, the author speaks to the public's responsibility for the violence in spectator sports and the effects of such violence.

WHO KILLED BENNY PARET?
NORMAN COUSINS

Sometime about 1935 or 1936 I had an interview with Mike Jacobs, the prize-fight promoter. I was a fledgling newspaper reporter at that time; my beat was education, but during the vacation season I found myself on varied assignments, all the way from ship news to sports reporting. In this way I found myself sitting opposite the most powerful figure in the boxing world.

There was nothing spectacular in Mr. Jacobs's manner or appearance, but when he spoke about prize fights, he was no longer a bland little man but a colossus who sounded the way Napoleon must have sounded when he reviewed a battle. You knew you were listening to Number One. His saying something made it true.

We discussed what to him was the only important element in successful promotion–how to please the crowd. So far as he was concerned, there was no mystery to it. You put killers in the ring and the people filled your arena. You hire boxing artists–men who are adroit at feinting, parrying, weaving, jabbing, and dancing, but who don't pack dynamite in their fists–and you wind up counting your empty seats. So you searched for the killers and sluggers and maulers–fellows who could hit with the force of a baseball bat.

I asked Mr. Jacobs if he was speaking literally when he said people came out to see the killer.

"They don't come out to see a tea party," he said evenly. "They come out to see the knockout. They come out to see a man hurt. If they think anything else, they're kidding themselves."

Recently a young man by the name of Benny Paret was killed in the ring. The killing was seen by millions; it was on television. In the twelfth round he was hit hard in the head several times, went down, was counted out, and never came out of the coma.

The Paret fight produced a flurry of investigations. Governor Rockefeller was shocked by what happened and appointed a committee to assess the responsibility. The New York State Boxing Commission decided to find out what was wrong. The District Attorney's office expressed its concern. One question that was solemnly studied in all three probes concerned the action of the referee. Did he act in time to stop the fight? Another question had to do with role of the examining doctors who certified the physical fitness of the fighters before the bout. Still another question involved Mr. Paret's manager; did he rush his boy into the fight without adequate time to recuperate from the previous one?

In short, the investigators looked into every possible cause except the real one. Benny Paret was killed because the human fist delivers enough impact, when directed against the head, to produce a massive hemorrhage in the brain. The human brain is the most delicate and complex mechanism in all creation. It has a lacework of millions of highly fragile nerve connections. Nature attempts to protect this exquisitely intricate machinery by encasing it in a hard shell. Fortunately, the shell is thick enough to withstand a great deal of pounding. Nature, however, can protect man against everything except man himself. Not every blow to the head will kill a man–but there is always the risk of concussion and damage to the brain. A prize fighter may be able to survive even repeated brain concussions and go on fighting, but the damage to his brain may be permanent.

In any event, it is futile to investigate the referee's role and seek to determine whether he should have intervened to stop the fight earlier. This is not where the primary responsibility lies. The primary responsibility lies with the people who pay to see a man hurt. The referee who stops a fight too soon from the crowd's viewpoint can expect to be booed. The crowd wants the knockout; it wants to see a man stretched out on the canvas. This is the supreme moment in boxing. It is nonsense to talk about prize fighting as a test of boxing skills. No crowd was ever brought to its feet screaming and cheering at the sight of two men beautifully dodging and weaving out of each other's jabs. The time the crowd comes alive is when a man is hit hard over the heart or the head, when his mouthpiece flies out, when blood squirts out of his nose or eyes, when he wobbles under the attack and his pursuer continues to smash at him with poleax impact.

Don't blame it on the referee. Don't even blame it on the fight managers. Put the blame where it belongs–on the prevailing mores that regard prize fighting as a perfectly proper enterprise and vehicle of entertainment. No one doubts that many people enjoy prize fighting and will miss it if it should be thrown out. And that is precisely the point.

1961

122

"My Wood," by E.M. Forster, investigates the different effects of property ownership on the author himself and on the individual in society. The author's focus is on the psychological effects of ownership. Consider the tone of the writer and its role in the development of the essay. Compare or contrast how ownership affects you with how it affects Forster.

MY WOOD
E.M. FORSTER

A few years ago I wrote a book which dealt in part with the difficulties of the English in India. Feeling that they would have had no difficulties in India themselves, the Americans read the book freely. The more they read it the better it made them feel, and a cheque to the author was the result. I bought a wood with the cheque. It is not a large wood—it contains scarcely any trees, and it is intersected, blast it, by a public footpath. Still, it is the first property that I have owned, so it is right that other people should participate in my shame, and should ask themselves, in accents that will vary in horror, this very important question: What is the effect of property upon the character? Don't let's touch economics; the effect of private ownership upon the community as a whole is another question—a more important question, perhaps, but another one. Let's keep to psychology. If you own things, what's their effect on you? What's the effect on me of my wood?

In the first place, it makes me feel heavy. Property does have this effect. Property produces men of weight, and it was a man of weight who failed to get into the Kingdom of Heaven. He was not wicked, that unfortunate millionaire in the parable, he was only stout; he stuck out in front, not to mention behind, and as he wedged himself this way and that in the crystalline entrance and bruised his well-fed flanks, he saw beneath him a comparatively slim camel passing through the eye of a needle and being woven into the robe of God. The Gospels all through couple stoutness and slowness. They point out what is perfectly obvious, yet seldom realized: that if you have a lot of things you cannot move about a lot, that furniture requires dusting, dusters require servants, servants require insurance stamps, and the whole tangle of them makes you think twice before you accept an invitation to dinner or go for a bathe in the Jordan. Sometimes the Gospels proceed further and say with Tolstoy that property is sinful; they approach the difficult ground of asceticism here, where I cannot follow them. But as to the immediate effects of property on people, they just show straightforward logic. It produces men of weight. Men of weight cannot, by definition, move like the lightning from the East unto the West, and the ascent of a fourteen-stone bishop into a pulpit is thus the exact antithesis of the coming of the Son of Man. My wood makes me feel heavy.

In the second place, it makes me feel it ought to be larger.

The other day I heard a twig snap in it. I was annoyed at first, for I thought that someone was blackberrying, and depreciating the value of the undergrowth. On coming nearer, I saw it was not a man who had trodden on the twig and snapped it, but a bird, and I felt pleased. My bird. The bird was not equally pleased. Ignoring the relation between us, it took fright as soon as it saw the shape of my face, and flew straight over the boundary hedge into a field, the property of Mrs. Henessy, where it sat down with a loud squawk. It had become Mrs. Henessy's bird. Something seemed grossly amiss here, something that would not have occurred had the wood been larger. I could not afford to buy Mrs. Henessy out, I dared not murder her, and limitations of this sort beset me on every side. Ahab did not want that vineyard–he only needed it to round off his property, preparatory to plotting a new curve–and all the land around my wood has become necessary to me in order to round off the wood. A boundary protects. But–poor little thing–the boundary ought in its turn to be protected. Noises on the edge of it. Children throw stones. A little more, and then a little more, until we reach the sea. Happy Canute! Happier Alexander! And after all, why should even the world be the limit of possession? A rocket containing a Union Jack, will, it is hoped, be shortly fired at the moon. Mars. Sirius. Beyond which . . .But these immensities ended by saddening me. I could not suppose that my wood was the destined nucleus of universal dominion–it is so very small and contains no mineral wealth beyond the blackberries. Nor was I comforted when Mrs. Henessy's bird took alarm for the second time and flew clean away from us all, under the belief that it belonged to itself.

In the third place, property makes its owner feel that he ought to do something to it. Yet he isn't sure what. A restlessness comes over him, a vague sense that he has a personality to express–the same sense which, without any vagueness, leads the artist to an act of creation. Sometimes I think I will cut down such trees as remain in the wood, at other times I want to fill up the gaps between them with new trees. Both impulses are pretentious and empty. They are not honest movements toward moneymaking or beauty. They spring from a foolish desire to express myself and from an inability to enjoy what I have got. Creation, property, enjoyment form a sinister trinity in the human mind. Creation and enjoyment are both very, very good, yet they are often unattainable without a material basis, and at such moments property pushes itself in as a substitute, saying, "Accept me instead–I'm good enough for all three." It is not enough. It is, as Shakespeare said of lust, "The expense of spirit in a waste of shame.": it is "Before, a joy proposed; behind, a dream." Yet we don't know how to shun it. It is forced on us by an internal defect in the soul, by the feeling that in property may lie the germs of self-development and of exquisite or heroic deeds. Our life on earth is, and ought to be, material and carnal. But we have not yet learned to manage our materialism and carnality properly; they are still entangled with the desire for ownership, where (in the words of Dante) "Possession is one with loss."

And this brings us to our fourth and final point: the blackberries. Blackberries are not plentiful in this meagre grove, but they are easily seen from the public footpath

124

which traverses it, and all too easily gathered. Foxgloves, too—people will pull up the foxgloves, and ladies of an educational tendency even grub for toadstools to show them on the Monday in class. Other ladies, less educated, roll down the bracken in the arms of their gentlemen friends. There is paper, there are tins. Pray, does my wood belong to me or doesn't it? And, if it does, should I not own it best by allowing no one else to walk there? There is a wood near Lyme Regis, also cursed by a public footpath, where the owner has not hesitated on this point. He had built high stone walls each side of the path, and has spanned it by bridges, so that the public circulate like termites while he gorges on the blackberries unseen. He really does own his wood, this able chap. Dives in Hell did pretty well, but the gulf dividing him from Lazarus could be traversed by vision, and nothing traverses it here. And perhaps I shall come to this in time. I shall wall in and fence out until I really taste the sweets of property. Enormously stout, endlessly avaricious, pseudocreative, intensely selfish, I shall weave upon my head the quadruple crown of possession until those nasty Bolshies come and take it off again and thrust me aside into the outer darkness.

CHAPTER 4
ARGUMENTATION

Argument usually suggests to us a negative activity. We tend to think of argument synonymously with a quarrel or disagreement; we argue with parents, spouses, or friends. This use of the term, however, differs from its original and still primary meaning, which is associated with reason and objectivity. It is defined as the process of demonstrating, through reason, the likelihood or necessity of a given proposition. The end of argument is persuasion, achieved through reasoning. It is the process of influencing others to respond as we wish them to respond, to assent to the proposition of the speaker or writer.

If everyone always agreed on everything, there would be no need for argument. But we know that disagreements do exist at all levels of life. The fact that some of our disagreements are ancient ones suggests the difficulty people have in reaching agreement. For example, consider a few of the present day controversial topics–abortion, censorship, capital punishment. These controversies will never approach resolution until the truth is discovered and there is agreement as to that truth. Yet how can truth be discovered until there is a free and open encounter between opposing views? This sincere encounter with our differences is the heart of argumentative discourse; therefore, it must be addressed reasonably, objectively, and thoroughly. Once we feel we have touched upon the truth of an argument, we must then strive for assent by persuading others of the correctness of that truth. This attempt at persuasion is a complicated undertaking. To gain our reader's assent to our propositions, we must organize them in a format that will present our ideas most effectively. Since rhetoric is the art of using language effectively, logically we would want to use a rhetorical format, a long-established method that would assist us in presenting our argument and in persuading the reader. The end of persuasion, after all, is assent to the proposition of the speaker or writer, while the end of argument is truth as determined through reasoning. Strictly speaking, then, logic is a means of persuasion. Although their differences are vast, both argument and persuasion have the same goal: to convince for the purpose of assent. Therefore, we will treat these two forms, argumentation and persuasion, as one in our discussion of argumentation.

IMPLEMENTATION

We are all expected on occasion to explain our ideas. When we engage in such an explanation, we call upon evidence to convince our listener or reader that our ideas are true and correct and, therefore, worthy of attention. Sometimes we are expected to present and defend our ideas in writing. For example, in your academic career and in the workplace you will be called upon to analyze situations and texts and to argue for or against certain ideas or opinions. From small businesses to large corporations, employees who can articulate their views logically have an advantage in being considered for advancement. As a student, a citizen, a parent, an employee, or a consumer, you will have many opportunities to express your ideas. Being familiar with argumentative skills will improve your chances of being convincing and persuasive. In addition, you will be able to use these same skills in distinguishing between truth and falsehood in the world around you. Being familiar with the tools of persuasive discourse, you will be able to determine the correctness of claims made by political figures, employers, salespeople, advertisers, and friends. You can then not only determine the validity of others' arguments, but also formulate your own strategy of reasoned argument to counter the beliefs with which you disagree.

In a composition class, however, you will most likely be asked to present your views on a given controversial issue. Based on the topic assigned to you or the topic you select, you must determine what your purpose is. Do you intend to persuade by offering a defense or an attack? Since you will be expected to argue your views in an attempt to persuade your reader to see the issues as you do and, possibly, to act upon the views or recommendations you have prescribed, you must understand and be able to use effectively the rhetorical elements involved in writing persuasive arguments. In addition, you will be expected to identify your specific audience for your essay. The audience determines the approach you take to your argument. With your purpose and audience in mind, you must take a stand on your topic, present a proposition that reflects your stand, and provide evidence to support that stand.

Audience

You must first have a clear understanding of who your audience will be. Your audience will shape a great deal of what you say and how you say it and will guide you in determining your particular approach to your topic. First, your language must be appropriate for your reader. It would be unwise to address a group of junior high school readers with complex language and reasoning, just as it would be imprudent to address a group of experts on your topic in a manner that assumes no knowledge on their part. You must always be both intelligible to and respectful of your audience. In addition, knowing who your audience is allows you to make certain assumptions about that audience in order to select the appropriate and most convincing points to be discussed and the particular appeals to use in the essay. It also gives you the ability to anticipate what objections your audience will have to your ideas. You must assume that your audience is intelligent, informed about your topic, and not only opposes your position but resists it. By assuming an opposing audience you most likely will be prompted to offer a better argument and counter argument (refutation), making your stand on a given topic stronger and more convincing.

While argument begins in conflict, it should end in some form of resolution. Even if your reader is yet unconvinced that you are right and he is wrong, the most you can realistically expect to achieve in a sound argument is that your reader is willing at least to admit to some credibility of your argument. Remember that the fact that your topic is centered in controversy suggests that both schools of thought believe themselves correct in their thinking. Your opponent will probably have at least one sound argument as well. Keep this fact in mind when you are organizing and presenting your argument: this assumption can work to your advantage.

Definition of Terms

Many arguments fail because the writer does not define the terms on which his essay is based. For your audience to understand your ideas, make certain you clearly define the terms you discuss. State, for example, what you mean by "sexual harassment," "censorship," "pornography," "aesthetic value," or "redeeming quality." You must define any term your audience, for one reason or another, risks misunderstanding. Consult a dictionary or construct your own definition based on your understanding of the term and on the manner in which you discuss the term in your argument. You might review the section on Definition in **Chapter Three** to familiarize yourself with the methods of defining a term.

METHODS OF APPEAL

Because persuasion is an attempt to make your ideas and proposals attractive to an audience, you should be familiar with the methods you might use to appeal to that audience. Aristotle identified these appeals as forms of argument: the emotional (pathos), ethical (ethos), and logical (logos) appeals. These three appeals are interwoven throughout the essay, but you must understand how each works and when to use it. With your audience and purpose clearly in mind, you must determine what effect you wish to achieve in your essay and integrate the appeals accordingly in your argument.

Emotional Appeal

When we want to persuade an audience, we often find it necessary to appeal to the personal nature of our topic. People are generally more interested in those matters that touch their hearts than in statistics or logic. The writer of a persuasive argument cannot ignore the fact that much of our identity resides in our emotions and imaginations. If we are to convince readers, we must appeal to their emotions, attempting to ascertain which of our emotions they will accept or approve. The clever writer can then use certain associations which will elicit the desired emotional response in his audience. For instance, if you are addressing a religious group, you might associate the idea of human leadership or fellowship with Christ. This reference links the writer's own propositions to what the audience already identifies with and respects. Sometimes a well-placed word or phrase will enhance the emotional appeal of an argument, as when a writer of an essay against pornography mentions "innocent" children. Conversely, you must remember that this same knowledge of the emotional character of your audience suggests what not to use in your appeal. It would be unwise to think that you could evoke a sympathetic response from a group of Republicans, for instance, by associating Dan Quayle with the importance of correct spelling.

The emotional appeal should never be used exclusively, however. Many feel that appealing to people's emotions is suspect because it can be considered an attempt to manipulate them. Using emotions to manipulate others cannot be condoned in any fashion, but when emotions are used appropriately and in accord with your audience, they can be a very powerful and persuasive element of argumentation.

Ethical Appeal

The ethical argument or appeal is, according to Aristotle, the most potent of all the means of persuasion. For writers' arguments to be effective, their ethos must be apparent in their work and realized by their readers. Simply because a writer presents an argument does not mean that he or she can expect the reader's assent, or even attention; nor can the mere presence of sincerity or emotion bring about the desired assent. To determine the nature of the ethical appeal, one must understand that the writer's words have emotional associations as well as definite meanings. Although the ethical appeal is not restricted by any given specific rules or qualities, certain components can be discussed. For example, three major qualities of the ethical appeal illustrate how the writer can reveal his or her character through the words the writer chooses.

These three components that the writer must make apparent to the reader might be called **good sense, good will**, and **good moral character**. **Good sense** suggests that the writer is capable of making practical decisions and choosing the proper means to achieve an end. It must be apparent to the reader that the writer is confident in his argument and that it is, in fact, correct and that he views his topic in the proper perspective. **Good will**, the second component, consists in the writer's making clear to his audience that he has nothing but good will towards them. He must demonstrate that he shares their good intentions and basic aspirations and that he shares, too, some of their biases and prejudices, if necessary. The third component,

good moral character, is successfully presented if the writer convinces his audience that he would not deceive them. To acquire this trust, the writer must be sincere and believable. He must show that he knows right from wrong. His attitude and presentation must convince the reader that he is fair and trustworthy.

Keep in mind that the ethical appeal emerges throughout the essay. It is not something a writer merely inserts between paragraphs or ideas. A writer's ethos develops as he or she makes clear to the reader the possession of all three of the components: the heart is genuine, the intentions good, and the recommendations worthy of the reader's attention.

Rational Appeal

The rational appeal is used to convince an audience that the writer's claims are true. To construct an argument using the rational appeal, the writer employs **induction** and **deduction,** both forms of logic. But in order to employ the rational appeal effectively, the writer must first understand some basic concepts and terms of logic:

Logic
A method of distinguishing between correct and incorrect reasoning. Since reasoning is represented in arguments, logic is a method for evaluating arguments.

Argument
An organized discussion of an idea or an issue. It can proceed from a premise or several premises to a conclusion, or it can start with a claim and then give evidence to support that claim. An argument is meant to persuade its readers or listeners that the belief or position held by the arguer is true.

Proposition.
A statement that affirms or denies the truth of something. It can be as concrete and as easily verified as the statement *Houston is the largest city in Texas*, or as abstract and difficult to prove as the statement *The soul is immortal.*

Arguments are composed of two types of propositions or claims.

Premises. The propositions stated by the arguer as evidence for the belief that he or she is trying to prove. If possible, the arguer should select premises that will be readily accepted by the audience. Otherwise it will be necessary for the arguer to devise side arguments to show that the premises of the main argument are true.

Conclusion. The proposition expressing the belief that the arguer is trying to persuade the hearer or reader to accept. In a good argument the conclusion follows logically from the premises.

A sound or cogent argument not only provides evidence that its claims are **true**, it also makes sure that its conclusions are **validly** drawn from its premises.

Truth

The situation in which a proposition corresponds to reality or expresses a tautology (truth by definition). Correspondence with reality can only be determined empirically, that is through observation and experience. For example, the statement that the sun is approximately 93,000,000 miles from earth can be verified by experiment. Truth by definition is a matter of how speakers of a language have agreed (often implicitly) upon meanings of words. For example, the statement that bachelors are unmarried men is true because "unmarried men" and "bachelors" mean the same thing in English.

Validity

The process by which arguments are determined to be correct. An argument is valid if its conclusion is properly drawn from its premises, if the rules of logic have been followed in proceeding from premise to conclusion.

DEDUCTIVE REASONING

Deduction is a strict form of argument aiming for the strongest possible connection between premises and conclusion. The writer using deductive reasoning aims to set forth evidence so that if the premises are true, the conclusion necessarily follows as true. Alternatively, the writer tries to make it impossible for the premises to be true and the conclusion false. For example, if

$$A = B$$
$$C = A$$

Necessarily $C = B$ is true

The above example is a *syllogism*, which is a form of deductive argument. There are several types of syllogisms, but the one most commonly known and used is the **categorical syllogism**. The categorical syllogism is composed of two premises and a conclusion, as in the following example:

Parts

Major Premise	All men are mortal.
Minor Premise	Socrates is a man.
Conclusion	Socrates is mortal.

Terms

Major term	The predicate of the conclusion (mortal)
Minor term	The subject of the conclusion (Socrates)
Middle term	The term common to both premises but not included in the conclusion (man/men)

Checklist for Categorical Syllogisms

1. The middle term must be distributed at least once. That is, we must say something about all or no members of the class to which the middle term belongs.
2. There must be only three terms.
3. If a term is distributed in the conclusion, it must be distributed in the premises.
4. If both premises are affirmative, the conclusion must be affirmative.
5. If one premise is negative, the conclusion must be negative.
6. If both premises are negative, no valid conclusion is possible.

Enthymemes

An enthymeme is a syllogism with one of its premises omitted. In order to test the validity of the syllogistic argument, we must supply the omitted premise.

> Example 1. He couldn't have stolen that money; he is a church deacon.
> Suppressed premise: Church deacons do not steal.
>
> Example 2. They must be rich because they spend every summer in Europe.
> Suppressed premise: People who spend their summers in Europe are rich.
>
> Example 3. You can't deny a criminal his natural rights; after all, he is a human being.
> Suppressed premise: Humans cannot be denied their natural rights.

A danger in using an enthymeme is that your readers may not recognize it as an enthymeme and, therefore, fail to realize the full import of your argument. The advantage, however, is that if the enthymeme is recognized, it creates greater reader involvement in the argument and the essay as a whole.

While your thesis can be a statement that contains the whole syllogism, it can be shortened to include only an enthymeme. If you choose to use the enthymeme as your thesis, as in the examples above, you must still discuss the omitted premise in the body of the essay. Sometimes you may not want to use the syllogism or enthymeme as your thesis. Even though you employ deductive argument and it is based on a syllogism, you may have a thesis statement independent of the syllogism. For example, suppose that your discussion is organized around a syllogism that shows the validity of an argument indicating the benefits of

America's space program. Your reason for using the syllogism is to suggest that Congress should increase NASA's long term appropriations. Your purpose, therefore, involves advocating more money for the program while the syllogism itself argues deductively that the United States benefits from such a program. Your thesis statement might look something like the following: "Because the United States benefits from the space program, Congress should consider increasing NASA's appropriations." Whichever method you choose, make sure your thesis is effective and supports your precise purpose.

A good deductive argument is a **sound argument**, that is one whose premises are all true and whose form is valid. The reader must be satisfied with both before he can give assent to the conclusion. The fact that an argument is valid does not make it automatically acceptable because the premises may be false. For example:

Major Premise	All college students must take American history.
Minor Premise	You are a college student.
Conclusion	You must take American history.

This argument/syllogism is valid in the sense that if the premises are true, the conclusion necessarily follows; remember that validity is about the connection between the premises and the conclusion. The problem here, however, is that the major premise is untrue. (American history is a Texas state requirement for a college degree.) This argument, then, would be classified as valid but not sound.

When you are evaluating a deductive argument, ask yourself two questions:

1. Is it valid? Is the connection between the premises and the conclusion logical?
2. Are the premises true?

If your answer to both questions is "yes," the argument is **sound**. If your answer to either question is "no," you have a basis for rejecting the argument. The fact that the argument is unsound, however, does not mean that the conclusion is false; it simply means that the logic of this particular attempt to prove the conclusion has failed.

INDUCTIVE REASONING

Induction is a less strict form of argument than deduction. The writer of an inductive essay aims to set forth evidence so that if the premises are true, the conclusion **probably** follows as true. Yet it is possible for the premises to be true and the conclusion false. Induction is often used in science, history, and everyday life when one cannot obtain enough evidence to make the conclusion absolutely certain. An inductive argument is **strong** when the writer has succeeded in the aim of arranging premises so that if they are true, the conclusion probably follows. Here are some examples of strong inductive arguments listed by type:

1. Generalization

   Mockingbird #1 was observed to eat worms.
   Mockingbird #2 was observed to eat worms.

   . . .

   Mockingbird #99 was observed to eat worms.
   Conclusion: All mockingbirds eat worms.

2. Prediction

   In the past, an increase in stock prices has been followed
   shortly by a decrease in bond prices.
   Stock prices increased last week.
   Conclusion: Bond prices will decrease this week.

3. Analogy

   The car I am now driving weighs 3500 pounds, has a fuel-
   injected V-8, has a wind resistance coefficient of .29, and gets
   30 mpg on the highway.
   The car I am about to buy has the same characteristics.
   Conclusion: The car I am about to buy will get 30 mpg on the
   highway.

4. Causal Inference

   The old bridge that was here yesterday is not here today. It was
   inspected last month and was found to be dangerously weak.
   We have had torrential rains for the past week, and the creek
   has risen up to a level above the roadway on the bridge.
   Conclusion: The old bridge was probably swept away by the
   floodwaters in the creek.

In addition, a **cogent** inductive argument is one which is strong and whose premises are all true.

When you are evaluating an inductive argument, ask yourself two questions:

1. Is it strong? Is the connection between the premises and the conclusion logical?
2. Are the premises true?

If your answer to both questions is "yes," the argument is **cogent**. If the answer to either question is "no," you have a basis for rejecting the argument. Once again, finding that an argument is not cogent does not mean that the conclusion is false; it merely means that this particular attempt to prove the conclusion has failed.

Evidence For Argumentation

The difficult part for the writer using inductive reasoning is to know whether he or she has sufficient evidence from which to draw a conclusion. All the writer can do is establish as high a degree of probability as possible. Once the writer is certain that the evidence provided for the inductive argument is sufficient, random (there are a variety of examples), accurate, and relevant, the writer must make what is known as the "inductive leap," a conclusion he or she reaches based on the evidence discussed. Unless the evidence meets these criteria, the argument will not be convincing and the writer will appear to have jumped to a conclusion.

If in developing evidence for an inductive argument, you discover an exception to your proposition, you should include it, too, in your discussion. A couple of reasons suggest this course of action. One, the inclusion of the single exception (negative evidence) can work to your advantage psychologically and ethically since, by including the exception with your evidence, you suggest to your reader that you are trustworthy in reporting such potentially damaging evidence. Second, you can take the opportunity to mitigate the force of the exception.

Assume, for example, you are asked to write an analysis of a poem. You might begin your analysis with the "facts" from the poem (the more the better); next you might provide an interpretation and analysis of these "facts"; finally you can construct your thesis, a generalization which covers your facts and analysis. In other words, you proceed inductively. For example, you might determine that the poem is a bad poem and, therefore, state this generalization in your proposition/thesis. Next, you offer the facts (evidence) from the poem that you have gathered based on your reading. Such evidence will include the fact that the poem (1) is structurally confusing, (2) is illogically developed, (3) is technically inaccurate, (4) contains imagery that is inconsistent, (5) suffers from immoderate sentimentalism for such a subject, (6) has a rhythm that is erratic and inconsistent, and (7) has a speaker who shifts tone throughout the poem. Based on this evidence, you conclude that the poem is a bad poem. Should the poem contain a single quality that does not support your conclusion, mention it, but point out that the success of one element is not enough to redeem the poem for its reader. If you suspect that your audience favors the poem, you may want to concede that the poem does have one good quality but then proceed to lay out the condemning evidence.

Sources

Since a crucial element of persuasive argumentation is the evidence you use to support your assertions, you must pay particular attention to the sources of that evidence. Ask yourself: "Is the source reliable, unbiased, authoritative?" Sources include reports in the media, statistics, testimonials, research, and authority. More weight is generally attributed to primary sources than to secondary sources. **Primary sources** include such things as original documents and eyewitness accounts. **Secondary sources** are those materials that are based on primary sources. For example, in a political science class you might be asked to write a paper on the freedom of religion in this country. One of your primary sources might be the Constitution itself; your secondary sources might include analyses and explanations of what the Constitution means by historians, scholars, and legal experts. Secondary sources should be assessed in relation to whatever primary evidence is accessible. You will find that among secondary sources there is usually disagreement, which makes your task of assessing them more difficult. Nevertheless, the more secondary sources you are able to accumulate, the better your chances are at arriving at some general assumptions regarding the general validity of your sources.

COMMON LOGICAL FALLACIES

A fallacy is a particular kind of defect in an argument, attributable to unsound and incomplete reasoning. It weakens an argument and makes it vulnerable to attack. Not only should you be familiar with the common fallacies so you can avoid them in your own argumentative essays, you should also be able to identify your opponent's defective arguments, allowing you to refute his assertions more easily. The following list includes a few of the most common fallacies in student argumentative essays.

Hasty Generalization. An argument that draws a conclusion based on insufficient or inappropriate samplings: "My Oldsmobile is a real lemon; therefore, General Motors manufactures inferior automobiles." "Students at the University of Houston are rude. Last night the guys in the room next to mine played their stereo at full blast until two in the morning, and as I was on my way to class this morning a bicyclist almost ran me down."

Red Herring. In hunting, a strongly scented object drawn across a trail will distract hounds and cause them to follow the new scent. In argument, a red herring is a different issue raised to lead attention away from the issue being debated or argued. Usually the new issue arouses an emotional response that creates a digression. "According to the newspapers, sexually transmitted diseases are climbing at an alarming rate among children in their teens. This raises a serious question about the wisdom of teaching sex-education in middle school."

Begging the Question. An argument based on an assumption that has yet to be proven: "The immoral experimentation on animals for research must be abolished"; "My narrow-minded English instructor seems to have forgotten how difficult it is to be a student."

Either/or Reasoning. An argument that suggests that only two alternatives exist when more than two actually exist. "If you quit college, you will never succeed in anything you do." "We can recognize that athletes who participate in major sports must be given special consideration at Texas A&M, or we can let the university sink into athletic oblivion."

Faulty Analogy. An argument based on a comparison of two things that share few or no common and relevant features. An analogy should be carefully examined to be sure that the things being compared are alike in ways essential to the conclusion being drawn. The fact that they are alike in some ways is not enough. "Since he was a good actor, I'm sure he will make a good President." "Bill, you are a superb computer technician. You seem to have a natural talent for analyzing system problems and remedying them. Surely, then, you should be able to analyze the problems in the rough drafts of your papers and turn them into polished essays."

Argumentum ad Hominem. The Latin phrase means *argument against the man* and names the fallacy of attacking the person rather than his argument. Such an attack may be legitimate when someone presents no argument but his own unsupported testimony. For example, the procedure is frequently used in courts to impeach witnesses who are testifying as experts. If it can be shown that they are not experts or that their testimony cannot be relied on, their trustworthiness as witnesses is seriously challenged. However, if someone presents evidence to support a claim, simply attacking his character is illegitimate. "Mr. Grumpky should not be allowed to serve on the school board because he is a nonChristian." "I went to a meeting on gender issues last night. The speakers were about as homely a group of women as I've ever seen. No wonder they hate men. Maybe if they dressed a little better and put on some makeup they wouldn't have to be concerned about gender issues."

Circular Reasoning. An argument based on the repetition of an assertion as a reason for accepting it: "Drugs are harmful because they injure the body." "The president would never lie to the public because he is an honest man."

False Cause. An argument that confuses a causal relationship (see Chapter 3). For example, one might mistake a contributory cause for a sufficient one, or assume that because one event occurred before a second event, the first caused the second (an example of the **Post Hoc, ergo Propter Hoc** fallacy, a Latin phrase meaning *after this; therefore because of this*.) "Because the city council outlawed firearms, the crime rate declined." "Research shows that successful people have large vocabularies; therefore, one way to become successful is to develop a large vocabulary."

PARTS OF AN ARGUMENTATIVE DISCOURSE

In his *Rhetoric,* Aristotle discusses the five parts of the deliberative discourse (a discussion of what we should or should not do to bring about some future goal), only two of which, **invention and disposition,** are relevant to the organization of the written essay.

Invention. Invention is the process or method writers use to discover arguments. Aristotle divided the process into finding arguments and devising arguments from scratch:

>**Non-artistic proofs** are arguments you discover that have already been formulated by others. We call this process research. For methods of developing non-artistic proofs, see your handbook on research strategies.
>**Artistic proofs** are arguments you develop yourself.
>>a. Pathos: Emotional Appeal
>>b. Ethos: Ethical Appeal
>>c. Logos: Logical Appeal

>You will be expected to use the logical appeal in your essay, to avoid overly emotional appeals, and to incorporate the ethical appeal throughout.

>**Topics** are proofs grouped under common headings. Under common topics Aristotle discusses such topics as definition, comparison-contrast, causal analysis, and the proper use of testimony or authority. See *Chapter Three* for detailed discussions of these methods of exposition. Under specific topics for deliberative discourse, Aristotle points out that the purpose of an argument is to persuade the reader that your solution to a particular problem is logical and just and that it will benefit him in some way. These are the twofold goals of your argument.

Disposition. Disposition is the way one disposes or organizes one's arguments. According to Aristotle, there are six parts to the disposition of an argument:

>**Introduction.** In your introduction you need to supply an attention-getting opener to your topic and a statement of your proposition/claim (the stand you intend to take).
>**Narration.** The narration is a discussion of the background of the issue under consideration. Readers, for example, may not know that there is a problem to be solved. The amount of background material you provide depends upon the knowledge of your audience and the complexity of the issue you are dealing with.
>**Division.** In the division you list the arguments you will advance in support of your proposition/claim.
>**Confirmation.** The confirmation is the longest and most important part of your argument. Here you give the evidence to support your proposition/claim arranged in the order you have listed in the division.

Refutation. The refutation is a discussion and rebuttal of your opponents' counter arguments. See below.

Conclusion. In your conclusion make a strong appeal for acceptance of your argument.

In a face-to-face argument, we have the advantage of responding directly to an opponent. In writing, however, we lack this advantage. Therefore, we must depend on **refutation** when we argue our ideas in writing. In your refutation, you take your opponents' arguments and prove they are, to some degree, wrong, invalid, or fallacious. Methods of refutation include pointing out an opponent's faulty premise, an error in deductive logic, a deficient definition, a logical fallacy, any inappropriate or inaccurate evidence, or a questionable authority, to name a few. For the most part, refutation involves undermining an opponent's argument. You might deny his proposition, showing that you cannot both be right. You might refute the truth of his premises or object to the inferences drawn from the premises, saying, in effect, "I admit the truth of your premise, but I challenge its validity in this particular instance because. . . ." Or you might undermine your opponent's insufficient evidence for such an argument. Let good judgment and common sense rule. Consider your audience and their emotional biases, the occasion, the subject, and your own personality to help you determine the best course of action regarding refutation.

Some instructors prefer that you refute the opposition before beginning your confirmation. There is reasonable cause for such placement, especially if your opponents' views are shared strongly by your audience. However, if your opponents' arguments are weak, you can afford to delay refutation until the end of your own argument, using your discussion to build a case against your opponents' views. If your audience is hostile to your views, it might work to your advantage, psychologically, to delay your refutation until the end of your argument, to keep the direct attack of your opposition out of sight as long as possible. You need not remind your audience at the outset of your opposition, thus closing their ears to the remainder of what you have to say. By placing the refutation at the end, you may dispose your audience momentarily to hear what you have to say without compounding their hostility. Finally, you can also incorporate refutation wherever it is needed in each paragraph, rather than placing it in a separate section.

OUTLINE FOR A DEDUCTIVE ARGUMENT ESSAY

I. Introduction
      A.   Lead-in to your topic
              1. Startling statistic and/or
              2. Interesting example
      B.   Statement of the conclusion of your syllogism; the proposition
              or claim you are going to defend

II. Narration

    A.   Statement of background information to clarify your topic and to illustrate the problem you are dealing with. You might need to include here definitions of terms relevant to your argument.

    B.   Statement of the major premise and the minor premise that lead to your conclusion.(Note: one option to this method is to combine paragraphs I and II into a single paragraph. Consult your instructor for preference.)

Confirmation

III.   Statement of major premise as topic sentence

  A. Evidence #1 supporting the truth of your major premise.
- 1. Examples
- 2. Statistics
- 3. Authority

  B. Evidence #2 supporting the truth of your major premise
- 1. Examples
- 2. Statistics
- 3. Authority

IV.   Statement of minor premise as topic sentence

  A. Evidence #1 supporting the truth of your minor premise
- 1. Examples
- 2. Statistics
- 3. Authority

  B. Evidence #2 supporting the truth of your minor premise
- 1. Examples
- 2. Statistics
- 3. Authority

V.   Restatement of conclusion of syllogism as topic sentence

  A. Evidence #1 supporting the benefits to your audience of accepting your conclusion.

  B. Evidence #2 supporting the benefits of your audience of accepting your conclusion.

VI.   **Refutation** (optional here–see discussion of refutation above)

  A. Statement of counter argument (alternative conclusion) #1
- 1. Evidence #1 to refute or mitigate the force of A
- 2. Evidence #2 to refute or mitigate the force of A

  B. Statement of counter argument (alternative conclusion) #2
- 1. Evidence #1 to refute or mitigate the force of B
- 2. Evidence #2 to refute or mitigate the force of B

VII.   **Conclusion** A strong appeal for acceptance of your conclusion and/or a call to action.

Note there exist at least two options available to you when constructing your deductive argument outline, the introductory paragraph and the refutation paragraphs. Your instructor will indicate his or her preferences regarding this format.

OUTLINE FOR AN INDUCTIVE ARGUMENT ESSAY

I. **Introduction**
    A.   Lead-in to your topic
        1. Startling statistic and/or
        2. Interesting example
    B.   Statement of the generalization you have reached through your research; the proposition or claim you are going to defend in your argument.

II. **Narration**
    A.   Statement of background information to clarify your topic and to illustrate the problem you are dealing with. You might need to include here definitions of terms relevant to your argument.
    B.   Statement listing in one sentence at least three major pieces of evidence (x,y, and z) that support your generalization or claim.

Confirmation
III.   First major piece of supporting evidence as topic sentence.
    A. Subtopic #1 supporting X
        1. Examples
        2. Statistics
        3. Authority
    B. Subtopic #2 supporting X
        1. Examples
        2. Statistics
        3. Authority

IV.   Second major piece of supporting evidence as topic sentence.
    A. Subtopic #1 supporting Y
        1. Examples
        2. Statistics
        3. Authority
    B. Subtopic #2 supporting Y
        1. Examples
        2. Statistics
        3. Authority

V.   Third major piece of supporting evidence as topic sentence.
    A. Subtopic #1 supporting Z
        1. Examples
        2. Statistics
        3. Authority

    B. Subtopic #2 supporting Z
          1. Examples
          2. Statistics
          3. Authority

VI. **Refutation** (optional here–see discussion of refutation above)
      A.   Statement of counter argument (alternative conclusion) #1
          1. Evidence #1 to refute or mitigate the force of A
          2. Evidence #2 to refute or mitigate the force of A
      B.   Statement of counter argument (alternative conclusion) #2
          1. Evidence #1 to refute or mitigate the force of B
          2. Evidence #2 to refute or mitigate the force of B

VII. **Conclusion**–strong appeal for acceptance of your generalization and/or a call
          to action.

While this format is the standard method of organizing an inductive essay, it offers options to the student in the construction of the introductory paragraph (you may wish to combine paragraphs I and II in the above outline), and you may prefer to insert your refutation into each of the body paragraphs rather than have a separate section for refutation at the end of the essay. Consult your instructor for guidelines and preferences.

CHECKLIST

1.   Are your premises true? Will your implied premises be clear to your reader?

2.   Did you check your premises and reasoning to make sure your argument is sound, true, and valid?

3.   Did you make certain that your enthymeme's missing portion does not alter the argument?

4.   Is your argument free of logical fallacies?

5.   Is your representation of the facts for your argument honest and accurate?

6.   Does your proposition or thesis statement say what you want it to say, and does it clearly indicate your purpose?

7.   Is your tone consistent with your purpose, audience, and subject matter? Does it contribute to the development of your ethos?

8.   Have you identified your audience and adopted the appropriate voice for your audience?

9.   Did you use restraint with your emotional appeals? Are your emotional appeals appropriate for your audience and subject matter?

10.   Is your argument supported with adequate and convincing examples?

11.   Have you indicated your order or pattern of development, either by listing reasons (inductive) or premises (deductive)?

12. Have you accounted for the arguments of the opposition and refuted them early in the essay, throughout your discussion, or before your conclusion?
13. Are your transitions clear and logical?
14. Does your conclusion make a significant contribution to your audience's understanding of your purpose?

H. L. Mencken's essay, "Reflections on War," is a deductive argument stating that war will not be easily abolished. The author states his major premise in the second sentence of the first paragraph. What are his minor premise and conclusion? Be prepared to discuss the truth and/or validity of Mencken's argument.

REFLECTIONS ON WAR
H. L. MENCKEN

The thing constantly overlooked by those hopefuls who talk of abolishing war is that it is by no means an evidence of decay but rather a proof of health and vigor. To fight seems to be as natural to man as to eat. Civilization limits and wars upon the impulse but it can never quite eliminate it. Whenever the effort seems to be most successful–that is, whenever man seems to be submitting most willingly to discipline, the spark is nearest to the powder barrel. Here repression achieves its inevitable work. The most warlike people under civilization are precisely those who submit most docilely to the rigid inhibitions of peace. Once they break through the bounds of their repressed but steadily accumulating pugnacity, their destructiveness runs to great lengths. Throwing off the chains of order, they leap into the air and kick their legs. Of all the nations engaged in the two World Wars the Germans, who were the most rigidly girded by conceptions of renunciation and duty, showed the most gusto for war for its own sake.

The powerful emotional stimulus of war, its evocation of motives and ideals which, whatever their error, are at least more stimulating than those which impel a man to get and keep a safe job–that is too obvious to need laboring. The effect on the individual soldier of its very horror, filling him with a sense of the heroic, increases enormously his self-respect. This increase in self-respect reacts upon the nation, and tends to save it from the deteriorating effects of industrial discipline. In the main, soldiers are men of humble position and talents–laborers, petty mechanics, young fellows without definite occupation. Yet no one can deny that the veteran shows a certain superiority in dignity to the average man of his age and experience. He has played his part in significant events; he has been a citizen in a far more profound sense than any mere workman can ever be. The effects of all this are plainly seen in his bearing and his whole attitude of mind. War may make a fool of man, but it by no means degrades him; on the contrary, it tends to exalt him, and its net effects are much like those of motherhood on women.

That war is a natural revolt against the necessary but extremely irksome discipline of civilization is shown by the difficulty with which men on returning from it re-adapt themselves to a round of petty duties and responsibilities. This was notably apparent after the Civil War. It took three or four years for the young men engaged in that conflict to steel themselves to the depressing routine of everyday endeavor. Many of them, in fact, found it quite impossible. They could not go back to shovelling coal or tending a machine without intolerable pain. Such men flocked the West, where adventure still awaited them and discipline was still slack. In the same way, after the Franco-Prussian War, thousands of young German veterans came to the United States, which seemed to them one vast Wild West. True enough, they soon found that discipline was necessary here as well as at home, but it was a slacker discipline and they themselves exaggerated its slackness in their imagination. At all events, it had the charm of the unaccustomed.

We commonly look upon the discipline of war as vastly more rigid than any discipline necessary in time of peace, but this is an error. The strictest military discipline imaginable is still looser than that prevailing in the average assembly-line. The soldier, at worst, is still able to exercise the highest conceivable functions of freedom–that is, he is permitted to steal and to kill. No discipline prevailing in peace gives him anything even remotely resembling this. He is, in war, in the position of a free adult; in peace he is almost always in the position of a child. In war things are excused by success, even violations of discipline. In peace, speaking generally, success is inconceivable except as a function of discipline.

The hope of abolishing war is largely based upon the fact that men have long since abandoned the appeal to arms in their private disputes and submitted themselves to the jurisdiction of courts. Starting from this fact, it is contended that disputes between nations should be settled in the same manner, and that the adoption of the reform would greatly promote the happiness of the world.

Unluckily, there are three flaws in the argument. The first, which is obvious, lies in the circumstances that a system of legal remedies is of no value if it is not backed by sufficient force to impose its decisions upon even the most powerful litigants–a sheer impossibility in international affairs, for even if one powerful litigant might be coerced, it would be plainly impossible to coerce a combination, and it is precisely a combination of the powerful that is most to be feared. The second lies in the fact that any legal system, to be worthy of credit, must be administered by judges who have no personal interest in the litigation before them–another impossibility, for all the judges in the international court, in the case of disputes between first-class powers, would either be appointees of those powers, or appointees of inferior powers that were under their direct influence, or obliged to consider the effects of their enmity. The third objection lies in the fact, frequently forgotten, that the courts of justice which now exist do not actually dispense justice, but only law, and that this law is frequently in direct conflict, not only with what one litigant honestly believes to be his rights, but also with what he believes to be his honor. Practically every litigation, in truth, ends with either one litigant or the other nursing what appears to him as an outrage upon him. For both litigants to go away satisfied that justice has been done is almost unheard of.

In dispute between man and man this dissatisfaction is not of serious consequence. The aggrieved party has no feasible remedy; if he doesn't like it, he must lump it. In particular, he has no feasible remedy against a judge or juryman who, in his view, has treated him ill; if he essayed vengeance, the whole strength of the unbiased masses of men would be exerted to destroy him, and that strength is so enormous, compared to his own puny might, that it would swiftly and certainly overwhelm him. But in the case of first-class nations there would be no such overwhelming force in restraint. In a few cases the general opinion of the world might be so largely against them that it would force them to acquiesce in the judgment rendered, but in perhaps a majority of important cases there would be sharply divided sympathies, and it would constantly encourage resistance. Against that resistance there would be nothing save the counter-resistance of the opposition–i.e., the judge against the aggrieved litigant, the twelve jurymen against the aggrieved litigant's friends, with no vast and impersonal force of neutral public opinion behind the former.

In his essay "The Right to Fail," William Zinsser approaches the college dropout from a rather unconventional perspective. Using the inductive argument, the author proposes that the dropout is not today's failure but rather tomorrow's symbol of individualism, self-awareness, and ambition.

THE RIGHT TO FAIL
WILLIAM ZINSSER

I like "dropout" as an addition to the American language because it's brief and it's clear. What I don't like is that we use it almost entirely as a dirty word.

We only apply it to people under twenty-one. Yet an adult who spends his days and nights watching mindless TV programs is more of a dropout than an eighteen-year-old who quits college, with its frequently mindless courses, to become, say, a VISTA volunteer. For the young, dropping out is often a way of dropping in.

To hold this opinion, however, is little short of treason in America. A boy or girl who leaves college is branded a failure–and the right to fail is one of the few freedoms that this country does not grant its citizens. The American dream is a dream of "getting ahead," painted in strokes of gold wherever we look. Our advertisements and TV commercials are a hymn to material success, our magazine articles a toast to people who made it to the top. Smoke the right cigarette or drive the right car–so the ads imply–and the girls will be swooning into your deodorized arms and caressing your expensive lapels. Happiness goes to the man who has the sweet smell of achievement. He is our national idol, and everybody else is our national fink.

I want to put in a word for the fink, especially the teen-age fink, because if we give him time to get through his finkdom–if we release him from the pressure of attaining certain goals by a certain age–he has a good chance of becoming our national idol, a Jefferson or a Thoreau, a Buckminster Fuller or an Adlai Stevenson, a man with a mind of his own. We need mavericks and dissenters and dreamers far more than we need junior vice-presidents, but we paralyze them by insisting that every step be a step up to the next rung of the ladder. Yet in the fluid years of youth, the only way for boys and girls to find their proper road is often to take a hundred side trips, poking out in different directions, faltering, drawing back, and starting again.

"But what if we fail?" they ask, whispering the dreadful word across the Generation Gap to their parents, who are back home at the Establishment, nursing their "middle-class values" and cultivating their "goal-oriented society." The parents whisper back: "Don't!"

What they should say is "Don't be afraid to fail!" Failure isn't fatal. Countless people have had a bout with it and come out stronger as a result. Many have even come out famous. History is strewn with eminent dropouts, "loners" who followed their own trail, not worrying about its odd twists and turns because they had faith in their own sense of direction. To read their biographies is always exhilarating, not only because they beat the system, but because their system was better than the one that they beat.

Luckily, such rebels still turn up often enough to prove that individualism, though badly threatened, is not extinct. Much has been written, for instance, about the fitful scholastic career of Thomas P.F. Hoving, New York's former Parks Commissioner and now director of the Metropolitan Museum of Art. Hoving was a dropout's dropout, entering and leaving schools as if they were motels, often at the request of the management. Still, he must have learned something during those unorthodox years, for he dropped in again at the top of his profession.

His case reminds me of another boyhood–that of Holden Caulfield in J.D.Salinger's *The Catcher in the Rye*, the most popular literary hero of the postwar period. There is nothing accidental about the grip that this dropout continues to hold on the affections of an entire American generation. Nobody else, real or invented, has made such an engaging shambles of our "goal-oriented society," so gratified our secret belief that the "phonies" are in power and the good guys up the creek. Whether Holden has also reached the top of his chosen field today is one of those speculations that delight fanciers of good fiction. I speculate that he has. Holden Caulfield, incidentally, is now thirty-six.

I'm not urging everyone to go out and fail just for the sheer therapy of it, or to quit college just to coddle some vague discontent. Obviously it's better to succeed than to flop, and in general a long education is more helpful than a short one. (Thanks to my own education, for example, I can tell George Eliot from T.S. Eliot, I can handle the pluperfect tense in French, and I know that Caesar beat the Helvetii because he had enough frumentum.) I only mean that failure isn't bad in itself or success automatically good.

Fred Zinnemann, who has directed some of Hollywood's most honored movies, was asked by a reporter, when *A Man for All Seasons* won every prize, about his previous film *Behold a Pale Horse*, which was a box-office disaster . "I don't feel any obligation to be successful," Zinnemann replied. "Success can be dangerous– you feel you know it all. I've learned a great deal from my failures." A similar point was made by Richard Brooks about his ambitious money loser, *Lord Jim*. Recalling the three years of his life that went into it, talking almost with elation about the troubles that befell his unit in Cambodia, Brooks told me that he learned more about his craft from this considerable failure than from his many earlier hits.

It's a point, of course, that applies throughout the arts. Writers, playwrights, painters, and composers work in the expectation of periodic defeat, but they wouldn't keep going back into the arena if they thought it was the end of the world. It isn't the end of the world. For an artist–and perhaps for anybody–it is the only way to grow.

Today's younger generation seems to know that this is true, seems willing to take risks in life that artists take in art. "Society," needless to say, still has the upper hand–it sets the goals and condemns as a failure everybody who won't play. But the dropouts and the hippies are not as afraid of failure as their parents and grandparents. This could mean, as their elders might say, that they are just plumb lazy, secure in the comforts of an affluent state. It could also mean, however, that they just don't buy the old standards of success and are rapidly writing new ones.

Recently it was announced, for instance, that more than two hundred thousand Americans have inquired about service in VISTA (the domestic Peace Corps) and that, according to a Gallup survey, "more than three million American college students would serve VISTA in some capacity if given the opportunity." This is hardly the road to riches or to an executive suite. Yet I have met many of these young volunteers, and they are not pining for traditional success. On the contrary, they appear more fulfilled than the average vice-president with a swimming pool.

Who is to say, then, if there is any right path to the top, or even to say what the top consists of? Obviously the colleges don't have more than a partial answer– otherwise the young would not be so disaffected with an education that they consider vapid. Obviously business does not have the answer–otherwise the young would not be so scornful of its call to be an organization man.

The fact is, nobody has the answer, and the dawning awareness of this fact seems to me one of the best things happening in America today. Success and failure are again becoming individual visions, as they were when the country was younger, not rigid categories. Maybe we are learning again to cherish this right of every person to succeed on his own terms and to fail as often as necessary along the way.

(1970)

CHAPTER FIVE

CRITICAL ANALYSIS OF AN ESSAY

You probably have already read, and written, a number of essays this semester, and you have probably had occasion throughout your career in school to read numerous short articles in magazines and newspapers or on your computer. In its broadest sense, the word *essay* can cover everything from a short report to a lengthy, technical article. The motives behind essays are also varied. Essays are written to entertain, to explain, to persuade, to justify one's actions, to beg for support or money, to sell, to condemn some person or action, to report on what has been done in an experiment or accomplished on a job, to encourage patriotism, to inflame one group of people against another, to deceive, to express adoration and love–the possibilities are myriad.

Teachers of rhetoric use the more inclusive term *text* to cover such variety, and they add oral communication to the list. Modern critics engage in analyses of such divergent texts as Fourth-of-July speeches, parking regulations, and recipes. Modern critics also approach their texts from an astonishing variety of perspectives: there are sociological critics, feminist critics, historical critics, psychological critics, Marxist critics, cultural critics, post-modern critics. A text to contemporary critics is anything but a group of words whose meaning is carved in stone, and just as there are common elements of fiction that help us to understand and analyze short stories, so there are, though perhaps less standardized than in fiction, elements common to all prose texts.

ELEMENTS OF RHETORIC

As Chapter One of this book explains, all written texts–whether they are essays or handwritten notes–contain certain common, rhetorical elements. As you analyze an essay or text, you should examine and identify each of the following:

Audience. When you analyze an essay, always try to identify the intended audience of a particular text. The intended audience of an essay, for example, may be identified by looking at the author's style (his diction and sentence structure), the complexity and type of ideas discussed, the essay's length, its purpose and situation, and the persona adopted by the writer. Where an essay is published, in *Time*, *Field and Stream*, or *Scientific American*, is also a clue to the educational level and

151

interests of the audience. The intended audience is discovered inductively; for example we might determine that the 5:30 evening news is aimed toward an older, conservative, affluent audience by noting the number of advertisements shown during the half-hour for such things as denture cream, investment opportunities, and luxury automobiles.

Purpose. In analyzing an essay you should always attempt to state the author's purpose. What does the writer want the reader to understand, to feel, to do? Writers want to change their readers' beliefs or attitudes, make them laugh, make them cry, make them understand a complex issue. A list of purposes would be very long: to entertain, to persuade, to explain, to frighten, to teach, to anger, to placate.

Situation. All discourse is constrained by the situation in which it appears. Situation, loosely defined, is the context in which a particular text appears or the occasion on which a discourse is delivered. For example, the following are different situations with different contexts: you are required to write a ten-page report on the causes of the Civil War in an American history class; you volunteer to speak to your younger brother's scout troop on tae kwon do; you write a letter applying for a summer job at Yellowstone National Park. Each situation or context demands a different response. In analyzing an essay, you should try to determine the situation or context in which the essay was written and the specific constraints such a situation places on what the writer says. Keys to context or situation for published essays include when it was published, in what magazine or journal it is published, and the tone and language employed by the writer.

Voice. The writer reveals his personality, his attitudes, his prejudices and desires through what he says and the way he says it. Just as there is a narrator who tells a story from a particular point of view, just as there is a "voice" in poetry, so there is a speaker in an essay, a **persona** (in Latin, literally "actor's mask"). A writer may unconsciously reveal the kind of person he is through what he writes. We may determine that he is arrogant, friendly, narrow-minded or flippant. More often the writer's purpose, his audience, and the writing situation cause him to assume or adopt a persona. Aristotle says, for example, that when trying to persuade an audience we should present ourselves as honest, open-minded, and knowledgeable, with the best interests of our audience in mind (see Chapter Four). The persona a writer adopts may also reflect his social or cultural role. For example, we expect a priest and a movie critic to write in certain ways reflecting their different roles and positions in society.

Tone, finally, is closely connected to persona. Writers may adopt tones that are serious, playful, ironic, antagonistic, or passionate, among others. In writing a critical analysis of an essay, you should determine the persona and tone of the writer. Whether consciously or unconsciously revealed, persona is crucial to the total effect a text has on its audience.

RATIONAL APPEALS

Aristotle believed that what separated mankind from other animals was the ability to reason. Many writers thus employ rational appeals in an attempt to convince their audiences to accept or reject particular beliefs, claims, or courses of action. When a scientist writes a paper claiming to have discovered a new sub-atomic particle, when a biotechnology lab claims to have discovered the gene that causes Huntington's disease, when an engineer claims that a system of mass-transit will solve a city's transportation problems--all support their claims with evidence and logic. If a writer provides little or no proof for the claims he or she makes, you should be wary of accepting those claims, even though the claims might seem to be true. Further, in writing a critical analysis of an essay that focuses on its rational appeal, you will first need to review Chapter Four, which defines *logic* and *argument*, as well as any section of the handbook that discusses logic. In addition you should consider the following:

Burden of Proof. A basic principle of reason, as of law, is that the burden of proof rests with the person making a claim. A claim is a proposition, a statement about what is or is not true. If the state claims that Joe Smith murdered his wife, for instance, then the state must prove beyond a reasonable doubt that Joe is guilty; Joe does not have to prove that he did *not* murder his wife. Careful writers will not make claims that they cannot back up. Thus, when you read essays, always look to see what **evidence and support** the writer provides to back up his claims. Further, be wary of non-testable claims. A non-testable claim is set up in such a way that no possible evidence or change in circumstances could render it false. As Stephen Jay Gould writes in *Evolution as Fact and Theory*: "A set of ideas that cannot, in principle, be falsified is not science. . . . Unbeatable systems are dogma. . . ." For example, if someone argues that people *always* act from selfish motives, and no counter example you come up with, no action or set of circumstances you devise, is ever accepted as an example of an unselfish action, it is a non-testable claim; that is, it is an assertion of belief. Beliefs are strongly held attitudes involving judgments about the world and are often accepted as articles of faith, beyond the realm of rational inquiry.

Fallacies. Logicians have identified a number of common fallacies (faulty reasoning that may appear to be good); you need to look for them when you analyze a writer's argument. Refer to Chapter Four and to your handbook for a list of the most common fallacies.

Toulmin Analysis. In an *Introduction to Reasoning* (1984), Steven Toulmin provides an attractive scheme for analyzing arguments:

First find the **claim**, the conclusion of the argument or the thesis of the essay. Make sure that the claim is a testable-claim (that it is possible to support the claim by evidence), and that it is not preposterous or whimsical. For example, the following claim was made by a student at North Harris College: *Women should not be allowed in ground combat units in the army.*

Next look for the **grounds** that support that claim, that is, the evidence the writer gives in support of his proposition. Again you should consult your handbook for ways of evaluating evidence. For example, the student supported the above claim with the following evidence: *The fact that a woman can get pregnant may keep her from performing her task, thus rendering the squad ineffective to perform in a combat situation. An example of this situation occurred when I was stationed at Ft. Rucker, Alabama; in my squad there were four men and each of us was assigned a different task: machine gunner, sniper, squad leader, and Dragon gunner. We went on an exercise and the machine gunner became ill. He was rushed to the hospital, and I had to take over his task. The result of his illness was a catastrophe. When we attacked the enemy we were slower because I had to perform the jobs of two men. Therefore, the squad lost the battle, which not only had an effect on the squad but produced a chain reaction and destroyed the whole company. Thus if a woman were to be assigned to a combat unit and she became pregnant, it would have a negative influence on the whole company."*

Third look for any **Warrant** that the writer gives to show that the evidence is relevant to the claim. For example, if the writer cites the statement of an authority, does he or she give the credentials of the authority? Is the authority speaking in his own field of expertise? If a major scientific study is discussed as evidence, are other confirming studies also cited? For example, the student writing on women in combat added the following to the evidence given above: *"More than 1,200 pregnant women were evacuated from the Gulf region during the Gulf War; that is the equivalent of two infantry battalions. If the loss of one man from a squad can cause a company's performance to drop, how much more harm would there be with the loss of two battalions of soldiers? It would have a devastating effect."*

Fourth look for **Backing**, information that gives added support to the Warrant. For example, our student next added the following sentence to the above warrant: *"The statistics on the number of women evacuated from the Gulf War were released in a report by the Pentagon."*

Finally, check to see if the writer has given a **Rebuttal** to counter claims and arguments; that is, has he mentioned and then refuted claims that contradict his own? Also see if the writer has explained apparent exceptions to his evidence or mitigated the force of the counter claim in some way. For example, our student included the following in a refutation section: *"Some women argue that many other countries use women in combat roles. This statement is not altogether true. There are very few countries that have women in combat roles. Israel was one of those countries who tried to put women in combat, but they quickly stopped the program because it was a catastrophe. Israel still uses women in its military, but does not allow them in combat."*

Using Toulmin's scheme will help you to see the structure of the argument you are analyzing and the strengths and weaknesses of that argument; however, simply because a writer supplies a warrant and backing for a claim does not mean that his argument is sound or cogent. Be sure to apply the standards of appropriate evidence and reasoning to the argument (see Chapter Four and your handbook). Finally, remember that arguments are made to be convincing and that we are daily inundated by the mass media with hundreds of claims. The only rational stance to adopt in a world such as ours is one based on a respect for truth and an attitude of skepticism. In his essay "Of Cannibals," Montaigne says,"We should be on our guard against clinging to vulgar opinions and . . . we should judge things by light of reason, and not from common rumor."

EMOTIONAL APPEALS

If all people were as dispassionate as Mr. Spock or Data on the *Star Trek* series, then an account of the argument of an essay, of its rational appeal, would be the only analysis we would need to make. Yet while all people may be born with the capacity to reason, reasoning well requires knowledge, training, and practice. However, to echo the French eighteenth-century writer Jean Jacques Rousseau, we *felt* before we *thought*. Feeling, Rousseau said, is primary; it, not reason, makes us human.

Emotions, therefore, are powerful forces in humans, and while we might think of some people as "lacking feeling," most people are strongly affected by their emotions. While an attempt to analyze the emotions is best left to psychologists, a primitive classification might group them in terms of opposites: love-hate, desire-fear, compassion-repulsion for example. Further, while we consider our emotions *natural*, we know that these emotions are conditioned by our culture, our social background, and our individual upbringing. Writers appeal to their particular audience's emotions in order to motivate them to action or to gain their commitment to a belief or a group. For example, writers are well-aware that people respond emotionally to words and images that appeal to certain deep-seated human desires for love, sex, nourishment, and pleasure. Conversely, people respond emotionally to what they fear: rejection, privation, pain, and death. On the one hand, writers appeal to their audience's sense of comfort which they derive from belonging to a group such as a family, city, state, or country, or their affiliation with a certain ethnic or linguistic group, economic class or political party; on the other hand, writers play on their audience's fear and distrust of things or people that are strange or foreign to them.

The language used in emotional appeals can be direct or subtle. Writers can use words that have an obvious and immediate emotional impact on their audience and which are calculated to provoke a strong and predictable response. For instance, how do you react to the following words: *jerk, extremist, atheist, bubba, dumb blonde*; or to *peace, patriot, Christian, entrepreneur, mother*? For example, note Richard Nixon's use of emotionally charged language in the following paragraph, the conclusion to a famous speech he made on television in September of 1952; at the time many people were calling for his resignation as candidate for vice-president under Dwight Eisenhower because of allegations of misappropriation of campaign funds:

> *But just let me say this last word. Regardless of what happens, I am going to continue this fight. I am going to campaign up and down America until we drive the crooks and the communists and those that defend them out of Washington, and remember, folks, Eisenhower is a great man, and a vote for Eisenhower is a vote for what is good for America.*

The words used in this passage depict two contrasting sets of images. The first set creates the image of a man battling against the forces of evil: "... I am going to continue this *fight* ... until *we* [Note the shift in person. He is one of us.] drive the *crooks* and the *communists* and *those that defend them* out of *Washington*...." Here is the image of a man trying to drive out evil from one of our political holy places, perhaps like Jesus drove the moneychangers out of the Temple. The second set of words–"*Eisenhower is a great man*" and "what is *good for America*"–evokes the feelings of pride we have in a renowned military leader and associates those feelings with our feelings of patriotism. These feelings of greatness, goodness, and loyalty to our homeland are linked to the lonely fight against evil conducted by this man on our behalf.

The emotion of a passage may also arise naturally from the writer's subject and the intensity of the writer's engagement with that subject. For example, few would question the sincerity of the emotion expressed in the following sentences by the Russian writer Leo Tolstoy who, at the peak of his career as a writer, with fame, wealth, an interesting circle of friends, a family–all that a person could desire– suddenly experienced a terrible, gripping sense of the utter futility of life. He wrote of this life-altering experience in *My Confession* (here translated by David Patterson):

> *If not today, then tomorrow sickness and death will come (indeed, they were already approaching) to everyone, to me, and nothing will remain except the stench and the worms. My deeds, whatever they may be, will be forgotten sooner or later, and I myself will be no more. Why, then, do anything? How can anyone fail to see this and live? That's what is amazing! It is possible to live only as long as life intoxicates us; once we are sober we cannot help seeing that it is all a delusion, a stupid delusion! Nor is there anything funny or witty about it; it is only cruel and stupid.*

The intensity of feeling in this passage arises from the writer's emotional involvement with his subjects, death and the meaning of life. Tolstoy conveys his fear of death and his sense of the utter meaninglessness of life in such phrases as "sickness and death will come," "the stench and the worms," and "I myself will be no more." These words are simple, direct, and unadorned. Tolstoy also employs an everyday image of a drunk versus a sober man to convey his feelings about everyman's blindness to the reality of his own death. The emotions we feel when we read such a passage arise directly from the subject and the writer's engagement with it. Tolstoy's primary purpose is to convey his feelings, to make us feel what he himself feels.

In writing a critical analysis of an essay that focuses on its emotional content, therefore, you will need to look carefully for any emotionally charged words used by the writer, at any images the writer creates through description, and at any figurative language the writer uses (see the section on analysis of style later in this chapter). In addition, ask yourself the following questions:

How important is the writer's use of emotion to the overall purpose of the essay? Is the writer's use of emotion appropriate to the subject and occasion? Does the writer's use of emotionally charged language dominate the essay, or is it subordinated to more rational arguments? Is the writer's use of emotion effective and consistent with his purpose?

Answering these questions will also help you decide what the writer's attitude is toward his material and his audience. For example, is the writer asking the reader to sympathize or be outraged? Is the writer being satiric or ironic?

Finally, what can an analysis of the emotional appeals made in an essay tell us? First, it can clarify a complex argument by helping us separate the emotional appeals from the logical ones. Focusing on the language and metaphors employed by the writer in developing his emotional appeal can help us gain emotional distance, and thus objectivity. Therefore we may begin to notice that the writer gives little solid evidence to support his claims and essentially begs the question he is trying to prove. Or we may find that the emotional language drives home a point abundantly supported by evidence and reason. Second, an analysis of the emotional language and appeals in a speech or an essay can sensitize us to the sometimes subtle assault on our emotions made in newspapers and magazines, or over television and radio by politicians, preachers, teachers, and radio talk show hosts (and overwhelmingly in advertisements). Studying the emotional appeals made even in a single essay can help us to understand and to arm ourselves against such assaults. Emotions are very powerful; be wary of allowing yours to be manipulated.

ETHICAL APPEALS

Besides being rational and emotional creatures, humans are also moral beings. We all like to think of ourselves as "being good" and "doing what is right." Thus, if writers can convince us that what they propose for us to do or believe is moral, just, or right, we will more easily go along with them. Such appeals are what Aristotle called *ethical appeals*. In making an ethical appeal, a writer may appeal to our religious beliefs (adultery may be condemned because it is forbidden in the Bible), to our sense of fair play (we may be told that eliminating the capital gains tax will unfairly benefit the very rich who already pay few taxes), to our belief in law (we may be told that we should not smoke marijuana because it is illegal), to our sense of loyalty to an ideal (it may be argued that political action committees should be severely curtailed because they are inherently undemocratic), or to our empathy for fellow humans (all people deserve to have food and shelter).

The power of ethical appeals comes from their assumption of moral authority. If a writer's audience is composed of strong believers in the Bible, for instance, the writer can use scripture as a source of authority. Yet someone who does not accept the moral force of the Bible will hardly be convinced by references to scripture. The same is true of other groups. Some of the most intractable of contemporary conflicts derive from the fact that different groups have different moral bases for their beliefs. Again, to echo Aristotle, in making an ethical appeal writers appeal to what their audience considers to be good or right over and above what they consider useful or in their own interest. For example, Jane Goodall makes an essentially ethical appeal when she states that "all except the most primitive of non-human animals experience pain, and . . . 'higher' animals have emotions similar to the human emotions that we label pleasure or sadness, fear or despair." She implies that, since animals have feelings just as we do, it is no more right for us to subject them to suffering than it would be for us to subject other humans to suffering. Rhetorically, she asks: "How can we, the citizens of civilized, western countries, tolerate laboratories which–from the point of view of animal inmates–are not unlike concentration camps?" Her point is that no matter what benefits we receive, it is simply wrong to experiment on animals.

Another way of making an ethical appeal is for writers to present themselves as knowledgeable, thorough, and fair. That is, they present themselves as reasonable and trustworthy. They do this, as you can in your own essays, first by showing that they know a lot about the subject. They may reveal their credentials (their college degrees, their current position in government or at a university for example), they may discuss the research they themselves have done or discuss a wide range of research conducted by others (up-to-date research, of course), or they may provide convincing examples and other support for their generalizations and conclusions. Second, they may show their thoroughness by their consideration of all relevant material and points of view that have a bearing on their subject. Finally, they may show their fairness by considering opposing points of view and differing interpretations of the facts, by discussing those other positions courteously, and by acknowledging the strengths of those positions where reason demands they should.

Writers are like trial lawyers; they must convince their readers. While it is a popular cliché that "facts speak for themselves," we should be mature enough to realize that they don't; they must be given a voice and a context by a speaker or a writer, and that voice shapes the way we understand the facts.

ANALYSIS OF STYLE

Jonathan Swift described style as proper words in proper places. Today the word *style* is used in a number of different ways to describe such things as fashion, written formats (as in letter style), and the way people live (as in lifestyle). Written prose style reflects the education, experience, and habits of thought of the writer as well as the basic elements of rhetoric: purpose, audience, and situation. Style is also part of the argumentative and emotional design of an essay. The clarity and force of an argument depend as much on style as on logic; likewise the emotional impact of an essay depends heavily on style. Before beginning your analysis of the style of an essay, you should refer to the section in your handbook that discusses style.

To analyze a writer's style you must focus on the words a writer uses and the way those words are arranged in phrases, clauses, sentences, and paragraphs. The purpose of a stylistic analysis is to show how a writer's language, sentence structure, and imagery contribute to his overall purpose and design (or how they contradict it) as well as the way they reveal the writer's attitude toward his subject matter and audience. You can approach a stylistic analysis in one of two ways:

1. You can take one element of style, say the writer's use of figurative language, and analyze the entire essay in terms of this one element alone.

2. You can take a single paragraph, or several related short paragraphs, and do a more complete analysis of several elements of style.

In general, a writer's style depends on the way he uses the following:

Diction. The kinds of words writers choose, their *diction*, depend upon their educational and linguistic background and upon the audience and purpose of their essay. We can arrange words along a scale based upon an analogy with social custom. For example, just as men wear suits and ties on serious and formal social occasions, so writers use formal diction on serious occasions and for serious purposes. Formal diction is characterized by polysyllabic words, many with Latin and Greek roots (*transference, multidimensional, orthodox*), abstract words (*cognitive, affective, discipline*) and words specific to a particular science or profession (medical terminology or computerese for example). Formal diction contributes to a formal style, which is also characterized by its objectivity and the writer's use of the third person, both of which distance the writer from the reader. Formal diction is often used in college textbooks, scientific journals, and philosophical essays; formal style is standard for exposition of serious subjects directed to educated audiences.

At the other end of the scale, comparable to men wearing T-shirts, cut-off shorts, and tennis shoes, is highly informal diction. Informal diction is characterized by monosyllabic words, many with Anglo-Saxon roots (short, familiar words such as *man, run, fish, speak*), colloquialisms, dialect (*"y'all"*), slang, contractions, and non-standard usage (*"ain't"*). Informal diction more closely copies everyday speech and contributes to an informal style, characterized by its subjectivity and the writer's use of first person, which brings the writer and the audience closer together. Informal diction is used in personal letters, the personal essay, and all sorts of short, written communication. As always, audience and purpose are important in the degree of informality of one's diction and one's style. In between these two poles (say, a man wearing loafers, slacks and an open-necked shirt) is a broad range of diction that incorporates words from both ends to a greater or lesser degree.

Besides the degree of formality or informality of the diction of an essay, you can also look at whether the words a writer chooses tend to be more abstract or more concrete, more general or more specific, or more dependent on denotation or connotation.

Concrete words stand for things that you can touch and see, such as *book, desk, cat,* and *fireplace*. Writers use concrete words to help us visualize what we read. **Abstract words,** such as *honor, justice, love,* and *discourse* do not call up specific images; nevertheless we have some way of visualizing them: we can picture a child in the arms of its mother when we read the word *love,* for example. Even more removed from our ability to visualize, however, are certain super-abstract words generally deplored by most good writers as **jargon;** *factor, case, condition,* and *degree* are examples. It is very hard to visualize a *factor*. Concrete diction contributes to a more familiar style and brings us closer to the writer: we see what the writer has seen; we feel what the writer has felt.

Likewise, **specific words** bring up specific images, while **general words** help us to group classes of things. Again, we can set up a scale with very general words on one end and very specific ones on the other: *creature, animal, human, male, boy, son, Daniel*. Good writers are always moving between the general and the specific, going from one end of the scale to the other as they move between broad statements of ideas and issues and specific, detailed examples. Specific language helps us see how large philosophical, moral, or political issues affect us on a personal level. We want a wide-angle lens to show us the big picture; we need a telephoto lens to show us the details.

Finally, writers use words for their limited, **denotative** meaning or for their emotional associations, their **connotations.** Think of another scale with scientists on one end using words for their specific meanings and poets on the other end using words that have multiple meanings and wide associations. A writer's purpose and audience are again extremely important. A politician at a political rally, for example, may use such evocative words as *freedom, democracy, free enterprise,* and *family*. A scientist at the other extreme may use words like *dorsal, ventral,* and *suture* that have precise meanings. Scientists want to communicate their ideas directly and clearly; they neither want the confusion that might arise from using words that have multiple meanings nor the emotional reactions that highly connotative words might create.

160

Syntax. Syntax designates the way words are combined to form phrases, clauses, and sentences. One way to analyze a writer's prose style is to look at the sentences he habitually uses. For example, some writers use longer sentences than others, piling up phrases and clauses within a single sentence. Others prefer short, more direct sentences. The sentences of the American authors William Faulkner and Ernest Hemingway provide a classic example of this contrast:

The boy, crouched on his nail keg at the back of the crowded room, knew he smelled cheese, and more: from where he sat he could see the ranked shelves close-packed with the solid, squat, dynamic shapes of tin cans whose labels his stomach read, not from the lettering which meant nothing to his mind but from the scarlet devils and the silver curve of fish–this, the cheese which he knew he smelled and the hermetic meat which his intestines believed he smelled coming in intermittent gusts momentary and brief between the other constant one, the smell and sense just a little of fear because mostly of despair and grief, the old fierce pull of blood ("Barn Burning").

The girl stood up and walked to the end of the station. Across, on the other side, were fields of grain and trees along the banks of the Ebro. Far away, beyond the river, were mountains. The shadow of a cloud moved across the field of grain and she saw the river through the trees ("Hills Like White Elephants").

The first passage from Faulkner shows his preference for complex sentences with clauses embedded within clauses. The sentence is evocative and rich with emotional overtones. The second passage from Hemingway, however, shows his preference for short, simple sentences. The prose is direct and disarmingly simple.

What can we learn from an analysis of the sentence structure of such writers? First, we can gain insight into what might be called the "world view" or the psychological perspective of the writer. Faulkner's complex sentences reflect the complex world portrayed in his novels–a world where narrators try to recapture the past in recursive attempts to understand and reinterpret the present. Hemingway's habitual use of short, simple, subject-verb-object sentences reflects his belief, also portrayed in his fiction, that life is lonely and harsh and must be confronted directly with simple dignity. Second, a study of sentence structure can help us understand the power, effectiveness, and emotional impact of writing as well as learn, through an understanding of such techniques as repetition and parallelism, how to replicate such effects in our own sentences.

To determine sentence length, for example, count the number of words in each sentence in several paragraphs and divide by the number of sentences to get an average word length per sentence. (Count all the words, including function words such as articles and prepositions.) You might also count the number of very short sentences, say those under eight words, and the number of very long sentences, say those over thirty words. Again, to determine the frequency of the different types of sentences, count the number of sentences by type in several paragraphs. Determining sentence length and type, for example, tells us how well writers develop their topics, how detailed their explanations are, and how much they qualify their generalizations. Some writers hammer home their points with short, direct blows; others allow us to follow the chain of reasoning that leads them to subtle and complex truths. One benefit of an analysis of this sort is that you can compare the length and type of your author's sentences to your own; you may find that clarity is not necessarily the result of short, simple sentences, nor is brevity always the soul of wit.

Sentences are also defined as being **loose**–where the main clause or idea comes first and qualifying statements and dependent clauses are tacked on, or **periodic**–where the dependent clauses and qualifying statements come first and the main clause comes at the end. For example, consider the following two sentences:

I waited three long days in your outer office, continually embarrassed by the number of people who came, waited a short while, and went in, smirked at by secretaries traipsing in and out, and feeling degraded by the position of beggar I had to assume.

Continually embarrassed by the number of people who came, waited a short while, and went in, smirked at by secretaries traipsing in and out, and feeling degraded by the position of beggar I had to assume, I waited three long days in your outer office.

The first sentence trails off after the main clause about waiting for three days in an outer office by simply adding details, one after the other. The reader focuses on each added detail but in the process relegates the earlier ones to the back of the mind. By the end of the sentence, the importance of the three-day wait has waned. In the second sentence, however, tension and suspense are built up as we add one detail to the next because we don't know what they refer to. The answer explodes at the end, and we feel the frustration and sense of indignity the writer has had to endure for three long days. We usually write words one after the other, adding details, descriptions, and explanations as we think of them, following the normal subject-verb-object pattern of English. Loose sentences are thus the workhorses of prose; periodic sentences add drama, suspense, and intensity.

There are other qualities of syntax that are important in analyzing prose style. Books on rhetoric devote much time to such qualities, including the methods writers use to expand and collapse sentences, the way they use particular punctuation marks to achieve certain effects, and their methods of opening and closing sentences. Prominent among these other qualities are the ways writers employ **parallel sentence structure, antithesis**, and **repetition**.

Parallel sentence structure is discussed in your handbook. English demands, for example, that parallel or equal grammatical structures be used on either side of a coordinating conjunction: *"cat and dog," "running and playing," "jump and shoot,"* but not *"running and jump."* English also demands parallel grammatical structures in series: *"books, magazines, newspapers and television,"* but not *"books,* *magazines, and decided to leave.*" Writers employ more elaborate schemes of parallelism to develop parallel ideas and to give force to them. Consider the emotional impact of the following two sentences:

But, in a larger sense, we cannot dedicate–we cannot consecrate–we cannot hallow–this ground. (Lincoln's *Gettysburg Address*). In this justly famous sentence, Lincoln emphasizes his inability to say anything that could remotely capture the sacrifice and heroism of the men who fought at Gettysburg. By repeating the same phrase, "we cannot," three times, and by raising the importance and force of the verb each time–going from the rather mundane "dedicate" to the more spiritual "consecrate" and finally to the holy and sanctified "hallow"– Lincoln's sentence does what he says he cannot do.

In such condition, there is no place for industry, because the fruit thereof is uncertain: and consequently no culture of the earth; no navigation, nor use of the commodities that may be imported by sea; no commodious building; no instruments of moving, and removing, such things as require much force; no knowledge of the face of the earth; no account of time; no arts, no letters; no society; and which is worst of all, continual fear, and danger of violent death; and the life of man, solitary, poor, nasty, brutish, and short. (Thomas Hobbes's *Leviathan*). In this sentence, Hobbes describes man in a state of nature, before the advent of civilization. The sentence builds on a series of parallel "no" clauses indicating the bareness and harshness of man's condition without the rules and laws of society. It ends in a climax of short, parallel adjectives that have the force of machine gun bullets.

Sentences employing **antithesis** balance contrasting ideas in parallel structures. We use *but* or *or* instead of *and* many times to signal a contrasting idea. In the following opening lines (the sentence continues), from *A Tale of Two Cities*, Charles Dickens expresses the glaring contradictions in French society on the eve of the French Revolution: *It was the best of times, it was the worst of times, it was the age of wisdom, it was the age of foolishness, it was the epoch of belief, it was the epoch of incredulity, it was the season of Light, it was the season of Darkness, it was the spring of hope, it was the winter of despair. . . .*

Repetition of words, phrases, and sometimes whole sentences is used to drive home a point or build suspense or tension within a paragraph or essay. A famous example is the speech of Marc Antony in Act III, scene ii of Shakespeare's *Julius Caesar* where Antony repeats the ironic phrase "Brutus is an honourable man" four times in a short speech to the Roman mob. Look at the repetition in the following lines by Martin Luther King:

I have a dream that one day on the red hills of Georgia, sons of former slaves and sons of former slave-owners will be able to sit down together at the table of brotherhood.

I have a dream that one day, even the state of Mississippi, a state sweltering with the heat of injustice, sweltering with the heat of oppression, will be transformed into an oasis of freedom and justice.

I have a dream my four little children will one day live in a nation where they will not be judged by the color of their skin but by the content of their character. I have a dream today!

The repetition of the phrase "I have a dream" emphasizes the fact that freedom, equality, and justice for African-Americans are still *only* dreams. Yet the repetition also affirms Dr. King's belief in change and the ultimate goodness and brotherhood of all men. The phrase, repeated a number of times in the entire speech, rings in the ear like the repetitions in a prayer.

Figures of Speech. Finally, writers many times use figures of speech to shock or surprise their readers, to emphasize a point, or to clarify their ideas. For example, Jane Goodall uses simile and metaphor when she speaks of laboratories that are "not unlike concentration camps," and says that many chimpanzees "live out their lives as prisoners, in bondage to man." See your handbook and Chapter 3 of this text for a list of the common figures of speech and examples.

In analyzing the style of an essay, you should not simply *point out* parallel sentence structures or figures of speech; you should explain how such elements of style contribute to the clarity, purpose, or force of the essay as a whole. For example: Does the writer use specific and concrete diction to help us visualize the ideas? Parallel sentence structure to help us grasp equal points? Repetition to help us keep complicated discussions in order? Further, does the style of the essay fit the purpose and situation of the essay? Does the writer use a formal style for a serious subject or formal occasion, or a formal, perhaps inflated style, for a trivial subject? (Sometimes a contrast between style and subject is a deliberate attempt to create humor or satire.) Finally, do the stylistic features of the essay contribute to or detract from the force or emotional impact of the essay? Is the writer deliberately trying to arouse our emotions with the choice of diction and sentence structure, or simply trying to convey his or her own feelings? Is the writer teaching us or preaching to us? As you can see, style is a complicated, integral part of all writing that directly creates meaning in an essay and not just a flourish added by a writer to make his prose "pretty" or "important."

WRITING A CRITICAL ANALYSIS OF AN ESSAY

Writing a critical analysis of an essay is not an easy task, but it can be made easier if you follow a plan and avoid some common mistakes. Keep in mind that your general purpose in writing a critical analysis is to explain and evaluate what the author has written.

First, follow a logical plan in preparing and writing your essay:

1. Read the essay to gain a general understanding of its purpose and meaning, underlining and writing notes in the margin to mark important passages.

2. Outline the essay, focusing on the thesis and the major supports of that thesis (evidence, examples, explanations, extended arguments, causes, effects, and so on). If the writer fails to support his or her claims, or if he or she uses colorful, emotional language, be sure to note these facts. Making this outline will give you a much clearer idea of the structure and scope of the essay.

3. Make a decision about what critical approach to take in analyzing your chosen essay. You might want to focus on the writer's use of the rational, emotional, or ethical appeals, or perhaps you might do an analysis of the author's style as it is exhibited in a single paragraph or several related paragraphs.

4. Now that you have chosen an approach, read the essay again, listing or otherwise noting examples of the types of support, instances of sound or cogent (or of fallacious) reasoning, or emotive language you want to emphasize in your essay.

5. Organize the material you have isolated, draw your conclusions, set up a thesis, and write your paper.

6. Be sure to mention the author's full name and the complete title of the essay in your introduction.

7. Finally, be sure you give your essay a precise, descriptive title such as *The Ethical Appeal in "Some Thoughts on the Exploitation of Non-Human Animals."*

Second, avoid the following mistakes in writing your critical analysis:

1. Be sure that you have a **critical** thesis and not a **descriptive** one. A critical thesis is one that states an *evaluation* or *judgment* of an essay based on your analysis of it. For example: *In "Some Thoughts on the Exploitation of Non-Human Animals," Jane Goodall mounts a strong emotional appeal by using highly connotative language, vivid figures of speech, and an effective moral analogy.* A descriptive thesis, however, merely summarizes what the author says in the essay: *In "Some Thoughts on the Exploitation of Non-Human Animals," Jane Goodall says that experimenting on animals, even if it benefits humans, is morally wrong.* This thesis will lead the writer merely to summarize what Goodall **says** in her essay; it provides no **analysis** of what she says.

2. Keep in mind that assertions are not arguments but judgments; they must be supported with details and examples drawn from the essay. For example, if you say that Goodall engages in fallacious reasoning, you must name the fallacies she uses and give examples of them drawn from the text. You must also tie in what the author says to the point you are making. Don't say merely that "Goodall uses emotionally charged words, such as 'concentration camps,'

'suffering,' and 'heartless monsters.'" Instead, for example, say that "Goodall's use of words and phrases such as 'concentration camps,' 'suffering,' and 'heartless monsters' helps to develop her emotional appeal by causing the reader to think of scientists as cruel and inhuman."

3.   Never use such phrases as "It is my opinion that . . ." or "I believe that. . . ." A critical analysis is written from a third-person, objective point of view.

4.   Do not write about your chosen essay in the past tense; use the historical present: "not "Goodall *said* . . ." but Goodall *says* . . . ."

Read Jane Goodall's article "Some Thoughts on the Exploitation of Non-Human Animals" and the two student-written analyses which follow it. Evaluate the effectiveness of the ethical and emotional appeals made in Ms. Goodall's essay and the soundness and cogency of her arguments. Next read the two student-written analyses of Ms. Goodall's essay. Does each have a clear thesis? Supporting examples? Are enough examples given to support the claim in the thesis? Are the writers' arguments sound and cogent? Do they themselves contain fallacies? Just as one should never accept a writer's claims uncritically, one should not accept a critic of that writer's claims uncritically.

SOME THOUGHTS ON THE EXPLOITATION OF
NON-HUMAN ANIMALS
JANE GOODALL

The more we learn of the true nature of non-human animals, especially those with complex brains and correspondingly complex social behavior, the more ethical concerns are raised regarding their use in the service of man–whether this be in entertainment, as "pets," for food, in research laboratories or any of the other uses to which we subject them. This concern is sharpened when the usage in question leads to intense physical or mental suffering–as is so often true with regard to vivisection.

Biomedical research involving the use of living animals began in an era when the man in the street, while believing that animals felt pain (and other emotions) was not, for the most part, much concerned by their suffering. Subsequently, scientists were much influenced by the Behaviorists, a school of psychologists which maintained that animals were little more than machines, incapable of feeling pain or any humanlike feelings or emotions. Thus it was not considered important, or even necessary, to cater to the wants and needs of experimental animals. There was, at that time, no understanding of the effect of stress on the endocrine and nervous systems, no inkling of the fact that the use of a stressed animal could affect the results of an experiment. Thus the conditions in which animals were kept–size and furnishings of cage, solitary versus social confinement–were designed to make the life of the caretaker and experimenter as easy as possible. The smaller the cage the cheaper it was to make, the easier to clean, and the simpler the task of handling its inmate. Thus it was hardly surprising that research animals were kept in tiny sterile

166

cages, stacked one on top of the other, usually one animal per cage. An ethical concern for the animal subjects was kept firmly outside the (locked) doors.

As time went on, the use of non-human animals in the laboratories increased, particularly as certain kinds of clinical research and testing on *human* animals became, for ethical reasons, more difficult to carry out legally. Animal research was increasingly perceived, by scientists and the general public, as being crucial to all medical progress. Today it is, by and large, taken for granted–the accepted way of gaining new knowledge about disease, its treatment and prevention. And, too, the accepted way of testing all manner of products, destined for human use, before they go on the market.

At the same time, thanks to a growing number of studies into the nature and mechanisms of animals' perceptions and intelligence, most people now believe that all except the most primitive of non-human animals experience pain, and that the "higher" animals have emotions similar to the human emotions we label pleasure or sadness, fear or despair. How is it, then, that scientists, at least when they put on their white coats and close the lab doors behind them, can continue to treat experimental animals as mere "things"? How can we, the citizens of civilized, western countries, tolerate laboratories which–from the point of view of animal inmates–are not unlike concentration camps? I think it is mainly because most people, even in these enlightened times, have little idea as to what goes on behind the closed doors of the laboratories, down in the basements. And even those who do have some knowledge, or those who are disturbed by the reports of cruelty that are occasionally released by animal rights organizations, believe that *all* animal research is essential to human health and progress in medicine and that the suffering so often involved is a *necessary* part of the research.

This is not true. Sadly, while some research is undertaken with a clearly defined objective that could lead to a medical breakthrough, a good many projects, some of which cause extreme suffering to the animals used, are of absolutely no value to human (or animal) health. Additionally, many experiments simply duplicate previous experiments. Finally, some research is carried out for the sake of gaining knowledge for its own sake. And while this is one of our more sophisticated intellectual abilities, should we be pursuing this goal at the expense of other living beings whom, unfortunately for them, we are able to dominate and control? Is it not an arrogant assumption that we have the *right* to (for example) cut up, probe, inject, drug and implant electrodes into animals of all species simply in our attempt to learn more about what makes them tick? Or what effect certain chemicals might have on them? And so on.

We may agree that the general public is largely ignorant of what is going on in the labs, and the reasons behind the research there, rather as the German people were mostly uninformed about the Nazi concentration camps. But what about the animal technicians, the veterinarians and the research scientists, those who are actually working in the labs and who know exactly what is going on? Are all those who use living animals as part of standard laboratory apparatus, heartless monsters?

Of course not. There may be some–there are occasional sadists in all walks of life. But they must be in the minority. The problem, as I see it, lies in the way we train young people in our society. They are victims of a kind of brainwashing that starts, only too often, in school and is intensified, in all but a few pioneering colleges and universities, throughout higher science education courses. By and large, students are taught that it is ethically acceptable to perpetrate, in the name of science, what, from the point of view of the animals, would certainly qualify as torture. They are encouraged to suppress their natural empathy for animals, and persuaded that animal pain and feelings are utterly different from our own–if, indeed, they exist at all. By the time they arrive in the labs these young people have been programmed to accept the suffering around them. And it is only too easy for them to justify this suffering on the grounds that the work being done is for the good of humanity. For the good of one animal species which has evolved a sophisticated capacity for empathy, compassion and understanding, attributes which we proudly acclaim as the hallmarks of humanity.

I have been described as a "rabid anti-vivisectionist." But my own mother is alive today because her clogged aortic valve was removed and replaced by that of a pig. The valve in question–a "bioplasticized" one, apparently–came, we were told, from a commercially slaughtered hog. In other words, the pig would have died anyway. This, however, does not eliminate my feeling of concern for that particular pig–I have always had a special fondness for pigs. The suffering of laboratory pigs and those who are raised in intensive farming units has become a special concern of mine. I am writing a book, *An Anthology of the Pig*, which, I hope, will help to raise public awareness regarding the plight of those intelligent animals.

Of course I should like to see the lab cages standing empty. So would every caring, compassionate human, including most of those who work with animals in biomedical research. But if all use of animals in the laboratory was *abruptly* stopped there would probably, for a while anyway, be a great deal of confusion, and many lines of inquiry would be brought to a sudden halt. This would inevitably lead to an increase in human suffering. This means that, until alternatives to the use of live animals in the research labs are widely available and, moreover, researchers and drug companies are legally compelled to use them, society will demand–and accept–the continued abuse of animals on its behalf.

Already, in many fields of research and testing, the growing concern for animal suffering has led to major advances in the development of techniques such as tissue culture, *in vitro* testing, computer simulation and so on. The day will eventually come when it will no longer be necessary to use animals at all. It must. But much more pressure should be brought to bear for the speedy development of additional techniques. We should put far more money into the research, and give due acknowledgment and acclaim to those who make new breakthroughs–at the very least a series of Nobel prizes. It is necessary to attract the brightest in the field. Moreover, steps should be taken to insist on the use of techniques already developed and proven. In the meantime, it is imperative that the numbers of animals used be reduced drastically. Unnecessary duplication of research must be avoided. There should be more stringent rules regarding what animals may and may not be used for. They should be used only for the most pressing projects that have clear-cut health benefits for many people, and contribute significantly to the alleviation of human suffering. Other use of animals in the labs should be stopped *immediately*, including the testing of cosmetics and household products. Finally, so long as animals are used in our labs, for any reason whatsoever, they should be given the most humane treatment possible, and the best possible living conditions.

Why is it that only relatively few scientists are prepared to back those who are insisting on better, more humane conditions for laboratory animals? The usual answer is that changes of this sort would cost so much that all progress in medical knowledge would come to an end. This is not true. Essential research would continue–the cost of building new cages and instigating better care-giving programmes would be considerable, but negligible, I am assured, when compared with the cost of sophisticated equipment used by research scientists today. Unfortunately, though, many projects are poorly conceived and often totally unnecessary. They might indeed suffer if the costs of maintaining the research animals are increased. People making their living from them would lose their jobs.

When people complain about the cost of introducing humane living conditions, my response is: "Look at your life-style, your house, your car, your clothes. Think of the administrative buildings in which you work, your salary, your expenses, the holidays you take. And, after thinking about those things, *then* tell me that we should begrudge the extra dollars spent in making a little less grim the lives of the animals used to reduce human suffering."

Surely it should be a matter of moral responsibility that we humans, differing from other animals mainly by virtue of our more highly developed intellect and, with it, our greater capacity for understanding and compassion, ensure that medical progress speedily detaches its roots from the manure of non-human animal suffering and despair. Particularly when this involves the servitude of our closest relatives.

In the United States, federal law still requires that every batch of hepatitis B vaccine be tested on a chimpanzee before it is released for human use. In addition, chimpanzees are still used in some highly inappropriate research–such as the effect on them of certain addictive drugs. There are no chimpanzees in the labs in Britain–British scientists use chimpanzees in the United States, or at the TNO Primate Centre in Holland where EEC funding has recently gone into a new chimpanzee facility. (British scientists do, of course, make massive use of other non-human primates and thousands of dogs, cats, rodents, and so forth.)

The chimpanzee is more like us than any other living being. Physiological similarities have been enthusiastically described by scientists for many years, and have led to the use of chimpanzees as "models" for the study of certain infectious diseases to which most non-human animals are resistant. There are, of course, equally striking similarities between humans and chimpanzees in the anatomy of the

brain and nervous system, and–although many have been reluctant to admit to these–in social behavior, cognition and emotionality. Because chimpanzees show intellectual abilities once thought unique to our own species, the line between humans and the rest of the animal kingdom, once thought to be so clear, has become blurred. Chimpanzees bridge the gap between "us" and "them."
Let us hope that this new understanding of the chimpanzees' place in nature will bring some relief to the hundreds who presently live out their lives as prisoners, in bondage to Man. Let us hope that our knowledge of their capacity for affection and enjoyment and fun, for fear and sadness and suffering, will lead us to treat them with the same compassion that we would show towards fellow humans. Let us hope that while medical science continues to use chimpanzees for painful or psychologically distressing experiments, we shall have the honesty to label such research for what, from the chimpanzees' point of view, it certainly is–the infliction of torture on innocent victims.

And let us hope that our understanding of the chimpanzee will lead also to a better understanding of the nature of other non-human animals, a new attitude towards the other species with which we share this planet. For, as Albert Schweitzer said, "We need a boundless ethic that includes animals too." And at the present time our ethic, where non-human animals are concerned, is limited and confused.

If we, in the western world, see a peasant beating an emaciated old donkey, forcing it to pull an oversize load, almost beyond its strength, we are shocked and outraged. That is cruelty. But taking an infant chimpanzee from his mother's arms, locking him into the bleak world of the laboratory, injecting him with human diseases–this, if done in the name of Science, is not regarded as cruelty. Yet in the final analysis, both donkey and chimpanzee are being exploited and misused for the benefit of humans. Why is one any more cruel that the other? Only because science has come to be venerated, and because scientists are assumed to be acting for the good of mankind, while the peasant is selfishly punishing a poor animal for his own gain. In fact, much animal research is self-serving too–many experiments are designed in order to keep the grant money coming in.

And let us not forget that we, in the west, incarcerate millions of domestic animals in intensive farm units in order to turn vegetable protein into animal protein for the table. While this is usually excused on grounds of economic necessity, or even regarded by some as sound animal husbandry, it is just as cruel as the beating of the donkey, the imprisonment of the chimpanzee. So are the fur farms. So is the abandonment of pets. And the illegal puppy farms. And fox hunting. And much that goes on behind the scenes when animals are trained to perform for our entertainment. The list could get very long.

Often I am asked whether I do not feel that it is unethical to devote time to the welfare of "animals" when so many human beings are suffering. Would it not be more appropriate to help starving children, battered wives, the homeless? Fortunately, there are hundreds of people addressing their considerable talents, humanitarian principles and fund-raising abilities to such causes. My own particular

170

energies are not needed there. Cruelty is surely the very worst of human sins. To fight cruelty, in any shape or form—whether it be towards other human beings or non-human beings—brings us into direct conflict with that unfortunate streak of *inhumanity* that lurks in all of us. If only we could overcome cruelty with compassion we should be well on the way to creating a new and boundless ethic—one that would respect all living beings. We should stand at the threshold of a new era in human evolution—the realization, at last, of our most unique quality: humanity. (1990)

The Emotional Appeal in "Some Thoughts on the Exploitation of Non-Human Animals"

In her essay, "Some Thoughts on the Exploitation of Non-Human Animals," Jane Goodall uses the rational appeal, the ethical appeal, and the emotional appeal; however, the emotional appeal is so strong that it overwhelms the rational appeal. This dominance is shown in three main ways: by Goodall's use of emotionally-charged language, her use of weak arguments, and her fallacious reasoning.

The first way in which Goodall reveals her emotions is through her choice of language. She uses descriptive words in order to show her readers exactly how cruel she thinks it is to use animals for research. For example, Goodall asks this question: "How can we, the citizens of civilized, western countries, tolerate laboratories which—from the point of view of animal inmates—are not unlike concentration camps?" The use of such words as "inmates" and "concentration camps" gives a person the idea that animals are kept like harmfully-treated prisoners, just as the Jews were during the Holocaust. This question, with its dramatic connotations, clearly illustrates how Goodall, through her choice of words, seeks to create a negative emotional attitude toward using animals in research. Because she chooses such emotionally charged words, the focus of the reader switches from looking for rational arguments to support Goodall's thesis to getting wrapped up in the emotions of the writer.

A second way in which emotion dominates Goodall's essay is that her arguments are very weak. There are two main examples in her essay that illustrate this point. Both focus on the same idea; Goodall gives no grounds, warrant, or backing as support for her thesis. In the first example, she says that "thanks to a growing number of studies into the nature and mechanisms of animals' perceptions and intelligence . . ." most people now realize that animals experience pain and other feelings. Nowhere in this statement does Goodall tell her readers who did the studies or when the studies were done, but she refers to these "studies" indirectly several times throughout her essay. For example, she says that students are taught that it is all right, as long as there is scientific benefit, to practice "what, from the point of view of the animals, would certainly qualify as torture." Here, Goodall is referring to the "studies" by saying that the animals can feel pain and are tortured. Again, because this statement is a reference to the "studies," it does not have sufficient grounds, warrant, or backing to make it a strong argument. The two previous examples also show that Goodall contradicts herself. The thesis of her essay is that animals should not be used in scientific testing, yet she praises the studies that were performed *on animals* to see if they experience pain. It certainly does not seem logical that an individual who is so strongly against testing on animals would give credit to such a practice. Her contradictions and the lack of support for her arguments are obscured by her use of emotion.

A final way in which Goodall's emotion overwhelms her reason is through her commission of fallacies. There are two main types of fallacies in her essay: *ad hominem* and begging the question. Goodall's use of the *ad hominem* argument is evident when she says that only a few scientists are willing to improve the living conditions of laboratory animals because of the cost involved. She criticizes scientists unwilling to pay for improving these conditions by saying that "the cost of building new cages and instigating better care-giving programs would be considerable, but negligible, I am assured, when compared with the cost of sophisticated equipment used by research scientists today." This statement shows that Goodall is attacking the scientists for not wanting to spend their money on improvements and not the actual issue of improvement itself. Therefore, this statement is an *ad hominem* fallacy. The second kind of fallacy that Goodall commits, begging the question, is seen in two statements. First, she says that "a good many projects . . . are of absolutely no value to human (or animal) health." This statement is clearly debatable because scientists and many other people would say that research experiments are quite beneficial to human and animal health. This statement is thus an example of the fallacy called "begging the question," stating a premise as if it were a conclusion. The second example of this kind comes when Goodall states that "many experiments simply duplicate previous experiments." Here Goodall implies, by using the word "simply," that duplicating experiments is also of no value. This implication is debatable because scientists would say that duplication is necessary in order to make sure that the results or effects of an experiment are as accurate as possible. Therefore, this statement is also an example of begging the question. All of these examples of fallacies show that Goodall is so emotionally involved in this issue that she tends to get off track and ends up using fallacies which weaken the arguments in support of her claim.

To conclude, Goodall's essay is very much dominated by emotion, which has left little room for strong argumentation. The overwhelming emotion can be seen in the use of extremely visual words, weak arguments, and fallacies. Overall, Goodall's argument could have used a little less emotion and more reason.

Amy Cain

The Ethical Appeal in "Some Thoughts on the Exploitation of Non-Human Animals"

Science is a double-edged sword. Scientists and researchers move in two directions at once. They attempt, sometimes, to save us; at other times, perhaps unwittingly in the service of curious brains, they destroy us or help us to destroy ourselves. From assaults on disease we have clearly benefited; from toying with atoms we now move weapons over the globe like deadly game pieces. Looking for keys to riddles by curiously observing the effects of experiments, scientists have assumed authority over many things; in so doing, they have reached into the animal kingdom for subjects on which to experiment. With the voracity of scientists in their search for answers, one wonders if ethical boundaries are being infringed upon by their use of animals in testing. In "Some Thoughts on the Exploitation of Non-Human Animals," Jane Goodall writes about the use of animals in research and voices her adamant objection to what she believes is outright torture to animals in the questionable service to man. Her argument contains a strong ethical appeal.

First, the title refers to "non-human animals." This is an important phrase, for humans on the whole, with their self-contemplative minds and perfect working thumbs, consider themselves above all other animals. But if one picks up any newspaper or watches a televised newscast he will see that humans are merely animals with tenure. Although Goodall gives no concrete examples of the types of torture inflicted on animals in research, one may choose to believe that if a woman who has spent thirty years studying the behavior of animals tells us they suffer, then one may accept it. If further proof is required, take a look at a deer's expression after it has been hit by a high-powered rifle shot, or listen to the cries of a dog when it has been hit on the backside too hard by its master's rolled-up newspaper. What could logic add?

Jane Goodall's claims in the text have support; she is not just a woman sitting at home petting her dog and possessing a more-than-average concern for animals. She is a scientist who has spent many years working with non-human animals, namely chimpanzees. Goodall is a scientist who has literally worked in the arena that she speaks of. From this knowledge, Ms. Goodall writes with stark emotional images and thus makes a strong ethical appeal.

For example, after establishing her argumentative goal in the first paragraph by writing that more knowledge of non-human animals leads to more concern about the ethics involved in using them in experiments, Goodall provides background on the early days of research and man's seeming obliviousness to non-human animals' feelings under testing. Goodall then poses a question, marked with an emotive comparison, that states her thesis: "How can we, the citizens of civilized, western countries, tolerate laboratories which–from the point of view of animal inmates–are not unlike concentration camps?". By creating images of animals as inmates in concentration camps, Goodall effectively pulls the reader into her concern over the use of animals in research experiments. In a second example near the end of her essay, Goodall asserts an ethical belief with which most people would readily agree: "Cruelty is surely the very worst of human sins". She then ends with a powerful emotional appeal directed at our sense of moral righteousness: "If only we could overcome cruelty with compassion we should be well on the way to creating a new and boundless ethic–one that would respect all living beings. We should stand at the threshold of a new era in human evolution–the realization, at last, of our most unique quality: humanity".

But Goodall does not remain mired in plaintive pleas to stop animal abuse in research; she discusses possible causes of the continued mass ignorance and lack of concern for what happens to animals in research environments. She believes that people fall under one or all of three basic categories of behavior towards animal abuse in research. People, she says, either have no idea what really happens to animals during research, they believe that all research is essential, or they are conditioned early in school to become convinced that to mistreat animals is all right in the name of science.

Goodall's entire position in the essay rests upon our beliefs that we are ethical creatures. This position she takes toward animal abuse is the pivotal point at which her readers will either turn away from the issue, believing that animals are far from the condition of humans, or read on in empathy for all living beings. Using emotional appeals in describing what animals are *in her belief* subjected to, Goodall's logical appeal, though subordinated in this essay, lies behind her personal research into the emotions and perceptions of animals. Although Goodall fails to provide well-defined answers to the problem of animal testing, she successfully paints an ominous picture of what science, curious for answers to human problems, does to animals in the name of humanity. Goodall knows that animals can suffer, so she believes it is cruel for animals to be subjected to torture in experiments that, on the whole, are not always necessary.

Finally, it must be noted that the crux of Goodall's essay, her belief that animals are tortured in experiments, lies unsupported by specific examples of abuse. One must go back to the title of the essay and see that Goodall's goal was to express "thoughts" on the subject, not to detail exact methods or to enumerate costs of alternative methods of research. Goodall is correct in saying that some animals suffer in scientific experiments; her arguments on chimpanzees and their similarities to humans "in social behavior, cognition, and emotion" are valid through her personal experience in studying them, and these arguments are a steppingstone for her from the suffering of humans to the suffering of animals.

Sifting through Goodall's essay, one finds her looking for *confirmation from the masses* on the issue of animal vivisection, not presenting exact solutions that, whether she has them or not, would probably make readers turn away from the issue without first accepting–and becoming ethically outraged at the fact–that animals suffer in the questionable name of science.

Terry Lee Thompson

174

FURTHER READINGS

DISPATCHES FROM A DYING GENERATION

NATHAN MCCALL

Two Christmases ago, I went home to Portsmouth, Va., and some of the boys from my old days on the block–Tony, Nutbrain and Roger–dropped by to check me out. We caught up on the years, and their stories revealed that not much with the old gang had changed. One had just gotten out of jail, he said, "for doing a rain dance" on his estranged girlfriend. Another had lost his house and family to a cocaine habit. A third friend, they said, had recently gotten his front teeth bashed out with a brick in a soured drug deal.

We learned that another old friend was back in town and decided to pay him a surprise visit. We crammed into my car, stopped at a store and bought a bottle of cheap wine–Wild Irish Rose, I think–just like the old days. I slid Marvin Gay's classic "What's Going On?" into the cassette player and, while cruising along, it struck me: It really *was* like old times–them passing the wine bottle from hand-to-hand; Roger and Nutbrain arguing and elbowing each other in the back seat; and everybody playing the dozens–trading insults left and right.

When our friend answered the door, he seemed surprised but not glad to see us. Within minutes, we knew the reason for his nervousness. There was a knock, followed by whispers and the stealthy entry of a scraggly-bearded man and a disheveled woman. Clearly, the three of them were about to do some drugs, *just like old times.*

What was different was that we left. And though I made a point of not being judgmental, I wondered, like Marvin Gaye had nearly two decades earlier, what *is* going on?

Lately, with the mounting toll of homicides, drug abuse and prison stints threatening to decimate a generation of young black men, I'm still wondering–not as an outsider but as one who came perilously close to becoming a fatal statistic myself.

These days, my visits home have become occasions for mourning, soul-searching and anger. On one recent visit, I saw a story, splashed across the top of the newspaper about the police busting up a $20-million narcotics ring. Listed in the article were several of the people I've known most of my life.

I sighed. It wasn't the first time that day I'd been hit with negative news about the neighborhood. And it wasn't the last. Before that day ended, family members and people I met on the streets told tale after tale of homeboys, young black men like me, living lives mired in lunacy.

Every day in D.C., I read dismal accounts of blacks murdered over trivia–drugs, a coat, a pair of sneakers, pocket change. The people in those stories are faceless to me. I peruse the accounts with detached sadness, then turn the page.

But in my hometown, 200 miles south, the names conjure images of real people who lived down the street, around the corner, on the next block.

Trips to my old neighborhood, a large black community called Cavalier Manor, bring a distressingly close-up view of black America's running tragedy. When I'm there, it dawns on me over and over again that this "endangered species" thing is no empty phrase.

Consider this: Most of the guys I hung out with are either in prison, dead, drug zombies or nickel-and-dime street hustlers. Some are racing full-throttle toward self-destruction. Others already have plunged into the abyss: Kenny Banks got 19 years for dealing drugs. Baby Joe just finished a 15-year bit for a murder beef. Charlie Gregg was in drug rehab. Bubba Majette was murdered. Teddy sleeps in the streets. Sherman is strung out on drink and drugs. Since I began writing this story several weeks ago, two former peers have died from drugs and alcohol.

Many of my former running pals are insane–literally; I'm talking overcoats in August and voices in their heads. Of the 10 families on my street that had young males in their households, four–including my own–have had one or more siblings serve time. One of my best buddies, Shane, was recently sent to prison. He shot a man several times, execution-style. He got life.

Often when I go home, as I did this past Christmas season, I prepare with a pep talk to myself and a pledge to focus on the positive–time spent with family and old friends who are doing well, and opportunities to lend a compassionate ear to those not so well off.

I know I will see former buddies. Some are old hoods, hanging on the same corners where I left them 15 years ago. I see in them how far I've come. I'm not sure what they see in me. In exchanges that are sometimes awkward, they recount their hard knocks. I say little about my establishment job or the new life I've found.

What should I say? Get a job? Go to college? Adopt my middle-class success strategies?

The fact is, I know what they've been through. And I understand what they face. I took the plunge myself, several times.

From a shoplifting charge, to stealing an ice-cream truck, to possession of a sawed-off shotgun and, ultimately, to armed robbery, I've had my share of clashes with the law.

Before I was 20, I'd seen people shot and was shot at myself. When I was 19, in a running rivalry with some other thugs, I shot a man in the chest at point-blank range. He survived, and the following year he shot and killed a man and went to prison.

When I read about the shootings in D.C. and at home, I often flash back to scenes in which I played a part. It's hard for me now to believe I was once very much a part of that world. Yet it's all too easy to understand how it came to be.

Many people are puzzled about the culture of violence pervading black communities; it's so foreign to them. Some wonder if there is something innately wrong with black males. And when all else fails, they reach for the easy responses: "Broken homes?" "Misplaced values?" "Impoverished backgrounds?"

I can answer with certainty only about myself. My background and those of my running partners don't fit all the convenient theories, and the problems among us are more complex than something we can throw jobs, social programs or more policeman at.

Portsmouth, a Navy town of nearly 103,000, is not the blighted big city that D. C. is. And Cavalier Manor is no ghetto or lair of single-parent homes. In fact, my old neighborhood is middle class by black standards and has long symbolized the quest for black upward mobility in Portsmouth. There are sprawling homes, manicured lawns and two-car garages. A scenic lake winds through part of the neighborhood. The homeowners are hardworking people who embrace the American dream and pursue it passionately.

Shane and I and the others in our loosely-knit gang started out like most other kids. Ebullient and naive, we played sandlot football, mowed neighbors' lawns for spending change and went to the movies. We devoured comic books, exchanged baseball cards and attended church.

Yet somewhere between adolescence and adulthood, something inside us changed. Our optimism faded. Our hearts hardened, and many of us went on to share the same fates as the so-called disadvantaged.

I'm not exactly sure why, but I've got a good idea.

A psychologist friend once explained that our fates are linked partly to how we perceive our choices in life. Looking back, the reality may well have been that possibilities for us were abundant. But in Cavalier Manor, we perceived our choices as being severely limited.

Nobody flatly said that. But in various ways, inside our community and out, it was communicated early and often that as black men in a hostile world our options would be few.

The perception was powerfully reinforced by what we saw in our families, where we had inherited a legacy of limited choices. My grandmother's parents were unschooled, and she spent her life as an uneducated domestic, working for white families. My stepfather left school after the 10th grade, and my mother, who dropped out after 11 years, did only slightly better. They all managed to exceed the

179

accomplishments of their forebears, but they lagged behind their white contemporaries.

What is not so easy for outsiders to grasp is why we did not follow our parents' lead and try to seize what we could with what we had. For us, somehow, growing up in the '70s, it was different. Our parents tried to insulate us from the full brunt of racism, but they could not counteract the flood of racial messages, subtle and blatant, filtering into our psyches–messages that artists like Richard Wright, James Baldwin and Ralph Ellison have documented, ones you never get accustomed to: the look in white storekeepers' eyes when you enter; the "click" of door locks when you walk past whites sitting in their cars.

Our parents, we believed, had learned to swallow pride for survival's sake. But my more militant generation seemed less inclined to make that compromise. In a curious way, we saw *anything* that brought us into the mainstream as a copout. We came to regard the establishment as the ubiquitous, all powerful "white man" who controlled our parents' lives and, we believed, determined our fates as well.

I think once we resigned ourselves to that notion, we became a lost and angry lot.

It is difficult to write this without sounding apologetic. But I know many of us could not bear to think about a future in which we were wholly subject to the whims of whites. We could not see a way out of that. Moreover, like many African Americans, then and now, we couldn't make the connection that seems so basic in the world where I now live and work.

For instance, the concept of education as a passport to a better life was vague to us. We saw no relation between school and our reality. That's why it was so easy for my buddies to drop out in our sophomore year. One day, as a group of us were walking to class, someone casually suggested we quit. I did not. (After all, I reasoned, you could find girls in school.) But one by one, the others tossed their books into the trash, just like that.

Still, there were plenty of role models in the neighborhood who were not our parents–teachers, postal workers and a smattering of professionals. But even those we respected seemed unable to articulate, or expose us to, choices they had not experienced themselves.

Besides, they were unappealing to us as heroes. They couldn't stand up to the white man. They didn't fulfill our notions about manhood.

Instead, we revered the guys on the streets, the thugs who were brazen and belligerent. They wore their hats backwards, left their belt buckles unfastened and shoelaces untied. They shunned the white establishment and worshipped violence.

In our eyes, they were real men. We studied their bouncy walk, known as the Pimp, and the slick, lyrical way they talked. Manhood became a measure of who could fight fiercest, shoot hoops best or get the most girls into bed. Our self-perceptions were reflected in the nicknames some of us took on: Dirty Stink, Whiskey Bottle, Bimbo, White Mouse, Turkey Buzzard, Rat Man, Scobie-D, Gruesome, Frank Nitty, Sweet Wolf, Black Sam, Sack Eye.

Our defiance may have stemmed partly from youthful rebellion, but it came mostly from rage at a world we sensed did not welcome us. And we knew there were countless others out there just like us, armed and on edge, and often all it took was an accidental brush against a coat sleeve or a misunderstood look to trigger a brawl or a shooting.

When your life in your own mind has no value, it becomes frighteningly easy to try to take another's life.

When I think about how to explain the carnage among young blacks in our cities—and how to stop—I think about my hometown. In Portsmouth, black males are assumed to have three post-high school options: the naval shipyard, the military or college. All of us knew that working in the system carried a price: humiliation on some level. Among us was the lingering fear that the racially integrated work world, with its relentless psychological assaults, was in some ways more perilous than life in the rough-and-tumble streets.

At least in the streets, the playing field is level and the rules don't change

Even among those of us who opted for college, there was the feeling that it was the place to stall. "We didn't know what to do or what we could do," Calvin Roberts, an old school friend told me recently. "We were in uncharted waters. Nobody we knew had been there, and we didn't know what to expect."

Perhaps for the first time in this nation's history, blacks began searching on a large scale for alternatives, and one option, of course, was the drug trade, the urban answer to capitalism. "The drug trade is one of the few places where young, uneducated blacks can say, 'I am the boss. This is *my* corporation,'" says Portsmouth Commonwealth Attorney Johnny Morrison, who has prosecuted some of his former friends for peddling drugs.

Contrary to some assumptions, there is no lack of work ethic in the drug trade. My best friend in school parlayed $20 into a successful drug operation. By the time we were both 18, he had employed a few people, bought a gold tooth and paid cash for a Buick Electra 225 (a deuce-and-a-quarter in street parlance). College students couldn't do that.

My friend didn't get caught, but others who were selling drugs, burglarizing and robbing did. I was one of them.

Often, during my teenage years, I felt like Bigger Thomas, the protagonist in Richard Wright's *Native Son*–propelled down a destructive road over which I had no control.

Seven months after being placed on probation for shooting a man, my journey ended: Nutbrain, Charlie Gregg and myself were caught after holding up a McDonald's. I was the gunman in the late night robbery, and I came so frighteningly close to pulling the trigger when the store manager tried to flee that my fingers moistened.

We actually got away with the money–about $2,000, I think–and were driving down the highway when several police cruisers surrounded us. After being searched, handcuffed and shoved into the back seat of the police car, I remember staring out the window and thinking that my life, at age 20, was over. How, I wondered, had it come to this? I had the strange, sudden wish that I could go back in time, perhaps to the year of my third-grade spelling bee, when I felt so full of hope.

In a weird way, I also felt relieved, as if I had been saved from something potentially worse. I truly had expected a more tragic fate: to go down in a shoot-out with police like Prairie Dog, a cross-town hood; to be caught by surprise one day, like Charles Lee, a neighborhood kid who was shot to death while burglarizing a home. When I read stories today in which shooting is involved, I think back to the moment when two lives could have been destroyed if I had put the slightest pressure on a trigger.

I realize that skeptics will say that nothing so concentrates the mind as getting caught. But in fact, that is exactly what happened. I realized that something in my life had gone terribly wrong. Prison was my wake-up call.

For nearly three years, I was forced to nurture my spirit and ponder all that had gone on before. A job in the prison library exposed me to a world of black literature that helped me understand who I was and why prison had become–literally–a rite of passage for so many of us. I sobbed when I read *Native Son* because it captured all those conflicting feelings–Bigger's restless anger, hopelessness, his tough facade among blacks and his morbid fear of whites–that I had often sensed in myself but was unable to express.

Malcolm X's autobiography helped me understand the devastating effects of self-hatred and introduced me to a universal principle: that if you change your self-perception, you can change your behavior. I concluded that if Malcolm X, who also went to prison, could pull his life out of the toilet, then maybe I could too.

My new life is still a struggle, harsher in some ways than the one I left. At times I feel suspended in a kind of netherworld, belonging fully to neither the streets nor the establishment.

I have come to believe two things that might seem contradictory: that some of our worst childhood fears *were* true–the establishment is teeming with racism. Yet I also believe whites are as befuddled about race as we are, and they're as scared of us as we are of them. Many of them are seeking solutions, just like us.

I am torn by a different kind of anger now: I resent suggestions that blacks enjoy being "righteous victims." And when people ask, "What is wrong with black men?" it makes me want to lash out. When I hear that question, I am reminded of something once said by Malcolm X: "I have no mercy or compassion in me for a society that will crush people and then penalize them for not being able to stand up under the weight."

Sometimes I wonder how I endured when so many others were crushed. I was not special. And when I hear the numbing statistics about black men, I often think of guys I grew up with who were smarter and more talented than me, but who will never realize their potential. Nutbrain, a mastermind in the ways of the streets, had the kind of raw intellect that probably could not be gauged in achievement tests. Shane, who often breezed effortlessly through tests in school, could have done anything he wanted with his life had he known what to do.

Now he has no choices.

When Shane was caught in a police manhunt a couple of years ago, I considered volunteering as a character witness, but dismissed the notion because I knew there was no way to tell a jury what I was unable to articulate to a judge at my own trial. How could I explain our anger and alienation from the rest of the world? Where was our common language?

Most people, I'm sure, would regard Shane's fate with the same detachment I feel when reading crime reports about people I don't know. But I hurt for Shane, who will likely spend the rest of his days behind bars and who must live with the agony of having taken a life. I hurt more for Shane's mother, who has now seen two of her four sons go to prison. A divorcee, she now delivers newspapers in Cavalier Manor.

I saw her recently after she tossed a paper onto my parents' doorstep. Her hair had grayed considerably. We hugged and chatted. She seemed proud that I had turned my life around, but I felt guilty and wondered again why I got a second chance and her sons did not.

After an awkward silence, I got Shane's prison address and said good-bye. I wrote to him but got no reply.

For those who'd like answers, I have no pithy social formulas to end black-on-black violence. But I do know that I see a younger, meaner generation out there now–more lost and alienated than we were–and placing even less value on life. We were at least touched by role models; this new bunch is totally estranged from the black mainstream. Crack has taken the drug game to a more lethal level and given young blacks far more economic incentive to opt for the streets.

I've come to fear that of the many things a black man can die from, the first may be rage–his own or someone else's.

For that reason, I seldom stick around when I stop on the block. One day not long ago, I spotted a few familiar faces hanging out at the old haunt, the local convenience store. I wheeled into the parking lot, strode over and high-fived the guys I knew. Within moments, I sensed that I was in danger.

I felt the hostile stares from those I didn't know. I was frightened by these younger guys, who now controlled my former turf. I eased back to my car and left, because I knew this: that if they saw the world as I once did, they believed they had nothing to lose, including life itself.

It made me wanna holler, and throw up both my hands. (1991)

CHICANO:
ORIGIN AND MEANING
EDWARD SIMMEN

Another minority group–the Mexican-American–is being heard on campuses in the Southwest and West. Following the blacks, this new voice–the Chicano–is now asking for special ethnic study programs. Surprising to many, he is receiving not only serious administrative attention, but action. And with it all, a new word has come into the printed English vocabulary–*Chicano*. Most often it is seen in the headlines of daily newspapers or national magazines leading to reports of incidents involving the actions of Mexican-Americans, such as those demonstrations that occurred in September 1970 in the streets of Los Angeles and at a school-board meeting in Houston.

However, the word, while freely used nationally by journalists, has little meaning for the general public who live outside the Southwest. Even those who live in the areas populated by the ten million Mexican-Americans in the United States do not fully understand the word.

Especially elusive are the origin and meaning of *Chicano*. Dictionaries are of no help; the word does not appear in even the most recently published English dictionaries. And as far as is known, its first appearance in print is the use of the term by Mario Suarez, a Mexican writer from Arizona, in a sketch entitled "El Hoyo," published in the *Arizona Quarterly*, Summer, 1947, to describe a barrio (a Mexican-American ghetto) in Tucson, whose inhabitants he refers to as "*chicanos* who raise hell on Saturday night, listen to Padre Estanislao on Sunday morning and then raise hell on Sunday night." But Suarez does not attempt to explain the origin of the word except to say that "the term *chicano* is a short way of saying *Mexicano*."

It can be safely said that no one knows for certain the origin of the word. Various theories do exist; of those suggested, scholars and students of Mexican-American life and literature generally accept one of two. Each is plausible, but neither has been proved.

According to Professor Philip D. Ortego of the University of Texas at El Paso, one theory "ascribes the word to Nahuatl origin, suggesting that Indians pronounce Mexicano as 'Me-shi-ca-noh'" (letter dated October 6, 1970). If such is the case, the first syllable was in time dropped and the soft "shi" was replaced with the hard "ch," and the word as it is known became commonly used in speech by Mexican-Americans within the barrios. The word then was merely a term of ethnic identification and not meant in any way to demean. More recently, however, *Chicano* has been used by other Mexican-Americans of a "lower" class who identify more with the Mexican-Indian culture than with the Mexican-Spanish culture.

Another theory asserts that the word was conventionally formed by suffixing *ano* to *chico* (a young boy), exactly as one would form, for example, Mexicano from Mexico. Thus, the word was used in the barrio for emphasis, to place in a special category an individual so called. A Chicano, then, would have been any Mexican-American who acted as a "young boy." Perhaps, in this sense, *Chicano* is related to *chicazo*, meaning "a poorly educated young man who aimlessly, as a vagabond, roams the streets."

Other problems arise with regard to meaning. Today, who is a Chicano? Certainly, the word is no longer used exclusively in speech by Mexican-Americans as an uncomplimentary term of address. In addition to newspapers and magazines, it is often seen in *El Grito*, a journal from the newly formed publishing house Quinto Sol Publication, Inc., of Berkeley, California. *Chicano* also is the title of a novel written by Richard Vasquez, published in 1970. *El Chicano* is a barrio newspaper published in the slums of San Bernardino, California.

To assist in understanding one popular meaning of *Chicano*, Professor Ortego has offered the following series of equivalents: "Negro/Mexican; Afro-American/Mexican-American; Black/Chicano" (letter dated May 26, 1970). In this sense, then, it describes the more radical and youthful Mexican-Americans whose controversial actions and statements often make the headlines. For example, in the June 4, 1969, issue of *The National Catholic Reporter*, an article on Mexican-American activities by Kathy Mulherin was headlined: CHICANOS TURN TO BROWN POWER: FIVE YEARS BEHIND THE BLACKS, BUT WE'LL CATCH UP VERY FAST. A year later, in an article entitled "Chicano Power: Militance Among the Mexican-Americans" (*The New Republic*, June 20, 1970), Stan Steiner wrote of the increasing "political revolt of the Chicanos, as the young Mexican-Americans call themselves throughout the Southwest." He quoted Bexar County (San Antonio) Commissioner Albert Pena on the subject: "These young people are the wave of the future. If things are going to change in Texas, they are going to do it. The Chicano is more determined and more militant. He is no longer asking, he is demanding." On October 5, 1970, the Houston *Chronicle* reported such an event which had occurred in a small Texas city on the Rio Grande. The headline read: CHICANOS HOLD PROTEST AT McALLEN. The Associated Press coverage began: "Some 250 young Mexican-Americans chanting 'Kill the Gringos' staged a protest rally and march here."

But many Mexican-Americans who would never be considered by the general public as lawless or irresponsible political activists are in increasing numbers calling themselves Chicanos, such as those individuals who attended a conference on Mexican-American studies at the University of Texas at Austin in November 1970. The participants, who came not only from inside the academic community but from outside as well, used the terms *Mexican-American* and *Chicano* interchangeably, with the emphasis on *Chicano*. Such individuals are attempting to discard a variety of other labels such as Latin, Latin-American, Spanish-American, and even Mexican-American and to replace them with one term—*Chicano*—to apply to all

Americans of Mexican descent, regardless of profession, education, or political persuasion.

Nevertheless, Mexican-Americans who would define *Chicano* in this way are presently in the minority. The vast majority of Americans, influenced by the press, believe that while all Chicanos are Mexican-Americans, not *all* Mexican-Americans are Chicanos. The term, for most Americans who hear and read it, seems to possess pejorative connotations. Today, the noun *Chicano* could well be defined: "A dissatisfied American of Mexican descent whose ideas regarding his position in the social or economic order are, in general, considered to be liberal or radical and whose statements and actions are often extreme and sometimes violent."

Yet even as the word is being used, the meaning is changing; amelioration is taking place as more Mexican-Americans in responsible educational, governmental, and professional positions begin to refer to themselves as *Chicanos*. We may assume that as more and more of these individuals use the term, the word will be defined as follows: "An American of Mexican descent who attempts through peaceful, reasonable, and responsible means to correct the image of the Mexican-American and to improve the position of this minority in the American social structure."

(1972)

FROM "THE MARKS
OF AN EDUCATED MAN"

Alan Simpson

Any education that matters is liberal. All the saving truths and healing graces that distinguish a good education from a bad one or a full education from a half-empty one are contained in that word. Whatever ups and downs the term "liberal" suffers in the political vocabulary, it soars above all controversy in the educational word. In the blackest pits of pedagogy the squirming victim has only to ask, "What's liberal about this?" to shame his persecutors. In times past a liberal education set off a free man from a slave or a gentleman from laborers and artisans. It now distinguishes whatever nourishes the mind and spirit from the training which is merely practical or professional or from the trivialities which are no training at all. Such an education involves a combination of knowledge, skills, and standards.

So far as knowledge is concerned, the record is ambiguous. It is sufficiently confused for the fact-filled freak who excels in quiz shows to have passed himself off in some company as an educated man. More respectable is the notion that there are some things which every educated man ought to know; but many highly educated men would cheerfully admit to a vast ignorance, and the framers of curriculums have differed greatly in the knowledge they prescribe. If there have been times when all the students at school or college studied the same things, as if it were obvious that without exposure to a common body of knowledge they would not be educated at all, there have been other times when specialization ran so wild that it might almost seem as if educated men had abandoned the thought of ever talking to each other once their education was completed.

If knowledge is one of our marks, we can hardly be dogmatic about the kind or the amount. A single fertile field tilled with care and imagination can probably develop all the instincts of an educated man. However, if the framer of a curriculum wants to minimize his risks, he can invoke an ancient doctrine which holds that an educated man ought to know a little about everything and a lot about something.

The "little about everything" is best interpreted these days by those who have given the most thought to the sort of general education an informed individual ought to have. More is required than a sampling of the introductory courses which specialists offer in their own disciplines. Courses are needed in each of the major divisions of knowledge–the humanities, the natural sciences, and social sciences–which are organized with the breadth of view and the imaginative power of competent staffs who understand the needs of interested amateurs. But, over and above this exciting smattering of knowledge, students should bite deeply into at least one subject and taste its full flavor. Its not enough to be dilettantes in everything without striving also to be craftsmen in something.

If there is some ambiguity about the knowledge an educated man should have, there is none at all about the skills. The first is simply the training of the mind in the capacity to think clearly. This has always been the business of education, but the way it is done varies enormously. Marshalling the notes of a lecture is one experience; the opportunity to argue with a teacher is another. Thinking within an accepted tradition is one thing; to challenge the tradition itself is another. The best results are achieved when the idea of the examined life is held firmly before the mind and when the examination is conducted with the zest, rigor, and freedom which really stretches everyone's capacities.

The vital aid to clear thought is the habit of approaching everything we hear and everything we are taught to believe with a certain skepticism. The method of using doubt as an examiner is a familiar one among scholars and scientists, but it is also the best protection which a citizen has against the cant and humbug that surround us.

To be able to listen to a phony argument and to see its dishonesty is surely one of the marks of an educated man. We may not need to be educated to possess some of this quality. A shrewd peasant was always well enough protected against impostors in the market place, and we have all sorts of businessmen who have made themselves excellent judges of phoniness without the benefit of a high-school diploma; but this kind of shrewdness goes along with a great deal of credulity. Outside the limited field within which experience has taught the peasant or the illiterate businessman his lessons, he is often hopelessly gullible. The educated man, by contrast, has tried to develop a critical faculty for general use, and he likes to think that he is fortified against imposture in all its forms.

It does not matter for our purposes whether the impostor is a deliberate liar or not. Some are, but the commonest enemies of mankind are unconscious frauds. Most salesmen under the intoxication of their own exuberance seem to believe in what they say. Most experts whose *expertise* is only a pretentious sham behave as if they had been solemnly inducted into some kind of priesthood. Very few demagogues are so cynical as to remain undeceived by their own rhetoric, and some of the worst tyrants in history have been fatally sincere. We can leave the disentanglement of motives to the students of fraud and error, but we cannot afford to be taken in by the shams.

We are, of course, surrounded by shams. Until recently the schools were full of them–the notion that education can be had without tears, that puffed rice is a better intellectual diet than oatmeal, that adjustment to the group is more important than knowing where the group is going, and that democracy has made it a sin to separate the sheep from the goats. Mercifully, these are much less evident now than they were before Sputnik startled us into our wits.

In front of the professor are the shams of the learned fraternity. There is the sham science of the social scientist who first invented a speech for fuddling thought and then proceeded to tell us in his lockjawed way what we already knew. There is the sham humanism of the humanist who wonders why civilization that once feasted at his table is repelled by the shredded and desiccated dishes that often lie on it today. There is the sham message of the physical scientist who feels that his mastery of nature has made him an expert in politics and morals, and there are all the other brands of hokum which have furnished material for satire since the first quacks established themselves in the first cloisters.

If this is true of universities with their solemn vows and limited temptations, how much truer is it of the naughty world outside, where the prizes are far more dazzling and the only protection against humbug is the skepticism of the ordinary voter, customer, reader, listener, and viewer? Of course, the follies of human nature are not going to be exorcised by anything that the educator can do, and I am not sure that he would want to exorcise them if he could. There is something irresistibly funny about the old Adam, and life would be duller without his antics. But they ought to be kept within bounds. We are none the better for not recognizing a clown when we see one.

The other basic skill is simply the art of self-expression in speech and on paper. A man is uneducated who has not mastered the elements of clean forcible prose and picked up some relish for style.

It is a curious fact that we style everything in this country–our cars, our homes, our clothes–except our minds. They still chug along like a Model T–rugged, persevering, but far from graceful.

No doubt this appeal for style, like the appeal for clear thinking, can be carried too far. There was once an American who said that the only important thing in life was "to set a chime of words ringing in a few fastidious minds." As far as can be learned, he left this country in a huff to tinkle his little bell in a foreign land. Most of us would think that he lacked a sense of proportion. After all, the political history of this country is full of good judgment expressed in bad prose, and business history has smashed through to some of its grandest triumphs across acres of broken syntax. But we can discard some of these frontier manners without becoming absurdly precious.

The road ahead bristles with obstacles. There is the reluctance of many people to use one word where they where they can get away with a half-dozen or a word of one syllable if they can find a longer one. No one has ever told them about the first rule in English composition: every slaughtered syllable is a good deed. The most persuasive teachers of this maxim are undoubtedly the commercial firms that offer a thousand dollars for the completion of a slogan in twenty-five words. They are the only people who are putting a handsome premium on economy of statement.

There is the decay of the habit of memorizing good prose and good poetry in the years when tastes are being formed. It is very difficult to write a bad sentence if the Bible has been a steady companion and very easy to imagine a well-turned phrase if the ear has been tuned on enough poetry.

There is the monstrous proliferation of gobbledy-gook in government, business, and the professions. Take this horrible example of verbal smog:

191

It is inherent to motivational phenomena that there is a drive for more gratification than is realistically possible, on any level or in any type of personality organization. Likewise it is inherent to the world of objects that not all potentially desirable opportunities can be realized within a human life span. Therefore, any personality must involve an organization that allocates opportunities for gratification, that systematizes precedence relative to the limited possibilities. The possibilities of gratification, simultaneously or sequentially, of all need-dispositions are severely limited by the structure of the object system and by the intra-systemic incompatibility of the consequences of gratifying them all.

What this smothered soul is trying to say is simply, "We must pick and choose, because we cannot have everything we want."

Finally there is the universal employment of the objective test as part of the price which has to be paid for mass education. Nothing but the difficulty of finding enough readers to mark essays can condone a system which reduces a literate student to the ignoble necessity of "blackening the answer space" when he might be giving his mind and pen free play. Though we have managed to get some benefits from these examinations, the simple fact remains that the shapely prose of the Declaration of Independence or the "Gettysburg Address" was never learned under an educational system which employed objective tests. It was mastered by people who took writing seriously, who had good models in front of them, good critics to judge them, and an endless capacity for taking pains. Without that sort of discipline, the arts of self-expression will remain as mutilated as they are now.

The standards which mark an educated man can be expressed in terms of three tests:

The first is a matter of sophistication. Emerson put it nicely when he talked about getting rid of "the nonsense of our wigwams." The wigwam may be an uncultivated home, a suburban conformity, a crass patriotism, or a cramped dogma. Some of this nonsense withers in the classroom. More of it rubs off by simply mixing with people, provided they are drawn from a wide range of back- grounds and exposed within a good college to a civilized tradition. An educated man can be judged by the quality of his prejudices. There is a refined nonsense which survives the raw nonsense which Emerson was talking about.

The second test is a matter of moral values. Though we all know individuals who have contrived to be both highly educated and highly immoral, and though we have all heard of periods in history when the subtlest resources of wit and sophistication were employed to make a mockery of simple values, we do not really believe that a college is doing its job when it is simply multiplying the number of educated scoundrels, hucksters, and triflers.

The health of society depends on simple virtues like honesty, decency, courage, and public spirit. There are forces in human nature which constantly tend to corrupt them, and every age has its own vices. The worst feature of ours is probably the obsession with violence. Up to some such time as 1914, it was possible to believe in a kind of moral progress. The quality which distinguished the Victorian from the

Elizabethan was a sensitivity to suffering and revulsion from cruelty which greatly enlarged the idea of human dignity. Since 1914 we have steadily brutalized ourselves The horrors of modern war, the bestialities of modern political creeds, the uncontrollable vices of modern cities, the favorite themes of modern novelists–all have conspired to degrade us. Some of the corruption is blatant. The authors of the best sellers, after exhausting all the possibilities of sex in its normal and abnormal forms and all the variations of alcoholism and drug addiction, are about to invade the recesses of the hospitals. A clinical study of a hero undergoing the irrigation of his colon is about all there is left to gratify a morbid appetite.

Some of the corruption is insidious. A national columnist recently wrote an article in praise of cockfighting. He had visited a cockfight in the company of Ernest Hemingway. After pointing out that Hemingway had made bullfighting respectable, he proceeded to describe the terrible beauty of fierce indomitable birds trained to kill each other for the excitement of the spectators. Needless to say, there used to be a terrible beauty about Christians defending themselves against lions or about heretics being burned at the stake, and there are still parts of the world where a public execution is regarded as a richly satisfying feast. But for three or four centuries the West taught itself to resist these excitements in the interest of a moral idea.

Educators are needlessly squeamish about their duty to uphold moral values and needlessly perplexed about how to implant them. The corruptions of our times are a sufficient warning that we cannot afford to abandon the duty to the homes and the churches, and the capacity which many institutions have shown to do their duty in a liberal spirit is a sufficient guaranty against bigotry.

Finally, there is the test imposed by the unique challenge of our own times. We are not unique in suffering from moral confusion–these crises are a familiar story–but we are unique in the tremendous acceleration of the rate of social change and in the tremendous risk of a catastrophic end to all our hopes. We cannot afford educated men who have every grace except the gift for survival. An indispensable mark of the modern educated man is the kind of versatile, flexible mind that can deal with new and explosive conditions.

With this reserve, there is little in this profile which has not been familiar for centuries. Unfortunately, the description which once sufficed to suggest its personality has been debased in journalistic currency. The "well-rounded man" has become the organization man, or the man who is so well rounded that he rolls wherever he is pushed. The humanists who invented the idea and preached it for centuries would recoil in contempt from any such notion. They understood the possibilities of the whole man and wanted an educational system which would give the many sides of his nature some chance to develop in harmony. They thought it a good idea to mix the wisdom of the world with the learning of the cloister, to develop the body as well as the mind, to pay a great deal of attention to character, and to neglect no art which could add to the enjoyment of living. It was a spacious idea which offered every hospitality to creative energy. Anyone who is seriously interested in liberal education must begin by rediscovering it.   (Spring 1961)

GRANT AND LEE:
A STUDY IN CONTRAST
BRUCE CATTON

When Ulysses S. Grant and Robert E. Lee met in the parlor of a modest house at Appomattox Court House, Virginia, on April 9, 1865, to work out the terms for the surrender of Lee's Army of Northern Virginia, a great chapter in American life came to a close, and a great new chapter began.

These men were bringing the Civil War to its virtual finish. To be sure, other armies had yet to surrender, and for a few days the fugitive Confederate government would struggle desperately and vainly, trying to find some way to go on living now that its chief support was gone. But in effect it was all over when Grant and Lee signed the papers. And the little room where they wrote out the terms was the scene of one of the poignant, dramatic contrasts in American History.

They were two strong men, these oddly different generals, and they represented the strengths of two conflicting currents that, through them, had come into final collision.

Back of Robert E. Lee was the notion that the old aristocratic concept might somehow survive and be dominant in American life.

Lee was tidewater Virginia, and in his background were family, culture, and tradition. . . the age of chivalry transplanted to a New World which was making its own legends and its own myths. He embodied a way of life that had come down through the age of knighthood and the English country squire. America was a land that was beginning all over again, dedicated to nothing much more complicated than the rather hazy belief that all men had equal rights and should have an equal chance in the world. In such a land Lee stood for the feeling that it was somehow of advantage to human society to have a pronounced inequality in the social structure. There should be a leisure class, backed by ownership of land; in turn, society itself should be keyed to the land as the chief source of wealth and influence. It would bring forth (according to this ideal) a class of men with a strong sense of obligation to the community; men who lived not to gain advantage for themselves, but to meet the solemn obligations which had been laid on them by the very fact that they were privileged. From them the country would get its leadership; to them it could look for the higher values–of thought, of conduct, or personal deportment–to give it strength and virtue.

Lee embodied the noblest elements of this aristocratic ideal. Through him, the landed nobility justified itself. For four years, the Southern states had fought a desperate war to uphold the ideals for which Lee stood. In the end, it almost seemed as if the Confederacy fought for Lee; as if he himself was the Confederacy. . .the best thing that the way of life for which the confederacy stood could ever have to offer. He had passed into legend before Appomattox. Thousands of tired, underfed, poorly clothed Confederate soldiers, long since past the simple enthusiasm of the early days of the struggle, somehow considered Lee the symbol of everything for which they had been willing to die. But they could not quite put this feeling into words. If the Lost Cause, sanctified by so much heroism and so many deaths, had a living justification, its justification was General Lee.

Grant, the son of a tanner on the Western frontier, was everything Lee was not. He had come up the hard way and embodied nothing in particular except the eternal toughness and sinewy fiber of the men who grew up beyond the mountains. He was one of a body of men who owed reverence and obeisance to no one, who were self-reliant to a fault, who cared hardly anything for the past but who had a sharp eye for the future.

These frontier men were the precise opposites of the tidewater aristocrats. Back of them, in the great surge that had taken people over the Alleghenies and into the opening Western country, there was a deep, implicit dissatisfaction with a past that had settled into grooves. They stood for democracy, not from any reasoned conclusion about the proper ordering of human society, but simply because they had grown up in the middle of democracy and knew how it worked. Their society might have privileges, but they would be privileges each man had won for himself. Forms and patterns meant nothing. No man was born to anything, except perhaps to a chance to show how far he could rise. Life was competition.

Yet along with this feeling had come a deep sense of belonging to a national community. The Westerner who developed a farm, opened a shop, or set up in business as a trader could hope to prosper only as his own community prospered—and this community ran from the Atlantic to the Pacific and from Canada down to Mexico. If the land was settled, with towns and highways and accessible markets, he could better himself. He saw his fate in terms of the nation's own destiny. As its horizons expanded, so did his. He had, in other words, an acute dollars-and-cents stake in the continued growth and development of his country.

And that, perhaps, is where the contrast between Grant and Lee becomes most striking. The Virginia aristocrat, inevitably, saw himself in relation to his own region. He lived in a static society which could endure almost anything except change. Instinctively, his first loyalty would go to the locality in which that society existed. He would fight to the limit of endurance to defend it, because in defending it he was defending everything that gave his own life its deepest meaning.

The Westerner, on the other hand, would fight with an equal tenacity for the broader concept of society. He fought so because everything he lived by was tied to growth, expansion, and a constantly widening horizon. What he lived by would survive or fall with the nation itself. He could not possibly stand by unmoved in the face of an attempt to destroy the Union. He would combat it with everything he had, because he could only see it as an effort to cut the ground out from under his feet.

So Grant and Lee were in complete contrast, representing two diametrically opposed elements in American life. Grant was the modern man emerging; beyond him, ready to come on the stage, was the great age of steel and machinery, of crowded cities and restless burgeoning vitality. Lee might have ridden down from the old age of chivalry, lance in hand, silken banner fluttering over his head. Each man was the perfect champion of his cause, drawing both his strengths and his weaknesses from the people he led.

Yet it was not all contrast, after all. Different as they were–in background, in personality, in underlying aspiration–these two great soldiers had much in common. Under everything else, they were marvelous fighters. Furthermore, their fighting qualities were really very much alike.

Each man had, to begin with, the great virtue of utter tenacity and fidelity. Grant fought his way down the Mississippi Valley in spite of acute personal discouragements and profound military handicaps. Lee hung on in the trenches at Petersburg after hope itself had died. In each man there was an indomitable quality . . .the born fighter's refusal to give up as long as he can still remain on his feet and lift his two fists.

Daring and resourcefulness they had, too: the ability to think faster and move faster than the enemy. These were the qualities which gave Lee the dazzling campaigns of Second Manassas and Chancellorsville and won Vicksburg for Grant.

Lastly, and perhaps greatest of all, there was the ability, at the end, to turn quickly from war to peace once the fighting was over. Out of the way these two men behaved at Appomattox came the possibility of a peace of reconciliation. It was a possibility not wholly realized, in the years to come, but which did, in the end, help the two sections to become one nation again. . . after a war whose bitterness might have seemed to make such a reunion wholly impossible. No part of either man's life became more than the part he played in their brief meeting in the McLean house at Appomattox. Their behavior there put all succeeding generations of Americans in their debt. Two great Americans, Grant and Lee–very different, yet under everything very much alike. Their encounter at Appomattox was one of the great moments of American History.

(1956)

HIS TALK, HER TALK
JOYCE MAYNARD

It can be risky these days to suggest that there are any innate differences between men and women, other than those of anatomy. Out the window go the old notions about man and aggression, woman and submission (don't even say the word), man and intellect, woman and instinct. If I observe that my infant son prefers pushing a block along the floor while making car noises to cradling a doll in his arms and singing lullabies (and he does)–well, I can only conclude that, despite all our earnest attempts at nonsexist child-rearing, he has already suffered environmental contamination. Some of it, no doubt unwittingly, came from my husband and me, reared in the days when nobody winced if you recited that old saw about what little girls and little boys are made of.

I do not believe, of course, that men are smarter, steadier, more high-minded than women. But one or two notions are harder to shake–such as the idea that there is such a thing as "men's talk" or "women's talk." And that it's a natural instinct to seek out, on occasion, the company of one's own sex, exclude members of the other sex and not feel guilty about it.

Oh, but we do. At a party I attended the other night, for instance, it suddenly became apparent that all the women were in one room and all the men were in the other. Immediately we redistributed ourselves, which was a shame. No one had suggested we segregate. The talk in the kitchen was simply, all the women felt, more interesting.

What was going on in the kitchen was a particular sort of conversation that I love and that most men I know would wash and wax the car, change the oil filter and vacuum the upholstery to avoid. There is a way women talk with other women, and, I gather, a way that men talk when in the company of other men. They are not at all the same.

I think I know my husband very well, but I have no idea what goes on when he and his male friends get together. Neither can he picture what can keep a woman friend and me occupied for three hours over a single pot of coffee.

The other day, after a long day of work, my husband, Steve, and his friend Dave stopped at a bar for a few beers. When he got home, I asked what they had talked about. "Oh, the usual." Like what? "Firewood. Central America. Trucks. The Celtics. Religion. You know."

No, not really. I had only recently met with my friend Ann and her friend Sally at a coffee shop nearby, and what we talked about was the workshop Sally would be holding that weekend concerning women's attitudes toward their bodies; Ann's 11-year-old daughter's upcoming slumber party, how hard it is buy jeans, and the recent dissolution of a friend's five-year marriage. Asked to capsulize our afternoon's discussion, in a form similar to my husband's outline of his night out, I would say we talked about life, love, happiness and heartbreak. Larry Bird's name never came up.

I don't want to reinforce old stereotypes of bubble-headed women (Lucy and Ethel), clinking their coffee cups over talk of clothes and diets while the men remove themselves to lean on mantels, puff on cigars and muse about world politics, machines and philosophy. A group of women talking, it seems to me, is likely to concern itself with matters just as pressing as those broached by my husband and his friends. It might be said, in fact, that we're really talking about the same eternal conflicts. Our styles are just different.

When Steve tells a story, the point is, as a rule, the ending, and getting there by the most direct route. It may be a good story, told with beautiful precision, but he tells it the way he eats a banana: in three efficient chews, while I cut mine up and savor it. He can (although this is rare) spend 20 minutes on the telephone with one of his brothers, tantalizing me with occasional exclamations of amazement or shock, and then after hanging up, reduce the whole conversation for me to a one-sentence summary. I, on the other hand, may take three quarters of an hour describing some figure from my past while he waits–with thinly veiled impatience–for the point to emerge. Did this fellow just get elected to the House of Representatives? Did he die and leave me his fortune?

In fairness to Steve, I must say that, for him, not talking about something doesn't necessarily mean not dealing with it. And he does listen to what I have to say. He likes a good story, too. It's just that, given a choice, he'd rather hear about quantum mechanics or the history of the Ford Mustang. Better yet, he'd rather play ball.

(1985)

200

KINDS OF DISCIPLINE
JOHN HOLT

A child, in growing up, may meet and learn from three different kinds of disciplines. The first and most important is what we might call the Discipline of Nature or of Reality. When he is trying to do something real, if he does the wrong thing or doesn't do the right one, he doesn't get the results he wants. If he doesn't pile one block on top of another, or tries to build on a slanting surface, his tower falls down. If he hits the wrong key, he hears the wrong note. If he doesn't hit the nail squarely on the head, it bends, and he has to pull it out and start with another. If he doesn't measure properly what he is trying to build, it won't open, close, fit, stand up, fly, float, whistle, or do whatever he wants it to do. If he closes his eyes when he swings, he doesn't hit the ball. A child meets this kind of discipline every time he tries to do something, which is why it is so important in school to give children more chances to do things, instead of just reading or listening to someone talk (or pretending to). This discipline is a great teacher. The learner never has to wait long for his answer; it usually comes quickly, often instantly. Also it is clear, and very often points toward the needed correction; from what happened he can not only see that what he did was wrong, but also why, and what he needs to do instead. Finally, and most important, the giver of the answer, call it Nature, is impersonal, impartial, and indifferent. She does not give opinions, or make judgments; she cannot be wheedled, bullied, or fooled; she does not get angry or disappointed; she does not praise or blame; she does not remember past failures or hold grudges; with her one always gets a fresh start, this time is the one that counts.

The next discipline we might call the Discipline of Culture, of Society, of What People Really Do. Man is a social, a cultural animal. Children sense around them this culture, this network of agreements, customs, habits, and rules binding the adults together. They want to understate it and be a part of it. They watch very carefully what people around them are doing and want to do the same. They want to do right, unless they become convinced they can't do right. Thus children rarely misbehave seriously in church, but sit as quietly as they can. The example of all those grownups is contagious. Some mysterious ritual is going on, and children, who like rituals, want to be part of it. In the same way, the little children that I see at concerts or operas, though they may fidget a little, or perhaps take a nap now and then, rarely make any disturbance. With all those grownups sitting there, neither moving nor talking, it is the most natural thing in the world to imitate them. Children who live among adults who are habitually courteous to each other, and to them, will soon learn to be courteous. Children who live surrounded by people who speak a certain way will speak that way, however much we try to tell them that speaking that way is bad or wrong.

The third discipline is the one most people mean when they speak of discipline–the Discipline of Superior Force, of sergeant to private, of "you do what I tell you or I'll make you wish you had." There is bound to be some of this in a child's life. Living as we do surrounded by things that can hurt children, or that children can

201

hurt, we cannot avoid it. We can't afford to let a small child find out from experience the danger of playing in a busy street, or of fooling with the pots on the top of a stove, or of eating up the pills in the medicine cabinet. So, along with other precautions, we say to him, "Don't play in the street, or touch things on the stove, or go into the medicine cabinet, or I'll punish you." Between him and the danger too great for him to imagine we put a lesser danger, but one he can imagine and maybe therefore wants to avoid. He can have no idea of what it would be like to be hit by a car, but he can imagine being shouted at, or spanked, or sent to his room. He avoids these substitutes for the greater danger until he can understand it and avoid it for its own sake. But we ought to use this discipline only when it is necessary to protect the life, health, safety, or well-being of people or other living creatures, or to prevent destruction of things that people care about. We ought not to assume too long, as we usually do, that a child cannot understand the real nature of the danger from which we want to protect him. The sooner he avoids the danger, not to escape our punishment, but as a matter of good sense, the better. He can learn that faster than we think. In Mexico, for example, where people drive their cars with a good deal of spirit, I saw many children no older than five or four walking unattended on the streets. They understood about cars, they knew what to do. A child whose life is full of the threat and fear of punishment is locked into babyhood. There is no way for him to grow up, to learn to take responsibility for his life and acts. Most important of all, we should not assume that having to yield to the threat of our superior force is good for the child's character. It is never good for *anyone's* character. To bow to superior force makes us feel impotent and cowardly for not having had the strength or courage to resist. Worse, it makes us resentful and vengeful. We can hardly wait to make someone pay for our humiliation, yield to us as we were once made to yield. No, if we cannot always avoid using the Discipline of Superior Force, we should at least use it as seldom as we can.

There are places where all three disciplines overlap. Any very demanding human activity combines in it the disciplines of Superior Force, of Culture, and of Nature. The novice will be told, "Do it this way, never mind asking why, just do it that way, that is the way we always do it." But it is probably just the way they always do it, and usually for the very good reason that it is a way that has been found to work. Think, for example, of ballet training. The student in a class is told to do this exercise, or that; to stand so; to do this or that with his head, arms shoulders, abdomen, hips, legs, feet. He is constantly corrected. There is no argument. But behind these seemingly autocratic demands by the teacher lie many decades of custom and tradition, and behind that, the necessities of dancing itself. You cannot make the moves of classical ballet unless over many years you have acquired, and renewed every day, the needed strength and suppleness in scores of muscles and joints. Nor can you do the difficult motions, making them look easy, unless you have learned hundreds of easier ones first. Dance teachers may not always agree on all the details of teaching these strengths and skills. But no novice could learn them all by himself. You could not go for a night or two to watch the ballet and then, without any other knowledge at all, teach yourself how to do it. In the same way, you would be unlikely to learn any complicated and difficult human activity without drawing heavily on the experience of those who know it better. But the point is that the authority of these experts or teachers stems from, grows out of their greater competence and experience, the fact that what they do *works*, not the fact that they happen to be the teacher and as such have the power to kick a student out of the class. And the further point is that children are always and everywhere attracted to the competence, and ready and eager to submit themselves to a discipline that grows out of it. We hear constantly that children will never do anything unless compelled to by bribes or threats. But in their private lives, or in extracurricular activities in school, in sports, music, drama, art, running a newspaper, and so on, they often submit themselves willingly and wholeheartedly to very intense disciplines, simply because they want to learn to do a given thing well. Our Little-Napoleon football coaches, of whom we have too many and hear far too much, blind us to the fact that millions of children work hard every year getting better at sports and games without coaches barking and yelling at them.

(1972, 1988)

WHY WE FALL IN LOVE
M. SCOTT PECK

Of all the misconceptions about love the most powerful and pervasive is the belief that "falling in love" is love or at least one of the manifestations of love. It is a potent misconception because falling in love is subjectively experienced in a very powerful fashion as an experience of love. When a person falls in love what he or she certainly feels is "I love him" or "I love her." But two problems are immediately apparent. The first is that the experience of falling in love is specifically a sex-linked erotic experience. We do not fall in love with our children though we may love them very deeply. We do not fall in love with our friends of the same sex–unless we are homosexually oriented–even though we may care for them greatly. We fall in love only when we are consciously or unconsciously sexually motivated. The second problem is that the experience of falling in love is invariably temporary. No matter whom we fall in love with, we sooner or later fall out of love if the relationship continues long enough. This is not to say that we invariably cease loving the person with whom we fell in love. But it is to say that the feeling of ecstatic lovingness that characterizes the experience of falling in love always passes. The honeymoon always ends. The bloom of romance always fades.

To understand the nature of the phenomenon of falling in love and the inevitability of its ending, it is necessary to examine the nature of what psychiatrists call ego boundaries. From what we can ascertain by indirect evidence, it appears that the newborn infant during the first few months of its life does not distinguish between itself and the rest of the universe. When it moves its arms and legs, the world is moving. When it is hungry, the world is hungry. When it sees its mother move, it is as if it is moving. When its mother sings, the baby does not know that it is itself not making the sound. It cannot distinguish itself from the crib, the room and its parents. The animate and inanimate are the same. There is no distinction yet between I and thou. It and the world are one. There are no boundaries, no separations. There is no identity.

But with experience the child begins to experience itself–namely, as an entity separate from the rest of the world. When it is hungry, mother doesn't always appear to feed it. When it is playful, mother doesn't always want to play. The child then has the experience of its wishes not being its mother's command. Its will is experienced as something separate from its mother's behavior. A sense of the "me" begins to develop. This interaction between the infant and the mother is believed to be the ground out of which the child's sense of identity begins to grow. It has been observed that when the interaction between the infant and its mother is grossly disturbed–for example, when there is no mother, no satisfactory mother substitute or when because of her own mental illness the mother is totally uncaring or uninterested–then the infant grows into a child or adult whose sense of identity is grossly defective in the most basic ways.

As the infant recognizes its will to be its own and not that of the universe, it begins to make other distinctions between itself and the world. When it wills movement, its arm waves before its eyes, but neither the crib nor the ceiling move. Thus the child learns that its arm and its will are connected, and therefore that its arm is its and not something or someone else's. In this manner, during the first year of life, we learn the fundamentals of who we are and who we are not, what we are and what we are not. By the end of our first year we know this is my arm, my foot, my head, my tongue, my eyes and even my viewpoint, my voice, my thoughts, my stomach-ache, and my feelings. We know our size and our physical limits. These limits are our boundaries. The knowledge of these limits inside our minds is what is meant by ego boundaries.

The development of ego boundaries is a process that continues through childhood into adolescence and even into adulthood, but the boundaries established later are more psychic than physical. For instance, the age between two and three is typically a time when the child comes to terms with the limits of its power. While before this time the child has learned that its wish is not necessarily its mother's command, it still clings to the possibility that its wish might be its mother's command and the feeling that its wish would be her command. It is because of this hope and feeling that the two-year-old usually attempts to act like a tyrant and autocrat, trying to give orders to its parents, siblings and family pets as if they were menials in its own private army, and responds with regal fury when they won't be dictated to. Thus parents speak of this age as "the terrible twos." By the age of three the child has usually become more tractable and mellow as a result of an acceptance of the reality of its own relative powerlessness. Still, the possibility of omnipotence is such a sweet, sweet dream that it cannot be completely given up even after several years of very painful confrontation with one's own impotence. Although the child of three has come to accept the reality of the boundaries of its power, it will continue to escape occasionally for some years to come into a world of fantasy in which the possibility of omnipotence (particularly its own) still exists. This is the world of Superman and Captain Marvel. Yet gradually even the superheroes are given up, and by the time of mid-adolescence, young people know that they are individuals, confined to the boundaries of their flesh and the limits of their power, each one a relatively frail and impotent organism, existing only by cooperation within a group of fellow organisms called society. Within this group they are not particularly distinguished, yet they are isolated from others by their individual identities, boundaries and limits.

It is lonely behind these boundaries. Some people–particularly those whom psychiatrists call schizoid–because of unpleasant, traumatizing experiences in childhood, perceive the world outside of themselves as unredeemably dangerous, hostile, confusing and unnurturing. Such people feel their boundaries to be protecting and comforting and find a sense of safety in their loneliness. But most of us feel our loneliness to be painful and yearn to escape from behind the walls of our individual identities to a condition in which we can be more unified with the world outside of ourselves. The experience of falling in love allows us this escape–temporarily. The essence of the phenomenon of falling in love is a sudden collapse

206

of a section of an individual's ego boundaries, permitting one to merge his or her identity with that of another person. The sudden release of oneself from oneself, the explosive pouring out of oneself into the beloved, and the dramatic surcease of loneliness accompanying this collapse of ego boundaries is experienced by most of us as ecstatic. We and our beloved are one! Loneliness is no more!

In some respects (but certainly not in all) the act of falling in love is an act of regression. The experience of merging with the loved one has in it echoes from the time when we were merged with our mothers in infancy. Along with the merging we also reexperience the sense of omnipotence which we had to give up in our journey out of childhood. All things seem possible! United with our beloved we feel we can conquer all obstacles. We believe that the strength of our love will cause the forces of opposition to bow down in submission and melt away into the darkness. All problems will be overcome. The future will be all light. The unreality of these feelings when we have fallen in love is essentially the same as the unreality of the two-year-old who feels itself to be king of the family and the world with power unlimited.

Just as reality intrudes upon the two-year-old's fantasy of omnipotence so does reality intrude upon the fantastic unity of the couple who have fallen in love. Sooner or later, in response to the problems of daily living, individual will reasserts itself. He wants to have sex; she doesn't. She wants to go to the movies; he doesn't. He wants to put money in the bank; she wants a dishwasher. She wants to talk about her job; he wants to talk about his. She doesn't like his friends; he doesn't like hers. So both of them, in the privacy of their hearts, begin to come to the sickening realization that they are not one with the beloved, that the beloved has and will continue to have his or her own desires, tastes, prejudices and timing different from the other's. One by one, gradually or suddenly, the ego boundaries snap back into place; gradually or suddenly, they fall out of love. Once again they are two separate individuals. At this point they begin either to dissolve the ties of their relationship or to initiate the work of real loving.

By my use of the word "real" I am implying that the perception that we are loving when we fall in love is a false perception–that our subjective sense of lovingness is an illusion. Full elaboration of real love will be deferred until later in this section. However, by stating that it is when a couple falls out of love they may begin to really love I am also implying that real love does not have its roots in a feeling of love. To the contrary, real love often occurs in a context in which the feeling of love is lacking, when we act lovingly despite the fact that we don't feel loving. Assuming the reality of the definition of love with which we started, the experience of "falling in love" is not real love for the several reasons that follow.

Falling in love is not an act of will. It is not a conscious choice. No matter how open to or eager for it we may be, the experience may still elude us. Contrarily, the experience may capture us at times when we are definitely not seeking it, when it is inconvenient and undesirable. We are as likely to fall in love with someone with whom we are obviously ill matched as with someone more suitable. Indeed, we may not even like or admire the object of our passion, yet, try as we might, we may not be able to fall in love with a person whom we deeply respect and with whom a deep relationship would be in all ways desirable. This is not to say that the experience of falling in love is immune to discipline. Psychiatrists, for instance, frequently fall in love with their patients, just as their patients fall in love with them, yet out of duty to the patient and their role they are usually able to abort the collapse of their ego boundaries and give up the patient as a romantic object. The struggle and suffering of the discipline involved may be enormous. But discipline and will can only control the experience; they cannot create it. We can choose how to respond to the experience of falling in love, but we cannot choose the experience itself.

Falling in love is not an extension of one's limits or boundaries; it is a partial and temporary collapse of them. The extension of one's limits requires effort; falling in love is effortless. Lazy and undisciplined individuals are as likely to fall in love as energetic and dedicated ones. Once the precious moment of falling in love has passed and the boundaries have snapped back into place, the individual may be disillusioned, but is usually none the larger for the experience. When limits are extended or stretched, however, they tend to stay stretched. Real love is a permanently self-enlarging experience. Falling in love is not.

Falling in love has little to do with purposively nurturing one's spiritual development. If we have any purpose in mind when we fall in love it is to terminate our own loneliness and perhaps insure this result through marriage. Certainly we are not thinking of spiritual development. To the contrary, we perceive him or her as perfect, as having been perfected. If we see any faults in our beloved, we perceive them as insignificant–little quirks or darling eccentricities that only add color and charm.

If falling in love is not love, then what is it other than temporary and partial collapse of ego boundaries? I do not know. But the sexual specificity of the phenomenon leads me to suspect that it is a genetically determined instinctual component of mating behavior. In other words, the temporary collapse of ego boundaries that constitutes falling in love is a stereotypic response of human beings to a configuration of internal sexual drives and external sexual stimuli, which serves to increase the probability of sexual pairing and bonding so as to enhance the survival of the species. Or to put it in another, rather crass way, falling in love is a trick that our genes pull on our otherwise perceptive mind to hoodwink or trap us into marriage. Frequently the trick goes awry one way or another, as when the sexual drives and stimuli are homosexual or when other forces–parental interference, mental illness, conflicting responsibilities or mature self-discipline–supervene to prevent the bonding. On the other hand, without this trick, this illusory and inevitably temporary (it would not be practical were it not temporary) regression to infantile merging and omnipotence, many of us who are happily or unhappily married today would have retreated in wholehearted terror from the realism of the marriage vows.

(1978)

WHY MEN MARRY
GEORGE GILDER

Men marry for love. But what does this mean beyond what they got in their lives as single men: the flash of a new face, new flesh across a room. The glimpse of breasts shifting softly in a silken blouse. The open sesame of a missing ring. The excited pursuit, the misunderstood meanings, the charged meetings. The telling touch of hands. The eyes welling open to the gaze. The scent of surrender. The pillowed splash of unbound hair. The ecstatic slipping between new sheets. The race. The winning. The chase and the conquest. . . and back on the road. Definitely back on the road. Free again. Strong again. For new women, new pursuit. What more is there in life–in love–than this?

Marriage means giving it all up. Giving up love? That is how it seems to the single man, and that is why he fears it. He must give up his hunter's heart, forgo the getaway Honda growl, shear off his shaggy hair, restrict his random eye, hang up his handgun, bow down and enter the cage. At bottom, what he is is hunter. No way he will be hubby.

And yet, he will. For years he lunges at women's surfaces, but as time passes he learns of a deeper promise. For years he may not know the reasons or believe them or care. The heart, it is said, has its reasons. They spring from the primal predicament of man throughout the history of the race: the need to choose a particular woman and stay by her and provide for her if he is to know his children and they are to love him and call him father.

In procreative love, both partners consciously or unconsciously glimpse a future infant–precarious in the womb, vulnerable in the world, and in need of nurture and protection. In the swelter of their bodies together, in the shape and softness of the woman, in the protective support of the man, the couple senses the outlines of a realm that can endure and perpetuate their union: a pattern of differences and complements that goes beyond the momentary pleasures of reciprocal sex.

Marriage asks men to give up their essential sexuality only as part of a clear scheme for replacing it with new, far more important, and ultimately far more sexual roles: husband and father. Without these roles, a woman can bear a child, but the man is able only to screw. He can do it a lot, but after his first years it will only get him unthreaded, and in the end he is disconnected and alone. In his shallow heats and frustrations, he all too often becomes a menace to himself and his community.

There are millions of single men, unlinked to any promising reality, dissipating their lives by the years, moving from job to job, woman to woman, illusion to embitterment. Yet they are not hopeless. Many more millions have passed through the same sloughs, incurred the same boozy dreams, marijuana highs, cocaine crashes, sex diseases, job vapors, legal scrapes, wanderings. They follow the entire syndrome and then break out of it. Normally they do not escape through psychiatrists' offices, sex-education courses, VISTA or Peace Corps programs, reformatories, or guidance-counseling uplift. What happens, most of the time–the only effective thing that happens, the only process that reaches the sources of motivation and character–is falling in love.

Love is effective because it works at a deeper, more instinctual level than the other modes of education and change. Love does not teach or persuade. It possesses and transforms. . . .

It is not just an intelligent appraisal of his circumstances that transforms the single man. It is not merely a desire for companionship or "growth." It is a deeper alchemy of change, flowing from a primal source. It seeps slowly into the flesh, the memory, the spirit; it rises through a life, until it can ignite. It is a perilous process, full of chances for misfire and mistake–or for an ever more mildewed middle age. It is not entirely understood. But we have seen it work, and so have we seen love. Love unifies reason and experience with the power to change a man caught in a morbid present into a man passionately engaged with the future.

The change that leads to love often comes slowly. Many of the girls a man finds will not help. They tend to go along with him and affirm his single life. But one morning he turns to the stranger sleeping next to him, who came to him as easily as a whiskey too many, and left him as heavy-headed, and decides he must seek a better way to live. One day he looks across the room over a pile of dirty dishes and cigarette butts and beer cans and sex magazines and bills and filthy laundry, and he does not see the evidence of happy carousing and bachelor freedom; he sees a trap closing in upon him more grimly than any marriage. One day while joking with friends about the latest of his acquaintances to be caught and caged, he silently wonders, for a moment, whether he really wishes it were he.

Suddenly he has a new glimpse of himself. His body is beginning to decline, grow weaker and slower, even if he keeps it fit. His body, which once measured out his few advantages over females, is beginning to intimate its terrible plan to become as weak as an older woman's. His aggressiveness, which burst in fitful storms throughout his young life but never seemed to cleanse him–his aggression for which he could so rarely find the adequate battle, the harmonious chase–is souring now. His job, so below his measure as a man, so out of tune with his body and his inspiration, now stretches ahead without joy or relief.

His sex, the force that drove the flower of his youth, drives still, drives again and again the same hard bargain–for which there are fewer and fewer takers, in a sexual arena with no final achievement for the single man, in which sex itself becomes work that is never done.

The single man is caught on a reef and the tide is running out. He is being biologically stranded and he has a hopeless dream. Studs Terkel's book *Working* registers again and again men's desire to be remembered. Yet who in this world is much remembered for his job?

Stuck with what he may sense as a choice between being trapped and being stranded, he still may respond by trying one more fling. The biological predicament can be warded off for a time, like Hemingway's hyena. Death often appears in the guise of eternal youth, at the ever-infatuating fountains: alcohol, drugs, hallucinogenic sex. For a while he may believe in the disguise. But the hyena returns and there is mortality in the air–diseases, accidents, concealed suicides, the whole range of the single man's aggression, turned at last against himself.

But where there is death, there is hope. For the man who is in touch with his mortality, but not in the grips of it, is also in touch with the sources of his love. He is in contact with the elements–the natural fires and storms so often used as metaphors for his passions. He is a man who can be deeply and effectively changed. He can find his age, his relation to the world, his maturity, his future. He can burn his signature into the covenant of a specific life.

The man has found a vital energy and a possibility of durable change. It has assumed the shape of a woman. It is the same form that has caught his eye and roiled his body all these years. But now there will be depths below the pleasing surfaces, meanings beyond the momentary ruttings. There will be a sense that this vessel contains the secrets of new life, that the womb and breasts bear a message of immortality. There will be a knowledge that to treat this treasure as an object–mere flesh like his own, a mere matrix of his pleasure–is to defile life itself. It is this recognition that she offers a higher possibility–it is this consciousness that he has to struggle to be worthy of her–that finally issues the spark. And then arises the fire that purges and changes him as it consumes his own death. His children... they will remember. It is the only hope.

The man's love begins in a knowledge of inferiority, but it offers a promise of dignity and purpose. For he then has to create, by dint of his own effort, and without the miracle of a womb, a life that a woman should choose. Thus are released and formed the energies of civilized society. He provides, and he does it for a lifetime, for a life. (1986)

WHY THE
JUSTICE SYSTEM FAILS
ROGER ROSENBLATT

Anyone who claims it is impossible to get rid of the random violence of today's mean streets may be telling the truth, but is also missing the point. Street crime may be normal in the U.S., but it is not inevitable at such advanced levels, and the fact is that there are specific reasons for the nation's incapacity to keep its street crime down. Almost all these reasons can be traced to the American criminal justice system. It is not that there are no mechanisms in place to deal with American crime, merely that the existing ones are impractical, inefficient, anachronistic, uncooperative, and often lead to as much civic destruction as they are meant to curtail.

Why does the system fail? For one thing, the majority of criminals go untouched by it. The police learn about one-quarter of the thefts committed each year, and about less than half the robberies, burglaries and rapes. Either victims are afraid or ashamed to report crimes, or they may conclude gloomily that nothing will be done if they do. Murder is the crime the police do hear about, but only 73% of the nation's murders lead to arrest. The arrest rates for lesser crimes are astonishingly low–59% for aggravated assault in 1979, 48% for rape, 25% for robbery, 15% for burglary.

Even when a suspect is apprehended, the chances of his getting punished are mighty slim. In New York State each year there are some 130,000 felony arrests; approximately 8,000 people go to prison. There are 94,000 felony arrests in New York City; 5,000 to 6,000 serve time. A 1974 study of the District of Columbia came up with a similar picture. Of those arrested for armed robbery, less than one-quarter went to prison. More than 6,000 aggravated assaults were reported; 116 people were put away. A 1977 study of such cities as Detroit, Indianapolis and New Orleans produced slightly better numbers, but nothing to counteract the exasperation of New York Police Commissioner Robert McGuire: "The criminal justice system almost creates incentives for street criminals."

It is hard to pinpoint any one stage of the system that is more culpable than any other. Start with the relationship between police and prosecutors. Logic would suggest that these groups work together like the gears of a watch since, theoretically, they have the same priorities: to arrest and convict. But prosecutors have enormous caseloads, and too often they simply focus on lightening them. Or they work too fast and lose a case; or they plea-bargain and diminish justice. The police also work too fast too often, are concerned with "clearing" arrests, for which they get credit. They receive no credit for convictions. Their work gets sloppy–misinformation recorded, witnesses lost, no follow-up. That 1974 study of the District of Columbia indicated that fully one-third of the police making arrests failed to process a single conviction. A study released this week of 2,418 police in seven cities showed that 15% were credited with half the convictions; 31% had no convictions whatever.

The criminal justice system is also debased by plea bargaining. At present nine out of ten convictions occur because of a guilty plea arrived at through a deal between the state and defendant, in which the defendant forgoes his right to trial. Of course, plea bargaining keeps the courts less crowded and doubtless sends to jail, albeit for a shorter stretch, some felons who might have gotten off if judged by their peers. And many feel that a bargain results in a truer level of justice, since prosecutors tend to hike up the charge in the first place in anticipation of defendant's copping a plea. Still, there are tricks like "swallowing the gun"–reducing the charge of armed robbery to unarmed robbery–that are performed for expediency, not for justice.

"Justice delayed is justice denied" is a root principle of common law, but nowadays the right to a speedy trial is so regularly denied that the thought seems antique. Last August 1, a witness was prepared to testify that Cornelius Wright, 18, shot him five times in the chest, stomach and legs. Because of a series of mishaps and continuances, Wright has been sitting in the Cook County jail for more than eight months. In fact, Wright's delay is the norm; eight months is the average time between arrest and trial. Continuances have so clogged Chicago's courts that the city's Crime Commission issues a monthly "Ten Most Wanted Dispositions" list in an effort to prod the system.

Detroit Deputy Police Chief James Bannon believes that trial delays work against the victim. "The judge doesn't see the hysterical, distraught victim. He sees a person who comes into court after several months or years who is totally different. He sees a defendant that bears no relationship to what he appeared to be at the time of the crime. He sits there in a nice three-piece suit and keeps his mouth shut. And the judge doesn't see the shouting, raging animal the victim saw when she was being raped, for example. Both the defendant and victim have lawyers, and that's what the court hears: law. It doesn't hear the guts of the crime."

Procedural concerns can cause delays, and in rare cases defendants' rights can be carried to absurd extremes. California Attorney General George Deukmejian tells of Willie Edward Level, who was convicted of beating a Bakersfield College woman student to death with a table leg. Level was informed of his right to remain silent and/or have an attorney present (the *Miranda* ruling). He waived these rights and confessed to the murder. Yet the California Court of Appeals threw out the conviction because Level had asked to speak to his mother at the time of his arrest and had not been permitted to; had he been able to do so, it was argued, he might not have made his confession.

"There's nothing in *Miranda* that says a defendant has the right to talk with his mother or a friend," says Deukmejian. "It says he can talk to a lawyer or not at all. It's so much of this kind of thing that makes a mockery of the system. And every time you have one these rulings it has the effect of dragging out the length of cases, which builds in more and more delays. We've got a murder case in Sacramento that's been in the pretrial state for four years."

Add to this the fact that witnesses are discouraged and lost by trial delays. In New York the average number of appearances a witness has to make in a given disposition is 17. Few people have the time or stamina to see a case through.

Then there is the matter of bail. In a recent speech before the American Bar Association, Chief Justice Warren Burger argued for tightening the standards for releasing defendants on bail, which seems justifiable. But the subject is complicated. Technically, judges are supposed to base their decisions about bail strictly on the likelihood of a defendant's appearing for trials. In practice, however, this is mere guesswork, and a great many serious crimes are committed by people out on bail or by bail jumpers, who are often given bail when rearrested. One sound reason for a bail system is to avoid locking up anyone before he is proved guilty. But it's simply unrealistic to disregard the criterion of likely dangerousness, even though it raises serious constitutional questions. It has probably resulted in more tragedies than a different standard would result in denials of civil liberties.

Judges blame the cops, and cops blame the judges. Patrick F. Healy, executive director of the Chicago Crime Commission, says judges are plain lazy. "Last year we did a spot check, and the judges' day on the bench totaled 3 hours 49 minutes." The judges will not concede laziness, but several of the nation's best, like Marvin Frankel, former federal judge in the District Court of Manhattan, admit to a "remarkable lack of consistency" in the judiciary. Judge Lois Forer, a most respected criminal-court justice in Philadelphia, contends that it "simply isn't true" that defendants get off on technicalities. It is just that "the system is overloaded."

She also emphasizes the problem of sloppy preparations: "It's truly painful when there's someone you're pretty sure committed a crime, and they [police, prosecutors] don't bring in the evidence."

Almost every critic of the system cites the lack of prison space. Despite the enormously high operating costs ($4 billion annually for all U.S. penal institutions), more prison space is an absolute necessity. New York State has between 22,000 and 24,000 jail cells. All are filled, some beyond proper capacity. Twice this year local officials in Missouri were asked not to send any more inmates to the state penitentiary. As a result the St. Louis county jail had to retain seven prisoners who ought to have been in the state pen, even though it meant holding eleven more inmates than the jail was intended to hold. Florida, which already has a higher proportion of its citizenry under lock and key than any other state, may need to spend $83 million on new prison construction and staff. This month 223 supposedly nonviolent inmates of Illinois' 13 prisons were given early release to make room for 223 newcomers. New York Police Inspector Richard Dillon, one of the nation's most thoughtful law officers, cites lack of prison space as the primary cause of city crime—the ultimate reason for inappropriate plea bargains, premature paroles, careless bail and too brief sentences.

Finally, the criminal justice system fails at its most sensitive level, that of juvenile crime. Until recently few juvenile courts admitted there was such a thing as a bad boy, restricting their vision of youthful offenders to memories of Father Flanagan's Boys Town or to Judge Tom Clark's quaint view that "every boy, in his heart, would rather steal second base than an automobile." In fact, there are several boys these days who would prefer to kill the umpire, and who have done so, only to receive light sentences or none at all A study by Marvin Wolfgang at the University of Pennsylvania traced the criminal careers of 10,000 males born in 1948. By the age of 16, 35% had one arrest, but then almost all stopped committing crimes. A small group, however, did not: 627 had five arrests by the time they were adults. They accounted for two-thirds of all the violent crime attributed to the group and almost all the homicides. "This is the group that society is afraid of, and rightly so," says Wolfgang. He is now studying a new group, born in 1958, which is "even nastier and more violent. We should concentrate on them and capture them as soon as possible."

Of course, there is no place to put this hard core, and that is part of the problem. The main difficulty, however, is a Pollyannish, outdated vision of youth, one that results in treating a child not as a potentially responsible human being but rather as some vague romantic entity, capable of continuous regeneration. An underage murderer may be put away for a few months or not at all. As Harvard's James Q. Wilson says, "The adult system is harsh, but before that it's a free ride." The ride is not only free, but clean. At the age of 18, juvenile criminals in many states start all over with unblemished records no matter how many crimes they have committed earlier.

In short, the criminal justice system is not really a system–at least not one in which the individual parts work well on their own or mesh effectively with each other. Few of the participants deny this, and while there is a natural tendency for each stratum–police, lawyers, prosecutors, judges, prison officials–to lay blame for the system's failures on one another, nobody is happy with the current situation. Reforming the system, however, is a tricky business, especially when reforms are likely to tend toward severity. "For my part," said Oliver Wendell Holmes in *Olmstead vs. U.S.*, "I think it a less evil that some criminals should escape than that the Government should play an ignoble part." Whatever reforms are contemplated, Justice Holmes will preside. (1981)

LETTER FROM BIRMINGHAM JAIL
MARTIN LUTHER KING, JR.

April 16, 1963

My Dear Fellow Clergymen:

WHILE CONFINED here in the Birmingham city jail, I came across your recent statement calling my present activities "unwise and untimely." Seldom do I pause to answer criticism of my work and ideas. If I sought to answer all the criticisms that cross my desk, my secretaries would have little time for anything other than such correspondence in the course of the day, and I would have no time for constructive work. But since I feel that you are men of genuine good will and that your criticisms are sincerely set forth, I want to try to answer your statement in what I hope will be patient and reasonable terms.

I think I should indicate why I am here in Birmingham, since you have been influenced by the view which argues against "outsiders coming in." I have the honor of serving as president of the Southern Christian Leadership Conference, and organization operating in every southern state, with headquarters in Atlanta, Georgia. We have some eighty-five affiliated organizations across the South, and one of them is the Alabama Christian Movement for Human Rights. Frequently we share staff, educational, and financial resources with our affiliates. Several months ago the affiliate here in Birmingham asked us to be on call to engage in a nonviolent direct-action program if such were deemed necessary. We readily consented, and when the hour came we lived up to our promise. So I, along with several members of my staff, am here because I was invited here. I am here because I have organizational ties here.

But more basically, I am in Birmingham because injustice is here. Just as the prophets of the eighth century B.C. left their villages and carried their "thus saith the Lord" far beyond the boundaries of their home towns, and just as the Apostle Paul left his village of Tarsus and carried the gospel of Jesus Christ to the far corners of the Greco-Roman world, so am I compelled to carry the gospel of freedom beyond my own home town. Like Paul, I must constantly respond to the Macedonian call for aid.

Moreover, I am cognizant of the interrelatedness of all communities and states. I cannot sit idly by in Atlanta and not be concerned about what happens in Birmingham. Injustice anywhere is a threat to justice everywhere. We are caught in an inescapable network of mutuality, tied in a single garment of destiny. Whatever affects one directly, affects all indirectly. Never again can we afford to live with the narrow, provincial "outside agitator" idea. Anyone who lives inside the United States can never be considered an outsider anywhere within its bounds.

You deplore the demonstrations taking place in Birmingham. But your statement, I am sorry to say, fails to express a similar concern for the conditions that brought about the demonstrations. I am sure that none of you would want to rest content with the superficial kind of social analysis that deals merely with effects and does not grapple with underlying causes. It is unfortunate that demonstrations are taking place in Birmingham, but it is even more unfortunate that the city's white power structure left the Negro community with no alternative.

In any nonviolent campaign there are four basic steps: collection of the facts to determine whether injustices exist; negotiation; self-purification; and direct action. We have gone through all these steps in Birmingham. There can be no gainsaying the fact that racial injustice engulfs this community. Birmingham is probably the most thoroughly segregated city in the United States. Its ugly record of brutality is widely known. Negroes have experienced grossly unjust treatment in the courts. There have been more unsolved bombings of Negro homes and churches in Birmingham than in any other city in the nation. These are the hard, brutal facts of the case. On the basis of these conditions, Negro leaders sought to negotiate with the city fathers. But the latter consistently refused to engage in good-faith negotiation.

Then, last September, came the opportunity to talk with leaders of Birmingham's economic community. In the course of the negotiations, certain promises were made by the merchants–for example, to remove the stores' humiliating racial signs. On the basis of these promises, the Reverend Fred Shuttlesworth and the leaders of the Alabama Christian Movement for Human Rights agreed to a moratorium on all demonstrations. As the weeks and months went by, we realized that we were the victims of a broken promise. A few signs, briefly removed, returned; the others remained.

As in so many past experiences, our hopes had been blasted, and the shadow of deep disappointment settled upon us. We had no alternative except to prepare for direct action, whereby we would present our very bodies as a means of laying our case before the conscience of the local and the national community. Mindful of the difficulties involved, we decided to undertake a process of self-purification. We began a series of workshops on nonviolence, and we repeatedly asked ourselves: "Are you able to accept blows without retaliating?" "Are you able to endure the ordeal of jail?" We decided to schedule our direct-action program for the Easter season, realizing that except for Christmas, this is the main shopping period of the year. Knowing that a strong economic-withdrawal program would be the by-product of the direct action, we felt that this would be the best time to bring pressure to bear on the merchants for the needed change.

Then it occurred to us that Birmingham's mayoral election was coming up in March, and we speedily decided to postpone action until after election day. When we discovered that the Commissioner of Public Safety, Eugene "Bull" Connor, had piled up enough votes to be in the run-off, we decided again to postpone action until the day after the run-off so that the demonstrations could not be used to cloud the issues. Like many others, we waited to see Mr. Connor defeated, and to this end we endured postponement after postponement. Having aided in this community need, we felt that our direct-action program could be delayed no longer.

You may well ask: "Why direct action? Why sit-ins, marches and so forth? Isn't negotiation a better path?" You are right in calling for negotiation. Indeed, this is the very purpose of direct action. Nonviolent direct action seeks to create such a crisis and foster such a tension that a community which has constantly refused to negotiate is forced to confront the issue. It seeks so to dramatize the issue that it can no longer be ignored. My citing the creation of tension as part of the work of the nonviolent-resister may sound rather shocking. But I must confess that I am not afraid of the word "tension." I have earnestly opposed violent tension, but there is a type of constructive, nonviolent tension which is necessary for growth. Just as Socrates felt that it was necessary to create a tension in the mind so that individuals could rise from the bondage of myths and half-truths to the unfettered realm of creative analysis and objective appraisal, so must we see the need for nonviolent gadflies to create the kind of tension in society that will help men rise from the dark depths of prejudice and racism to the majestic heights of understanding and brotherhood.

The purpose of our direct-action program is to create a situation so crisis-packed that it will inevitably open the door to negotiation. I therefore concur with you in your call for negotiation. Too long has our beloved Southland been bogged down in a tragic effort to live in monologue rather than dialogue.

One of the basic points in your statement is that the action that I and my associates have taken in Birmingham is untimely. Some have asked: "Why didn't you give the new city administration time to act?" The only answer that I can give to this query is that the new Birmingham administration must be prodded about as much as the outgoing one before it will act. We are sadly mistaken if we feel that the election of Albert Boutwell as mayor will bring the millennium to Birmingham. While Mr. Boutwell is a much more gentle person than Mr. Connor, they are both segregationists, dedicated to maintenance of the status quo. I have hope that Mr. Boutwell will be reasonable enough to see the futility of massive resistance to desegregation. But he will not see this without pressure from devotees of civil rights. My friends, I must say to you that we have not made a single gain in civil rights without determined legal and nonviolent pressure. Lamentably, it is an historical fact that privileged groups seldom give up their privileges voluntarily. Individuals may see the moral light and voluntarily give up their unjust posture; but, as Reinhold Niebuhr has reminded us, groups tend to be more immoral than individuals.

We know through painful experience that freedom is never voluntarily given by the oppressor; it must be demanded by the oppressed. Frankly, I have yet to engage in a direct-action campaign that was "well timed" in the view of those who have not suffered unduly from the disease of segregation. For years now I have heard the word "Wait!" It rings in the ear of every Negro with piercing familiarity. This

"Wait" has almost always meant "Never." We must come to see, with one of our distinguished jurists, that "justice too long delayed is justice denied."

We have waited for more than 340 years for our constitutional God-given rights. The nations of Asia and Africa are moving with jetlike speed toward gaining political independence, but we still creep at horse-and-buggy pace toward gaining a cup of coffee at a lunch counter. Perhaps it is easy for those who have never felt the stinging darts of segregation to say, "Wait." But when you have seen vicious mobs lynch your mothers and fathers at will and drown your sisters and brothers at whim; when you have seen hate-filled policemen curse, kick, and even kill your black brothers and sisters; when you see the vast majority of your twenty million Negro brothers smothering in an airtight cage of poverty in the midst of an affluent society; when you suddenly find your tongue twisted and your speech stammering as you seek to explain to your six-year-old daughter why she can't go to the public amusement park that has just been advertised on television, and see tears welling up in her eyes when she is told that Funtown is closed to colored children, and see ominous clouds of inferiority beginning to form in her little mental sky, and see her beginning to distort her personality by developing an unconscious bitterness toward white people; when you have to concoct an answer for a five-year-old son who is asking: "Daddy, why do white people treat colored people so mean?"; when you take a cross-country drive and find it necessary to sleep night after night in the uncomfortable corners of your automobile because no motel will accept you; when you are humiliated day in and day out by nagging signs reading "white" and "colored"; when your first name becomes "nigger," your middle name becomes "boy" (however old you are), and your last name becomes "John," and your wife and mother are never given the respected title "Mrs."; when you are harried by day and haunted by night by the fact that you are a Negro, living constantly at tiptoe stance, never quite knowing what to expect next, and are plagued with inner fears and outer resentments; when you are forever fighting a degenerating sense of "nobodiness"–then you will understand why we find it difficult to wait. There comes a time when the cup of endurance runs over, and men are no longer willing to be plunged into the abyss of despair. I hope, sirs, you can understand our legitimate and unavoidable impatience.

You express a great deal of anxiety over our willingness to break laws. This is certainly a legitimate concern. Since we so diligently urge people to obey the Supreme Court's decision of 1954 outlawing segregation in the public schools, at first glance it may seem rather paradoxical for us consciously to break laws. One may well ask: "How can you advocate breaking some laws and obeying others?" The answer lies in the fact that there are two types of laws: just and unjust. I would be the first to advocate obeying laws. Conversely, one has a moral responsibility to disobey unjust laws. I would agree with St. Augustine that "an unjust law is no law at all."

Now, what is the difference between the two? How does one determine whether a law is just or unjust? A just law is a man-made code that squares with the moral law or the law of God. An unjust law is a code that is out of harmony with the moral law. To put it in the terms of St. Thomas Aquinas: An unjust law is a human law that is not rooted in eternal law and natural law. Any law that uplifts human personality is just. Any law that degrades human personality is unjust. All segregation statutes are unjust because segregation distorts the soul and damages the personality. It gives the segregator a false sense of superiority and the segregated a false sense of inferiority. Segregation, to use the terminology of the Jewish philosopher Martin Buber, substitutes an "I-it" relationship for an "I-thou" relationship and ends up relegating persons to the status of things. Hence, segregation is not only politically, economically, and sociologically unsound, it is morally wrong and sinful. Paul Tillich has said that sin is separation. Is not segregation an existential expression of man's tragic separation, his awful estrangement, his terrible sinfulness? Thus it is that I can urge men to obey the 1954 decision of the Supreme Court, for it is morally right; and I can urge them to disobey segregation ordinances, for they are morally wrong.

Let us consider a more concrete example of just and unjust laws. An unjust law is a code that a numerical or power majority group compels a minority group to obey but does not make binding on itself. This is *difference* made legal. By the same token, a just law is a code that a majority compels a minority to follow and that it is willing to follow itself. This is *sameness* made legal.

Let me give another explanation. A law is unjust if it is inflicted on a minority that, as a result of being denied the right to vote, had no part in enacting or devising the law. Who can say that the legislature of Alabama which set up that state's segregation laws was democratically elected? Throughout Alabama all sorts of devious methods are used to prevent Negroes from becoming registered voters, and there are some counties in which, even though Negroes constitute a majority of the population, not a single Negro is registered. Can any law enacted under such circumstances be considered democratically structured?

Sometimes a law is just on its face and unjust in its application. For instance, I have been arrested on a charge of parading without a permit. Now, there is nothing wrong in having an ordinance which requires a permit for a parade. But such an ordinance becomes unjust when it is used to maintain segregation and to deny citizens the First-Amendment privilege of peaceful assembly and protest.

I hope you are able to see the distinction I am trying to point out. In no sense do I advocate evading or defying the law, as would the rabid segregationist. That would lead to anarchy. One who breaks an unjust law must do so openly, lovingly, and with a willingness to accept the penalty. I submit that an individual who breaks a law that conscience tells him is unjust, and who willingly accepts the penalty of imprisonment in order to arouse the conscience of the community over its injustice, is in reality expressing the highest respect for law.

Of course, there is nothing new about this kind of civil disobedience. It was evidenced sublimely in the refusal of Shadrach, Meshach, and Abednego to obey the laws of Nebuchadnezzar, on the ground that a higher moral law was at stake. It

221

was practiced superbly by the early Christians, who were willing to face hungry lions and the excruciating pain of chopping blocks rather than submit to certain unjust laws of the Roman Empire. To a degree, academic freedom is a reality today because Socrates practiced civil disobedience. In our own nation, the Boston Tea Party represented a massive act of civil disobedience.

We should never forget that everything Adolf Hitler did in Germany was "legal" and everything the Hungarian freedom fighters did in Hungary was "illegal." It was "illegal" to aid and comfort a Jew in Hitler's Germany. Even so, I am sure that, had I lived in Germany at the time, I would have aided and comforted my Jewish brothers. If today I lived in a Communist country where certain principles dear to the Christian faith are suppressed, I would openly advocate disobeying that country's antireligious laws.

I must make two honest confessions to you, my Christian and Jewish brothers. First, I must confess that over the past few years I have been gravely disappointed with the white moderate. I have almost reached the regrettable conclusion that the Negro's great stumbling block in his stride toward freedom is not the White Citizens' Counciler or the Ku Klux Klanner, but the white moderate, who is more devoted to "order" than to justice; who prefers a negative peace which is the presence of tension to a positive peace which is the presence of justice; who constantly says: "I agree with you in the goal you seek, but I cannot agree with your methods of direct action'" who paternalistically believes he can set the timetable for another man's freedom; who lives by a mythical concept of time and who constantly advises the Negro to wait for a "more convenient season." Shallow understanding from people of good will is more frustrating than absolute misunderstanding from people of ill will. Lukewarm acceptance is much more bewildering than outright rejection.

I had hoped that the white moderate would understand that law and order exist for the purpose of establishing justice and that when they fail in this purpose they become the dangerously structured dams that block the flow of social progress. I had hoped that the white moderate would understand that the present tension in the South is a necessary phase of the transition from an obnoxious negative peace, in which the Negro passively accepted his unjust plight, to a substantive and positive peace, in which all men will respect the dignity and worth of human personality. Actually, we who engage in nonviolent direct action are not the creators of tension. We merely bring to the surface the hidden tension that is already alive. We bring it out in the open, where it can be seen and dealt with. Like a boil that can never be cured so long as it is covered up but must be opened with all its ugliness to the natural medicines of air and light, injustice must be exposed, with all the tension its exposure creates, to the light of human conscience and the air of national opinion before it can be cured.

In your statement you assert that our actions, even though peaceful, must be condemned because they precipitate violence. But is this a logical assertion? Isn't this like condemning a robbed man because his possession of money precipitated the evil act of robbery? Isn't this like condemning Socrates because his unswerving commitment to truth and his philosophical inquiries precipitated the act by the misjudged populace in which they made him drink hemlock? Isn't this like condemning Jesus because his unique God-consciousness and never-ceasing devotion to God's will precipitated the evil act of crucifixion? We must come to see that, as the federal courts have consistently affirmed, it is wrong to urge an individual to cease his efforts to gain his basic constitutional rights because the quest may precipitate violence. Society must protect the robbed and punish the robber.

I had also hoped that the white moderate would reject the myth concerning time in relation to the struggle for freedom. I have just received a letter from a white brother in Texas. He writes: "All Christians know that the colored people will receive equal rights eventually, but it is possible that you are in too great a religious hurry. It has taken Christianity almost two thousand years to accomplish what it has. The teachings of Christ take time to come to earth." Such an attitude stems from a tragic misconception of time, from the strangely irrational notion that there is something in the very flow of time that will inevitably cure all ills. Actually, time itself is neutral; it can be used either destructively or constructively. More and more I feel that the people of ill will have used time much more effectively than have the people of good will. We will have to repent in this generation not merely for the hateful words and actions of the bad people but for the appalling silence of the good people. Human progress never rolls in on wheels of inevitability; it comes through the tireless efforts of men willing to be co-workers with God, and without this hard work, time itself becomes an ally of the forces of social stagnation. We must use time creatively, in the knowledge that the time is always ripe to do right. Now is the time to make real the promise of democracy and transform our pending national elegy into a creative psalm of brotherhood. Now is the time to lift our national policy from the quicksand of racial injustice to the solid rock of human dignity.

You speak of our activity in Birmingham as extreme. At first I was rather disappointed that fellow clergymen would see my nonviolent efforts as those of an extremist. I began thinking about the fact that I stand in the middle of two opposing forces in the Negro community. One is a force of complacency, made up in part of Negroes who, as a result of long years of oppression, are so drained of self-respect and a sense of "somebodiness" that they have adjusted to segregation; and in part of a few middle-class Negroes who, because of a degree of academic and economic security and because in some ways they profit by segregation, have become insensitive to the problems of the masses. The other force is one of bitterness and hatred, and it comes perilously close to advocating violence. It is expressed in the various black nationalists groups that are springing up across the nation, the largest and best-known being Elijah Muhammad's Muslim movement. Nourished by the Negro's frustration over the continued existence of racial discrimination, this movement is made up of people who have lost faith in America, who have absolutely repudiated Christianity, and who have concluded that the white man is an incorrigible "devil."

I have tried to stand between these two forces, saying that we need emulate neither the "do-nothingism" of the complacent nor the hatred and despair of the black nationalist. For there is the more excellent way of love and nonviolent protest. I am grateful to God that, through the influence of the Negro church, the way of nonviolence became an integral part of our struggle.

If this philosophy had not emerged, by now many streets of the South would, I am convinced, be flowing with blood. And I am further convinced that if our white brothers dismiss as "rabble-rousers" and "outside agitators" those of us who employ nonviolent direct action, and if they refuse to support our nonviolent efforts, millions of the Negroes will, out of frustration and despair, seek solace and security in black-nationalist ideologies–a development that would inevitably lead to a frightening racial nightmare.

Oppressed people cannot remain oppressed forever. The yearning for freedom eventually manifests itself, and that is what has happened to the American Negro. Something within has reminded him of his birthright of freedom, and something without has reminded him that it can be gained. Consciously or unconsciously, he has been caught up by the *Zeitgeist*, and with his black brothers of Africa and his brown and yellow brothers of Asia, South America, and the Caribbean, the United States Negro is moving with a sense of great urgency toward the promised land of racial justice. If one recognizes this vital urge that has engulfed the Negro community, one should readily understand why public demonstrations are taking place. The Negro has many pent-up resentments and latent frustrations, and he must release them. So let him march; let him make prayer pilgrimages to the city hall; let him go on freedom rides–and try to understand why he must do so. If his repressed emotions are not released in nonviolent ways, they will seek expression through violence; this is not a threat but a fact of history. So I have not said to my people: "Get rid of your discontent." Rather, I have tried to say that this normal and healthy discontent can be channeled into the creative outlet of nonviolent direct action. And now this approach is being termed extremist.

But although I was initially disappointed at being categorized as an extremist, as I continued to think about the matter I gradually gained a measure of satisfaction from the label. Was not Jesus an extremist for love: "Love your enemies, bless them that curse you, do good to them that hate you, and pray for them which despitefully use you, and persecute you." Was not Amos an extremist for justice: "Let justice roll down like waters and righteousness like an ever-flowing stream." Was not Paul an extremist for the Christian gospel: "I bear in my body the marks of the Lord Jesus." Was not Martin Luther an extremist: "Here I stand; I cannot do otherwise, so help me God." And John Bunyan: "I will stay in jail to the end of my days before I make a butchery of my conscience." And Abraham Lincoln: "This nation cannot survive half slave and half free." And Thomas Jefferson: "We hold these truths to be self-evident, that all men are created equal. . . ." So the question is not whether we will be extremists, but what kind of extremists we will be. Will we be extremists for hate or for love? Will we be extremists for the preservation of injustice or for the extension of justice? In that dramatic scene on

Calvary's hill three men were crucified. We must never forget that all three were crucified for the same crime–the crime of extremism. Two were extremists for immorality, and thus fell below their environment. The other, Jesus Christ, was an extremist for love, truth and goodness, and thereby rose above his environment. Perhaps the South, the nation and the world are in dire need of creative extremists.

I had hoped that the white moderate would see this need. Perhaps I was too optimistic; perhaps I expected too much. I suppose I should have realized that few members of the oppressor race can understand the deep groans and passionate yearnings of the oppressed race, and still fewer have the vision to see that injustice must be rooted out by strong, persistent, and determined action. I am thankful, however, that some of our white brothers in the South have grasped the meaning of this social revolution and committed themselves to it. They are still all too few in quantity, but they are big in quality. Some–such as Ralph McGill, Lillian Smith, Harry Golden, James McBride Dabbs, Ann Braden, and Sarah Patton Boyle–have written about our struggle in eloquent and prophetic terms. Others have marched with us down nameless streets of the South. They have languished in filthy, roach-infested jails, suffering the abuse and brutality of policemen who view them as "dirty nigger-lovers." Unlike so many of their moderate brothers and sisters, they have recognized the urgency of the moment and sensed the need for powerful "action" antidotes to combat the disease of segregation.

Let me take note of my other major disappointment. I have been so greatly disappointed with the white church and its leadership. Of course, there are some notable exceptions. I am not unmindful of the fact that each of you has taken some significant stands on this issue. I commend you, Reverend Stallings, for your Christian stand on this past Sunday, in welcoming Negroes to your worship service on a nonsegregated basis. I commend the Catholic leaders of this state for integrating Spring Hill College several years ago.

But despite these notable exceptions, I must honestly reiterate that I have been disappointed with the church. I do not say this as one of those negative critics who can always find something wrong with the church. I say this as a minister of the gospel who loves the church; who was nurtured in its bosom; who has been sustained by its spiritual blessings and who will remain true to it as long as the cord of life shall lengthen.

When I was suddenly catapulted into the leadership of the bus protest in Montgomery, Alabama, a few years ago, I felt we would be supported by the white church. I felt that the white ministers, priests, and rabbis of the South would be among our strongest allies. Instead, some have been outright opponents, refusing to understand the freedom movement and misrepresenting its leaders; all too many others have been more cautious than courageous and have remained silent behind the anesthetizing security of stained-glass windows.

In spite of my shattered dreams, I came to Birmingham with the hope that the white religious leadership of this community would see the justice of our cause and, with deep moral concern, would serve as the channel through which our just grievances could reach the power structure. I had hoped that each of you would understand. But again I have been disappointed.

I have heard numerous southern religious leaders admonish their worshipers to comply with a desegregation decision because it is the law, but I have longed to hear white ministers declare: "Follow this decree because integration is morally right and because the Negro is your brother." In the midst of blatant injustices inflicted upon the Negro, I have watched white churchmen stand on the sideline and mouth pious irrelevancies and sanctimonious trivialities. In the midst of a mighty struggle to rid our nation of racial and economic injustice, I have heard many ministers say: "Those are social issues, with which the gospel has no real concern." And I have watched many churches commit themselves to a completely otherworldly religion which makes a strange, un-Biblical distinction between body and soul, between the sacred and the secular.

I have traveled the length and breadth of Alabama, Mississippi, and all the other southern state. On sweltering summer days and crisp autumn mornings I have looked at the South's beautiful churches with their lofty spires pointing heavenward. I have beheld the impressive outlines of her massive religious-education buildings. Over and over I have found myself asking: "What kind of people worship here? Who is their God? Where were their voices when the lips of Governor Barnett dripped with words of interposition and nullification? Where were they when Governor Wallace gave a clarion call for defiance and hatred? Where were their voices of support when bruised and weary Negro men and women decided to rise from the dark dungeons of complacency to the bright hills of creative protest?"

Yes, these questions are still in my mind. In deep disappointment I have wept over the laxity of the church. But be assured that my tears have been tears of love. There can be no deep disappointment where there is not deep love. Yes, I love the church. How could I do otherwise? I am in the rather unique position of being the son, the grandson, and the great-grandson of preachers. Yes, I see the church as the body of Christ. But, oh! How we have blemished and scarred that body through neglect and through fear of being nonconformists.

There was a time when the church was very powerful–in the time when the early Christians rejoiced at being deemed worthy to suffer for what they believed. In those days the church was not merely a thermometer that transformed the mores of society. Whenever the early Christians entered a town, the people in power became disturbed and immediately sought to convict the Christians for being "disturbers of the peace" and "outside agitators." But the Christians pressed on, in the conviction that they were "a colony of heaven," called to obey God rather than man. Small in number, they were big in commitment. They were too God-intoxicated to be "astronomically intimidated." By their effort and example they brought an end to such ancient evils as infanticide and gladiatorial contests.

Things are different now. So often the contemporary church is a weak, ineffectual voice with an uncertain sound. So often it is an archdefender of the status quo. Far from being disturbed by the presence of the church, the power structure of the average community is consoled by the church's silent–and often even vocal–sanction of things as they are.

But the judgment of God is upon the church as never before. If today's church does not recapture the sacrificial spirit of the early church, it will lose its authenticity, forfeit the loyalty of millions, and be dismissed as an irrelevant social club with no meaning for the twentieth century. Every day I meet young people whose disappointment with the church has turned into outright disgust.

Perhaps I have once again been too optimistic. Is organized religion too inextricably bound to the status quo to save our nation and the world? Perhaps I must turn my faith to the inner spiritual church, the church within the church, as the true *ekklesia* and the hope of the world. But again I am thankful to God that some noble souls from the ranks of organized religion have broken loose from the paralyzing chains of conformity and joined us as active partners in the struggle for freedom. They have left their secure congregations and walked the streets of Albany, Georgia, with us. They have gone down the highways of the South on tortuous rides for freedom. Yes, they have gone to jail with us. Some have been dismissed from their churches, have lost the support of their bishops and fellow ministers. But they have acted in the faith that right defeated is stronger than evil triumphant. Their witness has been the spiritual salt that has preserved the true meaning of the gospel in these troubled times. They have carved a tunnel of hope through the dark mountain of disappointment.

I hope the church as a whole will meet the challenge of this decisive hour. But even if the church does not come to the aid of justice, I have no despair about the future. I have no fear about the outcome of our struggle in Birmingham, even if our motives are at present misunderstood. We will reach the goal of freedom in Birmingham and all over the nation, because the goal of America is freedom. Abused and scorned though we may be, our destiny is tied up with America's destiny. Before the pilgrims landed at Plymouth, we were here. Before the pen of Jefferson etched the majestic words of the Declaration of Independence across the pages of history, we were here. For more than two centuries our forebears labored in this country without wages; they made cotton king; they built the homes of their masters while suffering gross injustice and shameful humiliation–and yet out of a bottomless vitality they continued to thrive and develop. If the inexpressible cruelties of slavery could not stop us, the opposition we now face will surely fail. We will win our freedom because the sacred heritage of our nation and the eternal will of God are embodied in our echoing demands.

Before closing I feel impelled to mention one other point in your statement that has troubled me profoundly. You warmly commended the Birmingham police force for keeping "order" and "preventing violence." I doubt that you would have so warmly commended the police force if you had seen its dogs sinking their teeth into unarmed, nonviolent Negroes. I doubt that you would so quickly commend the policemen if you were to observe their ugly and inhumane treatment of Negroes here in the city jail; if you were to see them slap and kick old Negro men and young boys; if you were to observe them, as they did on two occasions, refuse to give us food because we wanted to sing our grace together. I cannot join you in your praise of the Birmingham police department.

It is true that police have exercised a degree of discipline in handling the demonstrators. In this sense they have conducted themselves rather "nonviolently" in public. But for what purpose? To preserve the evil system of segregation. Over the past few years I have consistently preached that nonviolence demands that the means we use must be as pure as the ends we seek. I have tried to make clear that it is wrong to use immoral means to attain moral ends. But now I must affirm that it is just as wrong, or perhaps even more so, to use moral means to preserve immoral ends. Perhaps Mr. Connor and his policemen have been rather nonviolent in public, as was Chief Pritchett in Albany, Georgia, but they have used the moral means of nonviolence to maintain the immoral end of racial injustice. As T.S. Eliot has said: "The last temptation is the greatest treason: To do the right deed for the wrong reason."

I wish you had commended the Negro sit-inners and demonstrators of Birmingham for their sublime courage, their willingness to suffer and their amazing discipline in the midst of great provocation. One day the South will recognize its heroes. They will be the James Merediths, with the noble sense of purpose that enables them to face jeering and hostile mobs, and with the agonizing loneliness that characterizes the life of the pioneer. They will be old, oppressed, battered Negro women, symbolized in a seventy-two-year-old woman in Montgomery, Alabama, who rose up with a sense of dignity and with her people decided not to ride segregated buses, and who responded with ungrammatical profundity to one who inquired about her weariness: "My feets is tired, but my soul is at rest." They will be the young high school and college students, the young ministers of the gospel and a host of their elders, courageously and nonviolently sitting in at lunch counters and willingly going to jail for conscience' sake. One day the South will know that when these disinherited children of God sat down at lunch counters, they were in reality standing up for what is best in the American dream and for the most sacred values in our Judaeo-Christian heritage, thereby bringing our nation back to those great wells of democracy which were dug deep by the founding fathers in their formulation of the Constitution and the Declaration of Independence.

Never before have I written so long a letter. I'm afraid it is much too long to take your precious time. I can assure you that it would have been much shorter if I had been writing from a comfortable desk, but what else can one do when he is alone in a narrow jail cell, other than write long letters, think long thoughts, and pray long prayers?

If I have said anything in this letter that overstates the truth and indicates an unreasonable impatience, I beg you to forgive me. If I have said anything that understates the truth and indicates my having a patience that allows me to settle for anything less than brotherhood, I beg God to forgive me.

I hope this letter finds you strong in faith. I also hope that circumstances will soon make it possible for me to meet each of you, not as an integrationist or a civil-rights leader but as a fellow clergyman and a Christian brother. Let us all hope that the dark clouds of racial prejudice will soon pass away and the deep fog of misunderstanding will be lifted from our fear-drenched communities, and in some not too distant tomorrow the radiant stars of love and brotherhood will shine over our great nation with all their scintillating beauty.

Yours for the cause of Peace and Brotherhood
MARTIN LUTHER KING, JR.

(1962)

WHY I QUIT
TEACHING THREE TIMES
MICHELLE BROCKWAY

"So you're a teacher," the receptionist at my doctor's office sighed. "You know, I thought about being a teacher once. But a friend who teaches in Baytown told me not to."

I laughed, sort of, and wrote my check. "A teacher's standard advice," I said. Noncommittal, just as I had been with a student that morning. Tim wants to be a coach, but every one of his teachers has urged him not to do it.

These days when the question of whether to teach arises, I keep my mouth shut. Given the reputation of the teaching profession, how could I ever advise a bright young person to pursue it? I would first have to warn him to brace himself for his friends' and family's assurances that he is "too smart" to be a teacher. Just last year when my brother informed me that he had met the perfect woman, he said, "She teaches elementary school." Then he added, "But she's not a bimbo." Goes with the territory, right?

One August, the time when teachers begin fantasizing about changing careers, I consulted an employment agency. He informed me that despite graduating *summa cum laude* and despite my master's degree in English, I had a huge handicap to overcome–the public's image of teachers.

Perhaps Americans assume teachers are intellectually handicapped because they've chosen a profession that is by no accounts lucrative. If they were smart, they would be making money, some people reason.

If we pin the decline in student achievement on inadequate teachers, shall we throw in drug abuse, teenage pregnancies and divorce rates for good measure? Why not blame teachers for vegetative TV brains and poverty as well?

In truth, most of the teachers I have met are completely capable of teaching their subjects; some are superb. Given the public school system and societal attitudes, it's simply damn good luck that any competent teachers exist at all. What intelligent 23-year-old wants to begin a low-paying career with the assurance that the educated community will perceive her as someone who can't do anything else?

Education is the keystone of democracy, yet we don't commit to it. The people who say education is too fat must spend their time hanging around the Texas Education Agency in Austin, because they certainly have not stepped into a school lately. According to the American Association of School Administrators, over 74 percent of schools in this country were built before World War II. The heaters in my classrooms still don't work and neither do the rusty locks on my file cabinets. That old hunk of Double Bubble is probably where you left it 20 years ago.

Part of becoming a teacher, then, is adjusting your ego, insulating yourself from the opinions of the uninformed, trusting yourself and your own work. What you are doing is crucial, and, a tad martyred, you carry on.

Meanwhile, in Austin, a group of people who theoretically are on your side have set out to subvert you. They stand reason on its head and leave your own good sense pinned and wiggling in frustration. These people are called administrators.

Administrators boast advanced degrees from the most scoffed-at department on any university campus, the college of education. They have the job of dreaming up new ways of putting things on paper. Some of it is necessary–attendance counts, registration forms, grade sheets–but most of it is not. Most of it, in fact, seems calculated to infuriate.

Administrators state the obvious–in many words–and neglect to offer any solutions. They labor over lengthy lists of goals for the schools–as if the goals were unclear. They force teachers to spend hours in in-service training sessions listening to "culture" experts sagely inform them that children from different backgrounds have different beliefs, that some people are morning people and some are evening people, that "cooperative discipline" is in and "assertive discipline" is out. Last year the state required that, after teaching all day, every teacher view a six-hour video of a talking head as it instructed them about revisions in the teacher assessment program, which few, if any, teachers respect. The head concluded that judging teachers' effectiveness was subjective (no kidding) and that none of the Texas Education Agency's trained assessors seemed to be able to agree whether the previous sample lesson was any good or not.

Unlike managers in the business world, administrators cannot rely on their good sense in judging a teacher's ability. Instead, they use their "instrument." At the end of last year my performance was summed up in a two-page form scattered with numbers: 12.0, 14.0, 3.64, 36.0. They were calculated after four visits by two assistant principals who arrived at my classroom with clipboards and counted the number of students called on and subtracted the number of correct responses, and who calculated the number of seconds I waited for students to answer questions. With practiced eyes they looked for evidence of "anticipatory sets," "closure" and "independent practice."

They told me my numbers were good, that I "exceeded expectations." But so did the teacher down the hall, the dingbat whose classes regularly collapse into ketchup fights and catcalls, the teacher who everyone on campus (including the kids) agrees deserves the bad press we all have been getting. Obviously, incompetence cannot be gauged in numbers. How much more honest and satisfying the process would be if it owned up to its subjectivity.

But administrators do not deal with intangibles or subjectivity. They therefore do not deal with the reality in which some students are poor, don't speak English, are beaten up or molested at home, or, believe it not, are not terribly intelligent. They demand that failure percentages decrease, but they can do nothing to reduce the number of bloated, childish faces and distended bellies or the number of harried mothers and angry adolescent boys who haven't seen Daddy in months or years–or ever.

They consult their figures and see that they do not match those of an ideal world. One of my former principals sent out a hand-written, photocopied memo to teachers in which he assumed that those with high failure rates must be teaching deconstructionism or quantum physics rather than high school level material. He never asked us about the staggering dropout rates among ninth and 10th graders (the grades with the highest failure rates), the number of students we saw once a week, the number who absolutely refused to put pen to paper, the number of parents who consoled us with, "I know, Miss, I can't get him to do anything either." He never asked us how much we ourselves grieved for the futures of these kids and of our own society. What he did subtly suggest was that if we wanted to keep our asses out of the office we'd take care of those figures.

Solutions are elusive, so many administrators resort to disguising the offensive odor of the numbers. One teacher supervisor informed me of exciting new research that recommended ways to decrease student failure rates: never telephoning parents with bad news, refusing to assign grades lower than a B, presenting work that is exceptional with a Q for "Quality!" Quite helpful.

Administrators insist that all students can learn, and in doing so they have turned egalitarianism into a four-letter word. The Ph.D.'s in Austin have decided that all students should attend regular classes, that they should be "mainstreamed." Thus in a typical ninth-grade class a teacher may have to attend to ESL students, E.D. ("emotionally disturbed," typically a code word for "bad personality") students and L.D. ("leaning disabled") students.

ESL students need to learn English, but no one is certain whether or not they belong in regular classrooms. The E.D. students are typically unmanageable. Once labeled, they are, according to state mandate, largely beyond the school's disciplinary process. Even if they achieve at college levels, classes are at their mercy if they become disruptive. One E.D. student in my class last year was on probation, had been rumored to deal drugs, had been caught on campus with a gun, and had threatened to kill a Spanish teacher after she took a radio from him. His own mother had rented him an apartment in order to get him out of her house.

True, most of the E.D. kids have led excruciatingly painful lives. We have to ask ourselves, though, if we are willing to sacrifice the education of 20 or 30 students to their anger. The Texas Education Agency has already answered this question. Society hasn't bothered.

The students who usually have the least business attending regular academic classes are the L.D. students, most of whom at best read only on elementary school levels. Commas and capital letters to them may as well be Celtic runes. They are mainstreamed not to improve their academic abilities (which research shows dwindle in a regular classroom setting), but to improve their social skills.

L.D. students arrive with forms that must be signed and lengthy checklists of "modifications" that teachers must implement. But most teachers find it difficult to modify algebra for students who cannot grasp basic addition. To teach *Romeo and Juliet* to kids who can't read *Green Eggs and Ham*, to administer essays to students who can perform no written exercises.

If an L.D. student fails a class, his or her teacher must provide detailed documentation as to why. "Can't read" won't cut it. If the student fails two terms in a row, the state requires the teacher and several other faculty members to attend an "Admission, Review and Dismissal" (ARD) meeting to offer justification. No one will officially say "Just pass them," but the machinery is arranged so that teachers feel they have few options. Meanwhile, society wants to know why so many illiterate students are receiving high-school diplomas.

The question to be asked here is not whether children with low IQs or learning disabilities deserve educations. The question is, what kind of an education do they deserve? Are we doing them and ourselves any favors by pretending to teach them skills they will never master and never be called upon to use?

On top of bureaucrats and students with individual needs, teachers must also cope with major discipline problems. And we're not talking spitballs and dipping braids into inkwells, either. One of my students last year was on probation for beating up his mother: a psychiatrist had diagnosed him as psychotic. Two years earlier I had a student who had just returned from the Texas Department of Corrections after serving time on an attempted murder charge. He was one step from being a murderer by virtue of missing his target! I didn't learn of his past until he disappeared from class after his parole was revoked; he had been arrested for burglarizing homes to feed his own and his mother's drug habits.

The effect of including so many academically or socially lacking students in regular classrooms is similar to what would occur if you attached a 50 pound weight to the back of a sprinter. It would slow him down. Teachers spend excessive amounts of time on discipline and are forced to reduce their standards to accommodate the low achievers; a 50 percent failure rate simply would not do. When you consider how many especially demanding children congregate in the average classroom, it's amazing that students can even spell their own names.

Teaching evokes a surplus of feeling, more than one wants at times. And yet to disregard your feelings as a doctor might in a cancer ward prevents you from being effective. If you want the kids with you, you've got to be there with them.

You're always on stage. Some days it can be fun, but there are also those when we, especially women, feel as if we have the terminal uglies, and every time we look in the mirror we want to dive back headfirst into bed. But still we have to drag in and perform, displaying our fat and pimples and our comfortable shoes to the most appearance-oriented group in our society. We cannot keep a low profile for the day; we cannot hide behind a desk, shut the door, tell our secretary "No calls."

In 1988, I experienced the worst year of my life while teaching in a district southeast of town. My classes were loaded with close to 40 students each. At the end of every day, I had to pretend to tutor a mandatory class of 50 students who had failed English. I, like five other teachers in the school, had been struggling with a very angry and out-of-control 17-year old freshman. He was a drug addict who had experienced all of the terrors that a violent alcoholic father had to inflict. I pitied him and I abhorred him. Daily I had to put on hold the education of my other students in order to deal with his outbursts. Talking with his parents was pointless, and every time I sent him to the principal's office he came back with a peppermint in his mouth.

I felt for Fernando the most extreme anger I have ever felt toward someone I did not love. One day, something bizarre and cruel and startling to every cell in my body occurred. As I sent Fernando out of the room, my head began to buzz and spin, my heart seemed to leap out in front of my body, and I began to sweat and pace the room like an anxious animal, fearful of the larger unknown, fiery beast staring in through a new ghostly door. My students marveled at my burning face while I pondered ways to flee. I felt confused, my voice trembled. Freddie lived.

That afternoon I went home and cried for eight straight hours. I called a friend of mine, a psychologist, and sobbed out my symptoms. The diagnosis: panic attack. I had many more after that, and almost always they occurred when I was on stage, when I was very angry or when I was giving a little piece of the core of personal truth and honesty and kindness that so many of us secret away.

I survived that year on mild tranquilizers and blood pressure medicine. Then I quit. And I've quit twice since then.

I began to appreciate the possibilities of less meaningful work. By May of last year I had sewn up a full scholarship to law school and had formally resigned from my last teaching position. I had given away all of the posters and books and crates and in-boxes I had collected over the years, commanding their recipients not to return them to me if I ever again succumbed to an insane desire to teach.

I felt somewhat guilty giving up my polyester pants for pinstripes, but as the news sped through the lounges I was greeted only with congratulations. Just one teacher asked "Why?" and she immediately burst into laughter.

Only when I returned to my school in August, having turned down the scholarship and accepted a new teaching position, did my amazed colleagues ask, quite sincerely, "Why?" Why, when I had options?

I couldn't admit this to them, but between you and me, I did it for Maria. Maria, who broke me up into laughter every time I tried to turn down her girlish decibels. Who dragged me out into the hall and pointed, "Look, Miss! Now there's a guy!" Who in that beautiful 16-year-old way frowned as she looked at my feet and demanded, "Uh–why don't you tie your shoelaces?" As if I had spinach between my teeth. So disgusted.

I did it for Fidel, a low-rider in black-and-white flannels, T-shirts and baggy pants. He drives a car with hydraulic lifts, a chain-link steering wheel, and a Madonna (the original virgin, that is) painted on the back window. The entire interior is cushioned in gold crushed velvet. With his devilish smile, he always seemed up to something, but he makes me laugh. The little s.o.b. only managed to pass three courses last year, but one of them was mine.

I did it for Kristie, who once innocently called from across the room, "Ms. Brockway, do you have sex?" And for Jesse, an all-around good-guy basketball player who never fails to wave when he passes my room; for the junior who tearfully passed me a note informing me she had failed the TAAS test ("Please don't tell anybody, Miss Brockway"), for pencil-thin Dana who is absolutely ridiculous and has yet to develop adolescent temerity, for Corey, whose lungs have collapsed twice this year and whose hollow eyes reflect the bewilderment and anguish of prematurely facing the ravages of time.

And then there's Lupe, the beautiful, absolutely lovely girl who's a good enough student, but not stellar, who is sometimes silly but generally shy, who doesn't demand attention but who is one of those people who touches me deeply and for whom I'd go the distance. That's one thing about teaching. Sometimes you do just get touched, and to try to reason it all out and explain it is asking too much.

When you teach, being touched has to be enough because that's all you'll get. I was surprised that Lupe and Jesse and Fidel could suffice for me. At least for now, I'm staying.

But take my advice.

Don't do it.

(1992)

ARE TELEVISION'S EFFECTS DUE TO TELEVISION?

HOWARD GARDNER

Nearly all of the ills of our sorely afflicted society have at one time or another been blamed on television. The drop in College Entrance Examination Board scores, the decline in literacy, the lack of political involvement on the part of many citizens, the upsurge in violent crimes, the mediocre artistic tastes of large segments of our culture–these and countless other lamentable trends have all been attributed to this pervasive medium. A deluge of articles, books, and even television programs have chronicled the evil effects of television. Marie Winn has deplored *The Plug-In Drug*, and Gerry Mander has issued *Four Arguments for the Elimination of Television.*

To be sure, one occasionally hears whispers about possible dividends from television: an earlier mastery of certain basic skills (courtesy of *Sesame Street*), greater access to information by neglected pockets within the society, an increase in the rate or efficiency of visual thinking, and, possibly the speedier erection of Marshal McLuhan's "global village." Yet for the most part, when television is spoken of, the medium that has been viewed by more individuals for longer periods of time than any other in human history receives a dismal press.

When such a consensus is voiced, it requires some boldness (or foolhardiness) to call it into question. Yet in my view we know astonishingly little about the actual effects of television. For the most part, we do not know what things are caused by television. And even when we can establish probable cause it is difficult to confirm that the medium of television *per se* is at fault. Put another way, it might be that any pursuit, or at least any medium with which one were engaged for twenty to thirty hours a week, would yield similar results–in which case the various trends cited above are hardly due to television itself. Our "vast wasteland" of ignorance about television's effects stems from the fact that researchers claiming to study television have failed to tease out those effects due directly to television from those that might have resulted from any mode of presentation. And so, to anticipate my conclusions, only if we systematically compare television to other media of communication will we be able to determine which sins–and which virtues–can legitimately be laid at the base of the ubiquitous console.

Television and Human Behavior, a recently published exhaustive compendium of more than 2,500 studies, provides an important case in point. This thoughtful book compiled by George Comstock and his colleagues inundates us with information about television in this country–the number of sets, the number of hours they are watched by members of every age and demographic group, and the preferences and dislikes of the gigantic viewing audience. Appropriately, the largest section of the book is devoted to the aspect of television that has generated the most controversy– the effects of the medium on children. In fact, it takes more than a hundred pages simply to survey the several hundred studies in this area.

I read through these pages with mounting disappointment. The millions of research dollars spent on this issue seem to have yielded only two major findings, each of which might easily have been anticipated by the experimenter's proverbial grandmother. As the authors constantly remind us, "it has now been established" that children will imitate behaviors they see on television, whether these actions be aggressive, violent, or benignly "prosocial." Moreover, "it has also been established" that the younger the child, the more likely it is that he will believe in the contents of commercials, urging parents to purchase what has been advertised and confusing commercial fare with other television content.

Some recent research efforts have adopted a more cognitive approach to children and television: they have implicitly viewed the child as a fledgling explorer trying to make sense of the mysterious lands visible on the handful of channels beamed to every household. And these studies have furnished the reassuring headline that, much as children pass through stages in the other realms of existence probed by psychologists, so children pass through "stages of television comprehension." But again, these pioneering studies have not revealed much that would surprise an observant parent or a shrewd grandparent.

Why do we know so little? Why have the thousands of studies failed to tell us more about television *per se* and about the minds of children who view it? A number of answers spring to mind. First of all, just as a new medium usually begins by presenting the contents previously transmitted through older media (for example, movies initially conveyed celluloid theater, and television at first amounted to visual radio), so, too, initial lines of research on television have largely adopted methods and questions that had once been applied to other media or to "unmediated" behavior. Only when a generation reared on television undertook research in this area did studies become attuned to the special or "defining" properties of television. Another limiting dimension has been the "mission" orientation of most television research. Because society has been (justifiably) vexed about violence and about commercials, it has twisted researchers' arms to grapple with these issues.

But probably the chief stumbling block to imaginative and generative television research has been the fact that everyone (and his grandmother) has a television set. Thus the crucial experimental control–comparing individuals with televisions to those without–cannot be done. The few eccentrics who do not have television are too different from their viewing counterparts to serve as a meaningful control group. Those scattered societies not yet blessed (or traumatized) with television are also sufficiently different to render comparisons of little value. When the gifted social psychologist Stanley Milgram was asked to study the effects of television on violence, he had a very logical idea which was, alas, soon dashed. Milgram's first impulse was to divide the country in half, remove all violence on television west of the Mississippi, enact laws so that no one could move from one part of the country to the other, and then observe what happened over a period of years. "It turned out not to be practical," he wryly admitted to an interviewer, "so I had to work with what I had."

I have recently encountered a few strands of research that address more directly the distinct features of television. In trying to determine which aspects of television compel children's attention, researchers Aletha Huston-Stein and John Wright of the University of Kansas have focused on the medium's "formal feature"–the quick cutaways, sound effects, and frenetic activity, in which commercial television revels. They have documented that the younger the child, the more likely he is to attend to these features of television, independent of the kind of content being presented. In contrast, older children will watch a program for extended periods of time even when such formal features are not heavily exploited. Huston-Stein and Wright make the interesting suggestion that violence or aggression are unnecessary for capturing the attention of preschool children. So long as a show is fast-paced, contains action, and is laced with interesting visual and sound effects (as is, for example, much of *Sesame Street*), the youngsters will remain hooked.

Another innovative researcher, Gavriel Salomon of the Hebrew University in Jerusalem, has also focused on those features that prove unique to television. He has paid special attention to such features as the zoom–the shot that begins with a panoramic overview and then rapidly "zooms" in upon a tell-tale detail. According to Salomon, children with difficulty attending to relevant detail can be greatly aided by a television segment replete with zooms: the medium can "supplant" a skill that the child needs but that, for one or another reason, he has not yet developed on his own. Salomon has not only documented an effect linked specifically to television but has also pointed the path to a positive pedagogical payoff.

Yet because they employ only television, even these isolated oases in the wasteland of research do not permit a determination of the effects of television *per se*. One line of research that does, however, was initiated by Laurene Meringoff, my colleague at Harvard Project Zero, and is now being continued in conjunction with several other colleagues. Exploiting the fact that television transmits certain contents, such as narratives, that have traditionally been conveyed by other media, these researchers have compared with as much precision as possible the differential effects wrought by such story content when it is presented on television, as opposed to when it is presented in book form. And they have uncovered some very intriguing findings.

Let me describe their procedures. To begin with, members of the research team select stories of high quality and interest. Using materials developed at Weston Woods, a studio which produces stories in various media for children, they prepare book and television versions that are virtually identical save in the medium of transmission.

As an example, the research team has worked extensively with *The Three Robbers* by Tomi Ungerer. In this tale three hitherto ferocious bandits abandon their violent ways after stopping a stagecoach that was carrying the charming orphan Tiffany. Turning their backs on a life of crime, the trio of robbers goes on to help abandoned boys and girls throughout the land. In a typical study, one group of subjects hears the story read by an experimenter and sees the accompanying pictures–the "book version." Another group of subjects views a film of equivalent length, based on the

239

book, on a television monitor; in this "television version, the specially recorded sound track uses the voice of the book narrator and the animated film presents the same illustrations that appear in the printed text. Thus, while respecting the essential properties of each medium (movement within the image in the case of television, discrete static imagery in the case of a picture book), the two versions are about as similar as can be imagined. (Of course, reading a book oneself is different from having it read aloud to one at a preordained rate, but the researchers were interested in attempting to simulate the latter experience.)

A quartet of studies carried out thus far by the Project Zero team revealed a consistent and instructive picture. To begin with, adults who watched the television program remembered about as much of the story on their own and were able to select as many items from multiple choice as did the matched adults who had the picture book read to them. But when subjects were asked to make inferences that went beyond the text, modest effects of medium were found. For example, subjects were asked to evaluate how a character felt or how difficult it was for the robbers to carry out an action. In these cases, adults who saw the story on television were more likely to make inferences based on the visual portions of the story (such as the expression on a character's face), while those exposed to the book were more likely to rely on the plot they heard (although both groups were exposed to identical sound tracks and saw a similar set of visual images, one static and one dynamic.)

With children the differences across the media proved far more dramatic. Compared to the video youngsters, the book children remembered much more of the story on their own and were also better able to recall information when they had been cued. When it came to recalling precise wordings and figures of speech, differences proved especially dramatic: the book children were surprisingly skilled at repeating just what they heard (phrases such as "visit her wicked aunt"), while the television children, when they remembered linguistically presented information at all, were prone to paraphrase.

To my mind, the most intriguing differences with children emerged when inferences were called for. Both groups of children tended to reach the same conclusion–for instance, an equal number of television and book children concluded that the robbers' axes were easy to wield or that Tiffany felt happy. But the lines of reasoning used to buttress the inferences were different. Television children relied overwhelmingly on what they had seen–how difficult an action looked, how someone appeared to feel. They rarely went beyond the video information, either to attend to what was said or to draw on their own experience. In contrast, book children were far more likely to draw on their own personal experiences or to apply their own real-world knowledge ("It's hard for me to hold an axe–it's way too heavy"). Estimates of time and space were also more constrained for the television children. That is, when asked how long an action took or how far from one another two sites were located, television children made more modest estimates, suggesting a reliance on the superficial flow of information rather than a consideration of what was plausible.

In all, television emerged as much more of a self-contained experience for children, and within this bounded realm the visual component emerged as paramount. The book experience, in contrast, allowed for greater access to the story's language and suggested greater expanses of time and space; it also encouraged connections to other realms of life–thus buttressing some of the very claims bibliophiles have made in the past.

One possible outcome of such research is to comfort critics of television–those troubled souls whose Cassandran cries I initially branded as premature. And it seems to be true that the younger the child, the greater the gap between comprehension of television and comprehension of books. Yet, in my own view, the significance of this research does not rest primarily in its favoring one medium over another. For one thing, the largely verbal measures used thus far could well be charged with being "pro book." It could be that other more visual measures might have favored television, as has in fact proved to be the case in subsequent studies. Or it could be that the kinds of skills actually engendered by television (for example, being able to create or recreate in one's mind a vivid visual sequence) cannot yet be tapped by our experimental methodology. Rather, the importance of the research may lie in its demonstration of qualitative differences in the effects of the media: exposure to television apparently highlights a set of contents and engenders a line of inference quite different from that stimulated by experience with books. Thus the individual who views television intensively and extensively may well develop different kinds of imaginative powers or, as Marshall McLuhan might have claimed, a different "ratio among imagination" from that of an individual weaned on another medium, such as books.

We are left with an even more tantalizing thought. Ever since the time of Immanuel Kant, it has been assumed by most philosophers that individuals perceive experience in terms of certain basic categories–time, space, and causality. Indeed, one has no choice but to conceive life in such terms–they are "givens." While psychologists do not necessarily accept these categories as part of the human birthright, they assume that eventually all normal individuals will come to possess similar versions of these basic categories of knowing.

If, however, one adopts an alternative perspective, if one affirms that some of our knowledge of time, space, and causality comes from the media of communication that happen to proliferate in one's culture, then this research has an additional implication. Put simply, it makes little sense to talk of the child's sense of time or space as a single undifferentiated entity. Rather, the ways in which we conceptualize our experience may reflect the kinds of media with which we have been engaged. And so the temporal and spatial outlook–and, *a fortiori*, the imagination of the television freak may have a different flavor from that of the bookworm. While such a finding from television research is perhaps not as immediately sensational as those involving violence or commercials, it can have potentially far-reaching educational implications. For instance, the way in which one teaches history (with its time frames) or geometry (with its spatial components) might differ depending on the media with which children have been raised and the media in which lessons are conveyed. And the findings can also help to reveal something about our own era. Based on comparisons between two pervasive cultural media–books and television– research results can pinpoint differences between individuals of our era and those of earlier times, and also suggest which of those differences might be due to television alone. (1982)

HOW THE SUPERWOMAN
MYTH PUTS WOMEN DOWN
SYLVIA RABINER

Sunday afternoon. I'm making my usual desultory way through the Sunday *Times* when I come upon Linda Kanner. Ms. Kanner is prominently on display in The National Economic Survey, where she is referred to as a woman "in the vanguard of women taking routes to the executive suite that were formerly traveled by men." A quick run-through of the article reveals that she is a marketing consultant with an M.B.A. degree from Harvard and a degree from the Simmons School of Social Work. She is married to a physician who has an M.B.A., too. Somewhere along the way she has managed to find time to produce two sons, and all this glory is hers at age 31.

Well, there goes my Sunday afternoon. After reading about Ms. Kanner, I will be in a muddy slump until nightfall at least. Every time I come across one of these proliferating articles about the successful woman of today, I am beset by feelings of self-contempt, loathing, and failure. Moreover, I hate Ms. Kanner, too, and if she were in my living room at the moment, I would set fire to her M.B.A. I am a six-year-old child once again, listening while my mother compares me to one of my flawless cousins.

Let me tell you, it's getting harder all the time to be a successful woman. In the old days, a woman was usually judged by the man she had ensnared. If he was a good provider and she kept the house clean, was a good cook, and raised a few decent children, she was well regarded by her peers and most likely by herself as well. Now the mainstream Women's Movement has thrust forth a new role model: the capitalist feminist. The career woman with a twist, she's not your old-time spinster who sacrificed marriage and motherhood for professional advancement, but a new, trickier model who has it all–a terrific career, a husband with a terrific career, and a couple of children as well.

We have Isabel Van Devanter Sawhill, successful economist, wife of New York University president John, and mother; or Laetty Cottin Pogrebin, successful author, editor, activist, wife of lawyer Bert, and mother. A recent article in *Newsweek* investigated the life-styles of working couples with children. Their random democratic sampling included Kathy Cosgrove, vice-president of a public relations firm, wife of Mark, an advertising executive; Consuelo Marshall, Superior Court commissioner, wife of George, Columbia Pictures executive; Charlotte Curtis, associate editor of the *New York Times*, wife of William Hunt, neurosurgeon; and Patricia Schroeder, congresswoman, wife of lawyer Jim. Patricia, the article gushed, managed at 35 to "gracefully combine career, marriage, and family." The article was capped by a description of Carla Hills, secretary of Housing and Urban Development, presidential possibility for the supreme court, wife of Roderick, chairman of the Securities and Exchange Commission, and mother of four. There was a photograph of Mrs. Hills presiding over her impeccable family at the dinner table. The article was swingy and upbeat. If they can do it, how about you?. . . Another afternoon ruined.

I turned for instruction to Letty Cottin Pogrebin, embodiment of the success game. Letty is now an editor at *Ms.* and author of two books–*How to Make It in a Man's World* and *Getting Yours*. Those titles reveal Letty's commitment to self-advancement. She doesn't hesitate to tell her readers that she is a woman to emulate. Letty was an executive at 21. She married a man whom she adores and has three "happy, well-behaved, bright, and spirited kids." I gleaned all this from Letty's first book. Since Letty was also gracefully combining career, marriage, and family, I thought I might get some pointers from her.

Letty Cottin arrived at Bernard Geis in 1960. After six months she was promoted to the position of director of publicity, advertising, and subsidiary rights. She met her husband at a party and married him a couple of months later. She proceeded to have her first children (twins) as planned "early in marriage but after one full year as newlyweds." Their next baby fit in perfectly after the three-year space between children which they deemed most desirable. She sums up: "It's better to be working than not working; it's better to be married than single; it's better to be a mommy as well as a Mrs. But it's best to be all four at once!"

Now, where does that leave me? My thumbnail autobiography follows: I am a child of my times, definitely more the rule than the exception to it. Raised in the '40s and '50s, the words *career* and *goal* were not spoken when I was in the room. I got the standard New York City College Jewish Parental Advice to Daughters. "Take a few education courses. Then if. . .God forbid. . .anything should happen, you can always take care of yourself." Nora Ephron said that she always knew she wanted to write (Dorothy Parker was her idol). When her less motivated college friends went off after graduation and got married, Nora went off and wrote. A few remarkable women like Nora and Letty undoubtedly knew at the age of 18 or younger what profession they wanted to pursue, but most of us at Hunter College, as I recall, were thundering off in a herd to stand under the marriage canopy. A bunch of simpletons, you say? Not so. We had produced the school plays, edited the school newspapers, put together the creative publications, belonged to Arista, and frequently had our names on the honor roll. What was happening, then? Well, let's call it economics. We were the children of immigrant or new immigrant parents. Hard-working, uneducated or self educated, they didn't know how to guide their bright daughters. The depression had been deeply felt and was well remembered. Their watchword was security. Dorothy Parker was my idol, too, but to my parents, writing was not a job. With encouragement from neither parents nor teachers, most of us sought security in marriage or teaching.

Now, I married neither wisely nor well, which to judge by current divorce statistics, proves me to be obstinately average. I worked to put my husband through graduate school, traveled where his career dictated, had two children as a matter of course and in the fall of 1969, although I had felt suffocated by my marriage, I protestingly and hysterically suffered its demise. My child support settlement would have done nicely to keep me in a cozy little tenement on Avenue C and 5th Street. I wanted to remain part of the middle class so I had to work: I had two children under the age of five and couldn't possibly pay a housekeeper. And I didn't really want a day-care center or baby-sitter with my boys eight or nine hours a day while I was at work. I wanted to be with them, so I found a job teaching night classes, and I tended home and sons during the day. A divorced woman with kids has a lot of things to think about. She is usually racing around trying to pay bills, do her job reasonably well, have some kind of social life, and be a loving mother too.

After 1969 I noticed that I never walked down a street, I ran. I ate standing up. I screamed at my sons a lot. The astute reader will detect here the subtle differences between Letty's life and mine. I admit I was failing in being a successful woman, I didn't have a terrific career, and I didn't have a husband with a terrific career. Where were all those dynamic, achieving wonderful men that the women in the news stories found and married? Not in the playgrounds and supermarkets where I spent my days, not in the classrooms where I spent my evenings, and not in any of the other places I checked out with varying degrees of enthusiasm on the weekends when I had a baby-sitter. As for my long-range career goals–well, to tell the truth, I was grateful to have my teaching contract renewed each semester. My concession to getting ahead was to return to graduate school to earn my M.A. degree. I was able to indulge in this luxury only because the university at which I taught offered me free tuition. At $91 a credit, graduate school is hardly a priority of the divorced working mother. It appears that in addition to all my other errors in judgment, I've made the mistake of living in New York City during a recession. Last June I lost the teaching job that was supposed to be my security in case. . . God forbid. . . anything happened. After collecting unemployment insurance for five months, I am now typing, filing, and serving my boss his coffee four times a day.

Now, I ask you–do I need to read about the triumphant lives of Helen Gurley Brown or Mary Wells Lawrence? Statistics currently indicate that there are 7.2 million families headed by women. Most of us are clerks, secretaries, waitresses, salesgirls, social workers, nurses, and–if lucky enough to still be working–teachers. For us, the superwoman who knits marriage, career, and motherhood into a satisfying life without dropping a stitch is as oppressive a role model as the airbrushed Bunny in the *Playboy* centerfold, or That *Cosmopolitan* Girl. While I struggle to keep my boat afloat in rough waters with prevailing high winds, I am not encouraged to row on by media hypes of ladies who run companies, serve elegant dinners for 30, play tennis with their husbands, earn advanced degrees, and wear a perfect size eight. They exist, I know, a privileged, talented minority, but to encourage me by lauding their achievements is like holding Sammy Davis, Jr., up as a model to a junior high school class in Bed.-Stuy. What does it really have to do with them?

Women are self-critical creatures. We can always find reasons to hate ourselves. Single women believe they are failing if they don't have a loving, permanent relationship; working mothers are conflicted about leaving their children; divorced women experience guilt over the break-up of their marriages; housewives feel inadequate because they don't have careers; career women are wretched if they aren't advancing, and everyone is convinced she is too fat!

It is ironic that feminism, finally respectable, has been made to backfire in this way. The superwoman image is a symbol of the corruption of feminist politics. It placed emphasis on a false ideal of individual success. We are led to believe that if we play our cards right, we'll get to the top, but in the present system it won't work; there just isn't that much room up there. And in our class society, those at the top probably were more than halfway up to start with. The superwoman image ignores the reality of the average working woman or housewife. It elevates an elite of upper-class women executives. The media love it because it is glamorous and false. In the end it threatens nothing in the system. In fact, all it does is give women like me a sense of inferiority.

(1976)

I BELIEVE IN GOD

GERALD KENNEDY

I never met an atheist. I have met a few people who claimed they were atheists. But when we talked it over, it always seemed to me they were objecting to someone else's idea of God rather than insisting that there was no God. There is a story about a man at a convention of atheists who became annoyed because he thought the other delegates were backing down from their atheism. He made a speech against this compromising attitude and ended by saying, "I am a real atheist, thank God!"

WE CANNOT LIVE WITHOUT GOD

There are people who will insist they are atheists. For them the words of Tolstoy are the point. He said that God is he without whom we cannot live. If some people insist there is no God and yet go on living, how shall we explain it? Let us say they go on living because they act as if they had not said it. Tolstoy was right. If a man really did not believe in God, he could not go on living as a man. We have to live as if we believe there is something in this universe that gives our life meaning. And when we face this basic fact in living as men, God has found us.

I do not see how anyone in a day like ours can doubt that God is real. We have been trying to get along without him for some time, and look at the sorry shape our world is in. We have felt that we ourselves could solve all our problems. We have set ourselves up high and worshipped gods made by our own hands–gods named Science, Progress, Money, Power, Prosperity, Pleasure, Reason, Education, Success. For a while these gods seemed to take the place of the God of our fathers well enough. But they have proved to be false gods. Worshipping them is superstition and not religion. Sometimes they turn their worshipers into monsters, madmen, or dull robots. If we follow them farther, we plunge into the abyss. God is he without whom men cannot live.

The point is that God is not a matter of choice; he is a matter of necessity. We cannot do as we please, cannot take him or leave him. When we go our own way, we go wrong. When we try to build a life or a society without coming to terms with him, we build on the sand. A civilization is always built on a religion. Once men begin to doubt their faith in God, they are on the way down. Experience shows that God is the reality on which life is built. Let a man doubt that he himself is real if he must, but never let him doubt that God is real.

It takes less effort to believe the most difficult doctrines of Christianity than it does to believe the universe began by chance. Men who accept that idea show more willingness to believe the unlikely than the most conservative of Christians. To put blind force in place of God calls for more blind credulity than a thinking man can muster. We turn from such nonsense to the opening words of Genesis, "In the beginning God . . ." The simple words shine in their own light and speak with conviction.

HOW SHALL WE DESCRIBE GOD?

I cannot undertake a profound, philosophical, exhaustive discussion of the nature of God. I am simply writing as a witness, telling what I believe about God. To the lazy, indifferent Christian people of our time I would like to say: "Why don't you take the time to find out what Christianity says about God? You would be ashamed to know as little about how your car operates as you know about what the great Christian thinkers have said about God." Christian people should not be content to take their ideas about God from experts in other fields–who mean well but do not know what the Church has been teaching.

Surely God has left enough signs of his presence to show plain men some things about his nature. For one thing, God is an artist who has given us beauty on every side. Painters, poets, and musicians know we can live in a world that is beyond the world our minds can grasp. It is the world of beauty. Sometimes we need help to see and hear, but you and I have enough appreciation in us to respond to the wonder of God's presence in Nature.

We remember autumn woods, mountains at sunrise, sunsets by the sea, forest groves at noontime, valleys by moonlight. Every place and every season has its special beauty for us. We cannot be a part of it without feeling our hearts rise up in worship. Admiral Byrd in his book *Alone* described his feelings as he watched a day die at the South Pole. He wrote: "The conviction came that that rhythm was too orderly, too harmonious, too perfect to be a product of blind chance–that, therefore, there must be purpose in the whole and that man was part of that whole and not an accidental offshoot."

GOD IS MIND

We cannot look at the wonders of the natural world without seeing a great Mind at work. Whether we think of the miracle of the atom or try vainly to understand what billions of light years mean, we cannot escape this conviction: the world reveals a Mind that makes our own minds count for something only as they can recognize this greater Mind. We do not create; we only discover. Most of our thinking is seeing and appreciating the marvels that prove a vast Intelligence at work. The glory of science is that it can reveal this truth. The weakness of science is its pride that assumes these marvels of nature are no longer God's because men have understood them. Nature's laws were not set up by men. They were operating a long time before man appeared.

The greatest scientists recognize how little their minds are beside the Mind revealed in the world of nature. They speak of "thinking the thoughts of God after him." They speak of standing on the ocean shore with a few shells in their hands while the great mystery of God stretches out before them. They speak of the universe as being not a great machine but a great thought. Men are growing dissatisfied with the nineteenth-century theory that nature is a substitute for God. They are driven at last to confess that nature is clear proof of a mighty Mind at work. In the words of Shakespeare, man increasingly

> Finds tongues in trees, books in the running brooks,
> Sermons in stones.

GOD IS RIGHTEOUSNESS

Beside the laws of nature there is the moral law. This would seem to say that God is the champion of the right. He has established an order that holds up good and tears down evil. Any man who is not an idiot knows that the sense of right and wrong is real.

The court of last appeal is the sense of "I ought." Against this we cannot argue, nor can we explain it apart from God. Some people have tried to make conscience out as merely social custom, but for his conscience's sake many a man defies social custom and goes against public opinion. Some people would say conscience is only a matter of education and home training. But every man recognizes the demands of conscience and sees them much alike no matter what his home training or cultural background has been. Every man has a conscience, and every man's conscience tells him he should do what is right and not do what is wrong.

Where does conscience come from? It comes from the God who created the world and men. We have a sense of owing something to the one who made us. Even when no man knows of our fault and there is no chance that any man will ever find it out, still we are guilty in our own eyes. We are guilty because we know there is Another who also knows all about it. How often a sensitive man who shrinks from an unpleasant duty says to himself: "If only God would leave me alone! If only he would let me be comfortable!" But God will not let us alone. When it comes to putting his demands upon us, God neither slumbers nor sleeps.

The moral law shows in the history of nations and societies. The children of Israel discovered it early. In Deborah's song of joy over the fall of an oppressor she says:

> From heaven fought the stars,
> from their courses they fought against Sisera.
> —Judg. 5:20

She knew that the universe itself is against wrong. Israel's prophets saw this so clearly that God became real to them in every event of history He was the deciding force in battles, in social life, in politics. We can be sure of one thing: no nation founded on injustice can long endure. When men or nations do wrong, they will be punished. In the words of the Old Testament:

> Righteousness exalteth a nation;
> But sin is a reproach to any people.
> —Prov. 14:34

None of this makes sense if we have a blind machine for a world. It makes sense only when we see that back of all our affairs there is God, who protects the good and destroys evil.

GOD IS A PERSON

The Christian truth that takes first place and includes all I have been saying is this: God is a person. This troubles a good many people. They suppose Christians are childish folk who think of God as if he were only a man. Such people prefer to talk about God as a "principle," or an "idea."

Let me make clear what I am *not* saying. I am not making God an old man with a long white beard. The Gospel of John saves us from that mistake by insisting that "God is a Spirit."

But I am saying God is a person. By this I mean he has will, mind, purpose, freedom, self-consciousness. The highest creation we know in the world is a person. The climax of the whole process of creation is a personality. Persons tower over nature and the animal kingdom. We must say God is at least a person, or we would be making him something of less value than a man. Principles and ideas do not mean as much as persons. God may be more than personal; but since we do not know anything that is more, we shall go as high as we know.

GOD FACES MEN

All of this becomes clear in the Christian experience of being found by God. When God finds a man, that man meets a Divine Person who faces him with personal claims. The man has to do much more than heed a moral principle or adjust his life to the law of right and wrong. He has to go through a personal experience. It is like David's experience when Nathan pointed to him and said, "Thou art the man." It is like Jesus' experience when he heard a voice from out the heavens say, "Thou art my beloved Son."

Until a man finds God and is found by God, he begins at no beginning and he works to no end. In other words, God is not one of the elective courses in the school of life; he is the one required course. Without this course we cannot pass our final examinations. There is nothing to take the place of God. Everything goes wrong without him. Nothing fits into place until a man has put God at the center of his thought and action.

Life has no purpose without God, and no generation should understand that better than ours. For we have most of the things we thought we wanted. We can travel swiftly; we can send messages over vast distances; we can produce more comforts of life than our fathers could imagine. Today the poor can enjoy things which would have been luxuries to the ancient kings. Yet something has gone wrong. We are no longer thrilled to think we will soon produce still more goods, more comforts. All our trinkets have not brought us peace of mind. In spite of our heroic conquests over nature, the feeling haunts us that we spend our time on toys and trivialities, and we are moved by no mighty purposes.

Only God can keep our sense of values straight. William Temple, late Archbishop of Canterbury, once said that the world is like a shop window where some prankster has gone in and changed all the price tags. On the expensive articles he has put the low prices, and on the cheap articles he has put the high prices. We pay more than we should for what does not satisfy us, and we neglect the things we really need. Isaiah's question is for us: "Wherefore do ye spend money for that which is not bread? and your labor for that which satisfieth not?" (Isa. 55:2). People who forget God also forget what is worth striving for.

Without God we cannot have human brotherhood, which is the recognition of each man's worth. If you can rob men of their belief that they are the sons of God, you pave the way for tyranny. This is not just somebody's opinion. This is history. We have only one bulwark against the cheapening of human life. It is to maintain at all costs the Christian belief that God created each man and made him a son of God. Like coins, men have value, not in themselves, but because they bear the stamp of the King.

We can find freedom only in God. God's demands often seem severe, yet they free us more than anything we know. When we try to get away from his demands, we end up as slaves to ourselves or to other men. But when we decide we must obey God rather than men, we feel we have been set free. It is like escaping from a prison. In God's service we find perfect freedom.

All the things that make us men have their roots in God. He is like the air we breathe and the water we drink. Eddie Rickenbacker, the famous flyer, drifted around on a life raft for twenty-one days, hopelessly lost in the Pacific. A friend later asked him what lesson he had learned. "The biggest lesson I learned from that experience," he said, "was that if you have all the fresh water you want to drink and all the food you want to eat, you ought never to complain about anything." So it is with the man who has lost God. He comes to know that God is man's one necessary possession.

I believe in God because he has faced men and laid his claims upon me. Just as a man knows it when he falls in love, or knows it when he thrills to the beauty of nature, so he knows it when God places his demand upon him. Maybe he cannot be as precise as John Wesley and say that it happened about a quarter of nine. But he knows that once he was lost and now he is found, and al his life is changed. The experience makes him humble. He may have learned enough about God to live by, but he now finds the ruling passion of his life is to learn *more* about him.

That is the hope of every Christian. It is the worthiest goal for any man's life. When we have gone far enough to be able to say, "I believe in God," we stand at the beginning of life's great adventure.

WHY I AM AN AGNOSTIC

CLARENCE DARROW (1875-1938)

An agnostic is a doubter. The word is generally applied to those who doubt the verity of accepted religious creeds or faiths. Everyone is an agnostic as to the beliefs or creeds they do not accept. Catholics are agnostic to the Protestant creeds, and the Protestants are agnostic to the Catholic creed. Anyone who thinks is an agnostic about something, otherwise he must believe that he is possessed of all knowledge. And the proper place for such a person is in the madhouse or the home for the feeble-minded. In a popular way, in the western world, an agnostic is one who doubts or disbelieves the main tenets of the Christian faith.

I would say that belief in at least three tenets is necessary to the faith of a Christian; a belief in God, a belief in immortality, and a belief in a supernatural book. Various Christian sects require much more, but it is difficult to imagine that one could be a Christian, under any intelligent meaning of the word, with less. Yet there are some people who claim to be Christians who do not accept the literal interpretation of all the Bible, and who give more credence to some portions of the book than to others.

I am an agnostic as to the question of God. I think that it is impossible for the human mind to believe in an object or thing unless it can form a mental picture of such object or thing. Since man ceased to worship openly an anthropomorphic God and talked vaguely and not intelligently about some force in the universe, he cannot be said to believe in God. One cannot believe in a force excepting as a force that pervades matter and is not an individual entity. To believe in a thing, an image of the thing must be stamped on the mind. If one is asked if he believes in such an animal as a camel, there immediately arises in his mind an image of the camel. This image has come from experience or knowledge of the animal gathered in some way or other. No such image comes, or can come, with the idea of a God who is described as a force.

Man has always speculated upon the origin of the universe, including himself. I feel, with Herbert Spencer, that whether the universe had an origin—and if it had—what the origin is will never be known by man. The Christian says that the universe could not make itself; that there must have been some higher power to call it into being. Christians have been obsessed for many years by Paley's argument that if a person passing through a desert should find a watch and examine its spring, its hands, its case and its crystal, he would at once be satisfied that some intelligent being capable of design had made the watch. The reason he would not doubt it is because he is familiar with watches and other appliances made by man. The savage was once unfamiliar with a watch and would have had no idea upon the subject. There are plenty of crystals and rocks of natural formation that are as intricate as a watch, but even to intelligent man they carry no implication that some intelligent power must have made them. They carry no such implication because no one has any knowledge or experience of someone having made these natural objects which everywhere abound.

To say that God made the universe gives us no explanation of the beginnings of things. If we are told that God made the universe, the question immediately arises: Who made God? Did he always exist, or was there some power back of that? Did he create matter out of nothing, or is his existence coextensive with matter? The problem is still there. What is the origin of it all? If, on the other hand, one says that the universe was not made by God, that it always existed he has the same difficulty to confront. To say that the universe was here last year, or millions of years ago, does not explain its origin. This is still a mystery. As to the question of the origin of things, man can only wonder and doubt and guess.

As to the existence of the soul, all people may either believe or disbelieve. Everyone knows the origin of the human being. They know that it came from a single cell in the body of the mother, and that the cell was one out of ten thousand in the mother's body. Before gestation the cell must have been fertilized by a spermatozoan from the body of the father. This was one out of perhaps a billion spermatozoa that was the capacity of the father. When the cell is fertilized a chemical process begins. The cell divides and multiplies and increases into millions of cells, and finally a child is born. Cells die and are born during the life of the individual until they finally drop apart, and this is death.

If there is a soul, what is it, and where did it come from, and where does it go? Can anyone who is guided by his reason possibly imagine a soul independent of a body, or other place of its residence, or the character of it, or anything concerning it? If man is justified in any belief or disbelief on any subject, he is warranted in the disbelief in a soul. Not one scrap of evidence exists to prove any such impossible thing.

Many Christians base the belief of a soul and God upon the Bible. Strictly speaking, there is no such book. To make the Bible, sixty-six books are bound into one volume. These books are written by many people at different times, and no one knows the time or the identity of any author. Some of the books were written by several authors at various times. These books contain all sorts of contradictory concepts of life and morals and the origin of things. Between the first and last nearly a thousand years intervened, a longer time than has passed since the discovery of America by Columbus.

When I was a boy the theologians used to assert that the proof of the divine inspiration of the Bible rested on miracles and prophecies. But a miracle means a violation of a natural law, and there can be no proof imagined that could be sufficient to show the violation of a natural law; even though proof seemed to show violation, it would only show that we were not acquainted with all natural laws. One believes in the truthfulness of a man because of his long experience with the man, and because the man has always told a consistent story. But no man has told so consistent a story as nature. If one should say that the sun did not rise, to use the ordinary expression, on the day before, his hearer would not believe it, even though he had slept all day and knew that his informant was a man of the strictest veracity.

He would not believe it because the story is inconsistent with the conduct of the sun in all the ages past.

Primitive and even civilized people have grown so accustomed to believing in miracles that they often attribute the simplest manifestations of nature to agencies of which they know nothing. They do this when the belief is utterly inconsistent with knowledge and logic. They believe in old miracles and new ones. Preachers pray for rain, knowing full well that no such prayer was ever answered. When a politician is sick, they pray for God to cure him, and the politician almost invariably dies. The modern clergyman who prays for rain and for the health of the politician is no more intelligent in this matter than the primitive man who saw a separate miracle in the rising and setting of the sun, in the birth of an individual, in the growth of a plant, in the stroke of lightning, in the flood, in every manifestation of nature and life.

As to prophecies, intelligent writers gave them up long ago. In all prophecies facts are made to suit the prophecy, or the prophecy was made after the facts, or the events have no relation to the prophecy. Weird and strange and unreasonable interpretations are used to explain simple statements, that a prophecy may be claimed.

Can any rational person believe that the Bible is anything but a human document? We now know pretty well where the various books came from, and about when they were written. We know that they were written by human beings who had no knowledge of science, little knowledge of life, and were influenced by the barbarous morality of primitive times, and were grossly ignorant of most things that men know today. For instance, Genesis says that God made the earth, and he made the sun to light the day and the moon to light the night, and in one clause disposes of the star by saying that "he made the stars also." This was plainly written by someone who had no conception of the stars. Man, by the aid of his telescope, has looked out into the heavens and found stars whose diameter is as great as the distance between the earth and the sun. We know that the universe is filled with stars and suns and planets and systems. Every telescope, looking further into the heavens only discovers more and more worlds and suns and systems in the endless reaches of space. The men who wrote Genesis believed, of course, that this tiny speck of mud that we call the earth was the center of the universe, the only world in space and made for man, who was the only being worth considering. These men believed that the stars were only a little way above the earth, and were set in the firmament for man to look at, and for nothing else. Everyone today knows that this conception is not true.

The origin of the human race is not as blind a subject as it once was. Let alone God creating Adam out of hand, from the dust of the earth, does anyone believe that Eve was made from Adam's rib–that the snake walked and spoke in the Garden of Eden–that he tempted Eve to persuade Adam to eat an apple, and it is on that account that the whole human race was doomed to hell–that for four thousand years there was no chance for any human to be saved, though none of them had anything

255

whatever to do with the temptation; and that finally men were saved only through God's son dying for them, and that unless human beings believed this silly, impossible and wicked story they were doomed to hell? Can anyone with intelligence really believe that a child born today should be doomed because the snake tempted Eve and Eve tempted Adam? To believe that is not God-worship, it is devil-worship.

Can anyone call this scheme of creation and damnation moral? It defies every principle of morality, as man conceives morality. Can anyone believe today that the whole world was destroyed by flood, save only Noah and his family and a male and female of each species of animal that entered the Ark? There are almost a million species of insects alone. How did Noah match these up and make sure of getting male and female to reproduce life in the world after the flood had spent its force? And why should all the lower animals have been destroyed? Were they included in the sinning of man? This is a story which could not beguile a fairly bright child of five years of age today.

Do intelligent people believe that the various languages spoken by man on earth came from the confusion of tongues at the Tower of Babel, some four thousand years ago? Human languages were dispersed all over the face of the earth long before that time. Evidences of civilizations are in existence now that were old long before the date that romancers fix for the building of the Tower, and even before the date claimed for the flood.

Do Christians believe that Joshua made the sun stand still, so that the day could be lengthened, that a battle might be finished? What kind of person wrote that story, and what did he know about astronomy? It is perfectly plain that the author thought that the earth was the center of the universe and stood still in the heavens, and that the sun either went around it or was pulled across its path each day, and that the stopping of the sun would lengthen the day. We know now that had the sun stopped when Joshua commanded it, and had it stood still until now, it would not have lengthened the day. We know that the day is determined by the rotation of the earth upon its axis, and not by the movement of the sun. Everyone knows that this story simply is not true, and not many even pretend to believe the childish fable.

What of the tale of Balaam's ass speaking to him, probably in Hebrew? Is it true, or is it a fable? Many asses have spoken, and doubtless some in Hebrew, but they have not been that breed of asses. Is salvation to depend on a belief in a monstrosity like this?

Above all the rest, would any human being today believe that a child was born without a father? Yet this story was not at all unreasonable in the ancient world; at least three or four miraculous births are recorded in the Bible, including John the Baptist and Samson. Immaculate conceptions were common in the Roman world at the time and at the place where Christianity really had its nativity. Women were taken to the temples to be inoculated of God so that their sons might be heroes, which meant, generally, wholesale butchers. Julius Caesar was a miraculous

256

conception–indeed, they were common all over the world. How many miraculous-birth stories is a Christian now expected to believe?

In the days of the formation of the Christian religion, disease meant the possession of human beings by devils. Christ cured a sick man by casting out the devils, who ran into the swine, and the swine ran into the sea. Is there any question but what that was simply the attitude and belief of a primitive people? Does anyone believe that sickness means the possession of the body by devils, and that devils must be cast out of the human being that he may be cured? Does anyone believe that a dead person can come to life? The miracles recorded in the Bible are not the only instances of dead men coming to life. All over the world one finds testimony of such miracles: miracles which no person is expected to believe, unless it is his kind of miracle. Still at Lourdes today, and all over the present world, from New York to Los Angeles and up and down the lands, people believe in miraculous occurrences, and even the return of the dead. Superstition is everywhere prevalent in the world. It has been so from the beginning, and most likely will be so unto the end.

The reasons for agnosticism are abundant and compelling. Fantastic and foolish and impossible consequences are freely claimed for the belief in religion. All the civilization of any period is put down as a result of religion. All the cruelty and error and ignorance of the period has no relation to religion. The truth is that the origin of what we call civilization is not due to religion but to skepticism. So long as men accepted miracles without question, so long as they believed in original sin and the road to salvation, so long as they believed in a hell where man would be kept for eternity on account of Eve, there was no reason whatever for civilization: life was short, and eternity was long, and the business of life was preparation for eternity.

When every event was a miracle, when there was no order or system or law, there was no occasion for studying any subject, or being interested in anything excepting a religion which took care of the soul. As man doubted the primitive conceptions about religion, and no longer accepted the literal, miraculous teachings of ancient books, he set himself to understand nature. We no longer cure disease by casting out devils. Since that time, men have studied the human body, have built hospitals and treated illness in a scientific way. Science is responsible for the building of railroads and bridges, of steamships, of telegraph lines, of cities, towns, large buildings and small, plumbing and sanitation, of the food supply, and the countless thousands of useful things that we now deem necessary to life. Without skepticism and doubt, none of these things could have been given to the world.

The fear of God is not the beginning of wisdom. The fear of God is the death of wisdom. Skepticism and doubt lead to study and investigation, and investigation is the beginning of wisdom.

The modern world is the child of doubt and inquiry, as the ancient world was the child of fear and faith. (1963)

EVOLUTION AS
FACT AND THEORY

STEPHEN JAY GOULD

Kirtley Mather, who died last year at age 89, was a pillar of both science and the Christian religion in America and one of my dearest friends. The difference of half a century in our ages evaporated before our common interests. The most curious thing we shared was a battle we each fought at the same age. For Kirtley had gone to Tennessee with Clarence Darrow to testify for evolution at the Scopes trial of 1925. When I think that we are enmeshed again in the same struggle for one of the best documented, most compelling and exciting concepts in all of science, I don't know whether to laugh or cry.

According to idealized principles of scientific discourse, the arousal of dormant issues should reflect fresh data that gives renewed life to abandoned notions. Those outside the current debate may therefore be excused for suspecting that creationists have come up with something new, or that evolutionists have generated some serious internal trouble. But nothing has changed; the creationists have not a single new fact or argument. Darrow and Bryan were at least more entertaining than we lesser antagonists today. The rise of creationism is politics, pure and simple; it represents one issue (and by no means the major concern) of the resurgent evangelical right. Arguments that seemed kooky just a decade ago have re-entered the mainstream.

CREATIONISM IS NOT SCIENCE

The basic attack of the creationists falls apart on two general counts before we even reach the supposed factual details of their complaints against evolution. First, they play upon a vernacular misunderstanding of the word *theory* to convey the false impression that we evolutionists are covering up the rotten core of our edifice. Second, they misuse a popular philosophy of science to argue that they are behaving scientifically in attacking evolution. Yet the same philosophy demonstrates that their own belief is not science, and that "scientific creationism" is therefore meaningless and self-contradictory, a superb example of what Orwell called "newspeak."

In the American vernacular, *theory* often means "imperfect fact"–part of a hierarchy of confidence running downhill from fact to theory to hypothesis to guess. Thus the power of the creationist argument: evolution is "only" a theory, and intense debate now rages about many aspects of the theory. If evolution is less than a fact, and scientists can't even make up their minds about the theory, then what confidence can we have in it? Indeed, President Reagan echoed this argument before an evangelical group in Dallas when he said (in what I devoutly hope was campaign rhetoric): "Well, it is a theory. It is a scientific theory only, and it has in recent years been challenged in the world of science–that is, not believed in the scientific community to be as infallible as it once was."

Well, evolution is a theory. It is also a fact. And facts and theories are different things, not rungs in a hierarchy of increasing certainty. Facts are world's data. Theories are structures of ideas that explain and interpret facts. Facts do not go away when scientists debate rival theories to explain them. Einstein's theory of gravitation replaced Newton's, but apples did not suspend themselves in mid-air pending the outcome. And human beings evolved from apelike ancestors whether they did so by Darwin's proposed mechanism or by some other, yet to be discovered.

Moreover, fact does not mean "absolute certainty." The final proofs of logic and mathematics flow deductively from stated premises and achieve certainty only because they are not about the empirical world. Evolutionists make no claim for perpetual truth, though creationists often do (and then attack us for a style of argument that they themselves favor). In science, fact can only mean "confirmed to such a degree that it would be perverse to withhold provisional assent." I suppose that apples might start to rise tomorrow, but the possibility does not merit equal time in physics classrooms.

Evolutionists have been clear about this distinction between fact and theory from the very beginning, if only because we have always acknowledged how far we are from completely understanding the mechanisms (theory) by which evolution (fact) occurred. Darwin continually emphasized the difference between his two great and separate accomplishments: establishing the fact of evolution, and proposing a theory–natural selection–to explain the mechanism of evolution. He wrote in *The Descent of Man*: " I had two distinct objects in view; firstly, to show that species had not been separately created, and secondly, that natural selection had been the chief agent of change. . . . Hence if I have erred in. . . . having exaggerated its [natural selection's] power. . .I have at least, as I hope, done good service in aiding to overthrow the dogma of separate creations."

Thus Darwin acknowledged the provisional nature of natural selection while affirming the fact of evolution. The fruitful theoretical debate that Darwin initiated has never ceased. From the 1940s through the 1960s, Darwin's own theory of natural selection did achieve a temporary hegemony that it never enjoyed in his lifetime. But renewed debate characterizes our decade, and, while no biologist questions the importance of natural selection, many now doubt its ubiquity. In particular, many evolutionists argue that substantial amounts of genetic change may not be subject to natural selection and may spread through populations at random. Others are challenging Darwin's linking of natural selection with gradual, imperceptible change through all intermediary degrees; they are arguing that most evolutionary events may occur far more rapidly than Darwin envisioned.

Scientists regard debates on fundamental issues of theory as a sign of intellectual health and a source of excitement. Science is–and how else can I say it?–most fun when it plays with interesting ideas, examines their implications, and recognizes that old information may be explained in surprisingly new ways. Evolutionary theory is now enjoying this uncommon vigor. Yet amidst all this turmoil no biologist has been led to doubt the fact that evolution occurred; we are debating how it happened. We are all trying to explain the same thing: the tree of evolutionary descent linking all organisms by ties of genealogy. Creationists pervert and caricature this debate by conveniently neglecting the common conviction that underlies it, and by falsely suggesting that we now doubt the very phenomenon we are struggling to understand.

Using another invalid argument, creationists claim that "the dogma of separate creations," as Darwin characterized it a century ago, is a scientific theory meriting equal time with evolution in high school biology curricula. But a prevailing viewpoint among philosophers of science belies this creationist argument. Philosopher Karl Popper has argued for decades that the primary criterion of science is the falsifiability of its theories. We can never prove absolutely, but we can falsify. A set of ideas that cannot, in principle, be falsified is not science.

The entire creationist argument involves little more than a rhetorical attempt to falsify evolution by presenting supposed contradictions among its supporters. Their brand of creationism, they claim, is "scientific" because it follows the Popperian model in trying to demolish evolution. Yet Popper's argument must apply in both directions. One does not become a scientist by the simple act of trying to falsify another scientific system; one has to present an alternative system that also meets Popper's criterion—it too must be falsifiable in principle.

"Scientific creationism" is a self-contradictory, nonsense phrase precisely because it cannot be falsified. I can envision observations and experiments that would disprove any evolutionary theory I know, but I cannot imagine what potential data could lead creationists to abandon their beliefs. Unbeatable systems are dogma, not science. Lest I seem harsh or rhetorical, I quote creationism's leading intellectual, Duane Gish, Ph.D., from his recent (1978) book *Evolution? The Fossils Say No!* "By creation we mean the bringing into being by a supernatural Creator of the basic kinds of plants and animals by the process of sudden, or fiat, creation. We cannot discover by scientific investigations anything about the creative processes used by the Creator." Pray tell, Dr. Gish, in the light of your last sentence, what then is "scientific" creationism?

THE FACT OF EVOLUTION

Our confidence that evolution occurred centers upon three general arguments. First, we have abundant, direct, observational evidence of evolution in action, from both the field and the laboratory. It ranges from countless experiments on change in nearly everything about fruit flies subjected to artificial selection in the laboratory to the famous British moths that turned black when industrial soot darkened the trees upon which they rest. (The moths gain protection from sharp-sighted bird predators by blending into the background.) Creationists do not deny these observations; how could they? Creationists have tightened their act. They now argue that God only created "basic kinds," and allowed for limited evolutionary meandering within them. Thus toy poodles and Great Danes come from the dog kind and moths can change color, but nature cannot convert a dog to a cat or a monkey to a man.

The second and third arguments for evolution—the case for major changes—do not involve direct observation of evolution in action. They rest upon inference, but are no less secure for that reason. Major evolutionary change requires too much time for direct observation on the scale of recorded human history. All historical sciences rest upon inference, and evolution is no different from geology, cosmology, or human history in this respect. In principle, we cannot observe processes that operated in the past. We must infer them from results that still survive: living and fossil organisms for evolution, documents and artifacts for human history, strata and topography for geology.

The second argument—that the imperfection of nature reveals evolution—strikes many people as ironic, for they feel that evolution should be most elegantly displayed in the nearly perfect adaptation expressed by some organisms—the chamber of a gull's wing, or butterflies that cannot be seen in ground litter because they mimic leaves so precisely. But perfection could be imposed by a wise creator or evolved by natural selection. Perfection covers the tracks of past history. And past history—the evidence of descent—is our mark of evolution.

Evolution lies exposed in the *imperfections* that record a history of descent. Why should a rat run, a bat fly, a porpoise swim, and I type this essay with structures built of the same bones unless we all inherited them from a common ancestor? An engineer, starting from scratch, could design better limbs in each case. Why should all the large native mammals of Australia be marsupials, unless they descended from a common ancestor isolated on this island continent? Marsupials are not "better," or ideally suited for Australia; many have been wiped out by placental mammals imported by man from other continents. This principle of imperfection extends to all historical sciences. When we recognize the etymology of September, October, November, and December (seventh, eighth, ninth, and tenth, from the Latin), we know that two additional items (January and February) must have been added to an original calendar of ten months.

The third argument is more direct: transitions are often found in the fossil record. Preserved transitions are not common—and should not be, according to our understanding of evolution (see next section)—but they are not entirely wanting, as creationists often claim. The lower jaw of reptiles contains several bones, that of mammals only one. The non-mammalian jawbones are reduced, step by step, in mammalian ancestors until they become tiny nubbins located at the back of the jaw. The "hammer" and "anvil" bones of the mammalian ear are descendants of these nubbins. How could such a transition be accomplished? the creationists ask. Surely a bone is either entirely in the jaw or in the ear. Yet paleontologists have discovered two transitional lineages of therapsids (the so-called mammal-like reptiles) with a double jaw joint—one composed of the old quadrate and articular bones (as in modern mammals). For that matter, what better transitional form could we desire than the oldest human, *Australopithecus afarensis*, with its apelike palate, its human upright stance, and a cranial capacity larger than any ape's of the same body size but a full 1,000 cubic centimeters below ours? If God made each of the half dozen human species discovered in ancient rocks, why did he create in an unbroken temporal sequence of progressively more modern features–increasing cranial capacity, reduced face and teeth, larger body size? Did he create to mimic evolution and test our faith thereby?

AN EXAMPLE OF CREATIONIST ARGUMENT
\
Faced with these facts of evolution and the philosophical bankruptcy of their own position, creationists rely upon distortion and innuendo to buttress their rhetorical claim. If I sound sharp or bitter, indeed I am–for I have become a major target of these practices.

I count myself among the evolutionists who argue for a jerky, or episodic, rather than a smoothly gradual, pace of change. In 1972 my colleague Niles Eldredge and I developed the theory of punctuated equilibrium [*Discover*, October]. We argued that two outstanding facts of the fossil record–geologically "sudden" origin of new species and failure to change thereafter (stasis)–reflect the predictions of evolutionary theory, not the imperfections of the fossil record. In most theories, small isolated populations are the source of new species, and the process of speciation takes thousands or tens of thousands of years. This amount of time, so long when measured against our lives, is a geological microsecond. It represents much less than 1 percent of the average life span for a fossil invertebrate species– more than 10 million years. Large, widespread, and well-established species, on the other hand, are not expected to change very much. We believe that the inertia of large populations explains the stasis of most fossil species over millions of years.

We proposed the theory of punctuated equilibrium largely to provide a different explanation for pervasive trends in the fossil record. Trends, we argued, cannot be attributed to gradual transformation within lineages, but must arise from the differential success of certain kinds of species. A trend, we argued, is more like climbing a flight of stairs (punctuations and stasis) than rolling up an inclined plane.

Since we proposed punctuated equilibria to explain trends, it is infuriating to be quoted again and again by creationists–whether through design or stupidity, I do not know–as admitting that the fossil record includes no transitional forms. Transitional forms are generally lacking at the species level, but are abundant between larger groups. The evolution from reptiles to mammals, as mentioned earlier, is well documented. Yet a pamphlet entitled "Harvard Scientists Agree Evolution is a Hoax" states: "The facts of punctuated equilibrium which Gould and Eldredge . . . are forcing Darwinists to swallow fit the picture that Bryan insisted on, and which God has revealed to us in the Bible."

Continuing the distortion, several creationists have equated the theory of punctuated equilibrium with a caricature of the beliefs of Richard Goldschmidt, a great early geneticist. Goldschmidt argued, in a famous book published in 1940, that new groups can arise all at once through major mutations. He referred to these suddenly transformed creatures as "hopeful monsters." (I am attracted to some aspects of the non-caricatured version, but Goldschmidt's theory still has nothing to do with punctuated equilibrium.) Creationist Luther Sunderland talks of the "punctuated equilibrium hopeful monster theory" and tells his hopeful readers that "it amounts to tacit admission that anti-evolutionists are correct in asserting there is no fossil evidence supporting the theory that all life is connected to a common ancestor." Duane Gish writes, "According to Goldschmidt, and now apparently according to Gould, a reptile laid an egg from which the first bird, feathers and all, was produced." Any evolutionist who believed such nonsense would rightly be laughed off the intellectual stage; yet the only theory that could ever envision such a scenario for the evolution of birds is creationism–God acts in the egg.

CONCLUSION

I am both angry at and amused by the creationists; but mostly I am deeply sad. Sad for many reasons. Sad because so many people who respond to creationist appeals are troubled for the right reason, but venting their anger at the wrong target. It is true that scientists have often been dogmatic and elitist. It is true that we have often allowed the white-coated, advertising image to represent us–"Scientists say that Brand X cures bunions ten times faster than . . . ." We have not fought it adequately because we derive benefits from appearing as a new priesthood. It is also true that faceless bureaucratic state power intrudes more and more into our lives and removes choices that should belong to individuals and communities. I can understand that requiring that evolution be taught in the schools might be seen as one more insult on all these grounds. But the culprit is not, and cannot be, evolution or any other fact of the natural world. Identify and fight your legitimate enemies by all means, but we are not among them.

I am sad because the practical result of this brouhaha will not be expanded coverage to include creationism (that would also make me sad), but the reduction or excision of evolution from high school curricula. Evolution is one of the half dozen "great ideas" developed by science. It speaks to the profound issues of genealogy that fascinate all of us–the "roots" phenomenon writ large. Where did we come from? Where did life arise? How did it develop? How are organisms related? It forces us to think, ponder, and wonder. Shall we deprive millions of this knowledge and once again teach biology as a set of dull and unconnected facts, without the thread that weaves diverse material into a supple unity?

But most of all I am saddened by a trend I am just beginning to discern among my colleagues. I sense that some now wish to mute the healthy debate about theory that has brought new life to evolutionary biology. It provides grist for creationist mills, they say, even if only by distortion. Perhaps we should lie low and rally round the flag of strict Darwinism, at least for the moment–a kind of old-time religion on our part.

263

But we should borrow another metaphor and recognize that we too have to tread a straight and narrow path, surrounded by roads to perdition. For if we ever begin to suppress our search to understand nature, to quench our own intellectual excitement in a misguided effort to present a united front where it does not and should not exist, then we are truly lost.

(1981)

DEATH AND JUSTICE

EDWARD I. KOCH

Last December a man named Robert Lee Willie, who had been convicted of raping and murdering an 18-year-old woman, was executed in the Louisiana state prison. In a statement issued several minutes before his death, Mr. Willie said: "Killing people is wrong. . . . It makes no difference whether it's citizens, countries, or governments. Killing is wrong." Two weeks later in South Carolina, an admitted killer named Joseph Carl Shaw was put to death for murdering two teenagers. In an appeal to the governor for clemency, Mr. Shaw wrote: "Killing is wrong when I did it. Killing is wrong when you do it. I hope you have the courage and moral strength to stop the killing."

It is a curiosity of modern life that we find ourselves being lectured on morality by cold-blooded killers. Mr. Willie previously had been convicted of aggravated rape, aggravated kidnapping, and the murders of a Louisiana deputy and a man from Missouri. Mr. Shaw committed another murder a week before the two for which he was executed, and admitted mutilating the body of the 14-year-old girl he killed. I can't help wondering what prompted these murderers to speak out against killing as they entered the death-house door. Did their new-found reverence for life stem from the realization that they were about to lose their own?

Life is indeed precious, and I believe the death penalty helps to affirm this fact. Had the death penalty been a real possibility in the minds of these murders, they might well have stayed their hand. They might have shown moral awareness before the victims died, and not after. Consider the tragic death of Rosa Velez, who happened to be home when a man named Luis Vera burglarized her apartment in Brooklyn. "Yeah, I shot her," Vera admitted. "She knew me, and I knew I wouldn't go to the chair."

During my 22 years in public service, I have heard the pros and cons of capital punishment expressed with special intensity. As a district leader, councilman, congressman, and mayor, I have represented constituencies generally thought of as liberal. Because I support the death penalty for heinous crimes of murder, I have sometimes been the subject of emotional and outraged attacks by voters who find my position reprehensible or worse. I have listened to their ideas. I have weighed their objections carefully. I still support the death penalty. The reasons I maintain my position can be best understood by examining the arguments most frequently heard in opposition.

1. *The death penalty is "barbaric."* Sometimes opponents of capital punishment horrify with tales of lingering death on the gallows, of faulty electric chairs, or of agony in the gas chamber. Partly in response to such protests, several states such as North Carolina and Texas switched to execution by lethal injection. The condemned person is put to death painlessly, without ropes, voltage, bullets, or gas. Did this answer the objections of death penalty opponents? Of course not. On June 22,

1984, the *New York Times* published an editorial that sarcastically attacked the new "hygienic" method of death by injection, and stated that "execution can never be made humane through science." So it's not the method that really troubles opponents. It's the death itself they consider barbaric.

Admittedly, capital punishment is not a pleasant topic. However, one does not have to like the death penalty in order to support it any more than one must like radical surgery, radiation, or chemotherapy in order to find necessary these attempts at curing cancer. Ultimately we may learn how to cure cancer with a simple pill. Unfortunately, that day has not yet arrived. Today we are faced with the choice of letting the cancer spread or trying to cure it with the methods available, methods that one day will almost certainly be considered barbaric. But to give up and do nothing would be far more barbaric and would certainly delay the discovery of an eventual cure. The analogy between cancer and murder is imperfect, because murder is not the "disease" we are trying to cure. The disease is injustice. We may not like the death penalty, but it must be available to punish crimes of cold-blooded murder, cases in which any other form of punishment would be inadequate and, therefore, unjust. If we create a society in which injustice is not tolerated, incidents of murder–the most flagrant form of injustice–will diminish.

2. *No other major democracy uses the death penalty.* No other major democracy– in fact, few other countries of any description–is plagued by a murder rate such as that in the United States. Fewer and fewer Americans can remember the days when unlocked doors were the norm and murder was a rare and terrible offense. In America the murder rate climbed 122 percent between 1963 and 1980. During the same period, the murder rate in New York City increased by almost 400 percent, and the statistics are even worse in many other cities. A study at MIT showed that based on 1970 homicide rates a person who lived in a large American city ran a greater risk of being murdered than an American soldier in World War II ran of being killed in combat. It is not surprising that the laws of each country differ according to differing conditions and traditions. If other countries had our murder problem, the cry for capital punishment would be just as loud as it is here. And I daresay that any other major democracy where 75 percent of the people supported the death penalty would soon enact it into law.

3. *An innocent person might be executed by mistake.* Consider the work of Adam Bedau, one of the most implacable foes of capital punishment in this country. According to Mr. Bedau, it is "false sentimentality to argue that the death penalty should be abolished because of the abstract possibility than an innocent person might be executed." He cites a study of the 7,000 executions in this country from 1893 to 1971, and concludes that the record fails to show that such cases occur. The main point, however, is this. If government functioned only when the possibility of error didn't exist, government wouldn't function at all. Human life deserves special protection, and one of the best ways to guarantee that protection is to assure that convicted murderers do not kill again. Only the death penalty can accomplish this end. In a recent case in New Jersey, a man named Richard Biegenwald was freed from prison after serving 18 years for murder; since his release he has been

convicted of committing four murders. A prisoner named Lemuel Smith, who, while serving four life sentences for murder (plus two life sentences for kidnapping and robbery) in New York's Green Haven Prison, lured a woman corrections officer into the chaplain's office and strangled her. He then mutilated and dismembered her body. An additional life sentence for Smith is meaningless. Because New York has no death penalty statute, Smith has effectively been given a license to kill.

But the problem of multiple murder is not confined to the nation's penitentiaries. In 1981, 91 police officers were killed in the line of duty in this country. Seven percent of those arrested in the cases that have been solved had a previous arrest for murder. In New York City in 1976 and 1977, 85 persons arrested for homicide had a previous arrest for murder. Six of these individuals had two previous arrests for murder, and one had four previous murder arrests. During those two years the New York police were arresting for murder persons with a previous arrest for murder on the average of one every 8.5 days. This is not surprising when we learn that in 1975, for example, the median time served in Massachusetts for homicide was less than two-and-a half years. In 1976 a study sponsored by the Twentieth Century Fund found that the average time served in the United States for first-degree murder is ten years. The median time served may be considerably lower.

4. *Capital punishment cheapens the value of human life.* On the contrary, it can be easily demonstrated that the death penalty strengthens the value of human life. If the penalty for rape were lowered, clearly it would signal a lessened regard for the victims' suffering, humiliation, and personal integrity. It would cheapen their horrible experience, and expose them to an increased danger of recurrence. When we lower the penalty for murder, it signals a lessened regard for the value of the victim's life. Some critics of capital punishment, such as columnist Jimmy Breslin, have suggested that a life sentence is actually a harsher penalty for murder than death. This is sophistic nonsense. A few killers may decide not to appeal a death sentence, but the overwhelming majority make every effort to stay alive. It is by exacting the highest penalty for the taking of human life that we affirm the highest value of human life.

5. *The death penalty is applied in a discriminatory manner.* This factor no longer seems to be the problem it once was. The appeals process for a condemned prisoner is lengthy and painstaking. Every effort is made to see that the verdict and sentence were fairly arrived at. However, assertions of discrimination are not an argument for ending the death penalty but for extending it. It is not justice to exclude everyone from the penalty of the law if a few are found to be so favored. Justice requires that the law be applied equally to all.

6. *Thou shalt not kill.* The Bible is our greatest source of moral inspiration. Opponents of the death penalty frequently cite the sixth of the Ten Commandments in an attempt to prove the capital punishment is divinely proscribed. In the original Hebrew, however, the Sixth Commandment reads "Thou Shalt Not Commit Murder," and the Torah specifies capital punishment for a variety of offenses. The

biblical viewpoint has been upheld by philosophers throughout history. The greatest thinkers of the 19th century–Kant, Locke, Hobbes, Rousseau, Montesquieu, and Mill–agreed that natural law properly authorizes the sovereign to take life in order to vindicate justice. Only Jeremy Bentham was ambivalent. Washington, Jefferson, and Franklin endorsed it. Abraham Lincoln authorized executions for deserters in wartime. Alexis de Tocqueville, who expressed profound respect for American institutions, believed that the death penalty was indispensable to the support of social order. The United States Constitution, widely admired as one of the seminal achievements in the history of humanity, condemns cruel and inhuman punishment, but does not condemn capital punishment.

7. *The death penalty is state-sanctioned murder.* This is the defense with which Messrs. Willie and Shaw hoped to soften the resolve of those who sentenced them to death. By saying in effect, "You're no better than I am," the murderer seeks to bring his accusers down to his own level. It is also a popular argument among opponents of capital punishment, but a transparently false one. Simply put, the state has rights that the private individual does not. In a democracy, those rights are given to the state by the electorate. The execution of a lawfully condemned killer is no more an act of murder than is legal imprisonment an act of kidnapping. If an individual forces a neighbor to pay him money under threat of punishment, it's called extortion. If the state does it, it's called taxation. Rights and responsibilities surrendered by the individual are what give the state its power to govern. This contract is the foundation of civilization itself.

Everyone wants his or her rights, and will defend them jealously. Not everyone, however, wants responsibilities, especially the painful responsibilities that come with law enforcement. Twenty-one years ago a woman named Kitty Genovese was assaulted and murdered on a street in New York. Dozens of neighbors heard her cries for help but did nothing to assist her. They didn't even call the police. In such a climate the criminal understandably grows bolder. In the presence of moral cowardice, he lectures us on our supposed failings and tries to equate his crimes with our quest for justice.

The death of anyone–even a convicted killer–diminishes us all. But we are diminished even more by a justice system that fails to function. It is an illusion to let ourselves believe that doing away with capital punishment removes the murderer's deed from our conscience. The rights of society are paramount. When we protect guilty lives, we give up innocent lives in exchange. When opponents of capital punishment say to the state: "I will not let you kill in my name," they are also saying to murderers: "You can kill in *your own* name as long as I have an excuse for not getting involved."

It is hard to imagine anything worse than being murdered while neighbors do nothing. But something worse exists. When those same neighbors shrink back from justly punishing the murderer, the victim dies twice. (1985)

NO DEATH PENALTY

DAVID BRUCK

Mayor Ed Koch contends that the death penalty "affirms life." By failing to execute murderers, he says, we "signal a lessened regard for the value of the victim's life." Koch suggests that people who oppose the death penalty are like Kitty Genovese's neighbors, who heard her cries for help but did nothing while an attacker stabbed her to death.

This is the standard "moral" defense of death as punishment: even if executions don't deter violent crime any more effectively than imprisonment, they are still required as the only means we have of doing justice in response to the worst of crimes.

Until recently, this " moral" argument had to be considered in the abstract since no one was being executed in the United States. But the death penalty is back now, at least in the southern states, where every one of the more than 30 executions carried out over the last two years has taken place. Those of us who live in those states are getting to see the difference between the death penalty in theory, and what happens when you actually try to use it.

South Carolina resumed executing prisoners in January with the electrocution of Joseph Carl Shaw. Shaw was condemned to death for helping to murder two teenagers while he was serving as a military policeman at Fort Jackson, South Carolina. His crime, propelled by mental illness and PCP, was one of terrible brutality. It is Shaw's last words ("Killing was wrong when I did it. It is wrong when you do it. . . .") that so outraged Mayor Koch: he finds it a "curiosity of modern life that we are being lectured on morality by cold-blooded killers." And so it is.

But it was not "modern life" that brought this curiosity into being. It was capital punishment. The electric chair was J.C. Shaw's platform. (The mayor mistakenly writes that Shaw's statement came in the form of a plea to the governor for clemency: actually Shaw made it only seconds before his death, as he waited, shaved and strapped into the chair, for the switch to be thrown.) It was the chair that provided Shaw with celebrity and an opportunity to lecture us on right and wrong. What made this weird moral reversal even worse is that J. C. Shaw faced his own death with undeniable dignity and courage. And while Shaw died, the TV crews recorded another "curiosity" of the death penalty–the crowd gathered outside the deathhouse to cheer on the executioner. Whoops of elation greeted the announcement of Shaw's death. Waiting at the penitentiary gates for the appearance of the hearse bearing Shaw's remains, one demonstrator started yelling, "Where's the beef?"

For those who had to see the execution of J. C. Shaw, it wasn't easy to keep in mind that the purpose of the whole spectacle was to affirm life. It will be harder still when Florida executes a cop-killer named Alvin Ford. Ford has lost his mind during his years of death-row confinement, and now spends his days trembling, rocking back and forth, and muttering unintelligible prayers. This has led to litigation over whether Ford meets a centuries-old legal standard for mental competency. Since the Middle Ages, the Anglo-American legal system has generally prohibited the execution of anyone who is too mentally ill to understand what is about to be done to him and why. If Florida wins its case, it will have earned the right to electrocute Ford in his present condition. If it loses, he will not be executed until the state has first nursed him back to some semblance of mental health.

We can at least be thankful that this demoralizing spectacle involves a prisoner who is actually guilty of murder. But this may not always be so. The ordeal of Lenell Jeter–the young black engineer who recently served more than a year of a life sentence for a Texas armed robbery that he didn't commit–should remind us that the system is quite capable of making the very worst sort of mistake. That Jeter was eventually cleared is a fluke. If the robbery had occurred at 7 p.m. rather than 3 p.m., he'd not have had an alibi, and would still be in prison today. And if someone had been killed in that robbery, Jeter probably would have been sentenced to death. We'd have seen the usual execution-day interviews with state officials and victim's relatives, all complaining that Jeter's appeals took too long. And Jeter's last words from the gurney would have taken their place among the growing literature of death-house oration that so irritates the mayor.

Koch quotes Hugo Adam Bedau, a prominent abolitionist, to the effect that the record fails to establish that innocent defendants have been executed in the past. But this doesn't mean, as Koch implies, that it hasn't happened. All Bedau was saying was that doubts concerning executed prisoners' guilt are almost never resolved. Bedau is at work now on an effort to determine how many wrongful death sentences may have been imposed: his list of murder convictions since 1900 in which the state eventually *admitted* error is some 400 cases long. Of course, very few of these cases involved actual executions: the mistakes that Bedau documents were uncovered precisely because the prisoner was alive and able to fight for his vindication. The cases where someone is executed are the very cases in which we're least likely to learn that we got the wrong man.

I don't claim that executions of entirely innocent people will occur very often. But they will occur. And other sorts of mistakes already have. Roosevelt Green was executed in Georgia two days before J. C. Shaw. Green and an accomplice kidnapped a young woman. Green swore that his companion shot her to death after Green had left, and that he knew nothing about the murder. Green's claim was supported by a statement that his accomplice made to a witness after the crime. The jury never resolved whether Green was telling the truth, and when he tried to take a polygraph examination a few days before his scheduled execution, the state of Georgia refused to allow the examiner into the prison. As the pressure for symbolic retribution mounts, the courts, like the public, are losing patience with such details.

Green was electrocuted on January 9, while members of the Ku Klux Klan rallied outside the prison.

Then there is another sort of arbitrariness that happens all the time. Last October, Louisiana executed a man named Ernest Knighton. Knighton had killed a gas station owner during a robbery. Like any murder, this was a terrible crime. But it was not premeditated, and is the sort of crime that very rarely results in a death sentence. Why was Knighton electrocuted when almost everyone else who committed the same offense was not? Was it because he was black? Was it because his victim and all 12 members of the jury that sentenced him were white? Was it because Knighton's court-appointed lawyer presented no evidence on his behalf at his sentencing hearing? Or maybe there's no reason except bad luck. One thing is clear: Ernest Knighton was picked out to die the way a fisherman takes a cricket out of a bait jar. No one cares which cricket gets impaled on the hook.

Not every prisoner executed recently was chosen that randomly. But many were. And having selected these men so casually, so blindly, the death penalty system asks us to accept that the purpose of killing each of them is to affirm the sanctity of human life.

The death penalty states are also learning that the death penalty is easier to advocate than it is to administer. In Florida, where executions have become almost routine, the governor reports that nearly a third of his time is spent reviewing the clemency requests of condemned prisoners. The Florida Supreme Court is hopelessly backlogged with death cases. Some have taken five years to decide, and the rest of the Court's work waits in line behind the death appeals. Florida's death row currently holds more than 230 prisoners. State officials are reportedly considering building a special "death prison" devoted entirely to the isolation and electrocution of the condemned. The state is also considering the creation of a special public defender unit that will do nothing else but handle death penalty appeals. The death penalty, in short, is spawning death agencies.

And what is Florida getting for all of this? The state went through almost all of 1983 without executing anyone: its rate of intentional homicide declined by 17 percent. Last year Florida executed eight people–the most of any state, and the sixth highest total for any year since Florida started electrocuting people back in 1924. Elsewhere in the U.S. last year, the homicide rate continued to decline. But in Florida, it actually rose by 5.1 percent.

But these are just the tiresome facts. The electric chair has been a centerpiece of each of Koch's recent political campaigns, and he knows better than anyone how little the facts have to do with the public's support for capital punishment. What really fuels the death penalty is the justifiable frustration and rage of people who see that the government is not coping with violent crime. So what if the death penalty doesn't work? At least it gives us the satisfaction of knowing that we got one or two of the sons of bitches.

Perhaps we want retribution on the flesh and bone of a handful of convicted murderers so badly that we're willing to close our eyes to all of the demoralization and danger that come with it. A lot of politicians think so, and they may be right. But if they are, then let's at least look honestly at what we're doing. This lottery of death both comes from and encourages an attitude toward human life that is not reverent, but reckless.

And that is why the mayor is dead wrong when he confuses such fury with justice. He suggests that we trivialize murder unless we kill murderers. By that logic, we also trivialize rape unless we sodomize rapists. The sin of Kitty Genovese's neighbors wasn't that they failed to stab her attacker to death. Justice does demand that murderers be punished. And common sense demands that society be protected from them. But neither justice nor self-preservation demands that we kill men whom we have already imprisoned.

The electric chair in which J. C. Shaw died earlier this year was built in 1912 at the suggestion of South Carolina's governor at the time, Cole Blease. Governor Blease's other criminal justice initiative was an impassioned crusade in favor of the lynch law. Any lesser response, the governor insisted, trivialized the loathsome crimes of interracial rape and murder. In 1912 a lot of people agreed with Governor Blease that a proper regard for justice required both lynching and the electric chair. Eventually we are going to learn that justice requires neither. (1985)

ANITA HILL'S STATEMENT
TO THE SENATE JUDICIARY
COMMITTEE
ANITA HILL

Mr. Chairman, Sen. Thurmond, members of the committee, my name is Anita F. Hill, and I am a professor of law at the University of Oklahoma. I was born on a farm in Okmulgee County, Okla., in 1956. I am the youngest of 13 children. I had my early education in Okmulgee County. My father, Albert Hill, is a farmer in that area. My mother's name is Erma Hill. She is also a farmer and a housewife.

My childhood was one of a lot of hard work and not much money, but it was one of solid family affection, as represented by my parents. I was reared in a religious atmosphere in the Baptist faith, and I have been a member of the Antioch Baptist Church in Tulsa, Okla., since 1983. It is a very warm part of my life at the present time.

For my undergraduate work, I went to Oklahoma State University and graduated from there in 1977. I am attaching to this statement a copy of my resume for further details of my education.

I graduated from the university with academic honors and proceeded to the Yale Law School, where I received my JD degree in 1980. Upon graduation from law school, I became a practicing lawyer with the Washington, D.C., firm of Ward, Hardraker & Ross.

In 1981, I was introduced to now Judge Thomas by a mutual friend. Judge Thomas told me that he was anticipating a political appointment, and he asked if I would be interested in working with him. He was, in fact, appointed as assistant secretary of education for civil rights. After he had taken that post, he asked if I would become his assistant, and I accepted that position.

In my early period there, I had two major projects. The first was an article I wrote for Judge Thomas's signature on the education of minority students. The second was the organization of a seminar on high-risk students which was abandoned because Judge Thomas transferred to the EEOC where he became chairman of that office.

During this period at the Department of Education, my working relationship with Judge Thomas was positive. I had a good deal of responsibility and independence. I thought he respected my work and that he trusted my judgment. After approximately three months of working there, he asked me to go out socially with him.

What happened next and telling the world about it are the two most difficult things, experiences of my life. It is only after a great deal of agonizing consideration and sleepless number–a great number of sleepless nights that I am able to talk of these unpleasant matters to anyone but my close friends.

I declined the invitation to go out socially with him and explained to him that I thought it would jeopardize what at the time I considered to be a very good working relationship. I had a normal social life with other men outside of the office. I believed then, as now, that having a social relationship with a person who was supervising my work would be ill-advised. I was very uncomfortable with the idea and told him so.

I thought that by saying no and explaining my reasons my employer would abandon his social suggestions. However, to my regret, in the following few weeks, he continued to ask me out on several occasions. He pressed me to justify my reasons for saying no to him. These incidents took place in his office or mine. They were in the form of private conversations which would not have been overheard by anyone else.

My working relationship became even more strained when Judge Thomas began to use work situations to discuss sex. On these occasions, he would call me into his office for reports on education issues and projects, or he might suggest that, because of the time pressures of his schedule, we go to lunch to a government cafeteria.

After a brief discussion of work, he would turn the conversations to a discussion of sexual matters.

His conversations were very vivid. He spoke about acts that he had seen in pornographic films involving such matters as women having sex with animals and films showing group sex or rape scenes.

He talked about pornographic materials depicting individuals with large penises or large breasts involved in various sex acts. On several occasions, Thomas told me graphically of his own sexual prowess.

Because I was extremely uncomfortable talking about sex with him at all and particularly in such a graphic way, I told him that I did not want to talk about these subjects. I would also try to change the subject to education matters or to non-sexual personal matters such as his background or his beliefs. My efforts to change the subject were rarely successful.

Throughout the period of these conversations, he also from time to time asked me for social engagements. My reaction to these conversations was to avoid them by eliminating opportunities for us to engage in extended conversations. This was difficult because at the time I was his only assistant at the Office of Education–or Office for Civil Rights.

During the latter part of my time at the Department of Education, the social pressures and any conversation of his offensive behavior ended. I began both to believe and hope that our working relationship could be a proper, cordial, and professional one.

When Judge Thomas was made chair of the EEOC, I needed to face the question of whether to go with him. I was asked to do so, and I did. The work itself was interesting, and at that time it appeared that the sexual overtures which had so troubled me had ended. I also faced the realistic fact that I had no alternative job. While I might have gone back to private practice, perhaps in my old firm or at another, I was dedicated to civil rights work, and my first choice was to be in that field. Moreover, the Department of Education itself was a dubious venture. President Reagan was seeking to abolish the entire department.

For my first months at the EEOC, where I continued to be an assistant to Judge Thomas, there were no sexual conversations or overtures. However, during the fall and winter of 1982, these began again. The comments were random and ranged from pressing me about why I didn't go out with him to remarks about my personal appearance. I remember his saying that some day I would have to tell him the real reason that I wouldn't go out with him.

He began to show displeasure in his tone and voice and his demeanor and his continued pressure for an explanation. He commented on what I was wearing in terms of whether it made me more or less sexually attractive. The incidents occurred in his inner office at the EEOC.

One of the oddest episodes I remember was an occasion in which Thomas was drinking a Coke in his office. He got up from the table at which we were working, went over to his desk to get the Coke, looked at the can and asked, "Who has put pubic hair on my Coke?" On other occasions, he referred to the size of his own penis as being larger than normal, and he also spoke on some occasions of the pleasures he had given to women with oral sex.

At this point, late 1982, I began to feel severe stress on the job. I began to be concerned that Clarence Thomas might take out his anger with me by degrading me or not giving me important assignments. I also thought that he might find an excuse for dismissing me.

In January of 1983, I began looking for another job. I was handicapped because I feared that, if he found out, he might make it difficult for me to find other employment and I might be dismissed from the job I had. Another factor that made my search more difficult was that there was a period–this was during a period of a hiring freeze in the government. In February of 1983, I was hospitalized for five days on an emergency basis for acute stomach pain which I attributed to stress on the job.

Once out of the hospital, I became more committed to find other employment and sought further to minimize my contact with Thomas. This became easier when Allison Duncan became the office director, because most of my work was then funneled through her and I had contact with Clarence Thomas mostly in staff meetings.

In the spring of 1983, an opportunity to teach at Oral Roberts University opened up. I participated in a seminar–taught an afternoon session and seminar at Oral Roberts University. The dean of the university saw me teaching and inquired as to whether I would be interested in furthering–pursuing a career in teaching, beginning at Oral Roberts University. I agreed to take the job in large part because of my desire to escape the pressures I felt at the EEOC due to Judge Thomas.

When I informed him that I was leaving in July, I recall that his response was that now I would no longer have an excuse for not going out with him. I told him that I still preferred not to do so.

At some time after that meeting, he asked if he could take me to dinner at the end of the term. When I declined, he assured me that the dinner was a professional courtesy only and not a social invitation.

I reluctantly agreed to accept that invitation, but only if it was at the very end of a working day.

On, as I recall, the last day of my employment at the EEOC in the summer of 1983, I did have dinner with Clarence Thomas. We went directly from work to a restaurant near the office. We talked about the work I had done, both at Education and at the EEOC. He told me that he was pleased with all of it except for an article and speech that I had done for him while we were in the Office for Civil Rights. Finally, he made a comment that I will vividly remember.

He said that if I ever told anyone of his behavior that it would ruin his career. This was not an apology, nor was it an explanation. That was his last remark about the possibility of our going out or reference to his behavior.

In July of 1983, I left the Washington, D.C., area and have had minimal contact with Judge Clarence Thomas since. I am of course aware from the press that some questions have been raised about conversations I had with Judge Clarence Thomas after I left the EEOC. From 1983 until today, I have seen Judge Thomas only twice.

On one occasion, I needed to get a reference from him, and on another he made a public appearance in Tulsa.

On one occasion he called me at home and we had an inconsequential conversation. On one occasion he called me without reaching me, and I returned the call without reaching him, and nothing came of it. I have on at least three occasions been asked to act as a conduit to him for others.

I knew his secretary, Diane Holt. We had worked together at both EEOC and Education. There were occasions on which I spoke to her, and on some of these occasions undoubtedly I passed on some casual comment to then Chairman Thomas. There were a series of calls in the first three months of 1985, occasioned by a group in Tulsa, which wished to have a civil rights conference. They wanted Judge Thomas to be the speaker and enlisted my assistance for this purpose.

I did call in January and February to no effect, and finally suggested to the person directly involved, Susan Cahal, that she put the matter into her own hands and call directly. She did so in March of 1985. In connection with that March invitation, Ms. Cahal wanted conference materials for the seminar and some research was needed. I was asked to try to get the information and did attempt to do so.

There was another call about another possible conference in July of 1985. In August of 1987, I was in Washington, D.C., and I did call Diane Holt. In the course of this conversation, she asked me how long I was going to be in town and I told her. It is recorded in the message as Aug. 15. It was, in fact, Aug. 20. She told me about Judge Thomas's marriage and I did say to congratulate him.

It is only after a great deal of agonizing consideration that I am able to talk of these unpleasant matters to anyone except my closest friends. As I've said before, these last few days have been very trying and very hard for me and it hasn't just been the last few days this week. It has actually been over a month now that I have been under the strain of this issue.

Telling the world is the most difficult experience of my life, but it is very close to having to live through the experience that occasioned this meeting. I may have used poor judgment early on in my relationship with this issue. I was aware, however, that telling at any point in my career could adversely affect my future career. And I did not want early on to burn all the bridges to the EEOC.

As I said, I may have used poor judgment. Perhaps I should have taken angry or even militant steps, both when I was in the agency, or after I left it. But I must confess to the world that the course that I took seemed the better as well as the easier approach.

I declined any comment to newspapers, but later when Senate staff asked me about these matters I felt I had a duty to report. I have no personal vendetta against Clarence Thomas. I seek only to provide the committee with information which it may regard as relevant.

It would have been more comfortable to remain silent. I took no initiative to inform anyone. But when I was asked by a representative of this committee to report my experience, I felt that I had to tell the truth. I could not keep silent.

(1991)

CLARENCE THOMAS'S STATEMENT TO THE SENATE JUDICIARY COMMITTEE

CLARENCE THOMAS

Mr. Chairman, Sen. Thurmond, members of the committee. As excruciatingly difficult as the last two weeks have been, I welcome the opportunity to clear my name today. No one other than my wife and Sen. Danforth, to whom I read this statement at 6:30 a.m., has seen or heard this statement. No handlers, no advisers.

The first I learned of the allegations by Prof. Anita Hill was on Sept. 25, 1991, when the FBI came to my home to investigate her allegations. When informed by the FBI agent of the nature of the allegations and the person making them, I was shocked, surprised, hurt and enormously saddened. I have not been the same since that day.

For almost a decade, my responsibilities included enforcing the rights of victims of sexual harassment. As a boss, as a friend and as a human being, I was proud that I had never had such an allegation leveled against me, even as I sought to promote women and minorities into non-traditional jobs.

In addition, several of my friends who are women have confided in me about the horror of harassment on the job or elsewhere. I thought I really understood the anguish, the fears, the doubts, the seriousness of the matter. But, since Sept. 25th, I have suffered immensely as these very serious charges were leveled against me. I have been racking my brains and eating my insides out trying to think of what I could have said or done to Anita Hill to lead her to allege that I was interested in her in more than a professional way and that I talked with her about pornographic or X-rated films.

Contrary to some press reports, I categorically denied all of the allegations and denied that I ever attempted to date Anita Hill when first interviewed by the FBI. I strongly reaffirm that denial.

Let me describe my relationship with Anita Hill. In 1981, after I went to the Department of Education as an assistant secretary in the Office of Civil Rights, one of my closest friends from both college and law school, Gil Hardy, brought Anita Hill to my attention. As I remember, he indicated that she was dissatisfied with her law firm and wanted to work in government.

Based primarily, if not solely, on Gil's recommendation, I hired Anita Hill.

During my tenure at the Department of Education, Anita Hill was an attorney adviser who worked directly with me. She worked on special projects, as well as day-to-day matters. As I recall, she was one of two professionals working directly with me at the time.

As a result, we worked closely on numerous matters. I recall being pleased with her work product and the professional but cordial relationship which we enjoyed at work. I also recall engaging in discussions about politics and current events.

Upon my nomination to become chairman of the Equal Employment Opportunity Commission, Anita Hill, to the best of my recollection, assisted me in the nomination and confirmation process. After my confirmation, she and Diane Holt, then my secretary, joined me at EEOC. I do not recall that there was any question or doubt that she would become a special assistant to me at EEOC, although, as a career employee, she retained the option of remaining at the Department of Education.

At EEOC, our relationship was more distant and our contacts less frequent as a result of the increased size of my personal staff and the dramatic increase and diversity of my day-to-day responsibilities. Upon reflection, I recall that she seemed to have had some difficulty adjusting to this change in her role. In any case, our relationship remained both cordial and professional.

At no time did I become aware, either directly or indirectly, that she felt I had said or done anything to change the cordial nature of our relationship. I detected nothing from her or from my staff, or from Gil Hardy, our mutual friend, with whom I maintained regular contact. I am certain that, had any statement or conduct on my part been brought to my attention, I would remember it clearly because of the nature and seriousness of such conduct, as well as my adamant opposition to sex discrimination and sexual harassment. But there were no such statements.

In the spring of 1983, Mr. Charles Kothe contacted me to speak at the law school at Oral Roberts University in Tulsa, Okla.

Anita Hill, who is from Oklahoma, accompanied me on that trip. It was not unusual that individuals on my staff would travel with me occasionally. Anita Hill accompanied me on that trip primarily because this was an opportunity to combine business and a visit to her home.

As I recall, during our visit at Oral Roberts University, Mr. Kothe mentioned to me the possibility of approaching Anita Hill to join the faculty at Oral Roberts University Law School. I encouraged him to do so and noted to him, as I recall, that Anita Hill would do well in teaching. I recommended her highly and she eventually was offered a teaching position.

Although I did not see Anita Hill often after she left EEOC, I did see her on one or two subsequent visits to Tulsa, Okla.

And, on one visit, I believe, she drove me to the airport. I also occasionally received telephone calls from her. She would speak directly with me or my secretary, Diane Holt. Since Anita Hill and Diane Holt had been with me at the Department of Education, they were fairly close personally and I believe they occasionally socialized together. I would also hear about her through Linda Jackson, then Linda Lambert, whom both Anita Hill and I met at the Department of Education, and I would hear of her from my friend, Gil.

Throughout the time that Anita Hill worked with me, I treated her as I treated my other special assistants. I tried to treat them all cordially, professionally and respectfully, and I tried to support them in their endeavors and be interested in and supportive of their success. I had no reason or basis to believe my relationship with Anita Hill was anything but this way until the FBI visited me a little more than two weeks ago.

I find it particularly troubling that she never raised any hint that she was uncomfortable with me. She did not raise or mention it when considering moving with me to EEOC from the Department of Education, and she'd never raised it with me when she left EEOC and was moving on in her life. And, to my fullest knowledge, she did not speak to any other women working with or around me who would feel comfortable enough to raise it with me, especially Diane Holt, to whom she seemed closest on my personal staff. Nor did she raise it with mutual friends such as Linda Jackson and Gil Hardy.

This is a person I have helped at every turn in the road since we met. She seemed to appreciate the continued cordial relationship we had since Day 1. She sought my advice and counsel, as did virtually all of the members of my personal staff.

During my tenure in the executive branch as a manager, as a policy-maker and as a person, I have adamantly condemned sex harassment. There is no member of this committee or this Senate who feels stronger about sex harassment than I do. As a manager, I made every effort to take swift and decisive action when sex harassment raised or reared its ugly head. The fact that I feel so very strongly about sex harassment and spoke loudly at EEOC has made these allegations doubly hard on me. I cannot imagine anything that I said or did to Anita Hill that could have been mistaken for sexual harassment.

But, with that said, if there is anything that I have said that has been misconstrued by Anita Hill or anyone else to be sexual harassment, then I can say that I am so very sorry and I wish I had known. If I did know, I would have stopped immediately and I would not, as I've done over the past two weeks, have to tear away at myself, trying to think of what I could possibly have done. But I have not said or done the things that Anita Hill has alleged. God has gotten me through the days since Sept. 25th, and he is my judge.

Mr. Chairman, something has happened to me in the dark days that have followed since the FBI agents informed me about these allegations. And the days have grown darker as this very serious, very explosive and very sensitive allegation—or these sensitive allegations were selectively leaked in a distorted way to the media over the past weekend. As if the confidential allegations themselves were not enough, this apparently calculated public disclosure has caused me, my family and

280

my friends enormous pain and great harm. I have never in all my life felt such hurt, such pain, such agony. My family and I have been done a grave and irreparable injustice.

During the past two weeks, I lost the belief that, if I did my best, all would work out. I called upon the strength that helped me get here from Pin Point, and it was all sapped out of me. It was sapped out of me because Anita Hill was a person I considered a friend whom I admired and thought I had treated fairly and with the utmost respect. Perhaps I could have been–better weathered this if it was from someone else. But here was someone I truly felt I had done my best with. Though I am by no means a perfect person, I have not done what she has alleged, and I still don't know what I could possibly have done to cause her to make these allegations.

When I stood next to the President in Kennebunkport being nominated to the Supreme Court of the United State, that was a high honor; but, as I sit here before you 103 days later, that honor has been crushed. From the very beginning, charges were leveled against me from the shadows, charges of drug abuse, anti-Semitism, wife beating, drug use by family members, that I was a quota appointment, confirmation conversion, and much, much more. And now, this.

I have complied with the rules. I responded to a document request that produced over 30,000 pages of documents, and I have testified for five full days under oath. I have endured this ordeal for 103 days. Reporters sneaking into my garage to examine books I read. Reporters and interest groups swarming over divorce papers looking for dirt. Unnamed people starting preposterous and damaging rumors. Calls all over the country specifically requesting dirt.

This is not American; this is Kafkaesque. It has got to stop. It must stop for the benefit of future nominees and our country. Enough is enough.

I'm not going to allow myself to be further humiliated in order to be confirmed. I am here specifically to respond to allegations of sex harassment in the workplace. I am not here to be further humiliated by this committee or anyone else, or to put my private life on display for prurient interests or other reasons. I will not allow this committee or anyone else to probe into my private life. This is not what America is all about.

To ask me to do that would be to ask me to go beyond fundamental fairness.

Yesterday, I called my mother. She was confined to her bed, unable to work and unable to stop crying. Enough is enough.

Mr. Chairman, in my 43 years on this Earth I have been able with the help of others and with the help of God to defy poverty, avoid prison, overcome segregation, bigotry, racism and obtain one of the finest educations available in this country, but I have not been able to overcome this process. This is worse than any obstacle or anything that I have ever faced.

Throughout my life, I have been energized by the expectation and the hope that in this country I would be treated fairly in all endeavors. When there was segregation, I hoped there would be fairness one day or some day. When there was bigotry and prejudice, I hoped that there would be tolerance and understanding some day.

Mr. Chairman, I am proud of my life, proud of what I have done and what I have accomplished, proud of my family—and this process, this process is trying to destroy it all. No job is worth what I have been through, no job. No horror in my life has been so debilitating. Confirm me if you want. Don't confirm me if you are so led, but let this process end. Let me and my family regain our lives.

I never asked to be nominated. It was an honor. Little did I know the price, but it is too high.

I enjoy and appreciate my current position and I am comfortable with the prospect of returning to my work as a judge on the U.S. Court of Appeals for the D.C. Circuit and to my friends there. Each of these positions is public service, and I have given at the office. I want my life and my family's life back, and I want them returned expeditiously. I have experienced the exhilaration of new heights from the moment I was called to Kennebunkport by the President to have lunch and he nominated me. That was the high point. At that time, I was told eye-to-eye that, "Clarence, you made it this far on merit. The rest is going to be politics." And it surely has been.

There have been other highs. The outpouring of support from my friends of long standing; a bonding like I have never experienced with my old boss, Sen. Danforth; the wonderful support of those who have worked with me. There have been prayers said for my family and me by people I know and people I will never meet, prayers that were heard and that sustained not only me, but also my wife and my entire family.

Instead of understanding and appreciating the great honor bestowed upon me, I find myself here today defending my name, my integrity, because somehow select portions of confidential documents dealing with this matter were leaked to the public.

Mr. Chairman, I am a victim of this process. My name has been harmed. My integrity has been harmed. My character has been harmed. My family has been harmed. My friends have been harmed.

There is nothing this committee, this body or this country can do to give me my good name back. Nothing.

I will not provide the rope for my own lynching or for further humiliation. I am not going to engage in discussions nor will I submit to roving questions of what goes on in the most intimate parts of my private life or the sanctity of my bedroom. These are the most intimate parts of my privacy, and they will remain just that, private.

———————————————————————————————

A MODEST PROPOSAL

JONATHAN SWIFT

For Preventing the Children of Poor People in Ireland
from Being a Burden to Their Parents or Country,
and for Making Them Beneficial to the Public.

It is a melancholy object to those who walk through this great town[1] or travel in the country, when they see the streets, the roads, and cabin doors, crowded with beggars of the female sex, followed by three, four, or six children, all in rags and importuning every passenger for an alms. These mothers, instead of being able to work for their honest livelihood, are forced to employ all their time in strolling to beg sustenance for their helpless infants: who as they grow up either turn thieves for want of work, or leave their dear native country to fight for the pretender in Spain,[2] or sell themselves to the Barbadoes.[3]

I think it is agreed by all parties that this prodigious number of children in the arms, or on the backs, or at the heels of their mothers, and frequently of their fathers, is in the present deplorable state of the kingdom a very great additional grievance; and, therefore, whoever could find out a fair, cheap, and easy method of making these children sound, useful members of the commonwealth, would deserve so well of the public as to have his statue set up for a preserver of the nation.

But my intention is very far from being confined to provide only for the children of professed beggars; it is of a much greater extent, and shall take in the whole number of infants at a certain age who are born of parents in effect as little able to support them as those who demand our charity in the streets.

As to my own part, having turned my thoughts for many years upon this important subject, and maturely weighed the several schemes of our projectors,[4] I have

---

[1] this great town: Dublin.–EDS.

[2] pretender in Spain: James Stuart (1688-1766); exiled in Spain, he laid claim to the English crown and had the support of many Irishmen who had joined an army hoping to restore him to the throne.–EDS.

[3] the Barbadoes: In habitants of the British colony in the Caribbean where Irishmen emigrated to work as indentured servants in exchange for their passage.–EDS.

[4] projectors: Planners.–EDS.

always found them grossly mistaken in their computation. It is true, a child just dropped from its dam may be supported by her milk for a solar year, with little other nourishment; at most not above the value of 2s.,[5] which the mother may certainly get, or the value in scraps, by her lawful occupation of begging; and it is exactly at one year old that I propose to provide for them in such a manner as instead of being a charge upon their parents or the parish, or wanting food and raiment for the rest of their lives, they shall on the contrary contribute to the feeding, and partly to the clothing, of many thousands.

There is likewise another great advantage in my scheme, that it will prevent those voluntary abortions, and that horrid practice of women murdering their bastard children, alas! too frequent among us! sacrificing the poor innocent babes I doubt more to avoid the expense than the shame, which would move tears and pity in the most savage and inhuman breast.

The number of souls in this kingdom being usually reckoned one million and a half, of these I calculate there may be about 200,000 couple whose wives are breeders; from which number I subtract 30,000 couple who are able to maintain their own children (although I apprehend there cannot be so many, under the present distress of the kingdom); but this being granted, there will remain 170,000 breeders. I again subtract 50,000 for those women who miscarry, or whose children die by accident or disease within the year. There only remain 120,000 children of poor parents annually born. The question therefore is, how this number shall be reared and provided for? which, as I have already said, under the present situation of affairs, is utterly impossible by all the methods hitherto proposed. For we can neither employ them in handicraft or agriculture; we neither build houses (I mean in the country) nor cultivate land; they can very seldom pick up a livelihood by stealing, till they arrive at six years old, except where they are of towardly parts;[6] although I confess they learn the rudiments much earlier; during which time they can, however, be properly looked upon only as probationers; as I have been informed by a principal gentleman in the county of Cavan, who protested to me that he never knew above one or two instances under the age of six, even in a part of the kingdom so renowned for the quickest proficiency in that art.

I am assured by our merchants, that a boy or a girl before twelve years old is no salable commodity; and even when they come to this age they will not yield above 3(. or 3(. 2s. 3d. at most on the exchange; which cannot turn to account either to the parents or kingdom, the charge of nutriment and rags having been at least four times that value.

---

[5]2s.: Two shillings; in Swift's time one shilling was worth less than twenty-five cents. Other monetary references in the essay are to pounds sterling ("£"), pence ("d"), a crown, and a groat. A pound consisted of twenty shillings; a shilling of twelve pence; a crown was five shillings; a groat was worth a few cents.–EDS.

[6]towardly parts: Natural abilities.–EDS.

I shall now therefore humbly propose my own thoughts, which I hope will not be liable to the least objection.

I have been assured by a very knowing American of my acquaintance in London, that a young healthy child well nursed is at a year old a most delicious, nourishing, and wholesome food, whether stewed, roasted, baked, or broiled; and I make no doubt that it will equally serve in a fricassee or a ragout.[7]

I do therefore humbly offer it to public consideration that of the 120,000 children already computed 20,000 may be reserved for breed, whereof only one-fourth part to be males; which is more than we allow to sheep, black cattle, or swine; and my reason is, that these children are seldom the fruits of marriage, a circumstance not much regarded by our savages; therefore one male will be sufficient to serve four females. That the remaining 100,000 may, at a year old, be offered in sale to the persons of quality and fortune through the kingdom; always advising the mother to let them suck plentifully in the last month, so as to render them plump and fat for a good table. A child will make two dishes at an entertainment for friends; and when the family dines alone, the fore and hind quarter will make a reasonable dish, and seasoned with a little pepper or salt will be very good boiled on the fourth day, especially in winter.

I have reckoned upon a medium that a child just born will weigh 12 pounds, and in a solar year, if tolerably nursed, will increase to 28 pounds.

I grant this food will be somewhat dear, and therefore very proper for landlords, who, as they have already devoured most of the parents, seem to have the best title to the children.

Infants' flesh will be in season throughout the year, but more plentiful in March, and a little before and after: for we are told by a grave author, an eminent French physician,[8] that fish being a prolific diet, there are more children born in Roman Catholic countries about nine months after Lent than at any other season; therefore, reckoning a year after Lent, the markets will be more glutted than usual, because the number of popish infants is at least three to one in this kingdom: and therefore it will have one other collateral advantage, by lessening the number of papists among us.

---

[7]ragout: A stew.–EDS.

[8]**French physician:** François Rabelais (c. 1494-1553), the great Renaissance humanist and author of the comic masterpiece *Gargantua and Pantagruel.* Swift is being ironic in calling Rabelais "grave." –EDS.

I have already computed the charge of nursing a beggar's child (in which list I reckon all cottagers, laborers, and four-fifths of the farmers) to be about 2s. per annum, rags included; and I believe no gentleman would repine to give 10s. for the carcass of a good fat child, which, as I have said, will make four dishes of excellent nutritive meat, when he has only some particular friend or his own family to dine with him. Thus the squire will learn to be a good landlord, and grow popular among the tenants; the mother will have 8s. net profit, and be fit for work till she produces another child.

Those who are more thrifty (as I must confess the times require) may flay the carcass; the skin of which artificially[9] dressed will make admirable gloves for ladies, and summer boots for fine gentlemen.

As to our city of Dublin, shambles[10] may be appointed for this purpose in the most convenient parts of it, and butchers we may be assured will not be wanting: although I rather recommend buying the children alive, and dressing them hot from the knife as we do roasting pigs.

A very worthy person, a true lover of his country, and whose virtues I highly esteem, was lately pleased in discoursing on this matter to offer a refinement upon my scheme. He said that many gentlemen of this kingdom, having of late destroyed their deer, he conceived that the want of venison might be well supplied by the bodies of young lads and maidens, not exceeding fourteen years of age nor under twelve; so great a number of both sexes in every country being now ready to starve for want of work and service; and these to be disposed of by their parents, if alive, or otherwise by their nearest relations. But with due deference to so excellent a friend and so deserving a patriot, I cannot be altogether in his sentiments; for as to the males, my American acquaintance assured me from frequent experience that their flesh was generally tough and lean, like that of our schoolboys by continual exercise, and their taste disagreeable; and to fatten them would not answer the charge. Then as to the females, it would, I think, with humble submission be a loss to the public, because they soon would become breeders themselves: and besides, it is not improbable that some scrupulous people might be apt to censure such a practice (although indeed very unjustly), as a little bordering upon cruelty; which, I confess, has always been with me the strongest objection against any project, how well soever intended.

[9]artifically: Artfully.–EDS.
[10]shambles: Slaughterhouses.–EDS.

But in order to justify my friend, he confessed that this expedient was put into his head by the famous Psalmanazar[11] a native of the island Formosa, who came from thence to London about twenty years ago: and in conversation told my friend, that in his country when any young person happened to be put to death, the executioner sold the carcass to persons of quality as a prime dainty; and that in his time the body of a plump girl of fifteen, who was crucified for an attempt to poison the emperor, was sold to his imperial majesty's prime minister of state, and other great mandarins of the court, in joints from the gibbet, at 400 crowns. Neither indeed can I deny, that if the same use were made of several plump young girls in this town, who without one single groat to their fortunes cannot stir abroad without a chair,[12] and appear at the playhouse and assemblies in foreign fineries which they never will pay for, the kingdom would not be the worse.

Some persons of a desponding spirit are in great concern about the vast number of poor people, who are aged, diseased, or maimed, and I have been desired to employ my thoughts what course may be taken to ease the nation of so grievous an encumbrance. But I am not in the least pain upon the matter, because it is very well known that they are every day dying and rotting by cold and famine, and filth and vermin, as fast as can be reasonably expected. And as to the young laborers, they are now in as hopeful a condition: They cannot get work,
and consequently pine away for want of nourishment, to a degree that if at any time they are accidentally hired to common labor, they have not strength to perform it; and thus the country and themselves are happily delivered from the evils to come.

I have too long digressed, and therefore shall return to my subject. I think the advantages by the proposal which I have made are obvious and many, as well as of the highest importance.

For first, as I have already observed, it would greatly lessen the number of papists, with whom we are yearly overrun, being the principal breeders of the nation as well as our most dangerous enemies; and who stay at home on purpose to deliver the kingdom to the Pretender, hoping to take their advantage by the absence of so many good Protestants, who have chosen rather to leave their country than stay at home and pay tithes against their conscience to an Episcopal curate.

Secondly, The poor tenants will have something valuable of their own, which by law may be made liable to distress[13] and help to pay their landlord's rent, their corn and cattle being already seized, and money a thing unknown.

---

[11]**Psalmanazar**: George Psalmanazar (c. 1679-1763) was a Frenchman who tricked London society into believing he was a native of Formosa (now Taiwan).–EDS.

[12]**a chair**: A sedan chair in which one is carried about.–EDS.

[13]**distress**: Seizure of payment of debt.–EDS.

Thirdly, whereas the maintenance of 100,000 children from two years old and upward, cannot be computed at less than 10s. a-piece per annum, the nation's stock will be thereby increased (50,000 per annum, beside the profit of a new dish introduced to the tables of all gentlemen of fortune in the kingdom who have any refinement in taste. And the money will circulate among ourselves, the goods being entirely of our own growth and manufacture.

Fourthly, The constant breeders beside the gain of 8s. sterling per annum by the sale of their children, will be rid of the charge of maintaining them after the first year.

Fifthly, This food would likewise bring great custom to taverns, where the vintners will certainly be so prudent as to procure the best receipts[14] for dressing it to perfection, and consequently have their houses frequented by all the fine gentlemen, who justly value themselves upon their knowledge in good eating; and a skillful cook who understands how to oblige his guests, will contrive to make it as expensive as they please.

Sixthly, This would be a great inducement to marriage, which all wise nations have either encouraged by rewards or enforced by laws and penalties. It would increase the care and tenderness of mothers toward their children, when they were sure of a settlement for life to the poor babes, provided in some sort by the public, to their annual profit instead of expense. We should see an honest emulation among the married women, which of them would bring the fattest child to the market. Men would become as fond of their wives during the time of their pregnancy as they are now of their mares in foal, their cows in calf, their sows when they are ready to farrow; nor offer to beat or kick them (as is too frequent a practice) for fear of a miscarriage.

Many other advantages might be enumerated. For instance, the addition of some thousand carcasses in our exportation of barreled beef, the propagation of swine's flesh, and improvement in the art of making good bacon, so much wanted among us by the great destruction of pigs, too frequent at our table; which are no way comparable in taste or magnificence to a well-grown, fat, yearling child, which roasted whole will make a considerable figure at a lord mayor's feast or any other public entertainment. But this and many others I omit, being studious of brevity.

Supposing that 1,000 families in this city would be constant customers for infants' flesh, besides others who might have it at merry-meetings, particularly at weddings and christenings, I compute that Dublin would take off annually about 20,000 carcasses; and the rest of the kingdom (where probably they will be sold somewhat cheaper) the remaining 80,000.

[14]receipts: Recipes.–EDS.

I can think of no one objection that will possibly be raised against this proposal, unless it should be urged that the number of people will be thereby much lessened in the kingdom. This I freely own, and it was indeed one principal design in offering it to the world. I desire the reader will observe, that I calculate my remedy for this one individual kingdom of Ireland and for no other that ever was, is, or I think ever can be upon earth. Therefore let no man talk to me of other expedients: of taxing our absentees at 5s. a pound: of using neither clothes nor household furniture except what is our own growth and manufacture: of utterly rejecting the materials and instruments that promote foreign luxury: of curing the expensiveness of pride, vanity, idleness, and gaming in our women: of introducing a vein of parsimony, prudence, and temperance: of learning to love our country, in the want of which we differ even from Laplanders and the inhabitants of Topinamboo:[15] of quitting our animosities and factions, nor acting any longer like the Jews, who were murdering one another at the very moment their city was taken:[16] of being a little cautious not to sell our country and conscience for nothing: of teaching landlords to have at least one degree of mercy toward their tenants: lastly, of putting a spirit of honesty, industry, and skill into our shopkeepers; who, if a resolution could now be taken to buy only our native goods, would immediately unite to cheat and exact upon us in the price the measure, and the goodness, nor could ever yet be brought to make one fair proposal of just dealing, though often and earnestly invited to it.

Therefore I repeat, let no man talk to me of these and the like expedients, till he has at least some glimpse of hope that there will be ever some hearty and sincere attempt to put them in practice.

But as to myself, having been wearied out for many years with offering vain, idle, visionary thoughts, and at length utterly despairing of success, I fortunately fell upon this proposal; which, as it is wholly new, so it has something solid and real, of no expense and little trouble, full in our power, and whereby we can incur no danger in disobliging England. For this kind of commodity will not bear exportation, the flesh being of too tender a consistence to admit a long continuance in salt, although perhaps I could name a country which would be glad to eat up our whole nation without it.

[15]**Laplanders and the inhabitants of Topinamboo**: Lapland is the area of Scandanavia above the Artic Circle; Topinamboo, in Brazil, was known in Swift's time for the savagery of its tribes.–EDS.
[16]**was taken**: A reference to the Roman seizure of Jerusalem (A.D. 70).–EDS.

After all, I am not so violently bent upon my own opinion as to reject any offer proposed by wise men, which shall be found equally innocent, cheap, easy, and effectual. But before something of that kind shall be advanced in contradiction to my scheme, and offering a better, I desire the author or authors will be pleased maturely to consider two points. First, as things now stand, how they will be able to find food and raiment for 100,000 useless mouths and backs. And secondly, there being a round million creatures in human figure throughout this kingdom, whose subsistence put into a common stock would leave them in debt 2,000,000(. sterling, adding those who are beggars by profession to the bulk of farmers, cottagers, and laborers, with the wives and children who are beggars in effect; I desire those politicians who dislike my overture, and may perhaps be so bold as to attempt an answer, that they will first ask the parents of these mortals, whether they would not at this day think it a great happiness to have been sold for food at a year old in the manner I prescribe, and thereby have avoided such a perpetual scene of misfortunes as they have since gone through by the oppression of landlords, the impossibility of paying rent without money or trade, the want of common sustenance, with neither house nor clothes to cover them from the inclemencies of the weather, and the most inevitable prospect of entailing the like or greater miseries upon their breed forever.

I profess, in the sincerity of my heart, that I have not the least personal interest in endeavoring to promote this necessary work, having no other motive than the public good of my country, by advancing our trade, providing for infants, relieving the poor, and giving some pleasure to the rich. I have no children by which I can propose to get a single penny; the youngest being nine years old, and my wife past childbearing.

(1729)

A PROPOSAL TO ABOLISH GRADING

PAUL GOODMAN

Let half a dozen of the prestigious Universities–Chicago, Stanford, the Ivy League–abolish grading, and use testing only and entirely for pedagogic purposes as teachers see fit.

Anyone who knows the frantic temper of the present schools will understand the transvaluation of values that would be effected by this modest innovation. For most of the students, the competitive grade has come to be the essence. The naive teacher points to the beauty of the subject and the ingenuity of the research; the shrewd student asks if he is responsible for that on the final exam.

Let me at once dispose of an objection whose unanimity is quite fascinating. I think that the great majority of professors agree that grading hinders teaching and creates a bad spirit, going as far as cheating and plagiarizing. I have before me the collection of essays, *Examining in Harvard College*, and this is the concensus. It is uniformly asserted, however, that the grading is inevitable; for how else will the graduate schools, the foundations, the corporations *know* whom to accept, reward, hire? How will the talent scouts know whom to tap?

By testing the applicants, of course, according to the specific task requirements of the inducting institution, just as applicants for the Civil Service or for licenses in medicine, law, and architecture are tested. Why should Harvard professors do the testing *for* corporations and graduate schools?

The objection is ludicrous. Dean Whitla, of the Harvard Office of Tests, points out that the scholastic-aptitude and achievement tests use for *admission* to Harvard are a super-excellent index for all-around Harvard performance, better than high school grades or particular Harvard course-grades. Presumably, these college-entrance tests are tailored for what Harvard and similar institutions want. By the same logic, would not an employer do far better to apply his own job-aptitude test rather than to rely on the vagaries of Harvard section-men? Indeed, I doubt that many employers bother to look at such grades; they are more likely to be interested merely in the fact of a Harvard diploma, whatever that connotes to them. The grades have most of their weight with the graduate schools–here, as elsewhere, the system runs mainly for its own sake.

It is really necessary to remind our academics of the ancient history of Examination. In the medieval university, the whole point of the gruelling trial of the candidate was whether or not to accept him as a peer. His disputation and lecture for the Masters was just that, a master-piece to enter the guild. It was not to make comparative evaluations. It was not to weed out and select for an extra-mural licensor or employer. It was certainly not to pit one young fellow against another in an ugly competition. My philosophic impression is that the medievals thought they knew what a good job of work was and that we are competitive because we do not know.

But the more status is achieved by largely irrelevant competitive evaluation, the less will we ever know.

(Of course, our American examinations never did have this purely guild orientation, just as our faculties have rarely had absolute autonomy; the examining was to satisfy Overseers, Elders, distant Regents–and they as paternal superiors have always doted on giving grades, rather than accepting peers. But I submit that this set-up itself makes it impossible for the student to *become* a master, to *have* grown up, and to commence on his own. He will always be making A or B for some overseer. And in the present atmosphere, he will always be climbing on his friend's neck.)

Perhaps the chief objectors to abolishing grading would be the students and their parents. The parents should be simply disregarded; their anxiety has done enough damage already. For the students, it seems to me that a primary duty of the university is to deprive them of their props, their dependence on extrinsic valuation and motivation, and to force them to confront the difficult enterprise itself and finally lose themselves in it.

A miserable effect of grading is to nullify the various uses of testing. Testing, for both student and teacher, is a means of structuring, and also of finding out what is blank or wrong and what has been assimilated and can be taken for granted. Review–including high-pressure review–is a means of bringing together the fragments, so that there are flashes of synoptic insight.

There are several good reasons for testing, and kinds of tests. But if the aim is to discover weakness, what is the point of down-grading and punishing it, and thereby inviting the student to conceal his weakness, by faking and bulling, if not cheating? The natural conclusion of synthesis is the insight itself, not a grade for having had it. For the important purpose of placement, if one can establish in the student the belief that one is testing *not* to grade and make invidious comparisons but for his own advantage, the student should normally seek his own level, where he is challenged and yet capable, rather than trying to get by. If the student dares to accept himself as he is, a teacher's grade is a crude instrument compared with a student's self-awareness. But it is rare in our universities that students are encouraged to notice objectively their vast confusion. Unlike Socrates, our teachers rely on power-drives rather than shame and ingenuous idealism.

Many students are lazy, so teachers try to goad or threaten them by grading. In the long run this must do more harm than good. Laziness is a character-defense. It may be a way of avoiding learning, in order to protect the conceit that one is already perfect (deeper, the despair that one *never* can be). It may be a way of avoiding just the risk of failing and being down-graded. Sometimes it is a way of politely saying, "I won't." But since it is the authoritarian grown-up demands that have created such attitudes in the first place, why repeat the trauma? There comes a time when we must treat people as adult, laziness and all. It is one thing courageously to fire a do-nothing out of your class; it is quite another thing to evaluate him with a lordly F.

Most important of all, it is often obvious that balking in doing the work, especially among bright young people who get to great universities, means exactly what it says: The work does not suit me, not this subject, or not at this time, or not in this school, or not in school altogether. The student might not be bookish; he might be school-tired; perhaps his development ought now to take another direction. Yet unfortunately, if such a student is intelligent and is not sure of himself, he *can* be bullied into passing, and this obscures everything. My hunch is that I am describing a common situation. What a grim waste of young life and teacherly effort! Such a student will retain nothing of what he has "passed" in. Sometimes he must get mononucleosis to tell his story and be believed.

And ironically, the converse is also probably commonly true. A student flunks and is mechanically weeded out, who is really ready and eager to learn in a scholastic setting, but he has not quite caught on. A good teacher can recognize the situation, but the computer wreaks its will. (1984)

THE CHILD BY TIGER

THOMAS WOLFE

> Tiger, tiger, burning bright
> In the forests of the night,
> What immortal hand or eye
> Could frame thy fearful symmetry?

One day after school, twenty-five years ago, several of us were playing with a football in the yard at Randy Shepperton's. Randy was calling signals and handling the ball. Nebraska Crane was kicking it. Augustus Potterham was too clumsy to run or kick or pass, so we put him at center, where all he'd have to do would be to pass the ball back to Randy when he got the signal.

It was late in October and there was a smell of smoke, of leaves, of burning in the air. Nebraska had just kicked to us. It was a good kick, too–a high, soaring punt that spiraled out above my head, behind me. I ran back and tried to get it, but it was far and away "over the goal line"–that is to say, out in the street. It hit the street and bounded back and forth with that peculiarly erratic bounce a football has.

The ball rolled away from me down toward the corner. I was running out to get it when Dick Prosser, Shepperton's new Negro man, came along, gathered it up neatly in his great black paw and tossed it to me. He turned in then, and came on down the alleyway, greeting us as he did. He called all of us "Mister" except Randy, and Randy was always "Cap'n–Cap'n Shepperton." This formal address– "Mr." Crane, "Mr." Potterham, "Mr." Spangler, "Cap'n" Shepperton–pleased us immensely, gave us a feeling of mature importance and authority.

"Cap'n Shepperton" was splendid! It had a delightful military association, particularly when Dick Prosser said it. Dick had served a long enlistment in the United States Army. He had been a member of a regiment of crack Negro troops upon the Texas border, and the stamp of the military man was evident in everything he did. It was a joy, for example, just to watch him split up kindling. He did it with a power, a kind of military order, that was astounding. Every stick he cut seemed to be exactly the same length and shape as every other one. He had all of them neatly stacked against the walls of the Shepperton basement with such regimented faultlessness that it almost seemed a pity to disturb their symmetry for the use for which they were intended.

It was the same with everything else he did. His little whitewashed basement room was as spotless as a barracks room. The bare board floor was always cleanly swept, a plain bare table and a plain straight chair were stationed exactly in the center of the room. On the table there was always just one object: an old Bible almost worn out by constant use, for Dick was a deeply religious man. There was a little cast-iron stove and a little wooden box with a few lumps of coal and a neat stack of kindling in it. And against the wall, to the left, there was an iron cot, always precisely made and covered cleanly with a coarse gray blanket.

The Sheppertons were delighted with him. He had come there looking for work just a month or two before, and modestly presented his qualifications. He had, he said, only recently received his discharge from the Army and was eager to get employment, at no matter what wage. He could cook, he could tend the furnace, he knew how to drive a car–in fact, it seemed to us boys that there was very little that Dick Prosser could not do. He could certainly shoot. He gave a modest demonstration of his prowess one afternoon, with Randy's .22, that left us gasping. He just lifted that little rifle in his powerful black hands as if it were a toy, without seeming to take aim, pointed it toward a strip of tin on which we had crudely marked out some bull's-eye circles, and he simply peppered the center of the bull's-eye, putting twelve holes through a space one inch square, so fast we could not even count the shots.

He knew how to box too. I think he had been a regimental champion. At any rate, he was as cunning and crafty as a cat. He never boxed with us, of course, but Randy had two sets of gloves, and Dick used to coach us while we sparred. There was something amazingly tender and watchful about him. He taught us many things–how to lead, to hook, to counter and to block–but he was careful to see that we did not hurt each other.

He knew about football, too, and today he paused, a powerful, respectable-looking Negro man of thirty years or more, and watched us for a moment as we played.

Randy took the ball and went up to him. "How do you hold it, Dick?" he said. "Is this right?"

Dick watched him attentively as he gripped the ball, and held it back above his shoulder. The Negro nodded approvingly and said, "That's right, Cap'n Shepperton. You've got it. Only," he said gently, and now took the ball in his own powerful hand, "when you gits a little oldah yo' handses gits biggah and you gits a bettah grip."

His own great hand, in fact, seemed to hold the ball as easily as if it were an apple. And, holding it so a moment, he brought it back, aimed over his outstretched left hand as if he were pointing a gun, and rifled it in a beautiful, whizzing spiral thirty yards or more to Gus. He then showed us how to kick, how to get the ball off of the toe in such a way that it would rise and spiral cleanly. He knew how to do this too. He must have got off kicks there, in the yard at Shepperton's, that traveled fifty yards.

He showed us how to make a fire, how to pile the kindling so that the flames shot up cone-wise, cleanly, without smoke or waste. He showed us how to strike a match with the thumbnail of one hand and keep and hold the flame in the strongest wind. He showed us how to lift a weight, how to tote a burden on our shoulders in

298

the easiest way. There was nothing that he did not know. We were all so proud of him. Mr. Shepperton himself declared that Dick was the best man he'd ever had, the smartest darky that he'd ever known.

And yet? He went too softly, at too swift a pace. He was there upon you sometimes like a cat. Looking before us, sometimes, seeing nothing but the world before us, suddenly we felt a shadow at our backs and, looking up, would find that Dick was there. And there was something moving in the night. We never saw him come or go. Sometimes we would waken, startled, and feel that we had heard a board creak, and the soft clicking of a latch, a shadow passing swiftly. All was still.

"Young white fokes, oh, young white gent'mun,"–his soft voice ending in a moan, a kind of rhythm in his hips– "oh, young white fokes, Ise tellin' you" –that soft low moan again– "you gotta love each othah like a brothah." He was deeply religious and went to church three times a week. He read his Bible every night. It was the only object on his square board table.

Sometimes Dick would come out of his little basement room, and his eyes would be red, as if he had been weeping. We would know, then, that he had been reading his Bible. There would be times when he would almost moan when he talked to us, a kind of hymnal chant that came from some deep and fathomless intoxication of the spirit, and that transported him. For us, it was a troubling and bewildering experience. We tried to laugh it off and make jokes about it. But there was something in it so dark and strange and full of a feeling that we could not fathom that our jokes were hollow, and the trouble in our minds and in our hearts remained.

Sometimes on these occasions his speech would be made up of some weird jargon of Biblical phrases, of which he seemed to have hundreds, and which he wove together in this strange pattern of his emotion in a sequence that was meaningless to us, but to which he himself had the coherent clue. "Oh, young white fokes," he would begin, moaning gently, "de dry bones in de valley. I tell you, white fokes, de day is comin' when He's comin' on dis earth again to sit in judgment. He'll put de sheep upon de right hand and de goats upon de left. Oh, white fokes, white fokes, de Armageddon day's a'comin', white fokes, an' de dry bones in de valley."

Or again, we could hear him singing as he went about his work, in his deep rich voice, so full of warmth and strength, so full of Africa, singing hymns that were not only of his own race but familiar to us all. I don't know where he learned them. Perhaps they were remembered from his Army days. Perhaps he had learned them in the service of former masters. He drove the Sheppertons to church on Sunday morning, and would wait for them throughout the morning service. He would come up to the side door of the church while the service was going on, neatly dressed in his good dark suit, holding his chauffeur's hat respectfully in his hand, and stand there humbly and listen during the course of the entire sermon.

And then, when the hymns were sung and the great rich sound would swell and roll out into the quiet air of Sunday, Dick would stand and listen, and sometimes he would join in quietly in the song. A number of these favorite Presbyterian hymns we heard him singing many times in a low rich voice as he went about his work around the house. He would sing "Who Follows in His Train?" or "Alexander's Glory Song," or "Rock of Ages," or "Onward, Christian Soldiers!"

And yet? Well, nothing happened–there was just "a flying hint from here and there," and the sense of something passing in the night. Turning into the square one day as Dick was driving Mr. Shepperton to town, Lon Everett skidded murderously around the corner, sideswiped Dick and took the fender off. The Negro was out of the car like a cat and got his master out. Shepperton was unhurt. Lon Everett climbed out and reeled across the street, drunk as a sot at three o'clock. He swung viciously, clumsily, at the Negro, smashed him in the face. Blood trickled from the flat black nostrils and from the thick liver-colored lips. Dick did not move. But suddenly the whites of his eyes were shot with red, his bleeding lips bared for a moment over the white ivory of his teeth. Lon smashed at him again. The Negro took it full in the face again; his hands twitched slightly, but he did not move. They collared the drunken sot and hauled him off and locked him up. Dick stood there for a moment, then he wiped his face and turned to see what damage had been done to the car. No more now, but there were those who saw it who remembered later how the eyes went red.

Another thing: Sheppertons had a cook named Pansy Harris. She was a comely Negro wench, young, plump, black as the ace of spades, a good-hearted girl with a deep dimple in her cheeks and faultless teeth, bared in the most engaging smile. No one ever saw Dick speak to her. No one ever saw her glance at him, or him at her, and yet that smilingly good-natured wench became as mournful-silent and as silent-sullen as midnight pitch. She went about her work as mournfully as if she were going to a funeral. The gloom deepened all about her. She answered sullenly now when spoken to.

One night toward Christmas she announced that she was leaving. In response to all entreaties, all efforts to find the reason for her sudden and unreasonable decision, she had no answer except a sullen repetition of the assertion that she had to leave. Repeated questionings did finally wring from her a sullen statement that her husband needed her at home. More than this she would not say, and even this excuse was highly suspect, because her husband was a Pullman porter, only home two days a week and well accustomed to do himself such housekeeping tasks as she might do for him.

The Sheppertons were fond of her. They tried again to find the reason for her leaving. Was she dissatisfied? "No'm"–an implacable monosyllable, mournful, unrevealing as the night. Had she been offered a better job elsewhere? "No'm"–as untelling as before. If they offered her more wages, would she stay with them? "No'm," again and again, sullen and unyielding, until finally the exasperated mistress threw her hands up in a gesture of defeat and said, "All right then, Pansy. Have it your own way, if that's the way you feel. Only for heaven's sake don't leave us in the lurch until we get another cook."

This, at length, with obvious reluctance, the girl agreed to. Then, putting on her hat and coat and taking the paper bag of "leavings" she was allowed to take home with her at night, she went out the kitchen door and made her sullen and morose departure.

This was on Saturday night, a little after eight o'clock. That afternoon Randy and I had been fooling around the basement and, seeing that Dick's door was slightly ajar, we looked in to see if he was there. The little room was empty, swept and spotless, as it had always been.

But we did not notice that! We saw it! At the same moment, our breaths caught sharply in a gasp of startled wonderment. Randy was the first to speak. "Look!" he whispered. "Do you see it?"

See it! My eyes were glued upon it. Squarely across the bare board table, blue-dull, deadly in its murderous efficiency, lay a modern repeating rifle. Beside it was a box containing one hundred rounds of ammunition, and behind it, squarely in the center, face downward on the table, was the familiar cover of Dick's worn old Bible.

Then he was on us like a cat. He was there like a great dark shadow before we knew it. We turned, terrified. He was there above us, his thick lips bared above his gums, his eyes gone small and red as rodents'.

"Dick!" Randy gasped, and moistened his dry lips. "Dick!" he fairly cried now.

It was all over like a flash. Dick's mouth closed. We could see the whites of his eyes again. He smiled and said softly, affably, "Yes, suh, Cap'n Shepperton. Yes, suh! You gent'mun lookin' at my rifle?" he said, and moved into the room.

I gulped and nodded my head and couldn't say a word, and Randy whispered, "Yes." And both of us still stared at him, with an expression of appalled and fascinated interest.

Dick shook his head and chuckled. "Can't do without my rifle, white fokes. No, suh!" he shook his head good-naturedly again. "Ole Dick, he's–he's–he's an ole Ahmy man, you know. If they take his rifle away from him, why, that's jest lak takin' candy from a little baby. Yes, suh!" he chuckled, and picked the weapon up affectionately. "Ole Dick felt Christmas comin' on–he-he–I reckon he must have felt it in his bones"–he chuckled– "so I been savin' up my money. I just thought I'd hide this heah and keep it as a big supprise fo' the young white fokes untwil Christmas morning. Then I was gonna take the young white fokes out and show 'em how to shoot."

We had begun to breathe more easily now and, almost as if we had been under the spell of the Pied Piper of Hamelin, we had followed him, step by step, into the room.

"Yes, suh," Dick chuckled, "I was just fixin' to hide this gun away twill Christmas Day, but Cap'n Shepperton—hee!" He chuckled heartily and slapped his thigh. "You can't fool ole Cap'n Shepperton. He just must've smelled this ole gun right out. He comes right in and sees it befo' I has a chance to tu'n around. . . . Now, white fokes"–Dick's voice fell to a tone of low and winning confidence– "now that you's found out, I'll tell you what I'll do. If you'll just keep it a supprise from the other white fokes twill Christmas Day, I'll take all you gent'mun out and let you shoot it. Now, cose," he went on quietly, with a shade of resignation, "if you want to tell on me, you can, but"–here his voice fell again, with just the faintest, yet most eloquent shade of sorrowful regret– "old Dick was looking fahwad to this; hopin' to give all the white fokes a supprise Christmas Day."

We promised earnestly that we would keep his secret as if it were our own. We fairly whispered our solemn vow. We tiptoed away out of the little basement room as if we were afraid our very footsteps might betray the partner of our confidence.

This was four o'clock on Saturday afternoon. Already, there was a somber moaning of the wind, gray storm clouds sweeping over. The threat of snow was in the air.

Snow fell that night. It came howling down across the hills. It swept in on us from the Smokies. By seven o'clock the air was blind with sweeping snow, the earth was carpeted, the streets were numb. The storm howled on, around houses warm with crackling fires and shaded light. All life seemed to have withdrawn into thrilling isolation. A horse went by upon the streets with muffled hoofs. Storm shook the houses. The world was numb. I went to sleep upon this mystery, lying in the darkness, listening to that exultancy of storm, to that dumb wonder, that enormous and attentive quietness of snow, with something dark and jubilant in my soul I could not utter.

A little after one o'clock that morning I was awakened by the ringing of a bell. It was the fire bell of the city hall, and it was beating an alarm–a hard fast stroke that I had never heard before. Bronze with peril, clangorous through the snow-numbed silence of the air, it had a quality of instance and menace I had never known before. I leaped up and ran to the window to look for the telltale glow against the sky. But almost before I looked, those deadly strokes beat in upon my brain the message that this was no alarm for fire. It was a savage clangorous alarm to the whole town, a brazen tongue to warn mankind against the menace of some peril, secret, dark, unknown, greater than fire or flood could ever be.

I got instantly, in the most overwhelming and electric way, the sense that the whole town had come to life. All up and down the street the houses were beginning to light up. Next door, the Shepperton house was ablaze with light from top to bottom. Even as I looked, Mr. Shepperton, wearing an overcoat over his pajamas, ran down the snow-covered steps and padded out across the snow-covered walk toward the street.

People were beginning to run out of doors. I heard excited shouts and questions everywhere. I saw Nebraska Crane come pounding down the middle of the street. I knew that he was coming for me and Randy. As he ran by Shepperton's, he put his fingers to his mouth and whistled piercingly. It was a signal we all knew.

I was all ready by the time he came running down the alley toward our cottage. He hammered at the door; I was already there.

"Come on!" he said, panting with excitement, his black eyes burning with an intensity I'd never seen before. "Come on!" he cried. We were halfway out across the yard by now. "It's that nigger. He's gone crazy and is running wild."

"Wh-wh-what nigger?" I gasped, pounding at his heels.

Even before he spoke, I had the answer. Mr. Crane had already come out of his house, buttoning his heavy policeman's overcoat as he came. He had paused to speak for a moment to Mr. Shepperton, and I heard Shepperton say quickly, in a low voice, "Which way did he go?"

Then I heard somebody cry, "It's that nigger of Shepperton's!"

Mr. Shepperton turned and went quickly back across his yard toward the house. His wife and two girls stood huddled in the open doorway, white, trembling, holding themselves together, their arms thrust into the wide sleeves of their kimonos.

The telephone in Shepperton's house was ringing like mad, but no one was paying any attention to it. I heard Mrs. Shepperton say quickly, as he ran up the steps, "Is it Dick?" He nodded and passed her brusquely, going toward the phone.

At this moment, Nebraska whistled piercingly again upon his fingers and Randy Shepperton ran past his mother and down the steps. She called sharply to him. He paid no attention to her. When he came up, I saw that his fine thin face was white as a sheet. He looked at me and whispered, "It's–it's Dick!" And in a moment, "They say he's killed four people."

"With–" I couldn't finish.

Randy nodded dumbly, and we both stared there for a minute, aware now of the murderous significance of the secret we had kept, with a sudden sense of guilt and fear, as if somehow the crime lay on our shoulders.

Across the street a window banged up in the parlor of Sugg's house, and Old Man Suggs appeared in the window, clad only in his nightgown, his brutal old face inflamed with excitement, his shock of silvery white hair awry, his powerful shoulders, and his thick hands gripping his crutches.

"He's coming this way!" he bawled to the world in general. "They say he lit out across the square! He's heading out in this direction.!"

Mr. Crane paused to yell back impatiently over his shoulder, "No, he went down South Dean Street! He's heading for Wilton and the river! I've already heard from headquarters!"

Automobiles were beginning to roar and sputter all along the street. Across the street I could hear Mr. Potterham sweating over his. He would whirl the crank a dozen times or more; the engine would catch for a moment, cough and sputter, and then die again. Gus ran out-of-doors with a kettle of boiling water and began to pour it feverishly down the radiator spout.

Mr. Shepperton was already dressed. We saw him run down the back steps toward the carriage house. All three of us, Randy, Nebraska, and myself, streaked down the alleyway to help him. We got the old wooden doors open. He went in and cranked the car. It was a new one, and started up at once. Mr. Shepperton backed out into the snowy drive. We all clambered up on the running board. He spoke absently, saying, "You boys stay here. . . . Randy, your mother's calling you," but we all tumbled in and he didn't say a word.
He came backing down the alleyway at top speed. We turned into the street and picked up Mr. Crane at the corner. We lit out for town, going at top speed. Cars were coming out of alleys everywhere. We could hear people shouting questions and replies at one another. I heard one man shout, "He's killed six men!"

I don't think it took us over five minutes to reach the square, but when we got there, it seemed as if the whole town was there ahead of us. Mr. Shepperton pulled the car up and parked in front of the city hall. Mr. Crane leaped out and went pounding away across the square without another word to us.

From every corner, every street that led into the square, people were streaking in. One could see the dark figures of running men across the white carpet of the square. They were all rushing in to one focal point.

The southwest corner of the square where South Dean Street came into it was like a dog fight. Those running figures streaking toward that dense crowd gathered there made me think of nothing else so much as a fight between two boys upon the playgrounds of the school at recess time. The way the crowd was swarming in was just the same.

But then I *heard* a difference. From that crowd came a low and growing mutter, an ugly and insistent growl, of a tone and quality I had never heard before. But I knew instantly what it meant. There was no mistaking the blood note in that foggy growl. And we looked at one another with the same question in the eyes of all.

Only Nebraska's coal-black eyes were shining now with a savage sparkle even they had never had before. "Come on," he said in a low tone, exultantly. "They mean business this time, sure. Let's go." And he darted away toward the dense and sinister darkness of the crowd.

Even as we followed him we heard coming toward us now, growing, swelling at every instant, one of the most savagely mournful and terrifying sounds that night can know. It was the baying of the hounds as they came up upon the leash from Niggertown. Full-throated, howling deep, the savagery of blood was in it, and the savagery of man's guilty doom was in it too.

They came up swiftly, fairly baying at our heels as we sped across the snow-white darkness of the square. As we got up to the crowd, we saw that it had gathered at the corner where my uncle's hardware store stood. Cash Eager had not yet arrived, but, facing the crowd which pressed in on them so close and menacing that they were almost flattened out against the glass, three or four men were standing with arms stretched out in a kind of chain, as if trying to protect with the last resistance of their strength and eloquence the sanctity of private property.

Will Hendershot was mayor at that time, and he was standing there, arm to arm with Hugh McNair. I could see Hugh, taller by half a foot than anyone around him, his long gaunt figure, the gaunt passion of his face, even the attitude of his outstretched bony arms, strangely, movingly Lincolnesque, his one good eye blazing in the cold glare of the corner lamp with a kind of cold inspired Scotch passion.

"Wait a minute! You men wait a minute!" he cried. His words cut out above the clamor of the mob like an electric spark. "You'll gain nothing, you'll help nothing if you do this thing!"

They tried to drown him out with an angry and derisive roar. He shot his big fist up into the air and shouted at them, blazed at them with that cold single eye, until they had to hear. "Listen to me!" he cried. "This is no time for mob law! this is no case for lynch law! This is a time for law and order! Wait till the sheriff swears you in! Wait until Cash Eager comes! Wait–"

He got no farther. "Wait, hell!" cried someone. "We've waited long enough! We're going to get that nigger!"

The mob took up the cry. The whole crowd was writhing angrily now, like a tormented snake. Suddenly there was a flurry in the crowd, a scattering. Somebody yelled a warning at Hugh McNair. He ducked quickly, just in time. A brick whizzed past him, smashing the plate-glass window into fragments.

And instantly a bloody roar went up. The crowd surged forward, kicked the fragments of jagged glass away. In a moment the whole mob was storming into the dark store. Cash Eager got there just too late. He arrived in time to take out his keys and open the front doors, but as he grimly remarked it was like closing the barn doors after the horse had been stolen.

The mob was in and helped themselves to every rifle they could find. They smashed open cartridge boxes and filled their pockets with the loose cartridges. Within ten minutes they had looted the store of every rifle, every cartridge in the stock. The whole place looked as if a hurricane had hit it. The mob was streaming out into the street, was already gathering round the dogs a hundred feet or so away, who were picking up the scent at that point, the place where Dick had halted last before he had turned and headed south, downhill along South Dean Street toward the river.

The hounds were scampering about, tugging at the leash, moaning softly with their noses pointed to the snow, their long ears flattened down. But in that light and in that snow it almost seemed no hounds were needed to follow Dick. Straight as a string right down the center of the sheeted car tracks, the Negro's footsteps led away until they vanished downhill in the darkness.

But now, although the snow had stopped, the wind was swirling through the street and making drifts and eddied in the snow. The footprints were fading rapidly. Soon they would be gone.

The dogs were given their head. They went straining on softly, sniffing at the snow; behind them the dark masses of the mob closed in and followed. We stood there watching while they went. We saw them go on down the street and vanish. But from below, over the snow-numbed stillness of the air, the vast low mutter of the mob came back to us.

Men were clustered now in groups. Cash Eager stood before his shattered window, ruefully surveying the ruin. Other men were gathered around the big telephone pole at the corner, pointing out two bullet holes that had been drilled cleanly through it.

And swiftly, like a flash, running from group to group, like a powder train of fire, the full detail of that bloody chronicle of night was pieced together.

This was what had happened. Somewhere between nine and ten o'clock that night, Dick Prosser had gone to Pansy Harris's shack in Niggertown. Some said he had been drinking when he went there. At any rate, the police had later found the remnants of a gallon jug of raw corn whiskey in the room. What happened, what passed between them, was never known. And, besides, no one was greatly interested. It was a crazy nigger with "another nigger's woman."

Shortly after ten o'clock that night, the woman's husband appeared upon the scene. The fight did not start then. According to the woman, the real trouble did not come until an hour or more after his return.

The men drank together. Each was in an ugly temper. Shortly before midnight, they got into a fight. Harris slashed at Dick with a razor. In a second they were locked together, rolling about and fighting like two madmen on the floor. Pansy Harris went screaming out-of-doors and across the street into a dingy little grocery store.

A riot call was telephoned at once to police headquarters on the public square. The news came in that a crazy nigger had broken loose on Gulley Street in Niggertown, and to send help at once. Pansy Harris ran back across the street toward her little shack.

As she got there, her husband, with blood streaming from his face, staggered out into the street, with his hands held up protectively behind his head in a gesture of instinctive terror. At the same moment, Dick Prosser appeared in the doorway of the shack, deliberately took aim with his rifle and shot the fleeing Negro squarely through the back of the head. Harris dropped forward on his face into the snow. He was dead before he hit the ground. A huge dark stain of blood-soaked snow widened out around him. Dick Prosser seized the terrified Negress by the arm, hurled her into the shack, bolted the door, pulled down the shades, blew out the lamp and waited.

A few minutes later, two policemen arrived from town. They were a young constable named Willis, and John Grady, a lieutenant of police. The policemen took one look at the bloody figure in the snow, questioned the frightened keeper of the grocery store and, after consulting briefly, produced their weapons and walked out into the street.

Young Willis stepped softly down on to the snow-covered porch of the shack, flattened himself against the wall between the window and the door, and waited. Grady went around to the side and flashed his light through the window, which, on this side, was shadeless. Grady said in a loud tone: "Come out of there!"

Dick's answer was to shoot him cleanly through the wrist. At the same moment Willis kicked the door in and, without waiting, started in with pointed revolver. Dick shot him just above the eyes. The policeman fell forward on his face.

Grady came running out around the house, rushed into the grocery store, pulled the receiver of the old-fashioned telephone off the hook, rang frantically for headquarters and yelled out across the wire that a crazy nigger had killed Sam Willis and a Negro man, and to send help.

At this moment Dick stepped out across the porch into the street, aimed swiftly through the dirty window of the little store and shot John Grady as he stood there at the phone. Grady fell dead with a bullet that entered just below his left temple and went out on the other side.

Dick, now moving in a long, unhurried stride that covered the ground with catlike speed, turned up the long snow-covered slope of Gulley Street and began his march toward town. He moved right up the center of the street, shooting cleanly from left to right as he went. Halfway up the hill, the second-story window of a two-story Negro tenement flew open. An old Negro man stuck out his ancient head of cotton wool. Dick swiveled and shot casually from his hip. The shot tore the top of the old Negro's head off.

307

By the time Dick reached the head of Gulley Street, they knew he was coming. He moved steadily along, leaving his big tread cleanly in the middle of the sheeted street, shifting a little as he walked, swinging his gun cross wise before him. This was the Negro Broadway of the town, but where those poolrooms, barbershops, drugstores and fried-fish places had been loud with dusky life ten minutes before, they were now silent as the ruins of Egypt. The word was flaming through the town that a crazy nigger was on the way. No one showed his head.

Dick moved on steadily, always in the middle of the street, reached the end of Gulley Street and turned into South Dean—turned right, uphill, in the middle of the car tracks, and started toward the square. As he passed the lunchroom on the left, he took a swift shot through the window at the counter man. The fellow ducked behind the counter. The bullet crashed into the wall above his head.

Meanwhile, at police headquarters, the sergeant had sent John Chapman out across the square to head Dick off. Mr. Chapman was perhaps the best-liked man upon the force. He was a pleasant florid-faced man of forty-five, with curling brown mustaches, congenial and good-humored, devoted to his family, courageous, but perhaps too kindly and too gentle for a policeman.

John Chapman heard the shots and ran. He came up to the corner by Eager's hardware store just as Dick's last shot went crashing through the lunchroom window. Mr. Chapman took up his post there at the corner behind the telephone post that stood there at that time. Mr. Chapman, from his vantage point behind this post, took out his revolver and shot directly at Dick Prosser as he came up the street.

By this time Dick was not more than thirty yards away. He dropped quietly upon one knee and aimed. Mr. Chapman shot again and missed. Dick fired. The high-velocity bullet bored through the post a little to one side. It grazed the shoulder of John Chapman's uniform and knocked a chip out of the monument sixty yards or more behind him in the center of the square.

Mr. Chapman fired again and missed. And Dick, still coolly poised upon his knee, as calm and steady as if he were engaging in a rifle practice, fired again, drilled squarely through the center of the post and shot John Chapman through the heart. Then Dick rose, pivoted like a soldier in his tracks and started down the street, straight as a string, right out of town.

This was the story as we got it, pieced together like a train of fire among the excited groups of men that clustered there in trampled snow before the shattered glass of Eager's store.

But now, save for these groups of talking men, the town again was silent. Far off in the direction of the river, we could hear the mournful baying of the hounds. There was nothing more to see or do. Cash Eager stopped, picked up some fragments of the shattered glass and threw them in the window. A policeman was left on guard, and presently all five of us–Mr. Shepperton, Cash Eager and we three boys–walked back across the square and got into the car and drove home again.

But there was no more sleep, I think, for anyone that night. Black Dick had murdered sleep. Toward daybreak, snow began to fall again. The snow continued through the morning. It was piled deep in gusting drifts by noon. All footprints were obliterated, the town waited, eager, tense, wondering if the man could get away.

They did not capture him that day, but they were on his trail. From time to time throughout the day, news would drift back to us. Dick had turned east along the river and gone out for some miles along the Fairchilds road. There, a mile or two from Fairchilds, he crossed the river at the Rocky Shallows.

Shortly after daybreak, a farmer from the Fairchilds section had seen him cross a field. They picked the trail up there again and followed it across the field and through a wood. He had come out on the other side and got down into the Cane Creek section, and there, for several hours, they lost him. Dick had gone right down into the icy water of the creek and walked upstream a mile or so. They brought the dogs down to the creek, to where he broke the trail, took them over to the other side and scented up and down.

Toward five o'clock that afternoon they picked the trail up on the other side, a mile or more upstream. From that point on, they began to close in on him. The dogs followed him across the fields, across the Lester road, into a wood. One arm of the posse swept around the wood to head him off. They knew they had him. Dick, freezing, hungry and unsheltered, was hiding in that wood. They knew he couldn't get away. The posse ringed the wood and waited until morning.

At 7:30 the next morning he made a break for it. He got through the line without being seen, crossed the Lester road and headed back across the field in the direction of Cane Creek. And there they caught him. They saw him plunging through the snowdrift of a field. A cry went up. The posse started after him.

Part of the posse were on horseback. The men rode in across the field. Dick halted at the edge of the wood, dropped deliberately upon one knee and for some minutes held them off with rapid fire. At two hundred yards he dropped Doc Lavender, a deputy, with a bullet through the throat.

The posse came in slowly, in an encircling, flankwise movement. Dick got two more of them as they closed in, and then, as deliberately as a trained soldier retreating in good order, still firing as he went, he fell back through the wood. At the other side he turned and ran down through a sloping field that bordered on Cane Creek. At the creek edge, he turned again, knelt once more in the snow and aimed.

It was Dick's last shot. He didn't miss. The bullet struck Wayne Foraker, a deputy, dead center in the forehead and killed him in his saddle. Then the posse saw

309

the Negro aim again, and nothing happened. Dick snapped the breech open savagely, then hurled the gun away. A cheer went up. The posse came charging forward. Dick turned, stumblingly, and ran the few remaining yards that separated him from the cold and rock-bright waters of the creek.

And here he did a curious thing–a thing that no one ever wholly understood. It was thought that he would make one final break for freedom, that he would wade the creek and try to get away before they got him. Instead, he sat down calmly on the bank and, as quietly as if he were seated on his cot in an Army barracks, he unlaced his shoes, took them off, placed them together neatly at his side, and then stood up like a soldier, erect, in his bare bleeding feet, and faced the mob.

The men on horseback reached him first. They rode up around him and discharged their guns into him. He fell forward in the snow, riddled with bullets. The men dismounted, turned him over on his back, and all the other men came in and riddled him. They took his lifeless body, put a rope around his neck and hung him to a tree. Then the mob exhausted all their ammunition on the riddled carcass.

By nine o'clock that morning the news had reached town. Around eleven o'clock, the mob came back along the river road. A good crowd had gone out to meet it at the Wilton Bottoms. The sheriff rode ahead. Dick's body had been thrown like a sack and tied across the saddle of the horse of one of the deputies he had killed.

It was in this way, bullet-riddled, shot to pieces, open to the vengeful and the morbid gaze of all, that Dick came back to town. The mob came back right to its starting point in South Dean Street. They halted there before an undertaking parlor, not twenty yards away from where Dick knelt to kill John Chapman. They took that ghastly mutilated thing and hung it in the window of the undertaker's place, for every woman, man, and child in town to see.

And it was so we saw him last. We said we wouldn't look. But in the end we went. And I think it has always been the same with people. They protest. They shudder. And they say they will not go. But in the end they always have their look.

At length we went. We saw it, tried wretchedly to make ourselves believe that once this thing had spoken to us gently, had been partner to our confidence, object of our affection and respect. And we were sick with nausea and fear, for something had come into our lives we could not understand.

We looked and whitened to the lips, craned our necks and looked away, and brought unwilling, fascinated eyes back to the horror once again, and craned and turned again, and shuffled in the slush uneasily, but could not go. And we looked up at the leaden reek of day, the dreary vapor of the sky, and, bleakly, at these forms and faces all around us–the people come to gape and stare, the poolroom loafers, the town toughs, the mongrel conquerors of earth–and yet, familiar to our lives and to the body of our whole experience, all known to our landscape, all living men.

And something had come into life–into our lives–that we had never known about before. It was a kind of shadow, a poisonous blackness filled with bewildered loathing. The snow would go, we knew; the reeking vapors of the sky would clear away. The leaf, the blade, the bud, the bird, then April, would come back again, and all of this would be as it had ever been. The homely light of day would shine again familiarly. And all of this would vanish as an evil dream. And yet not wholly so. For we would still remember the old dark doubt and loathing of our kind, of something hateful and unspeakable in the souls of men. We knew that we should not forget.

Beside us, a man was telling the story of his own heroic accomplishments to a little group of fascinated listeners. I turned and looked at him. It was Ben Pounders of the ferret face, the furtive and uneasy eye, Ben Pounders of the mongrel mouth, the wiry muscles of the jaw, Ben Pounders, the collector of usurious lendings to the blacks, the nigger hunter. And now Ben Pounders boasted of another triumph. He was the proud possessor of another scalp.

"I was the first one to git in a shot," he said. "You see that hole there?" He pointed with a dirty finger. "That big hole right above the eye?" They turned and goggled with a drugged and feeding stare.

"That's mine," the hero said, turned briefly to the side and spat tobacco juice into the slush. "That's where I got him. Hell, after that he didn't know what hit him. He was dead before he hit the ground. We all shot him full of holes then. We sure did fill him full of lead. Why, hell, yes," he declared, with a decisive movement of his head, "we counted up to two hundred and eighty seven. We must have put three hundred holes in him."

And Nebraska, fearless, blunt, outspoken as he always was, turned abruptly, put two fingers to his lips and spat between them, widely and contemptuously.

"Yeah–*we!*" he grunted. "*We* killed a big one! We–we killed a b'ar, we   did! . . .Come on, boys," he said gruffly. "Let's be on our way!"

And, fearless and unshaken, untouched by any terror or any doubt, he moved away. And two white-faced, nauseated boys went with him.

A day or two went by before anyone could go into Dick's room again. I went in with Randy and his father. The little room was spotless, bare and tidy as it had always been. But even the very austerity of that little room now seemed terribly alive with the presence of its black tenant. It was Dick's room. We all knew that. And somehow we all knew that no one else could ever live there again.

Mr. Shepperton went over to the table, picked up Dick's old Bible that still lay there, open and face downward, held it up to the light and looked at it, at the place that Dick had marked when he last read in it. And in a moment, without speaking to us, he began to read in a quiet voice:

311

"The Lord is my shepherd; I shall not want.

"2. He maketh me to lie down in green pastures: he leadeth me beside the still waters.

"3. He restoreth my soul: he leadeth me in the paths of righteousness for his name's sake.

"4. Yea, though I walk through the valley of the shadow of death, I will fear no evil: for thou art with me—"

Then Mr. Shepperton closed the book and put it down upon the table, the place where Dick had left it. And we went out the door, he locked it, and we went back into that room no more forever.

The years passed, and all of us were given unto time. We went our ways. But often they would turn and come again, these faces and these voices of the past, and burn there in my memory again, upon the muted and immortal geography of time.

And all would come again—the shout of the young voices, the hard thud of the kicked ball, and Dick moving, moving steadily, Dick moving, moving, silently, a storm-white world and silence, and something moving, moving in the night. Then I would hear the furious bell, the crowd a-clamor and the baying of the dogs, and feel the shadow coming that would never disappear. Then I would see again the little room that we would see no more, the table and the book. And the pastoral holiness of that old psalm came back to me and my heart would wonder with perplexity and doubt.

For I had heard another song since then, and one that Dick, I know, had never heard, and one perhaps he might not have understood; but one whose phrases and whose imagery it seemed to me would suit him better:

> What the hammer? What the chain?
> In what furnace was thy brain?
> What the anvil? What dread grasp
> Dare its deadly terrors clasp?
>
> When the stars threw down their spears,
> And water'd heaven with their tears,
> Did he smile His work to see?
> Did He who made the lamb make thee?

"*What* the hammer? *What* the chain?" No one ever knew. It was a mystery and a wonder. There were a dozen stories, a hundred clues and rumors; all came to nothing in the end. Some said that Dick had come from Texas, others that his home had been in Georgia. Some said that it was true that he had been enlisted in the Army, but that he had killed a man while there and served a term at Leavenworth. Some said he had served in the Army and had received an honorable discharge, but had later killed a man and had served a term in a state prison in Louisiana. Others said that he had been an Army man, but that he had gone crazy, that he had served a period in an asylum, that he had escaped from prison, that he was a fugitive from justice at the time he came to us.

But all these stories came to nothing. Nothing was ever proved. Men debated and discussed these things a thousand times–who and what he had been, what he had done, where he had come from–and all of it came to nothing. No one knew the answer. But I think that I have found the answer. I think I know from where he came.

He came from darkness. He came out of the heart of darkness, from the dark heart of the secret and undiscovered South. He came by night, just as he passed by night. He was night's child and partner, a token of the other side of man's dark soul, a symbol of those things that pass by darkness and that still remain, a symbol of man's evil innocence, and the token of his mystery, a projection of his own unfathomed quality, a friend, a brother and a mortal enemy, an unknown demon, two worlds together–a tiger and a child.

(1937)

———————————————————————

HILLS LIKE
WHITE ELEPHANTS

ERNEST HEMINGWAY

The hills across the valley of the Ebro were long and white. On this side there was no shade and no trees and the station was between two lines of rails in the sun. Close against the side of the station there was the warm shadow of the building and a curtain, made of strings of bamboo beads, hung across the open door into the bar, to keep out flies. The American and the girl with him sat at a table in the shade, outside the building. It was very hot and the express from Barcelona would come in forty minutes. It stopped at this junction for two minutes and went on to Madrid.

"What should we drink?" the girl asked. She had taken off her hat and put it on the table.

"It's pretty hot," the man said.

"Let's drink beer."

"Dos cervezas," the man said into the curtain.

"Big ones?" a woman asked from the doorway.

"Yes. Two big ones."

The woman brought two glasses of beer and two felt pads. She put the felt pads and the beer glasses on the table and looked at the man and the girl. The girl was looking off at the line of hills. They were white in the sun and the country was brown and dry.

"They look like white elephants," she said.

"I've never seen one," the man drank his beer.

"No, you wouldn't have."

"I might have," the man said. "Just because you say I wouldn't have doesn't prove anything."

The girl looked at the bead curtain. "They've painted something on it," she said. "What does it say?"

"Anis del Toro. It's a drink."

"Could we try it?"

The man called "Listen" through the curtain. The woman came out from the bar.

"Four reales."

"We want two Anis del Toro."

"With water?"

"Do you want it with water?"

"I don't know," the girl said. "Is it good with water?"

"It's all right."

"You want them with water?" asked the woman.

"Yes, with water."

"It tastes like licorice," the girl said and put the glass down.

"That's the way with everything."

"Yes," said the girl. "Everything tastes of licorice. Especially all the things you've waited so long for, like absinthe."

"Oh, cut it out."

"You started it," the girl said. "I was being amused. I was having a fine time."

"Well, let's try to have a fine time."

"All right. I was trying. I said the mountains looked like white elephants. Wasn't that bright?"

"That was bright."

"I wanted to try this new drink. That's all we do, isn't it–look at things and try new drinks."

"I guess so."

The girl looked across at the hills.
"They're lovely hills," she said. "They don't really look like white elephants. I just meant the coloring of their skin through the trees."

"Should we have another drink?"

"All right."

The warm wind blew the bead curtain against the table.

"The beer's nice and cool," the man said.

"It's lovely," the girl said.

"It's really an awfully simple operation, Jig," the man said. "It's not really an operation at all."

The girl looked at the ground the table legs rested on.

"I know you wouldn't mind it, Jig. It's really not anything. It's just to let the air in."

The girl did not say anything.

"I'll go with you and I'll stay with you all the time. They just let the air in and then it's all perfectly natural."

"Then what will we do afterward?"

"We'll be fine afterward. Just like we were before."

"What makes you think so?"

"That's the only thing that bothers us. It's the only thing that's made us unhappy."

The girl looked at the bead curtain, put her hand out and took hold of two of the strings of beads.

"And you think then we'll be all right and be happy."

"I know we will. You don't have to be afraid. I've known lots of people that have done it."

"So have I," said the girl. "And afterward they were all so happy."

"Well," the man said, "if you don't want to you don't have to. I wouldn't have you do it if you didn't want to. But I know it's perfectly simple."

"And you really want to?"

"I think it's the best thing to do. But I don't want you to do it if you don't really want to."

"And if I do it you'll be happy and things will be like they were and you'll love me?"

"I love you now. You know I love you."

"I know. But if I do it, then it will be nice again if I say things are like white elephants, and you'll like it?"

"I'll love it. I love it now but I just can't think about it. You know how I get when I worry."

"If I do it you won't ever worry."

"I won't worry about that because it's perfectly simple."

"Then I'll do it. Because I don't care about me."

"What do you mean?"

"I don't care about me."

"Well, I care about you."

"Oh, yes. But I don't care about me. And I'll do it and then everything will be fine."

"I don't want you to do it if you feel that way."

The girl stood up and walked to the end of the station. Across, on the other side, were fields of grain and trees along the banks of the Ebro. Far away, beyond the river, were mountains. The shadow of a cloud moved across the field of grain and she saw the river through the trees.

"And we could have all this," she said. "And we could have everything and every day we make it more impossible."

"What did you say?"
"I said we could have everything."

"We can have everything."

"No, we can't."

"We can have the whole world."

"No, we can't."

"We can go everywhere."

"No, we can't. It isn't ours any more."

"It's ours."

"No, it isn't. And once they take it away, you never get it back."

"But they haven't taken it away."

"We'll wait and see."

"Come on back in the shade," he said. "You mustn't feel that way."

"I don't feel any way," the girl said. "I just know things."

"I don't want you to do anything that you don't want to do–"

"Nor that isn't good for me," she said. "I know. Could we have another beer."

"All right. But you've got to realize–"

"I realize," the girl said. "Can't we stop talking?"

They sat down at the table and the girl looked across at the hills on the dry side of the valley and the man looked at her and at the table.

"You've got to realize," he said, "that I don't want you to do it if you don't want to. I'm perfectly willing to go through with it if it means anything to you."

"Doesn't it mean anything to you? We could get along."

"Of course it does. But I don't want anybody but you. I don't want any one else. And I know it's perfectly simple."

"Yes, you know it's perfectly simple."

"It's all right for you to say that, but I do know it."

"Would you do something for me now?"

"I'd do anything for you."

"Would you please please please please please please please stop talking?"

He did not say anything but looked at the bags against the wall of the station. There were labels on them from all the hotels where they had spent nights.

319

"But I don't want you to," he said. "I don't care anything about it."

"I'll scream," said the girl.

The woman came out through the curtains with two glasses of beer and put them down on the damp felt pads. "The train comes in five minutes," she said.

"What did she say?" asked the girl.

"That the train is coming in five minutes."

The girl smiled brightly at the woman to thank her.

"I'd better take the bags over to the other side of the station," the man said. She smiled at him.

"All right. Then come back and we'll finish the beer."

He picked up the two heavy bags and carried them around the station to the other tracks. He looked up the tracks but could not see the train. Coming back, he walked through the barroom, where people waiting for the train were drinking. He drank an Anis at the bar and looked at the people. They were all waiting reasonably for the train. He went out through the bead curtain. She was sitting at the table and smiled at him.

"Do you feel better?" he asked.

"I feel fine," she said. "There's nothing wrong with me. I feel fine." (1927)

DOVER BEACH

Matthew Arnold

The sea is calm tonight,
The tide is full, the moon lies fair
Upon the straits;—on the French coast the light
Gleams and is gone; the cliffs of England stand,
Glimmering and vast, out in the tranquil bay.
Come to the window, sweet is the night-air!
Only, from the long line of spray
Where the sea meets the moon-blanched land,
Listen! you hear the grating roar
Of pebbles which the waves draw back, and fling,
At their return, up the high strand,
Begin, and cease, and then again begin,
With tremulous cadence slow, and bring
The eternal note of sadness in.

Sophocles long ago
Heard it on the Aegean, and it brought
Into his mind the turbid ebb and flow
Of human misery; we
Find also in the sound a thought,
Hearing it by this distant northern sea.

The Sea of Faith
Was once, too, at the full, and round earth's shore
Lay like the folds of a bright girdle furled.
But now I only hear
Its melancholy, long, withdrawing roar,
Retreating, to the breath
Of the night-wind, down the vast edges drear
And naked shingles of the world.

Ah, love, let us be true
To one another! for the world, which seems
To lie before us like a land of dreams,
So various, so beautiful, so new,
Hath really neither joy, nor love, nor light,
Nor certitude, nor peace, nor help for pain;
And we are here as on a darkling plain
Swept with confused alarms of struggle and flight,
Where ignorant armies clash by night.

(1867)

LIVING IN SIN

ADRIENNE RICH

She had thought the studio would keep itself,
no dust upon the furniture of love.
Half heresy, to wish the taps less vocal,
the panes relieved of grime. A plate of pears,
a piano with a Persian shawl, a cat
stalking the picturesque amusing mouse
had risen at his urging.
Not that at five each separate stair would writhe
under the milkman's tramp; that morning light
so coldly would delineate the scraps
of last night's cheese and three sepulchral bottles;
that on the kitchen shelf among the saucers
a pair of beetle-eyes would fix her own—
envoy from some village in the moldings . . .
Meanwhile, he, with a yawn,
sounded a dozen notes upon the keyboard,
rubbed at his beard, went out for cigarettes;
while she, jeered by the minor demons,
pulled back the sheets and made the bed and found
a towel to dust the table-top,
and let the coffee-pot boil over on the stove.
By evening she was back in love again,
though not so wholly but throughout the night
she woke sometimes to feel the daylight coming
like a relentless milkman up the stairs. (1975)

RICHARD CORY
EDWIN ARLINGTON ROBINSON

Whenever Richard Cory went down town,
We people on the pavement looked at him:
He was a gentleman from sole to crown,
Clean favored, and imperially slim.

And he was always quietly arrayed,
And he was always human when he talked;
But still he fluttered pulses when he said,
"Good-morning," and he glittered when he walked.

And he was rich—yes, richer than a king—
And admirably schooled in every grace:
In fine, we thought that he was everything
To make us wish that we were in his place.

So on we worked, and waited for the light,
And went without the meat, and cursed the bread;
And Richard Cory, one calm summer night,
Went home and put a bullet through his head.

(1897)

EXERCISE 1: OUTLINING

Arrange the following sentences in order by putting the number of the sentence in the proper place in the outline. Remember to look specifically for **levels of generality.**

(1)   The existing programs were discarded when the cost of upkeep became prohibitive or when more immediate, pressing concerns vied for attention.

(2)   Suddenly public and private funds became available for crash programs, especially in science and technology.

(3)   The launching of Sputnik caused widespread public concern for the status of education in the United States, especially education of the best and brightest.

(4)   More professional literature on the gifted and talented was published between 1956 and 1959 than had been in the previous thirty years.

(5)   In spite of this interest, no comprehensive, central philosophy or program emerged.

(6)   The position of the United States in the world was perceived as in danger unless our educational standards were raised, especially for the gifted student.

(7)   Research on the needs of the gifted was not translated into the curriculum, and not much attention was paid to the talented student or to the gifted student who was disadvantaged.

I.   Topic sentence: _____

        A. _____

                1. _____

                2. _____

        B. _____

                1. _____

                2. _____

EXERCISE 2: PARAGRAPHING

Consider the topic of "MTV Programming." Brainstorm this topic for a few minutes and then write a topic sentence that states precisely what you want to say about programming. Next, write THREE sentences that best support the view presented in your topic sentence. These three sentences will serve as your subtopics A, B, and C (major supports) for the paragraph. Finally, offer at least two examples in complete sentences that specifically develop each of the three subtopic statements.

MTV Programming

Topic Sentence: _____

_____

A. _____

1. _____

2. _____

3. _____

B. _____

1. _____

2. _____

3. _____

C. _____

1. _____

2. _____

3. _____

EXERCISE 3: TOPIC SENTENCES

Construct an appropriate sentence based on the evidence given.

1. Topic Sentence: _____

_____

    a. Kate's toys always seem to be misplaced.
    b. She is usually late for dinner.
    c. She sometimes forgets her homework assignments.
    d. Her room, despite her mother's pleadings, is a mess.

2. Topic sentence: _____

_____

    a. Colleen is always available to talk to about one's problems.
    b. Colleen never judges anyone.
    c. She is dependable and reliable.
    d. Colleen is very trustworthy.

3. Topic sentence: _____

_____

    a. I once forgot to feed my kids' parakeet and it died.
    b. One rainy day I accidentally ran over my dog Fido.
    c. Even goldfish float on their backs at my house.
    d. The crabs I bring home from the beach won't eat anything I give them.

4. Topic sentence: _____

_____

    a. Bubba chews tobacco and dips snuff.
    b. He drives an extended cab pick-up truck.
    c. Bubba's belt buckle is larger than his truck's chrome rims.
    d. He has nothing but contempt for any kind of music other than country and western.

5. Topic sentence: _____

_____

      a. My kids ignore me all the time.
      b. I never get to use the telephone at all.
      c. None of the things I like to eat can be found in the refrigerator.
      d. My family went on vacation and didn't notice that I was missing until they had traveled 200 miles.

6. Topic sentence: _____

_____

      a. Mrs. Bone lies about insignificant things.
      b. Mrs. Bone never lets her friends lead their own lives without offering some form of advice.
      c. She has a volatile temper and has never learned to discuss problems without shouting at the top of her voice.
      d. She expects more from others than she is capable of giving herself.
      e. She likes to pit her friends against one another.

7. Topic sentence: _____

_____

      a. Mr. Legree requires every employee to present a doctor's note for each absence.
      b. In a dispute between a supervisor and an employee, he always takes sides with the supervisor.
      c. The last time he recommended anyone for a raise in salary was ten years ago.
      d. Mr. Legree was recognized by the President of the company for leading the firm in productivity and cost control.

8. Topic sentence: _____

_____

      a. Many critics of the U.S. space program feel that NASA is more concerned with public relations than with space exploration.
      b. These critics believe that most of the tasks now performed by the astronauts could be handled by robotics and computers.

c. They feel that the money spent on each shuttle flight could be
better spent on the homeless.
d. Critics of NASA feel that no real benefits have come from the program as a whole.

9. Topic sentence: _____

_____

a. Rush Limbaugh has implied that there is murder and drug abuse in the White House.
b. Gordon Liddy told his radio program listeners how to wound federal agents.
c. The Oklahoma bombers have been linked to an extreme right wing talk show host on the Internet.

10. Topic sentence: _____

_____

a. Edward's apartment is completely without dust.
b. He cannot tolerate dirty dishes in the sink.
c. He vacuums his apartment everyday.
d. All the canned goods in his pantry are neatly arranged.

EXERCISE 4:
PARAGRAPH DEVELOPMENT

Complete each of the sections below by providing appropriate subtopics and examples to support the topic sentence given.

1. College registration is often a frustrating process.

    A. The amount of time it takes to register is daunting.

        1. _____

        2. _____

    B. Critical courses are often unavailable.

        1. _____

        2. _____

    C. The registrant often finds he does not have all the necessary paperwork.

        1. _____

        2. _____

        3. _____

Clincher: _____

_____

2. One of the disadvantages of living in a large city is the traffic problems.

    A. _____

        1. There often are bottle necks on major thoroughfares that have no apparent cause.

        2. _____

        3. _____

    B. _____

1. _____

2. _____

3. _____

C. _____

1. _____

2. The Interstate has been under construction since the 1950s.

3. _____

Clincher: _____

_____

3. Working while attending college creates several hardships for the student.

A. Budgeting and allotting time for everything is a problem.

1. _____

2. _____

3. _____

B. _____

1. _____

2. _____

3. _____

C. The most severe hardship is _____?

1. _____

2. _____

3. _____

Clincher: _____

EXERCISE 5: TOPIC SENTENCES

Narrow the subject and limit the focus of each of the following general
statements so they could serve as effective topic sentences for paragraphs.

1. Ted is a fascinating man.

_____

_____

2. Longhorn football games are a lot more fun than Aggie football games.

_____

_____

3. Tommy's character seems a little shady to me.

_____

_____

4. Teens today face many challenges.

_____

_____

5. My parents' tastes in music stink.

_____

_____

6. I tend to favor the Democratic candidate more than the Republican.

_____

_____

7. Computer labs are quite helpful.

_____

_____

8. High school, when compared to college, was a real drag.

_____

_____

9. A girlfriend/boyfriend is awfully expensive.

_____

_____

10. Living in an apartment is more fun than living at home.

_____

_____

EXERCISE 6: THESIS STATEMENTS

Compose a precise thesis statement based on the topic given. Remember to include a narrowed subject and a limited focus in each statement. Underline your controlling idea, or focus.

1. High school graduation night.

Thesis: _____

_____

2. Family life

Thesis: _____

_____

3. The anxieties of social dating.

Thesis: _____

_____

4. Advantages of attending a community college.

Thesis: _____

_____

5. Peer pressure

Thesis: _____

_____

6. Television commercials

Thesis: _____

_____

7. Careers

Thesis: _____

_____

8. Sports

Thesis: _____

_____

9. Love

Thesis: _____

_____

10. Death

Thesis: _____

_____

EXERCISE 7:
INTRODUCTION AND CONCLUSIONS

Take ONE of the above topics and thesis statements (Exercise 6) and construct both an introductory and concluding paragraph for an essay. Although the essay is not required here, assume you will write it, using these two paragraphs to introduce and conclude your essay. Your thesis should appear in your introduction.

Introductory paragraph: _____

Concluding paragraph: _____

EXERCISE 8: DESCRIPTION

1. Go somewhere on campus. The place may be inside or outside. Make yourself comfortable for a minute and decide whether the place impresses you favorably or unfavorably. On this sheet jot down as many specific details, observations, and ideas as you can in ten minutes or so. Focus on your senses, what can you see, touch, taste, hear, or smell?

2. Go somewhere else where you have a good writing surface, space, quiet. Review your list. Now go through your jottings and make a specific figure of speech of at least ten of them. Create at least ten vivid images of at least ten other details. Do not use clichés.

3. Now write your subjective dominant impression of the place to describe it to your audience.

4. Then choose specific details, images, and figures of speech to support your dominant impression.

5. Finally, write a paragraph in which you convince your audience to perceive a place on campus the way you do. Include your dominant impression, specific details, vivid language, logical transitions, and a clincher to emphasize your purpose.

EXERCISE 9: DESCRIPTION

Here is a simple declarative sentence:

The man and his daughter walked through the shopping mall.

Write a paragraph in which you use the basic idea above but you describe the circumstances. You will want to consider what the man and his daughter look like (How old are they? What are they wearing? Who are they?), how they are walking (Are they striding? lolling? Are they happy? upset? afraid?), and what is the mall like? (What will happen at the end of their shopping trip?). You may want to answer all the questions; your purpose and your point will determine the way you focus your description. Use and identify at least one literal comparison, two figures of speech, and three images in your description. Underline all the verbs. Change any you have used more than once.

EXERCISE 10:
DESCRIPTIVE TECHNIQUES

In the following paragraph from E. B. White's "Once More to the Lake," identify and underline the descriptive devices used.

One afternoon while we were at that lake a thunderstorm came up. It was like the revival of an old melodrama that I had seen long ago with childish awe. The second-act climax of the drama of the electrical disturbance over a lake in America had not changed in any important respect. This was the big scene, still the big scene. The whole thing was so familiar, the first feeling of oppression and heat and a general air around camp of not wanting to go very far away. In midafternoon (it was all the same) a curious darkening of the sky, and a lull in everything that had made life tick; and then the way the boats suddenly swung the other way at their moorings with the coming of a breeze out of the new quarter, and the premonitory rumble. Then the kettle drum, then the snare, then the bass drum and cymbals, then crackling light against the dark, and the gods grinning and licking their chops in the hills. Afterward the calm, the rain steadily rustling in the calm lake, the return of light and hope and spirits, and the campers running out in joy and relief to go swimming in the rain, their bright cries perpetuating the deathless joke about how they were getting simply drenched, and the children screaming with delight at the new sensation of bathing in the rain, and the joke about getting drenched linking the generations in a strong indestructible chain. And the comedian who waded in carrying an umbrella.

1. To what does he compare the storm? Is the comparison literal or figurative?

2. What images does he use?

3. Which figures of speech are employed?

4. What transitional devices does he use in this paragraph? Why does he repeat "then" in sentence 7?

EXERCISE 11: PROCESS

Below are several scrambled steps listing a series of events that makes up a process sequence. Unscramble these items and arrange them in chronological order. Then outline the process, indicating how you would group the events and what you would call each group. Make sure each level is parallel.

1. Pour a cup of coffee.
2. Re-wet hair and try again.
3. Put on shirt and tie after brushing lint off pants.
4. Dry off
5. Turn on light while rubbing knot on forehead
6. Start car
7. Brush teeth after changing shirts
8. Arrive at class 10 minutes late
9. Find key in sofa
10. Dodge vicious squirrel on the way to the car
11. Scald yourself in the shower–you forgot to check the temp before getting in
12. Spill coffee on shirt while putting lint brush away
13. Hit "snooze" on clock again
14. Fall over tub edge trying to get out of shower
15. Get stuck in traffic on FM 1960
16. Burn tongue with hot coffee
17. Put pants on after putting on socks
18. Bathe
19. Drag yourself out of bed
20. Turn off lights after finding keys in sofa
21. Change tie
22. Adjust water temperature
23. Put socks on after hair is dried the second time
24. Stumble back into the kitchen again with hair still dripping wet
25. Fix coffee
26. Search frantically for the keys
27. Drive 75 mph in a 55 mph zone to make up for lost time changing clothes
28. Change shirt
29. Having selected your wardrobe, time to dry hair
30. Shower after coffee begins to brew
31. Lock house
32. Drip toothpaste on tie
33. Hit snooze on alarm clock
34. With tongue still burning from coffee, pick out clothes for the day
35. Bump into wall as you move toward the kitchen
(continued on next page)
36. Run over neighbor's cat but no time to stop now

37. Class canceled because professor's favorite cat was run over in neighbor's driveway
38. Back out of driveway.

EXERCISE 12: PROCESS

Assume you have been offered jobs from three different companies at one
time. What are the steps in deciding with which company to work? List the
steps and then group them into logical categories. Finally, outline the
process based on these steps and supply a thesis.

Thesis:_____

_____

I. _____

_____

_____

II. _____

_____

_____

III. _____

_____

_____

EXERCISE 13: DEFINITION

Provide the missing sections of the following definitions. Remember that each term must be put into its class and then be distinguished from other items of the same class.

1. A bachelor is _____who _____.

2. A sitcom is _____ that _____.

3. A conspiracy is _____that _____.

4. Genius is _____that _____.

5. Graffiti is _____that _____.

6. Compassion is _____that _____.

7. A hypothesis is _____ that _____.

8. Take one of the above definitions and construct THREE topic sentences that would support and develop your thesis. Be precise in your sentences.

Thesis: (Your choice from list above.)

I. _____

II. _____

III. _____

EXERCISE 14:
COMPARISON/CONTRAST

Several pairs of items are listed below. Some of the items can be
compared, some contrasted. Follow the suggestions of each and list under
the items those bases of comparison you would use in an essay. For
example, if you are asked to compare two military leaders of the American
Civil War, you might select their origins, educational backgrounds,
personalities, and military experiences. You would simply list these four
bases of comparisons under the items.

1. Compare a computer repairman and a medical surgeon

    a. _____   b. _____

    c. _____   d. _____

2. Compare a loving relationship with a roller coaster.

    a. _____   b. _____

    c. _____   d. _____

3. Compare the O. J. Simpson trial with a circus.

    a. _____   b. _____

    c. _____   d. _____

4. Contrast high school students and college students.

    a. _____   b. _____

    c. _____   d. _____

5. Compare or contrast your private self with your public self.

    a. _____   b. _____

    c. _____   d. _____

Now write an appropriate thesis statement for each of the exercises listed above. Make certain that each thesis reflects your purpose and that each has a definite focus. The focus should contain each of the bases of comparison.

1. _____

   _____

2. _____

   _____

3. _____

   _____

4. _____

   _____

5. _____

   _____

EXERCISE 15:
CLASSIFICATION/DIVISION

Circle the item in each grouping below that violates the unity of classification and briefly explain your choice.

Topic: Friends
Classes: intimate friends
            social friends
            weird friends
            work friends

Topic: Students
Classes: metal heads
            preppies
            kickers
            jocks
            lazy

Topic: Movies
Classes: adventure
            romantic
            blockbusters
            horror
            suspense

Topic: Trees
Classes: exotic
            maple
            oak
            pine
            birch

Topic: Schools
Classes: elementary
            private
            secondary
            college
            technical

Topic: Tree
Division: leaf
            root
            trunk

                    fungus

Topic: Clothes
Division: jeans
                formal
                shorts
                shirt

EXERCISE 16: CAUSES & EFFECTS

List in the space below as many causes as you can for your success or failure (effect) in some personal project in your past.

1.   6.

2.   7.

3.   8.

4   9.

5.   10.

Can you determine which of the causes you listed above are necessary causes, contributing causes, and sufficient causes? Try to group your causes.

List in the space below what you think might be some of the eventual <u>effects</u> of your acquiring a college diploma. Then arrange the effects of your choice in a causal chain sequence, starting with the immediate effect and ending with the remote effect.

1.   6.

2.   7.

3.   8.

4.   9.

5.   10.

Now put your effects into a causal chain sequence, listing on the left the first effect and moving to the right toward the remote effect.

Event (Effect 1 (Effect 2 (Effect 3 (remote)

EXERCISE 17:
INDUCTIVE REASONING

I. Assume you are a detective. Based on what you find listed below in the garbage can of a family, determine the type of inhabitants in the house. How many people live in the house? What are their approximate ages and interests? Explain your findings/conclusions in a well-structured paragraph, providing sufficient evidence to support your conclusion.

Grocery Receipts

Clearasil
styling gel
Oil of Olay
diet sodas
AAA batteries
jello
Gummy Bears
tuna
Polo cologne
decaf coffee
Lean Cuisine
sugar-coated cereal
Bran flakes
donuts
case of beer
low-cholesterol products
ulcer medicine

Discarded Mail

college recruitments
military recruitments
University alumni magazines
   from Sarah Lawrence and
   Texas A & M
Stockholder reports

Magazines

Field and Stream
Cosmopolitan
Rolling Stone
Better Homes and Gardens
TV Guide
Sassy
Golf Digest
Vogue

Canceled Checks

dance lessons
The Gap
2 County Sheriff's Dept./
   Traffic Div. citations
Neiman Marcus
Hair Salon
Orthodontist
Country Club
car insurance (3 cars)
Clinique Cosmetics
Alimony Checks to Mrs. X

Paycheck Stubs

Exxon
McDonalds

_____

_____

_____

_____

_____

_____

_____

_____

_____

_____

_____

Write a paragraph in which you indicate how you arrived at your inductive
conclusions. State the evidence.

_____

_____

_____

_____

_____

_____

_____

_____

EXERCISE 18:
DEDUCTION/SYLLOGISMS

I. Consider each of the following syllogisms and indicate in the blank whether each is valid or not valid and true or not true.

1.

Major Premise (MP):	All persons will die.
Minor Premise (mp):	Mrs. Bone is a person.
Conclusion (C):	Mrs. Bone will die.

_____

2.

(MP):	All Baptists are Protestants.
(mp):	All Methodists are Protestants.
(C):	All Baptists are Methodists.

_____

3.

(MP):	Free speech is protected under the Constitution.
(mp):	Flag burning is an expression of free speech.
(C):	Flag burning is protected under the Constitution.

_____

4.

(MP):	Tyranny deserves no loyalty.
(mp):	King George III is a tyrant.
(C):	King George III deserves no loyalty.

_____

5.

(MP):	All rabbits have red eyes.
(mp):	Gomer is a rabbit.
(C):	Therefore, Gomer has red eyes.

_____

6.
(MP):   Policemen who commit a crime should be punished severely.
(mp):   Those policemen just beat a man to death.
(C):   Those policemen should be punished severely.

_____

II. Enthymemes: Explain in the first provided blank what the assumed
    premise is, and in the second blank explain why or why not the
    following enthymemes are valid and true.

7. My father is absent-minded because he is an English professor.

    a. _____

    b. _____

8. Percy Pinkus must be a Communist since he opposed organized
    religion.

    a. _____

    b. _____

9. Since he was an athlete in college, he must not be very smart.

    a. _____

    b. _____

10. Those students are not serious about school because they always sit
    at the back of the classroom.

    a. _____

    b. _____

Can you identify any of the logical fallacies in these enthymemes? Select
one of the above and discuss its error in reasoning.

_____

_____

_____

III. Evaluate the following deductive arguments as either valid or invalid. Among those which are valid, can you identify any that are sound as well?

1. The only way to manage a company effectively is to instill fear in your workers. Either you treat your employees kindly and they take advantage of you and goof off, or you are tough on them and they work hard for you.

_____

_____

2. I had a bad time with my first two husbands. From these experiences I have learned that men are all egotistical, inconsiderate philanderers who just want to score with as many "chicks" as possible.

_____

_____

3. Walter has always been a supporter of minimum wage laws, but we shouldn't pay any attention to his arguments. He has a couple of illegal aliens tending to his kids whom he pays only $2.00 an hour.

_____

_____

EXERCISE 19: ARGUMENTATION

Identify and underline the <u>conclusion</u> of each of the following arguments.

1. <u>Former Warsaw pact nations should be offered a limited "partnership" in NATO rather than full membership</u>, inasmuch as full membership would fuel Russian phobias about invasion from Eastern Europe.

2. <u>Philosophy is the best subject in which to major</u> because it teaches one to reason, an essential skill for a good life.

3. Cutting wage rates may enable one employer to hire more workers, but <u>cutting the wages of all workers may lead to fewer jobs, not more</u>, since workers would have less to spend on goods.

4. <u>The human mind is not the same thing as the human brain.</u> The human body, including the brain, is a material thing. The human mind is a spiritual thing. Nothing is both a material thing and a spiritual thing.

5. All 70 students who ate dinner at the fraternity house on Friday became ill during the night. None of the students who live at the house but didn't dine there that night became ill, so <u>the illness must have been food poisoning caused by something served for dinner at the house on Friday.</u>

6. In spite of the general's years, <u>he is evidently a little vain of his person and ambitious of conquests.</u> I observed him Sunday in church eyeing the county girls most suspiciously and have seen him leer upon them with a downright amorous look, even when he has been gallanting Lady Lilycraft with great ceremony through the churchyard.

7. The investigation of supernatural phenomena lies outside the realm of science. Therefore, <u>science can neither prove nor disprove the existence of God.</u>

8. Moreover, <u>cutting Social Security will not help the deficit problem.</u> As Martin Feldstein, chairman of the Council of Economic Advisors, has noted, Social Security is funded by separate payroll taxes and contributes not a cent to the deficit.

9. But <u>the particular evil of silencing opinion is that it is robbing the human race, posterity as well as the existing generation, those who dissent from the opinion, still more than those who hold it.</u> If the opinion is right, they are deprived of the opportunity of exchanging error for truth; if wrong, they lose what is almost as great a benefit, the clearer perception and livelier impression of truth, produced by its collision with error.

10. In England under the blasphemy laws it is illegal to express disbelief in the Christian religion. It is also illegal to teach what Christ taught us on the subject of nonresistance. . .[W]hoever wishes to avoid being a criminal must profess to agree with Christ's teaching but avoid saying so.

11. A coin has been tossed 12 times and has shown a head every time. The next time it is tossed, it will also show a head.

12. Archaeology is truly an infant discipline. Its parent, anthropology, is scarcely a century old; as the child it is even younger. Stratigraphic excavation was not done systematically until the early years of the twentieth century; carbon-14 dating is but 18 years old and the corpus of anthropological theory upon which sound archaeology must rest has only become truly useful during the past 30 years.

PERMISSIONS

Goodall, Jane. "Some thoughts on the Exploitation of Non-Human Animals" from *Through a Window: My Thirty Years with the Chimpanzees of Gombe* by Jane Goodall. Copyright © 1990 by Soko Publications, Ltd. Reprinted by permission of Houghton Mifflin Company. All rights reserved.

Goodman, Paul. "A Proposal to Abolish Grading" from *Compulsory Education.* Copyright © 1984 by Horizon Press. Reprinted with permission.

Gould, Stephen Jay. "Evolution as Fact and Theory" reprinted in its entirety from *Discover* magazine, May 1981. Reprinted with permission.

Hall, Edward T. "The English and the Americans" from *The Hidden Dimension.* Copyright © 1966, 1982 by Edward T. Hall. Used by permission of Doubleday, a division of Bantam Doubleday Dell Publishing Group, Inc.

Hemingway, Ernest. "Hills Like White Elephants" reprinted with permission of Charles Scribner's Sons, an imprint of Macmillan Publishing Company, from *Men Without Women.* Copyright © 1927 by Charles Scribner's Sons; renewal copyright 1955 by Ernest Hemingway.

Highet, Gilbert. "Diogenes and Alexander" reprinted by permission of *American Heritage* magazine, a division of Forbes, Inc., copyright © Forbes, Inc., 1963.

Hill, Anita. "Opening Statement" reprinted by permission of Associated Press. 1991.

Holt, John. "Kinds of Discipline" from *Freedom and Beyond.* Copyright © 1972 by John Holt, © 1988 by Holt Associates, Inc. Reprinted with permission.

"Horror Novels as Therapy." Student essay.

Kennedy, Gerald. "I Believe in God", Chapter One from *I Believe.* Copyright © renewal 1986 by Mary Kennedy. Used by permission of the publisher, Abingdon Press.

Kiechel, Walter A. III. "How to Give a Speech" from *Fortune*, June 8, 1987. Copyright © 1987 by Time Inc. All rights reserved.

King, Martin Luther, Jr. "Letter from Birmingham Jail." *Why We Can't Wait. Harper Collins Publishers.* Public domain. Copyright © 1963.

Koch, Edward. "Death and Justice" reprinted by permission of *The New Republic*, © 1985, The New Republic, Inc.

Lerner, Max. "Some American Types" from *America as a Civilization*. Copyright © 1985 by Max Lerner. Reprinted by permission of Simon & Schuster, Inc.

McCall, Nathan. *Dispatches from A Dying Generation*. Copyright © *Washington Post*, 1991. Reprinted by permission.

Maynard, Joyce. "His Talk, Her Talk" from Special Features newspaper column, copyright © 1985. Reprinted with permission.

Mencken, H.L. "Reflections on War" from *Minority Report: H. L. Mencken's Notebooks*. Copyright © 1956 by Alfred A. Knopf, Inc. Reprinted by permission of the publisher.

Mitford, Jessica. "Behind the Formaldehyde Curtain" from *The American Way of Death*. Copyright © 1963 by Jessica Mitford. All rights reserved. Reprinted by permission of Jessica Mitford.

" A New Career." Student essay.

Peck, M. Scott. "Why We fall in Love" from *The Road Less Traveled*. Copyright © 1978 by M. Scott Peck, M.D. Reprinted by permission of Simon and Schuster, Inc.

"Planting a Vegetable Garden." Student essay.

"Pumpers." Student essay.

Rabiner, Sylvia. "How the Superwoman Myth Puts Women Down" from *The Village Voice*, May 24, 1976. Reprinted with permission of the author and The Village Voice.

Rich, Adrienne. "Living in Sin" from *The Fact of a Doorframe: Poems Selected and New 1950-1984*. Reprinted by permission of W. W. Norton & Company, Inc. Copyright © 1984 by Adrienne Rich. Copyright © 1975, 1978 by W. W. Norton & Company, Inc. Copyright © 1981 by Adrienne Rich.

Robinson, E. A. "Richard Cory." Public domain.

Rosenblatt, Roger. "Why the Justice System Fails." Copyright © 1981 by Time Inc. Reprinted by permission.